LOWE'S

Home Plans

Single Story

HOMES FROM 624-4,826 SQ. FT.

Home Plans - Single Story - This book is a collection of best-selling single story plans from some of the nation's leading designers and architects. Only quality plans with sound design, functional layout, energy efficiency and affordability have been selected.

These plans cover a wide range of architectural styles in a popular range of sizes. A broad assortment is presented to match a wide variety of lifestyles and budgets. Each design page features floor plans, a front view of the house, and a list of special features. All floor plans show room dimensions, exterior dimensions and the interior square footage of the home.

Technical Specifications - At the time the construction drawings were prepared, every effort was made to ensure that these plans and specifications meet nationally recognized building codes (BOCA, Southern Building Code Congress and others). Because national building codes change or vary from area to area some drawing modifications and/or the assistance of a professional designer or architect may be necessary to comply with your local codes or to accommodate specific building site conditions. We advise you to consult with your local building official for information regarding codes governing your area.

Blueprint Ordering - Fast and Easy - Your ordering is made simple by following the instructions on page 288. See page 287 for more information on which types of blueprint packages are available and how many plan sets to order.

Your Home, Your Way - The blueprints you receive are a master plan for building your new home. They start you on your way to what may well be the most rewarding experience of your life.

House shown on front cover is Plan #530-007D-0010 and is featured on page 11. Photo Courtesy of Bill Wood Remodeling, St. Louis, Missouri.

Lowe's Home Plans Single Story Homes is published by HDA, Inc. (Home Design Alternatives) 944 Anglum Road, St. Louis, MO 63042. Artist drawings and photos shown in this publication may vary slightly from the actual working drawings. Some photos are shown in mirror reverse. Please refer to the floor plan for accurate layout.

CONTENTS

Current Printing 5 4

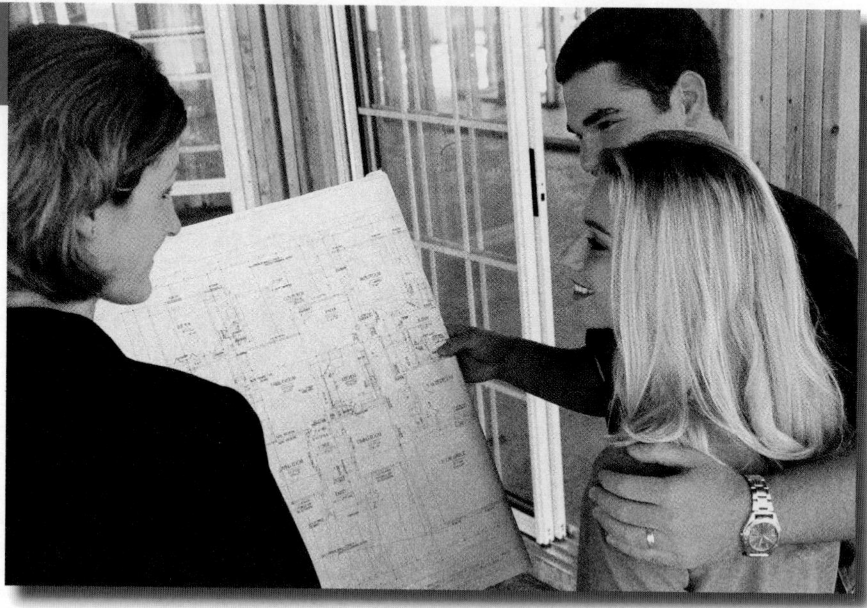

Signature SERIES

HDA is proud to bring you this unprecedented offer of our Lowe's Signature Series featuring our most popular single story home plans. Never before has there been a compilation of home plans as you will find in this publication.

Home plans included in the Lowe's Signature Series are indicated by the Lowe's Signature Series logo shown above and are found on pages 5 through 144. The series is a special collection of our most popular and unique plans. This is the ideal place to begin your search for a new home. Browse the plans in the Lowe's Signature Series collection to discover a home with the options and special characteristics you need.

One of the main reasons for purchasing home plans from a publication such as this is to save you time and money. And you will discover the extra benefits of the unique services offered through our Lowe's Signature Series of home plans.

Besides providing the expected beauty and functional efficiency of all our home plans, the Lowe's Signature Series offers detailed material lists unmatched in the industry today.

Material Lists

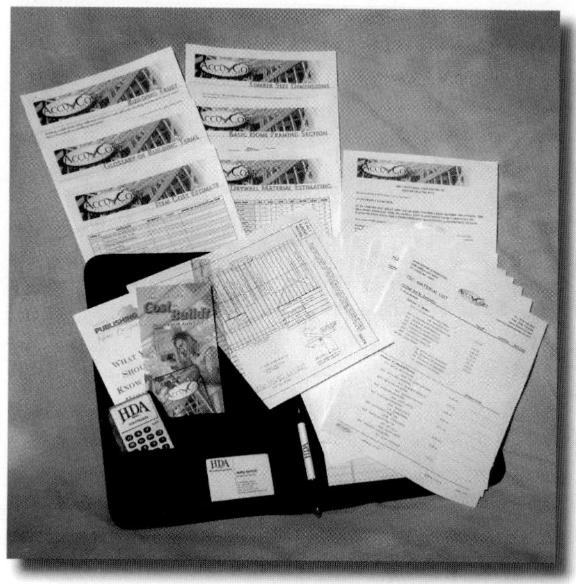

An accurate and detailed material list can save you a considerable amount of time and money. Our material lists give you the quantity, dimensions and descriptions of the major building materials necessary to construct your home. You'll get faster and more accurate bids from contractors and material suppliers, and you'll save money by paying for only the materials you need. Our package includes the material list, residential building resources, architect's scale, handy calculator, and convenient pen and paper all wrapped neatly in a durable leather portfolio. For availability and more information see the Index on page 286 and the Order Form on page 288.

Quick & Easy Customizing

Make Changes To Your Home Plan In 4 Steps

Here's an affordable and efficient way to make changes to your plan.

1. Select the house plan that most closely meets your needs. Purchase of a reproducible master is necessary in order to make changes to a plan.

2. Call 1-800-373-2646 or e-mail customize@hdainc.com to place your order. Tell the sales representative you're interested in customizing a plan. A $50 nonrefundable consultation fee will be charged. You will then be instructed to complete a customization checklist indicating all the changes you wish to make to your plan. You may attach sketches if necessary. If you proceed with the custom changes the $50 will be credited to the total amount charged.

3. FAX the completed customization checklist to our design consultant. Within 24-48* business hours you will be provided with a written cost estimate to modify your plan. Our design consultant will contact you by phone if you wish to discuss any of your changes in greater detail.

4. Once you approve the estimate, a 75% retainer fee is collected and customization work gets underway. Preliminary drawings can usually be completed within 5-10* business days. Following approval of the preliminary drawings your design changes are completed within 5-10* business days. Your remaining 25% balance due is collected prior to shipment of your completed drawings. You will be shipped five sets of revised blueprints or a reproducible master, plus a customized materials list if required.

Before

After

Sample Modification Pricing Guide

The average prices specified below are provided as examples only. They refer to the most commonly requested changes, and are subject to change without notice. Prices for changes will vary or differ, from the prices below, depending on the number of modifications requested, the plan size, style, quality of original plan, format provided to us (originally drawn by hand or computer), and method of design used by the original designer. To obtain a detailed cost estimate or to get more information, please contact us.

Categories	Average Cost*
Adding or removing living space	Quote required
Adding or removing a garage	Starting at $400
Garage: Front entry to side load or vice versa	Starting at $300
Adding a screened porch	Starting at $280
Adding a bonus room in the attic	Starting at $450
Changing full basement to crawl space or vice versa	Starting at $495
Changing full basement to slab or vice versa	Starting at $495
Changing exterior building material	Starting at $200
Changing roof lines	Starting at $360
Adjusting ceiling height	Starting at $280
Adding, moving or removing an exterior opening	$65 per opening
Adding or removing a fireplace	Starting at $90
Modifying a non-bearing wall or room	$65 per room
Changing exterior walls from 2"x4" to 2"x6"	Starting at $200
Redesigning a bathroom or a kitchen	Starting at $120
Reverse plan right reading	Quote required
Adapting plans for local building code requirements	Quote required
Engineering and Architectural stamping and services	Quote required
Adjust plan for handicapped accessibility	Quote required
Interactive Illustrations (choices of exterior materials)	Quote required
Metric conversion of home plan	Starting at $400

*Prices and Terms are subject to change without notice.

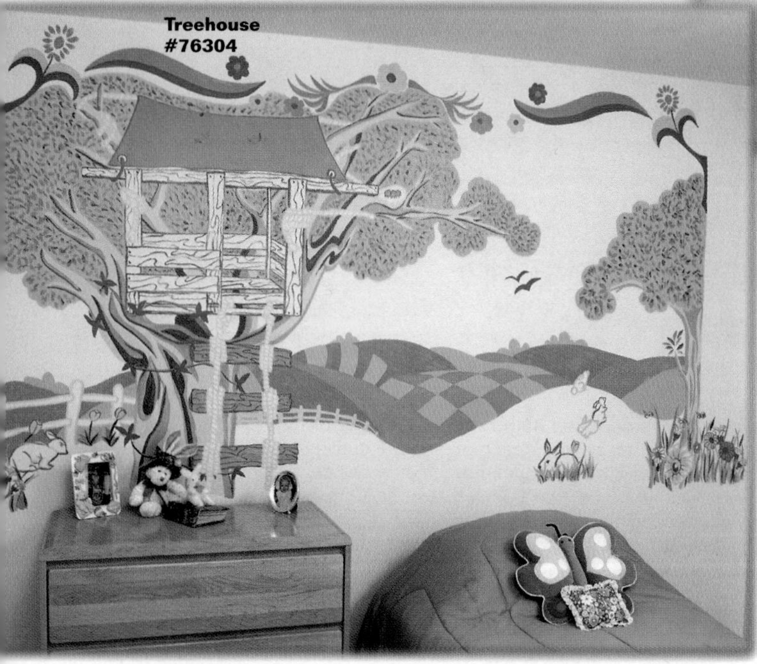

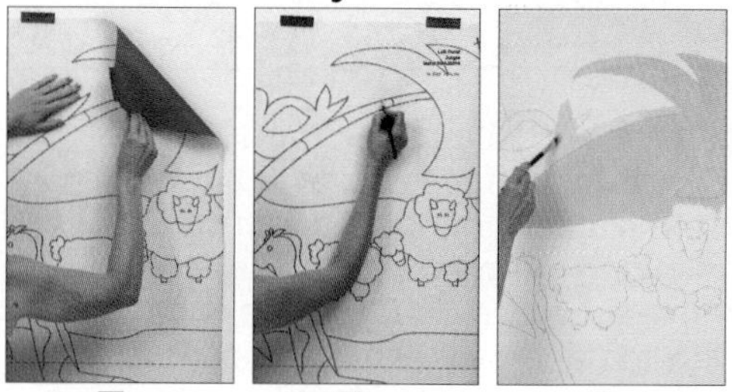

LOWE'S

Signature SERIES

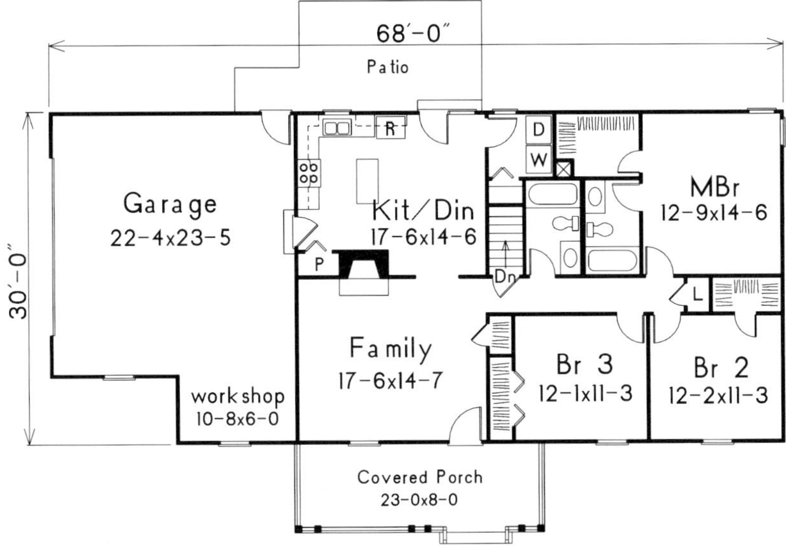
68'-0"
Patio
Garage
22-4x23-5
R
D
W
Kit/Din
17-6x14-6
P
Dn
MBr
12-9x14-6
L
30'-0"
Family
17-6x14-7
Br 3
12-1x11-3
Br 2
12-2x11-3
workshop
10-8x6-0
Covered Porch
23-0x8-0

Plan #530-001D-0024

Price Code A

Total Living Area: 1,360 Sq. Ft.

Home has 3 bedrooms, 2 baths, 2-car side entry garage and basement foundation, drawings also include crawl space and slab foundations.

Special features

- Kitchen/dining room features island workspace and plenty of dining area
- Master bedroom has a large walk-in closet and private bath
- Laundry room is adjacent to the kitchen for easy access
- Convenient workshop in the garage
- Large closets in secondary bedrooms

LOWE'S

Signature
SERIES

Plan #530-007D-0062

Price Code D

Total Living Area: 2,483 Sq. Ft.

Home has 4 bedrooms, 2 baths, 2-car side entry garage and basement foundation.

Special features

- A large entry porch with open brick arches and palladian door welcomes guests
- The vaulted great room features an entertainment center alcove and the ideal layout for furniture placement
- The dining room is extra large with a stylish tray ceiling
- A convenient kitchen with wrap-around counter, menu desk and pantry opens to the cozy breakfast area

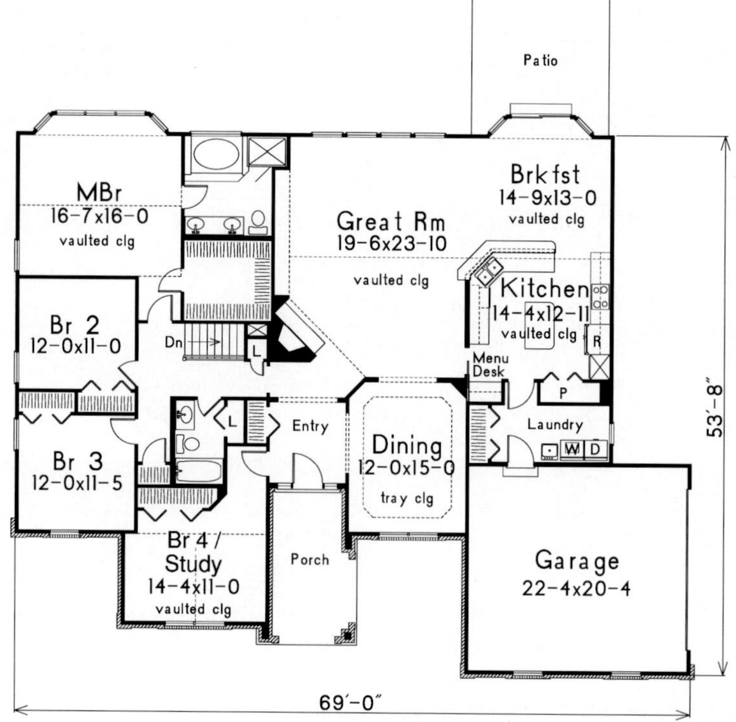
Patio
MBr
16-7x16-0
vaulted clg
Great Rm
19-6x23-10
vaulted clg
Brk fst
14-9x13-0
vaulted clg
Kitchen
14-4x12-11
vaulted clg
Br 2
12-0x11-0
Dn
Menu Desk
Br 3
12-0x11-5
Entry
Dining
12-0x15-0
tray clg
Laundry
Br 4 / Study
14-4x11-0
vaulted clg
Porch
Garage
22-4x20-4
69'-0"
53'-8"

Large Front Porch

LOWE'S

Signature SERIES

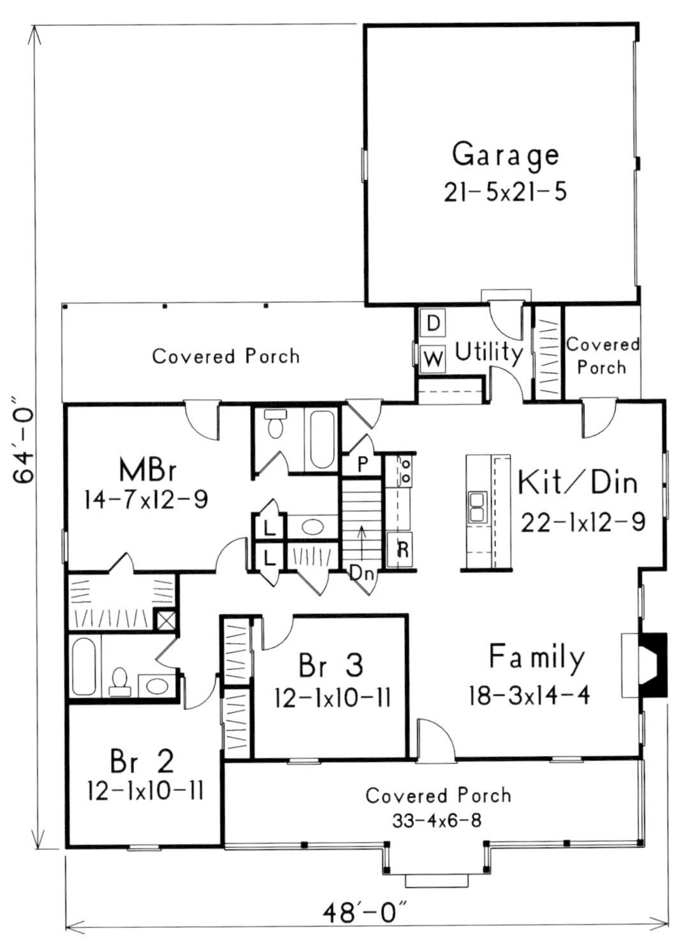
Garage
21-5x21-5
Covered Porch
D
W
Utility
Covered Porch
MBr
14-7x12-9
P
Kit/Din
22-1x12-9
L
L
R
Dn
Br 3
12-1x10-11
Family
18-3x14-4
Br 2
12-1x10-11
Covered Porch
33-4x6-8
64'-0"
48'-0"

Plan #530-001D-0031

Price Code B

Total Living Area:	1,501 Sq. Ft.

Home has 3 bedrooms, 2 baths, 2-car side entry garage and basement foundation, drawings also include crawl space and slab foundations.

Special features

- Spacious kitchen with dining area is open to the outdoors
- Convenient utility room is adjacent to garage
- Master bedroom features a private bath, dressing area and access to the large covered porch
- Large family room creates openness

LOWE'S

Signature SERIES

Plan #530-005D-0001

Price Code B

Total Living Area: 1,400 Sq. Ft.

Home has 3 bedrooms, 2 baths, 2-car garage and basement foundation, drawings also include crawl space foundation.

Special features

- Master bedroom is secluded for privacy
- Large utility room has additional cabinet space
- Covered porch provides an outdoor seating area
- Roof dormers add great curb appeal
- Living room and master bedroom feature vaulted ceilings
- Oversized two-car garage has storage

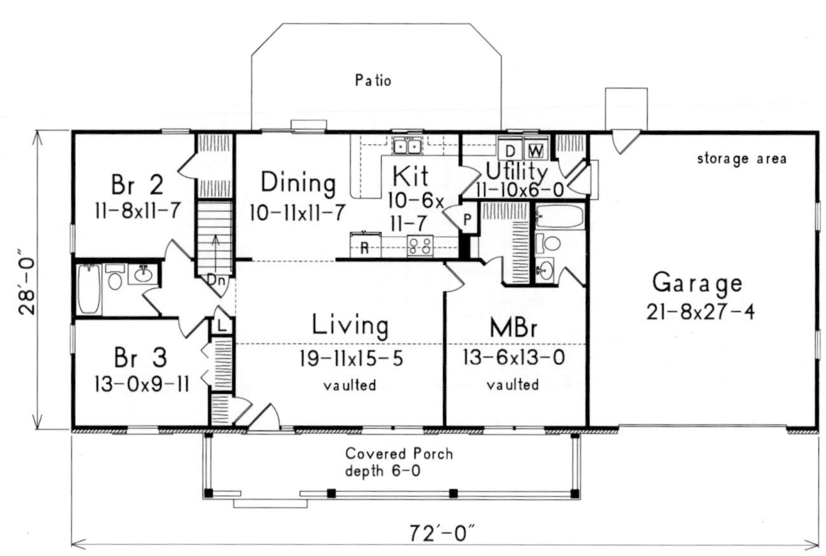
Patio
storage area
Br 2
11-8x11-7
Dining
10-11x11-7
Kit
10-6x
11-7
Utility
11-10x6-0
D
W
P
R
Dn
L
Garage
21-8x27-4
28'-0"
Living
19-11x15-5
vaulted
MBr
13-6x13-0
vaulted
Br 3
13-0x9-11
Covered Porch
depth 6-0
72'-0"

TO ORDER BLUEPRINTS USE THE FORM ON PAGE 288 OR CALL TOLL-FREE **1-800-DREAM HOME** (373-2646)

Double Atrium

LOWE'S

Signature
SERIES

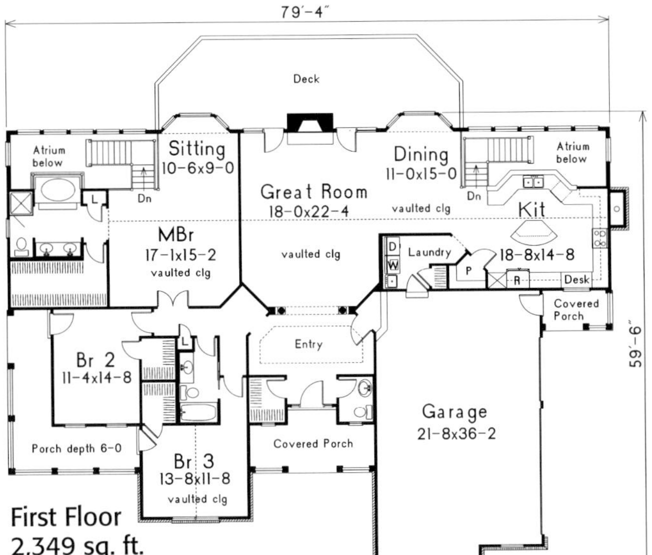
79'-4"
Deck
Atrium below
Sitting 10-6x9-0
Great Room 18-0x22-4
Dining 11-0x15-0
Atrium below
Dn
vaulted clg
Dn
Kit
MBr 17-1x15-2 vaulted clg
vaulted clg
Laundry
18-8x14-8
Desk
Covered Porch
59'-6"
Entry
Br 2 11-4x14-8
Garage 21-8x36-2
Porch depth 6-0
Covered Porch
Br 3 13-8x11-8 vaulted clg

First Floor
2,349 sq. ft.

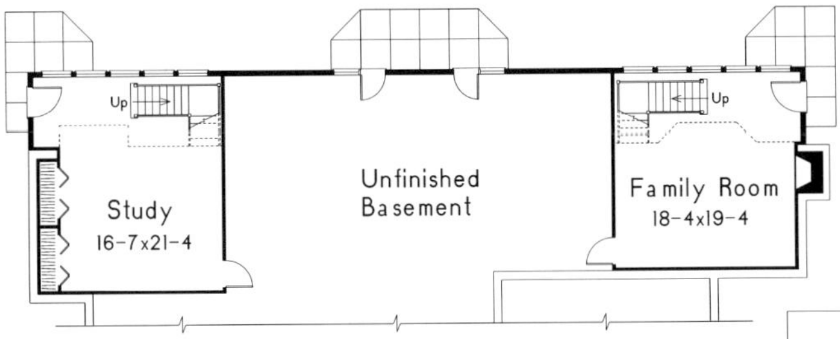

Up
Up
Study 16-7x21-4
Unfinished Basement
Family Room 18-4x19-4

Lower Level
850 sq. ft.

Plan #530-007D-0056

Price Code E

Total Living Area: 3,199 Sq. Ft.

Home has 3 bedrooms, 2 1/2 baths, 3-car side entry garage and walk-out basement foundation.

Special features

- Grand-scale kitchen features bay-shaped cabinetry built over an atrium that overlooks a two-story window wall
- A second atrium dominates the master bedroom that boasts a sitting area with bay window as well as a luxurious bath that has a whirlpool tub open to the garden atrium and lower level study

Rear View

LOWE'S

Signature SERIES

Charming Country Styling

Plan #530-021D-0006

Price Code C

Total Living Area: 1,600 Sq. Ft.

Home has 3 bedrooms, 2 baths, 2-car side entry garage and slab foundation, drawings also include crawl space and basement foundations.

Special features

- Impressive sunken living room features a massive stone fireplace and 16' vaulted ceiling
- The dining room is conveniently located next to the kitchen and divided for privacy
- Energy efficient home with 2" x 6" exterior walls
- Special amenities include a sewing room, glass shelves in kitchen and master bath and a large utility area
- Sunken master bedroom features a distinctive sitting room

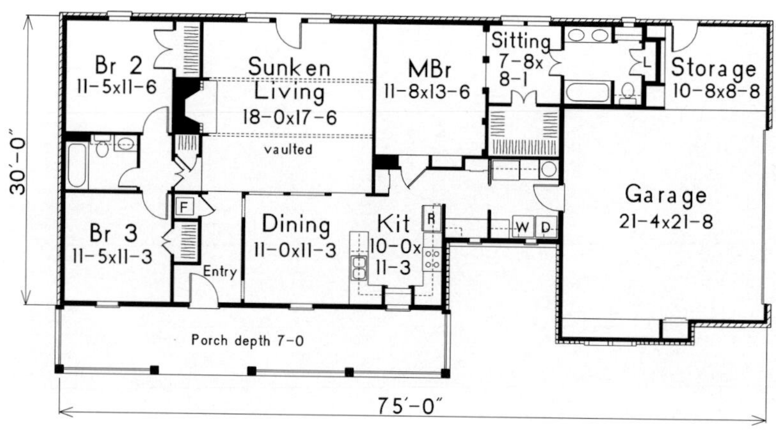
Br 2
11-5x11-6
Sunken Living
18-0x17-6
vaulted
MBr
11-8x13-6
Sitting
7-8x
8-1
Storage
10-8x8-8
Garage
21-4x21-8
Br 3
11-5x11-3
Entry
Dining
11-0x11-3
Kit
10-0x
11-3
W D
Porch depth 7-0
30'-0"
75'-0"

Atrium's Dramatic Ambiance

LOWE'S

Signature
SERIES

Plan #530-007D-0010

Price Code C

Total Living Area: 1,721 Sq. Ft.

Home has 3 bedrooms, 2 baths, 3-car garage and walk-out basement foundation, drawings also include crawl space and slab foundations.

Special features

- Roof dormers add great curb appeal
- Vaulted dining and great rooms are immersed in light from the atrium window wall
- Breakfast room opens onto the covered porch
- Functionally designed kitchen
- 1,604 sq. ft. on the first floor and 117 square feet on the lower level

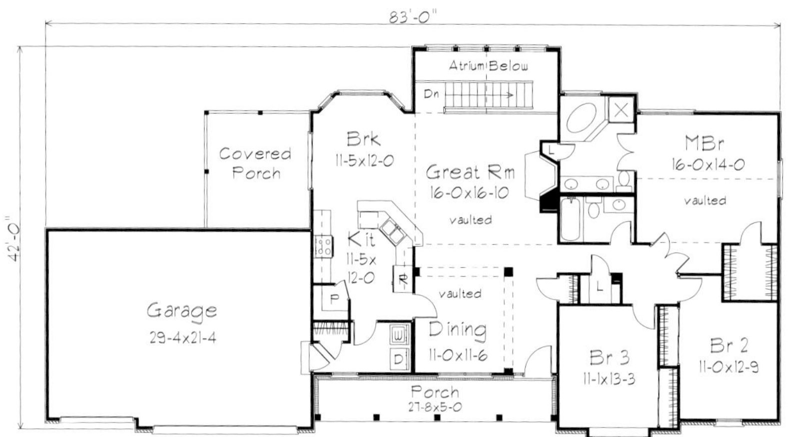
83'-0"
42'-0"
Atrium Below
Dn
Covered Porch
Brk
11-5x12-0
Great Rm
16-0x16-10
vaulted
MBr
16-0x14-0
vaulted
Kit
11-5x
12-0
Garage
29-4x21-4
vaulted
Dining
11-0x11-6
Br 3
11-1x13-3
Br 2
11-0x12-9
Porch
27-8x5-0

Rear View

Plan #530-007D-0002

Price Code G

Total Living Area: 3,814 Sq. Ft.

Home has 3 bedrooms, 2 1/2 baths, 3-car side entry garage and walk-out basement foundation.

Special features

- Massive sunken great room with vaulted ceiling includes exciting balcony overlook of towering atrium window wall
- Breakfast bar adjoins open "California" kitchen
- Seven vaulted rooms for drama and four fireplaces for warmth
- Master bath is complemented by the colonnade and fireplace surrounding the sunken tub and deck

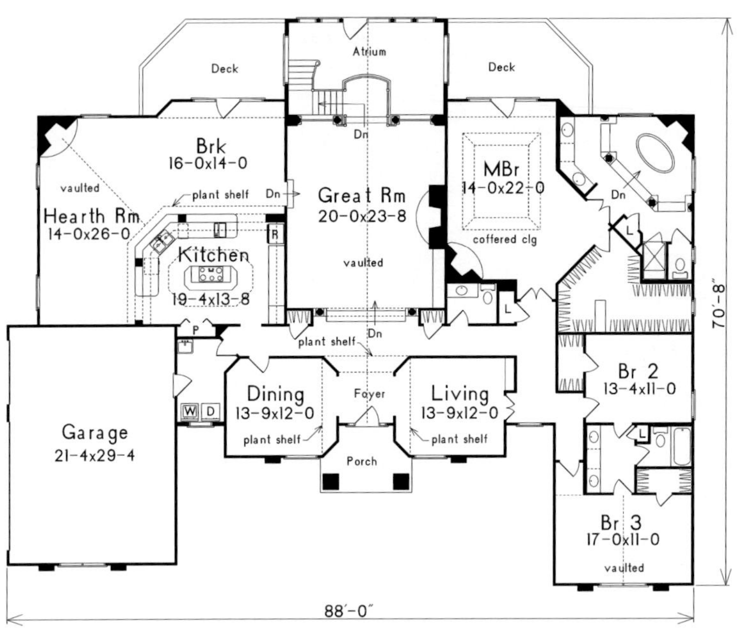
Deck
Atrium
Deck
Brk
16-0x14-0
vaulted
plant shelf
Dn
Hearth Rm
14-0x26-0
Kitchen
19-4x13-8
Great Rm
20-0x23-8
vaulted
MBr
14-0x22-0
coffered clg
Dn
plant shelf
Dn
Dining
13-9x12-0
plant shelf
Foyer
Living
13-9x12-0
plant shelf
Porch
Garage
21-4x29-4
W D
Br 2
13-4x11-0
Br 3
17-0x11-0
vaulted
88'-0"
70'-8"

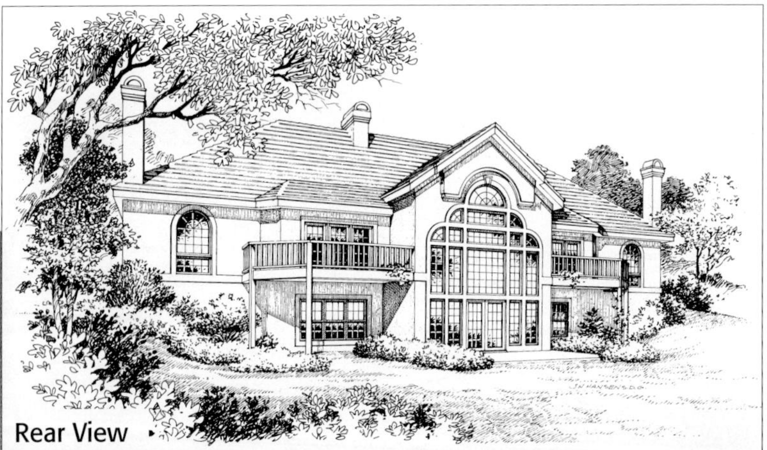

Rear View

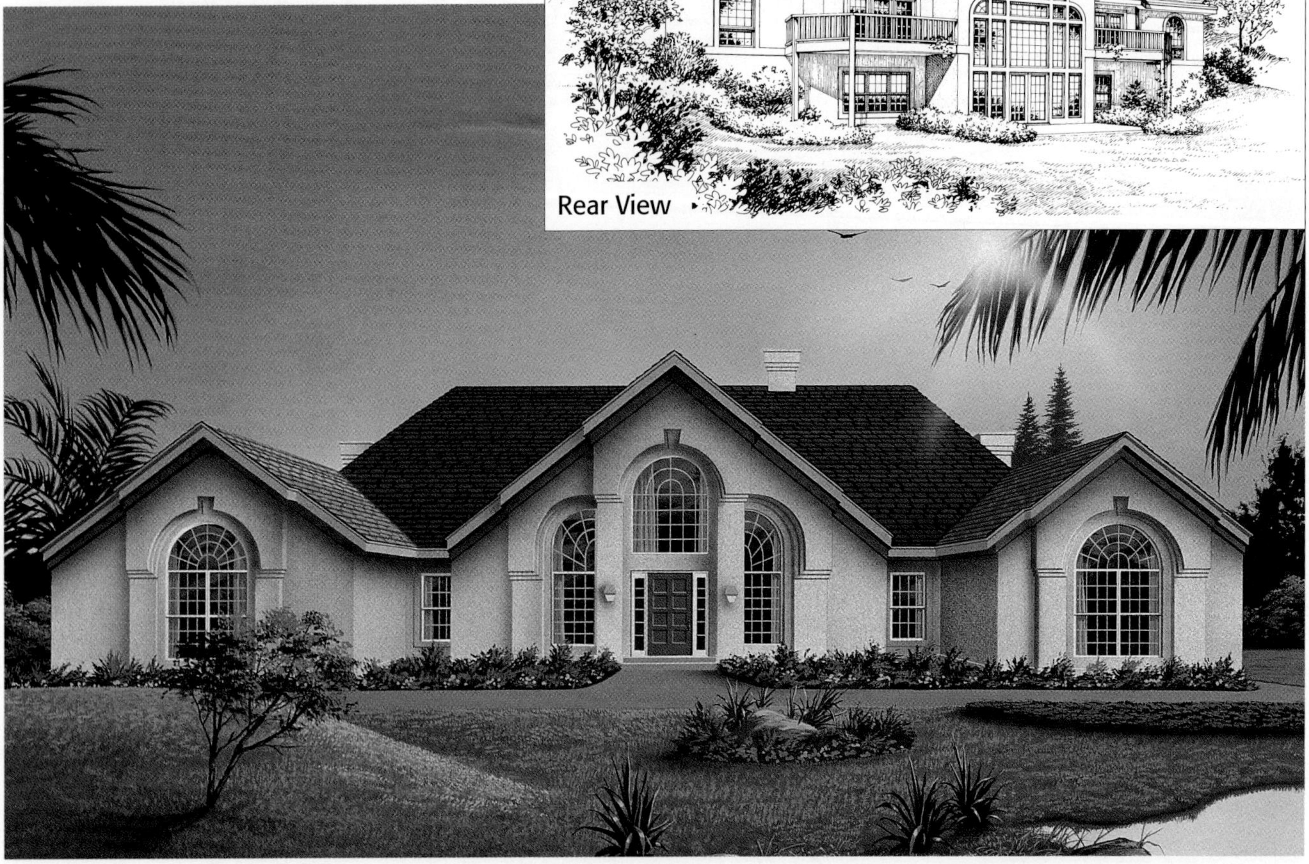

TO ORDER BLUEPRINTS USE THE FORM ON PAGE 288 OR CALL TOLL-FREE **1-800-DREAM HOME** (373-2646)

Floridian Architecture With Mother-In-Law Suite

LOWE'S

Signature SERIES

Plan #530-007D-0066

Price Code D

Total Living Area: 2,408 Sq. Ft.

Home has 4 bedrooms, 3 baths, 3-car side entry garage and walk-out basement foundation.

Special features

- Large vaulted great room overlooks atrium and window wall, adjoins dining room, spacious breakfast room with bay and pass-through kitchen
- A special private bedroom with bath, separate from other bedrooms, is perfect for mother-in-law suite or children home from college
- Atrium opens to 1,100 square feet of optional living area below

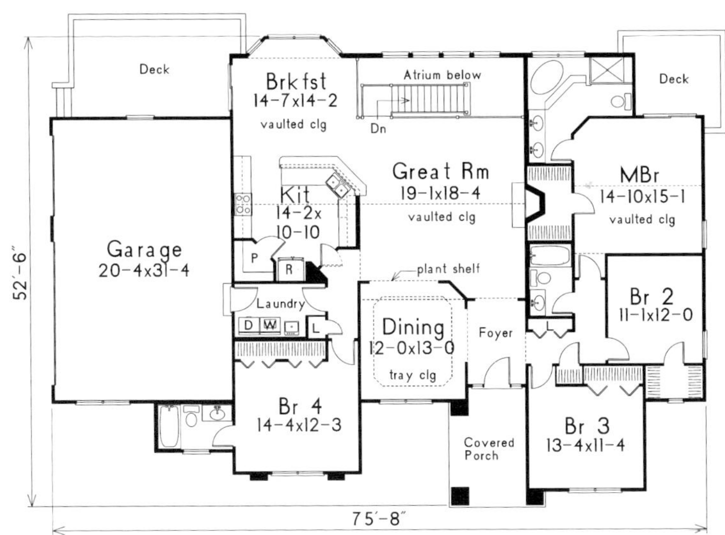

Deck
Brk fst
14-7x14-2
vaulted clg
Atrium below
Dn
Deck
Great Rm
19-1x18-4
vaulted clg
MBr
14-10x15-1
vaulted clg
Kit
14-2x
10-10
Garage
20-4x31-4
P
R
plant shelf
Laundry
D
W
L
Dining
12-0x13-0
tray clg
Foyer
Br 2
11-1x12-0
Br 4
14-4x12-3
Covered Porch
Br 3
13-4x11-4
52'-6"
75'-8"

First Floor
2,408 sq. ft.

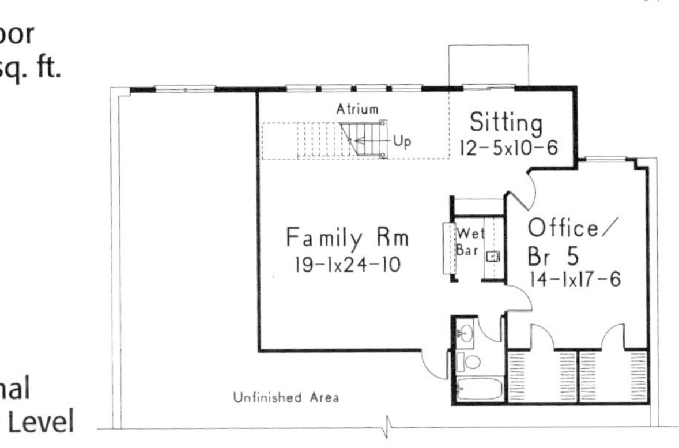

Atrium
Up
Sitting
12-5x10-6
Family Rm
19-1x24-10
Wet Bar
Office/
Br 5
14-1x17-6
Unfinished Area

Optional
Lower Level

LOWE'S

Signature
SERIES

Plan #530-007D-0050

Price Code E

Total Living Area: 2,723 Sq. Ft.

Home has 4 bedrooms, 2 1/2 baths, 3-car side entry garage and basement foundation.

Special features

- Large porch invites you into an elegant foyer which accesses a vaulted study with private hall and coat closet
- Great room is second to none, comprised of a fireplace, built-in shelves, vaulted ceiling and a 1 1/2 story window wall
- A spectacular hearth room with vaulted ceiling and masonry fireplace opens to an elaborate kitchen featuring two snack bars, a cooking island and walk-in pantry

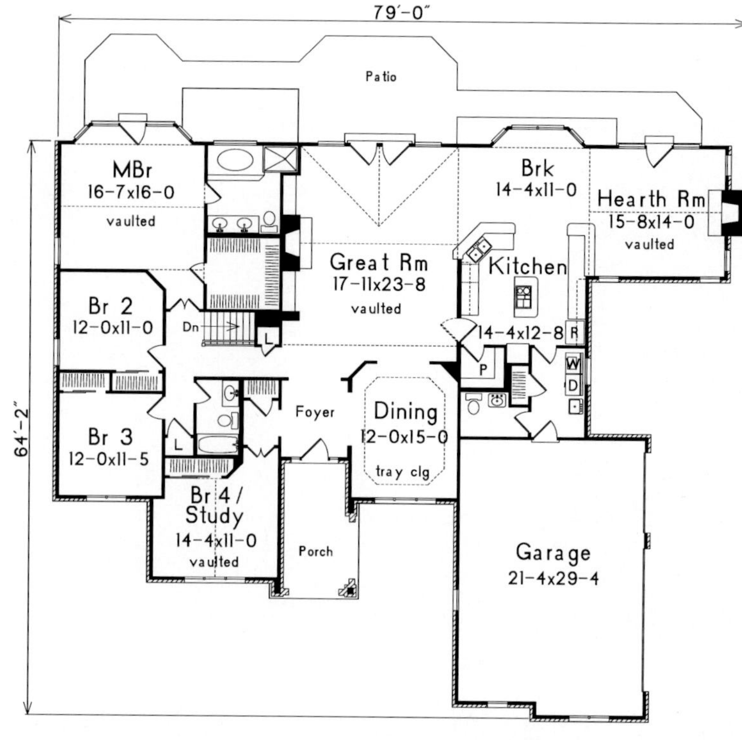
79'-0"
64'-2"
Patio
MBr
16-7x16-0
vaulted
Brk
14-4x11-0
Hearth Rm
15-8x14-0
vaulted
Great Rm
17-11x23-8
vaulted
Kitchen
14-4x12-8
Br 2
12-0x11-0
Dn
Br 3
12-0x11-5
Foyer
Dining
12-0x15-0
tray clg
Br 4 /
Study
14-4x11-0
vaulted
Porch
Garage
21-4x29-4

TO ORDER BLUEPRINTS USE THE FORM ON PAGE 288 OR CALL TOLL-FREE **1-800-DREAM HOME** (373-2646)

LOWE'S

Signature SERIES

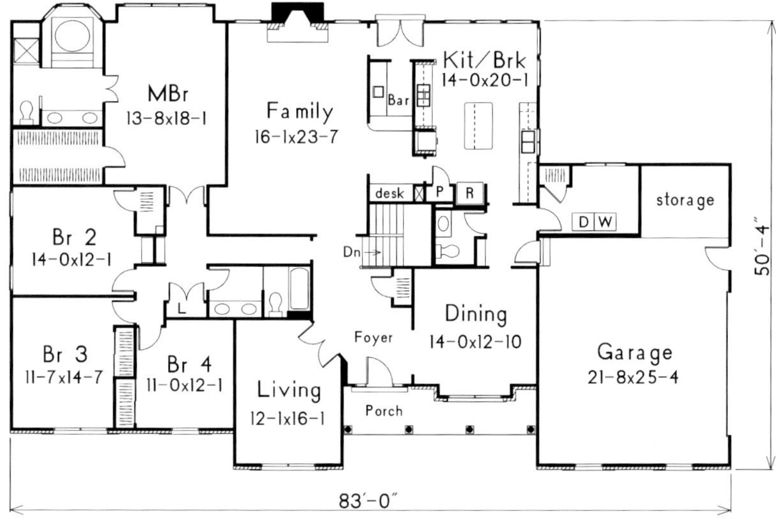
MBr
13-8x18-1
Family
16-1x23-7
Kit/Brk
14-0x20-1
Bar
desk
P
R
storage
D W
Br 2
14-0x12-1
Dn
L
Br 3
11-7x14-7
Br 4
11-0x12-1
Foyer
Dining
14-0x12-10
Garage
21-8x25-4
Living
12-1x16-1
Porch
50'-4"
83'-0"

Plan #530-001D-0007

Price Code E

Total Living Area: 2,874 Sq. Ft.

Home has 4 bedrooms, 2 1/2 baths, 2-car side entry garage and basement foundation.

Special features

- Large family room with sloped ceiling and wood beams adjoins the kitchen and breakfast area with windows on two walls
- Large foyer opens to family room with massive stone fireplace and open stairs to the basement
- Private master bedroom includes a raised tub under the bay window, dramatic dressing area and a huge walk-in closet

LOWE'S

Signature
SERIES

Plan #530-003D-0002

Price Code B

Total Living Area: 1,676 Sq. Ft.

Home has 3 bedrooms, 2 baths, 2-car garage and basement foundation, drawings also include crawl space and slab foundations.

Special features

- The living area skylights and large breakfast room with bay window provide plenty of sunlight
- The master bedroom has a walk-in closet and both the secondary bedrooms have large closets
- Vaulted ceilings, plant shelving and a fireplace provide a quality living area

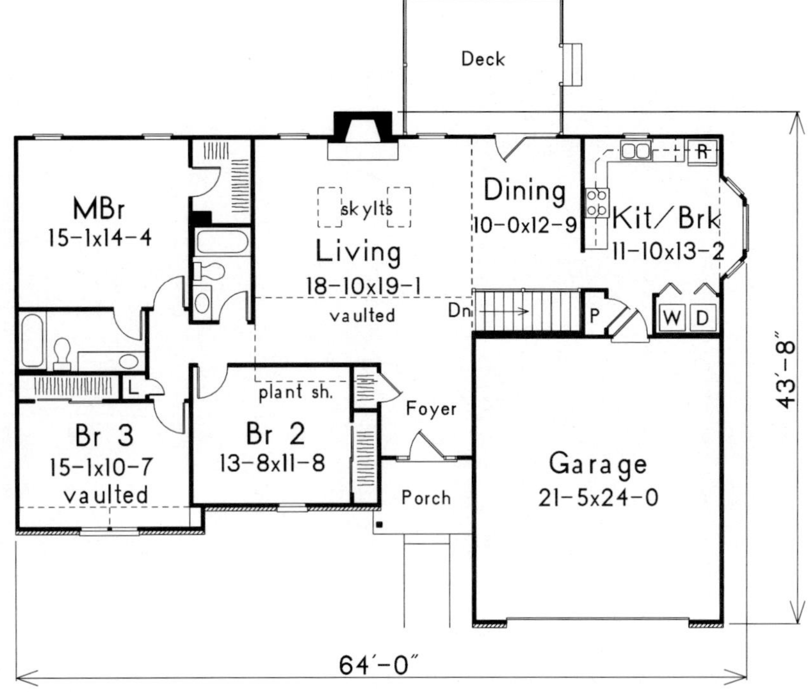
Deck
MBr
15-1x14-4
skylts
Living
18-10x19-1
vaulted
Dining
10-0x12-9
Kit/Brk
11-10x13-2
R
Dn
P
W
D
L
plant sh.
Foyer
Br 3
15-1x10-7
vaulted
Br 2
13-8x11-8
Porch
Garage
21-5x24-0
43'-8"
64'-0"

TO ORDER BLUEPRINTS USE THE FORM ON PAGE 288 OR CALL TOLL-FREE **1-800-DREAM HOME** (373-2646)

Gabled And Arched Brick Entry

LOWE'S

Signature
SERIES

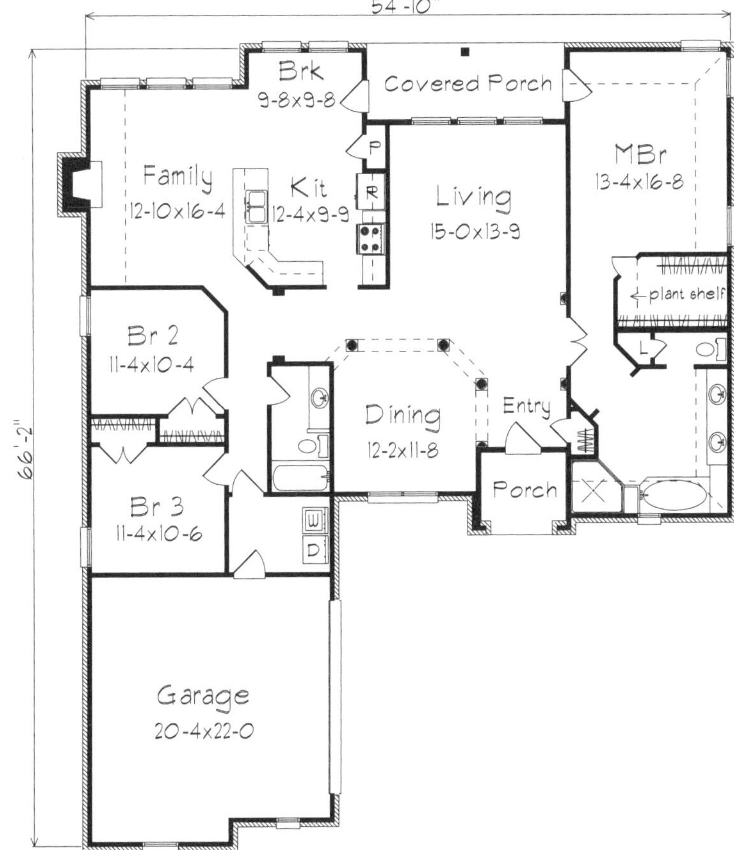
54'-10"
66'-2"
Brk
9-8x9-8
Covered Porch
Family
12-10x16-4
Kit
12-4x9-9
P
R
Living
15-0x13-9
MBr
13-4x16-8
plant shelf
L
Br 2
11-4x10-4
Dining
12-2x11-8
Entry
Porch
Br 3
11-4x10-6
W
D
Garage
20-4x22-0

Plan #530-018D-0008

Price Code C

Total Living Area: 2,109 Sq. Ft.

Home has 3 bedrooms, 2 baths, 2-car side entry garage and slab foundation, drawings also include crawl space foundation.

Special features

- 12' ceilings in the living and dining rooms
- The kitchen is designed as an integral part of the family and breakfast rooms
- The secluded and generously sized master bedroom includes a plant shelf, walk-in closet and private bath with separate tub and shower
- Stately columns and circle-top window frame the dining room

Signature SERIES

Unique Step Up

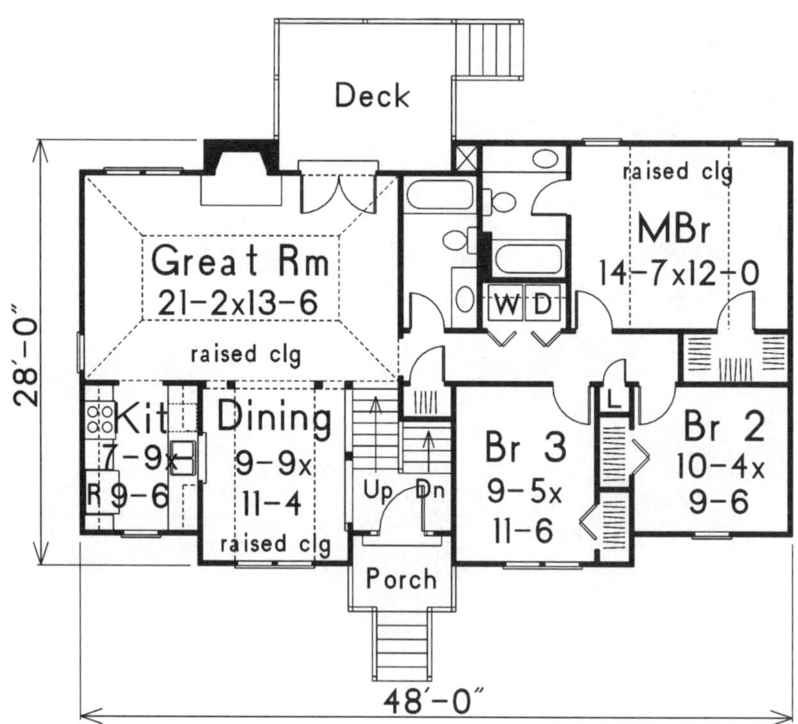

Deck
raised clg
MBr
14-7x12-0
Great Rm
21-2x13-6
raised clg
W D
Kit
7-9x
9-6
R
Dining
9-9x
11-4
raised clg
Up
Dn
Br 3
9-5x
11-6
L
Br 2
10-4x
9-6
Porch
28'-0"
48'-0"

Plan #530-053D-0049

Price Code A

Total Living Area: 1,261 Sq. Ft.

Home has 3 bedrooms, 2 baths, 2-car drive under garage and basement foundation.

Special features

- Great room, brightened by windows and doors, features a vaulted ceiling, fireplace and access to the deck
- Vaulted master bedroom enjoys a private bath
- Split-level foyer leads to the living space or basement
- Centrally located laundry area is near the bedrooms

Covered Arched Entry

LOWE'S
Signature
SERIES

Rear View

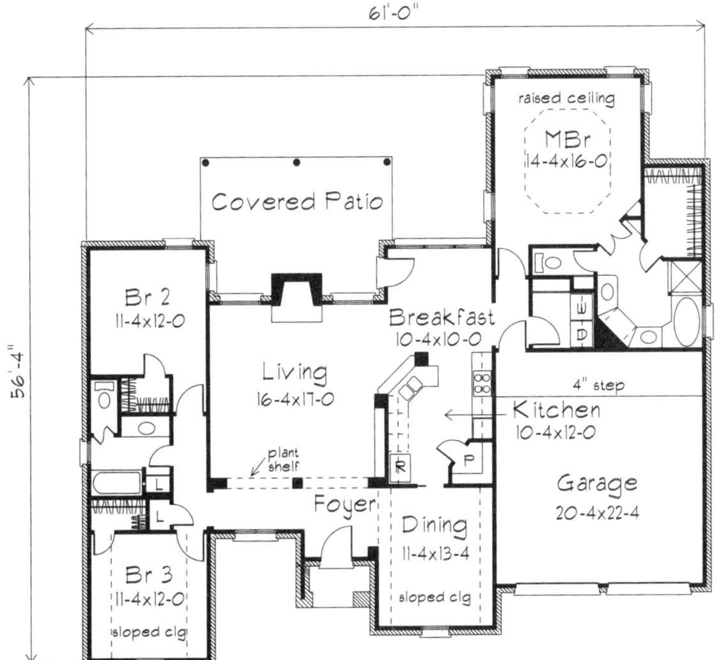
61'-0"
56'-4"
raised ceiling
MBr
14-4x16-0
Covered Patio
Br 2
11-4x12-0
Breakfast
10-4x10-0
Living
16-4x17-0
4" step
Kitchen
10-4x12-0
plant shelf
Garage
20-4x22-4
Foyer
Dining
11-4x13-4
sloped clg
Br 3
11-4x12-0
sloped clg

Plan #530-037D-0031

Price Code C

Total Living Area: 1,923 Sq. Ft.

Home has 3 bedrooms, 2 baths, 2-car garage and slab foundation.

Special features

- The foyer opens into a spacious living room with fireplace and splendid view of the covered porch
- Kitchen has a walk-in pantry adjacent to the laundry area and breakfast room
- All bedrooms feature walk-in closets
- Secluded master bedroom includes unique angled bath with spacious walk-in closet

Plan #530-048D-0005

Price Code E

Total Living Area: 2,287 Sq. Ft.

Home has 4 bedrooms, 2 1/2 baths, 2-car side entry garage and slab foundation.

Special features

- A double-door entry leads into an impressive master bedroom which accesses the covered porch and features a deluxe bath with double closets and a step-up tub
- Kitchen easily serves formal and informal areas of home
- The spacious foyer opens into formal dining and living rooms

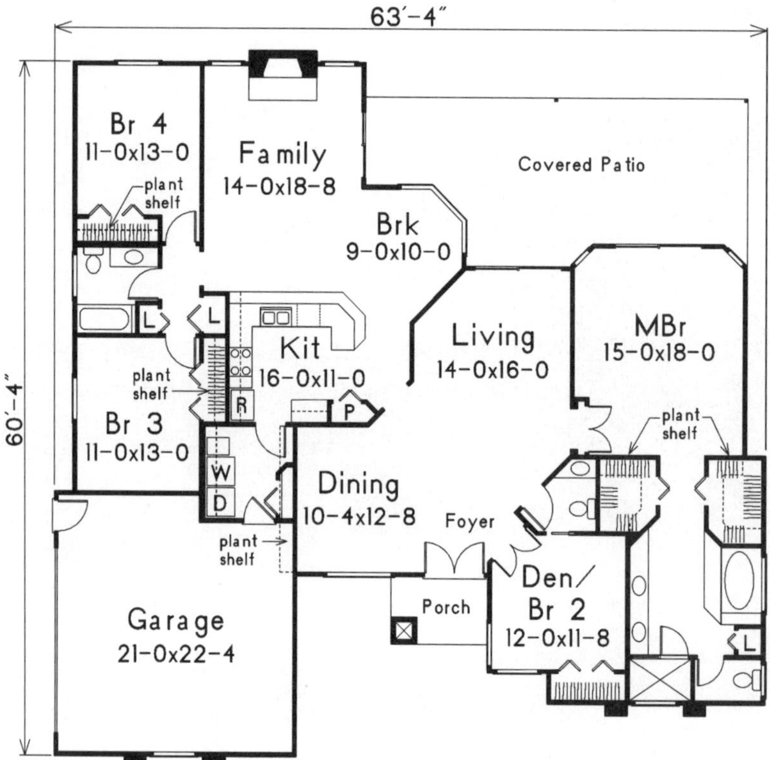
63′-4″
60′-4″
Br 4
11-0x13-0
plant shelf
Family
14-0x18-8
Covered Patio
Brk
9-0x10-0
Living
14-0x16-0
MBr
15-0x18-0
Kit
16-0x11-0
plant shelf
Br 3
11-0x13-0
L
R
P
W
D
Dining
10-4x12-8
Foyer
plant shelf
Den/
Br 2
12-0x11-8
Porch
Garage
21-0x22-4

J.N. HANSEN P.T.L.

TO ORDER BLUEPRINTS USE THE FORM ON PAGE 288 OR CALL TOLL-FREE **1-800-DREAM HOME** (373-2646)

Country Style With Spacious Rooms

LOWE'S

Signature SERIES

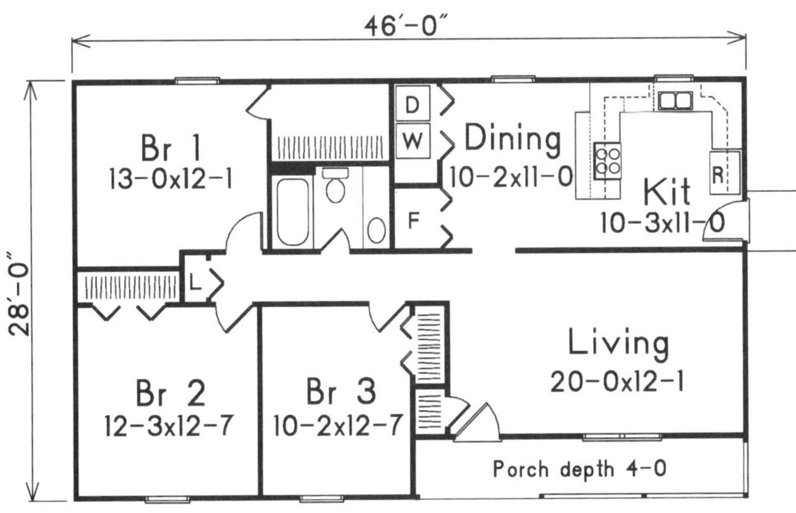
46'-0"
28'-0"
Br 1
13-0x12-1
D
W
Dining
10-2x11-0
Kit
10-3x11-0
R
F
L
Living
20-0x12-1
Br 2
12-3x12-7
Br 3
10-2x12-7
Porch depth 4-0

Plan #530-001D-0045

Price Code AA

Total Living Area: 1,197 Sq. Ft.

Home has 3 bedrooms, 1 bath and crawl space foundation, drawings also include basement and slab foundations.

Special features

- U-shaped kitchen includes ample workspace, breakfast bar, laundry area and direct access to the outdoors
- Large living room has a convenient coat closet
- Bedroom #1 features a large walk-in closet

LOWE'S

Signature SERIES

Traditional Exterior, Handsome Accents

Plan #530-001D-0013

Price Code D

Total Living Area: 1,882 Sq. Ft.

Home has 3 bedrooms, 2 baths, 2-car garage and basement foundation.

Special features

- Wide, handsome entrance opens to the vaulted great room with fireplace
- Living and dining areas are conveniently joined but still allow privacy
- Private covered porch extends breakfast area
- Practical passageway runs through the laundry and mud room from the garage to the kitchen
- Vaulted ceiling in master bedroom

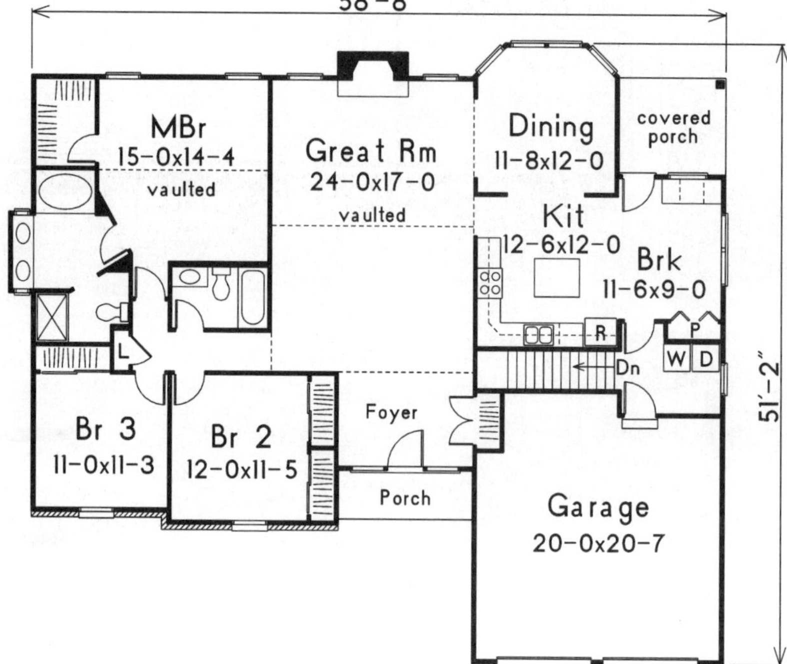
58′-8″
51′-2″
MBr
15-0x14-4
vaulted
Great Rm
24-0x17-0
vaulted
Dining
11-8x12-0
covered porch
Kit
12-6x12-0
Brk
11-6x9-0
R
P
W
D
Dn
L
Br 3
11-0x11-3
Br 2
12-0x11-5
Foyer
Porch
Garage
20-0x20-7

Accented By Bay Windows

LOWE'S

Signature SERIES

Plan #530-053D-0002

Price Code C

Total Living Area: 1,668 Sq. Ft.

Home has 3 bedrooms, 2 baths, 2-car drive under garage and basement foundation.

Special features

- Large bay windows grace the breakfast area, master bedroom and dining room
- Extensive walk-in closets and storage spaces are located throughout the home
- Handy covered entry porch
- Large living room has a fireplace, built-in bookshelves and sloped ceiling

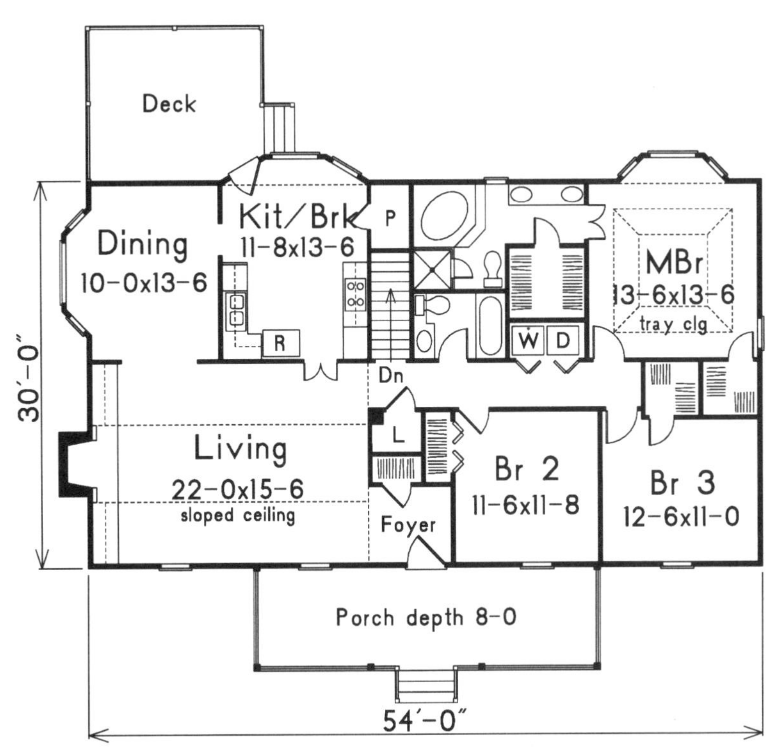
Deck
Dining
10-0x13-6
Kit/Brk
11-8x13-6
P
R
MBr
13-6x13-6
tray clg
W
D
Dn
Living
22-0x15-6
sloped ceiling
L
Br 2
11-6x11-8
Br 3
12-6x11-0
Foyer
Porch depth 8-0
30'-0"
54'-0"

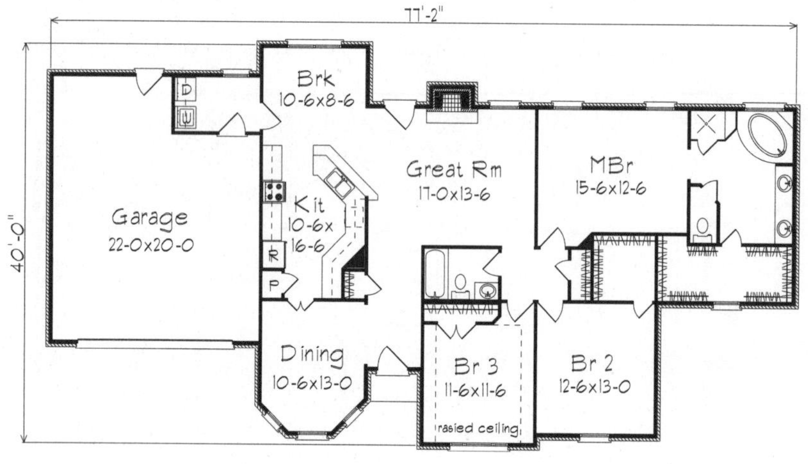
77'-2"
40'-0"
Brk
10-6x8-6
Great Rm
17-0x13-6
MBr
15-6x12-6
Kit
10-6x
16-6
Garage
22-0x20-0
Dining
10-6x13-0
Br 3
11-6x11-6
rasied ceiling
Br 2
12-6x13-0

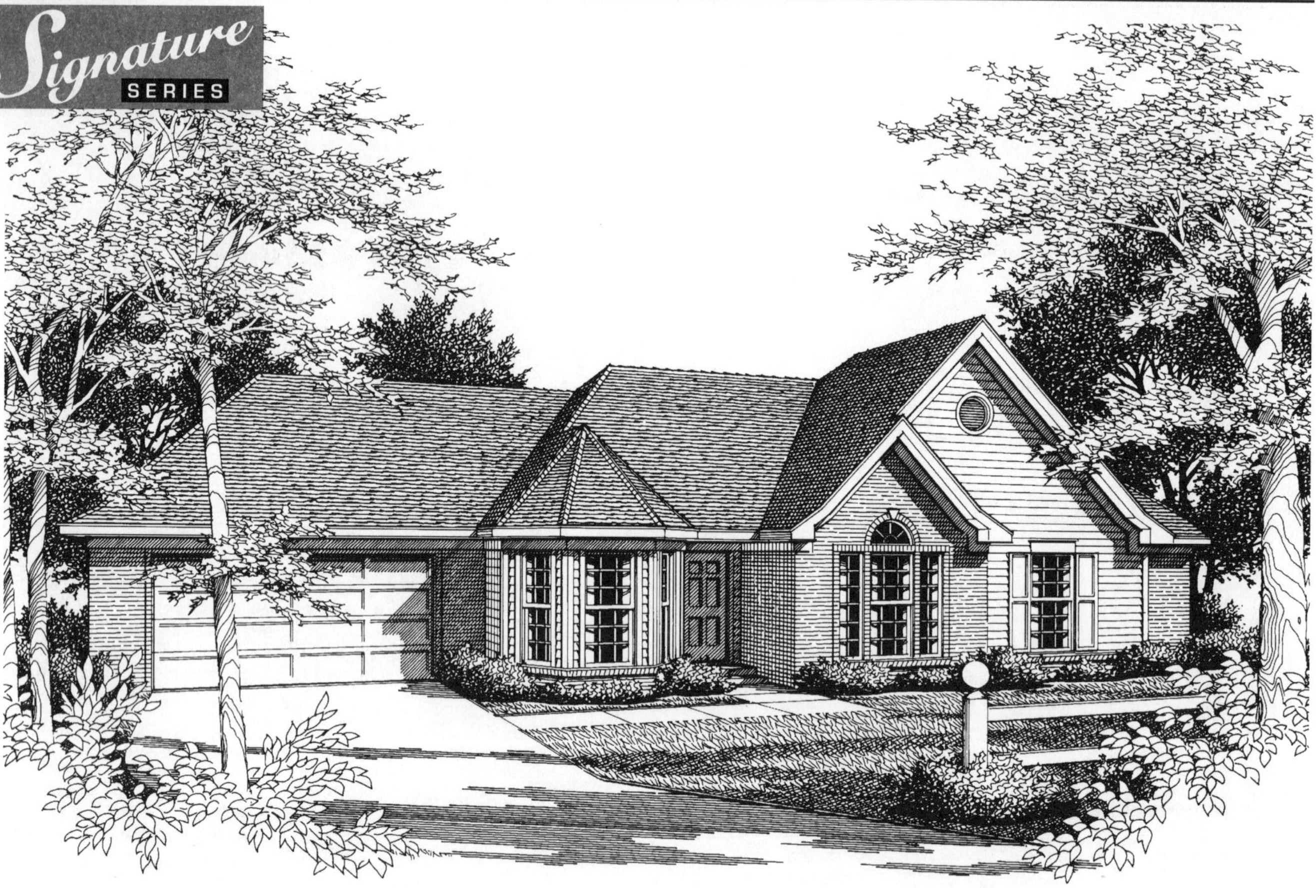

Plan #530-018D-0006

Price Code B

Total Living Area: 1,742 Sq. Ft.

Home has 3 bedrooms, 2 baths, 2-car garage and slab foundation, drawings also include crawl space foundation.

Special features

- Efficient kitchen combines with the breakfast area and great room creating a spacious living area
- Master bedroom includes a private bath with huge walk-in closet, shower and corner tub
- Great room boasts a fireplace and access outdoors
- Laundry room is conveniently located near the kitchen and garage

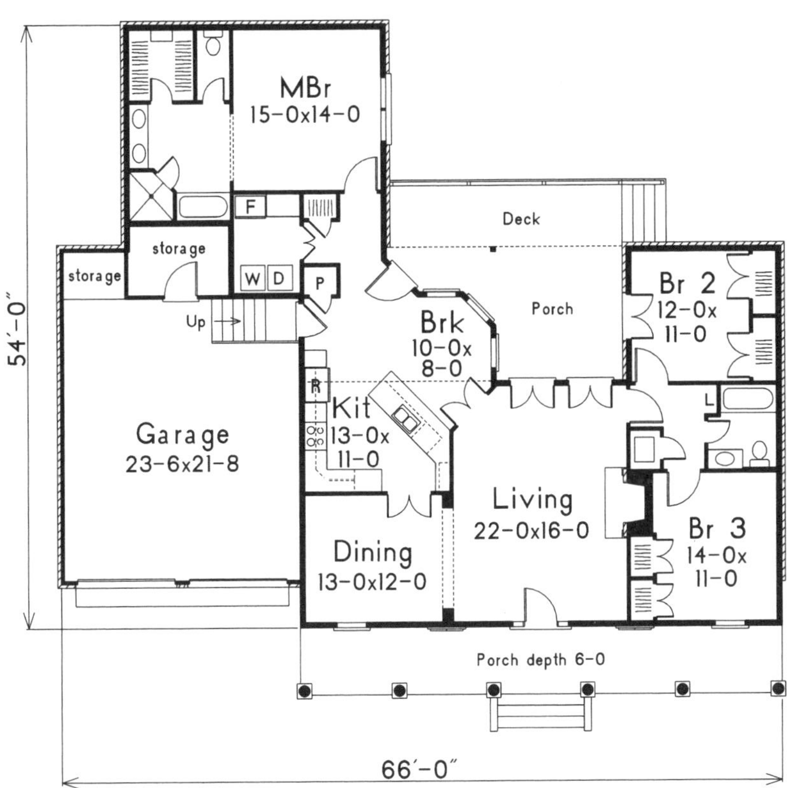
MBr
15-0x14-0
storage
storage
F
W D
P
Up
Deck
Porch
Brk
10-0x
8-0
Br 2
12-0x
11-0
Kit
13-0x
11-0
Garage
23-6x21-8
Living
22-0x16-0
Br 3
14-0x
11-0
Dining
13-0x12-0
Porch depth 6-0
54'-0"
66'-0"

Plan #530-021D-0004

Price Code C

Total Living Area: 1,800 Sq. Ft.

Home has 3 bedrooms, 2 baths, 2-car garage and crawl space foundation, drawings also include slab foundation.

Special features

- The stylish kitchen and breakfast area feature large windows that allow a great view outdoors
- Covered front and rear porches provide an added dimension to this home's living space
- Generous storage areas and a large utility room
- Energy efficient home with 2" x 6" exterior walls
- Large separate master bedroom with adjoining bath has a large tub and corner shower

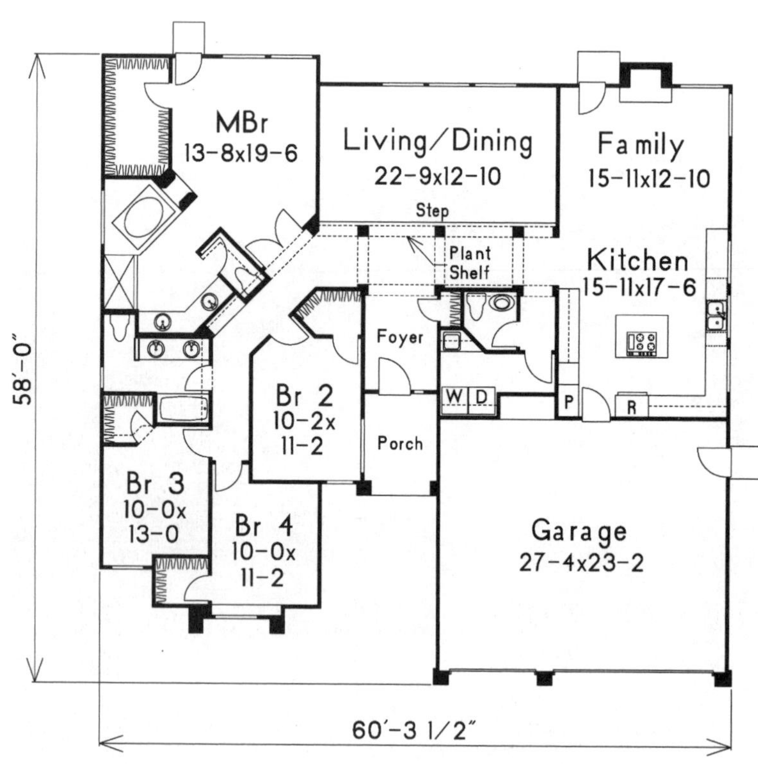
MBr
13-8x19-6
Living/Dining
22-9x12-10
Family
15-11x12-10
Step
Plant Shelf
Kitchen
15-11x17-6
Foyer
W D
P
R
Br 2
10-2x
11-2
Porch
Br 3
10-0x
13-0
Br 4
10-0x
11-2
Garage
27-4x23-2
58'-0"
60'-3 1/2"

Plan #530-061D-0003

Price Code D

Total Living Area: 2,255 Sq. Ft.

Home has 4 bedrooms, 2 1/2 baths, 3-car garage and slab foundation.

Special features

- Walk-in closets in all bedrooms
- Plant shelf graces hallway
- Large functional kitchen adjoins the family room which features a fireplace and access outdoors
- Master bath comes complete with a double vanity, enclosed toilet, separate tub and shower and cozy fireplace
- Living/dining room combine for a large formal gathering room

TO ORDER BLUEPRINTS USE THE FORM ON PAGE 288 OR CALL TOLL-FREE **1-800-DREAM HOME** (373-2646)

LOWE'S

Signature
SERIES

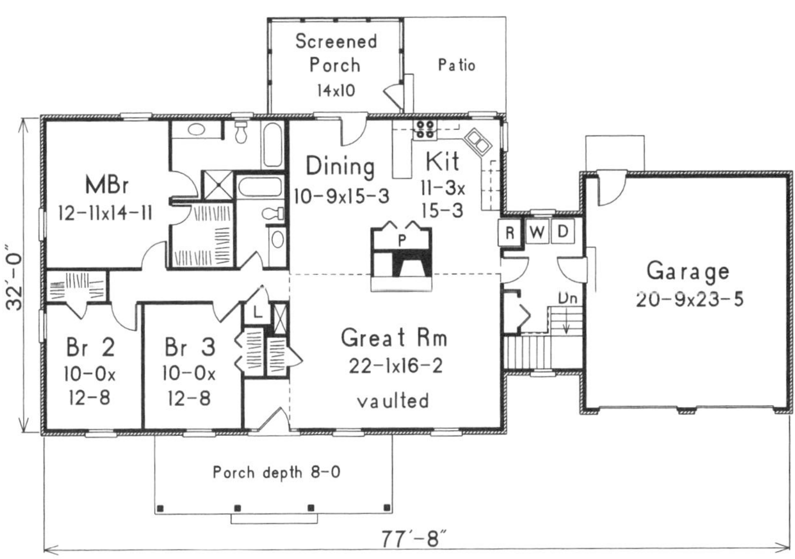
Screened
Porch
14x10
Patio
MBr
12-11x14-11
Dining
10-9x15-3
Kit
11-3x
15-3
R
W
D
Garage
20-9x23-5
Dn
Br 2
10-0x
12-8
Br 3
10-0x
12-8
L
Great Rm
22-1x16-2
vaulted
Porch depth 8-0
32'-0"
77'-8"

Plan #530-006D-0003

Price Code B

Total Living Area: 1,674 Sq. Ft.

Home has 3 bedrooms, 2 baths, 2-car garage and basement foundation, drawings also include crawl space and slab foundations.

Special features

- Vaulted great room, dining area and kitchen all enjoy a central fireplace and log bin
- Convenient laundry/mud room is located between the garage and family area with handy stairs to the basement
- Easily expandable screened porch and adjacent patio access the dining area
- Master bedroom features a full bath with tub, separate shower and walk-in closet

Window Adds Character Inside And Out

Plan #530-022D-0018

Price Code A

Total Living Area: 1,368 Sq. Ft.

Home has 3 bedrooms, 2 baths, 2-car garage and basement foundation.

Special features

- Entry foyer steps down to open living area which combines great room and formal dining area
- Vaulted master bedroom includes a box-bay window, large vanity, separate tub and shower
- Cozy breakfast area features direct access to the patio and pass-through kitchen
- Handy linen closet is located in the hall

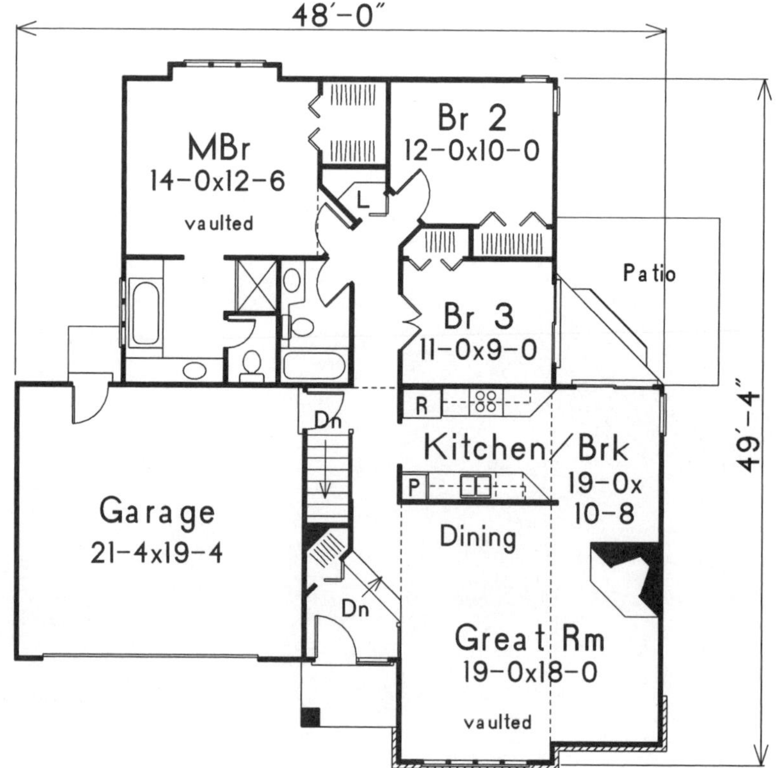
48'-0"
49'-4"
MBr
14-0x12-6
vaulted
Br 2
12-0x10-0
L
Patio
Br 3
11-0x9-0
R
Dn
Kitchen/Brk
19-0x
10-8
P
Garage
21-4x19-4
Dining
Dn
Great Rm
19-0x18-0
vaulted

TO ORDER BLUEPRINTS USE THE FORM ON PAGE 288 OR CALL TOLL-FREE **1-800-DREAM HOME** (373-2646)

LOWE'S

Signature
SERIES

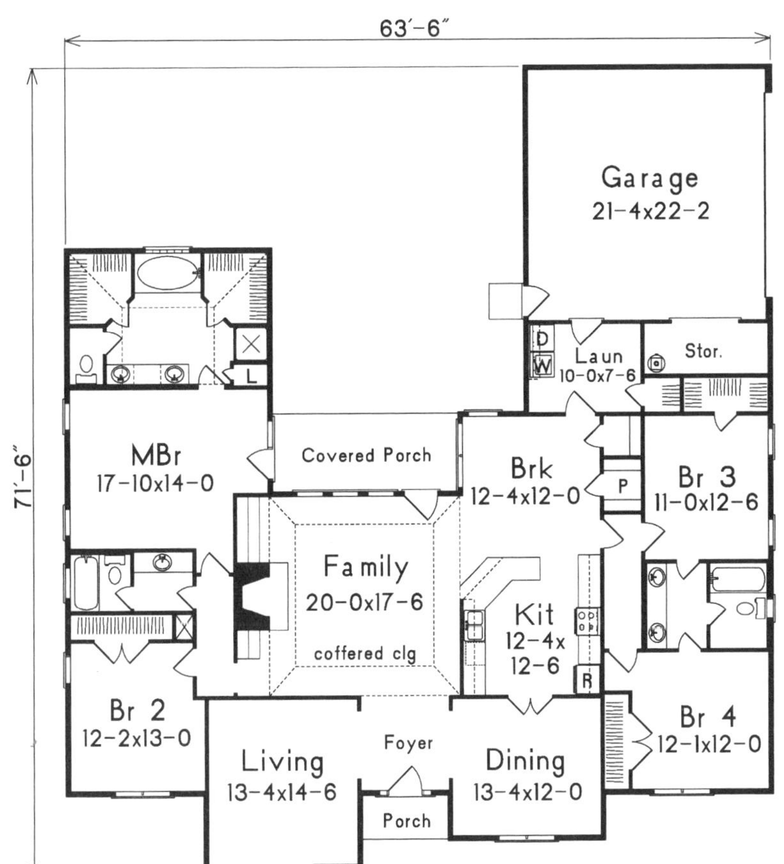
63'-6"
71'-6"
Garage
21-4x22-2
D
W
Laun
10-0x7-6
Stor.
L
MBr
17-10x14-0
Covered Porch
Brk
12-4x12-0
P
Br 3
11-0x12-6
Family
20-0x17-6
coffered clg
Kit
12-4x
12-6
R
Br 2
12-2x13-0
Living
13-4x14-6
Foyer
Dining
13-4x12-0
Br 4
12-1x12-0
Porch

Plan #530-023D-0010

Price Code D

Total Living Area: 2,558 Sq. Ft.

Home has 4 bedrooms, 3 baths, 2-car side entry garage and slab foundation, drawings also include crawl space foundation.

Special features

- 9' ceilings throughout the home
- Angled counter in the kitchen serves breakfast and family rooms
- The entry foyer is flanked by formal living and dining rooms
- Garage includes storage space

Enchanting Country Cottage

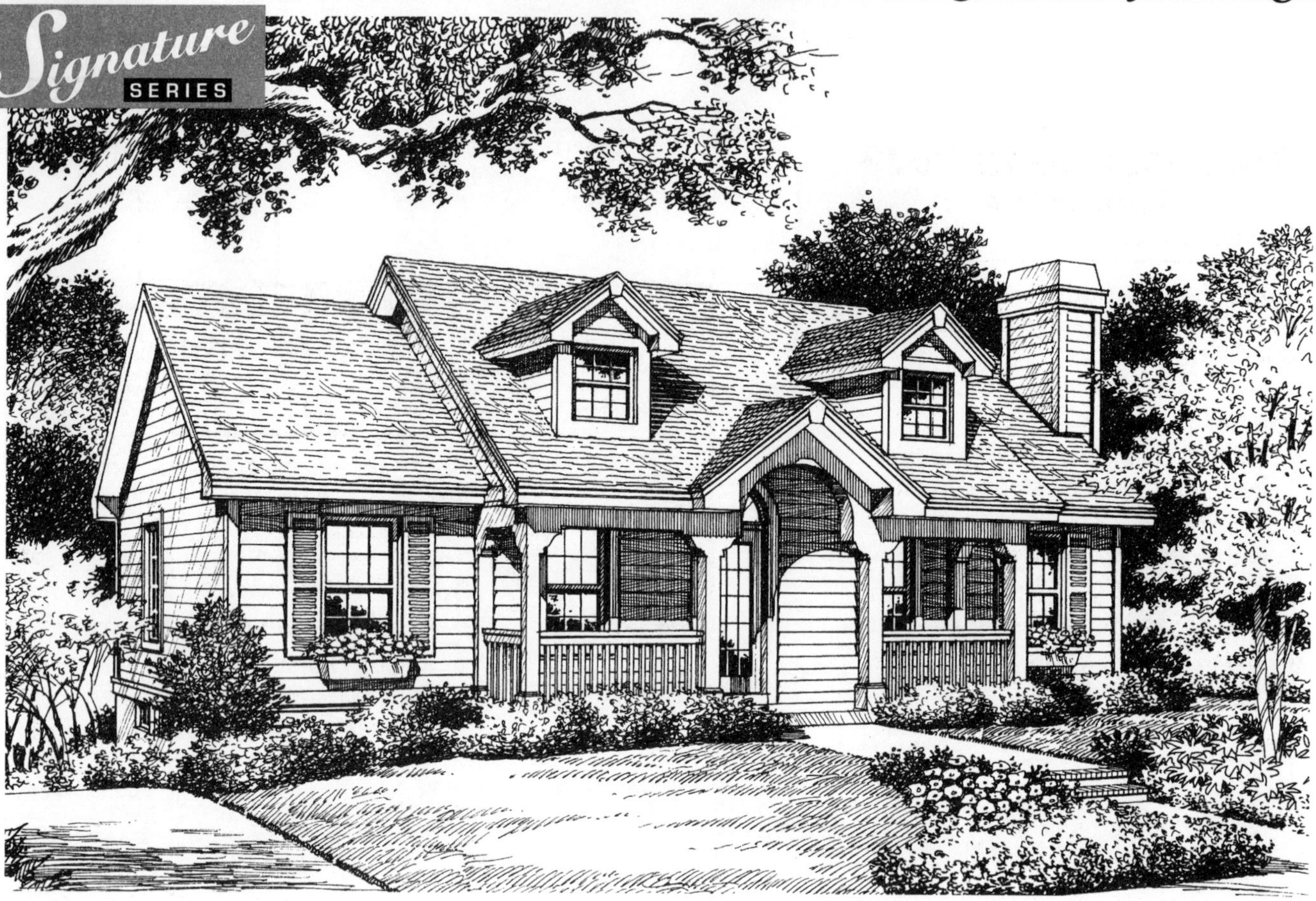

Plan #530-007D-0030
Price Code AA

Total Living Area: 1,140 Sq. Ft.

Home has 3 bedrooms, 2 baths, 2-car drive under garage and basement foundation.

Special features

- Open and spacious living and dining areas for family gatherings
- Well-organized kitchen with an abundance of cabinetry and a built-in pantry
- Roomy master bath features a double-bowl vanity

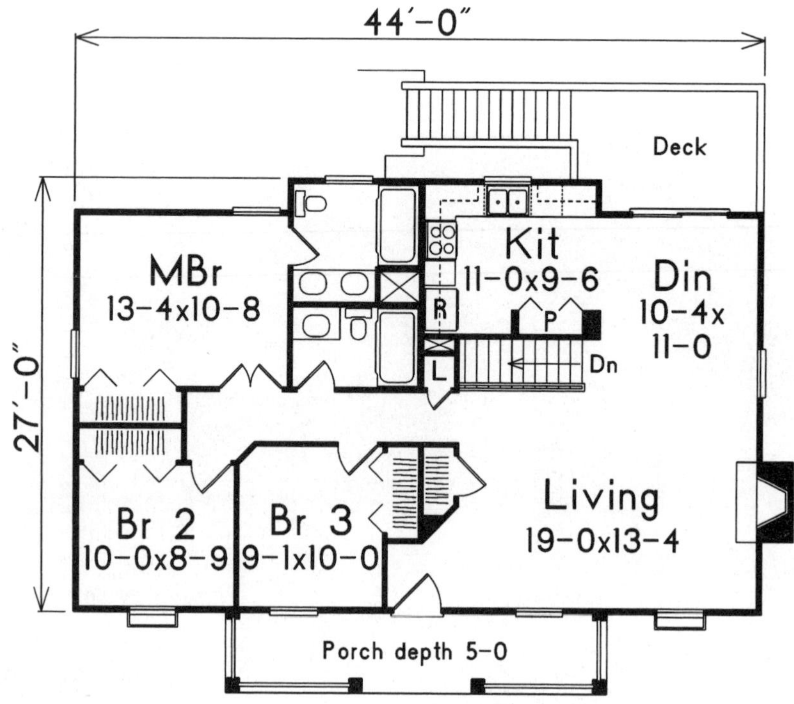

44′-0″
27′-0″
Deck
MBr
13-4x10-8
Kit
11-0x9-6
Din
10-4x
11-0
R
P
L
Dn
Br 2
10-0x8-9
Br 3
9-1x10-0
Living
19-0x13-4
Porch depth 5-0

LOWE'S

Signature
SERIES

Plan #530-053D-0029

Price Code A

Total Living Area: 1,220 Sq. Ft.

Home has 3 bedrooms, 2 baths, 2-car drive under garage and basement foundation.

Special features

- Vaulted ceilings add luxury to the living room and master bedroom
- Spacious living room is accented with a large fireplace and hearth
- Gracious dining area is adjacent to the convenient wrap-around kitchen
- Washer and dryer are handy to the bedrooms
- Covered porch entry adds appeal

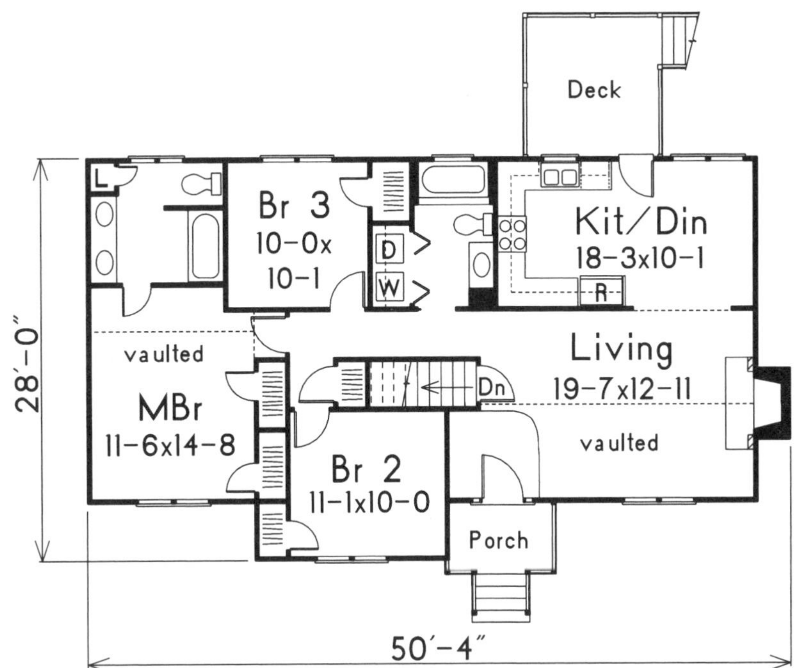
Deck
L
Br 3
10-0x
10-1
D
W
Kit/Din
18-3x10-1
R
vaulted
MBr
11-6x14-8
Dn
Living
19-7x12-11
vaulted
Br 2
11-1x10-0
Porch
28'-0"
50'-4"

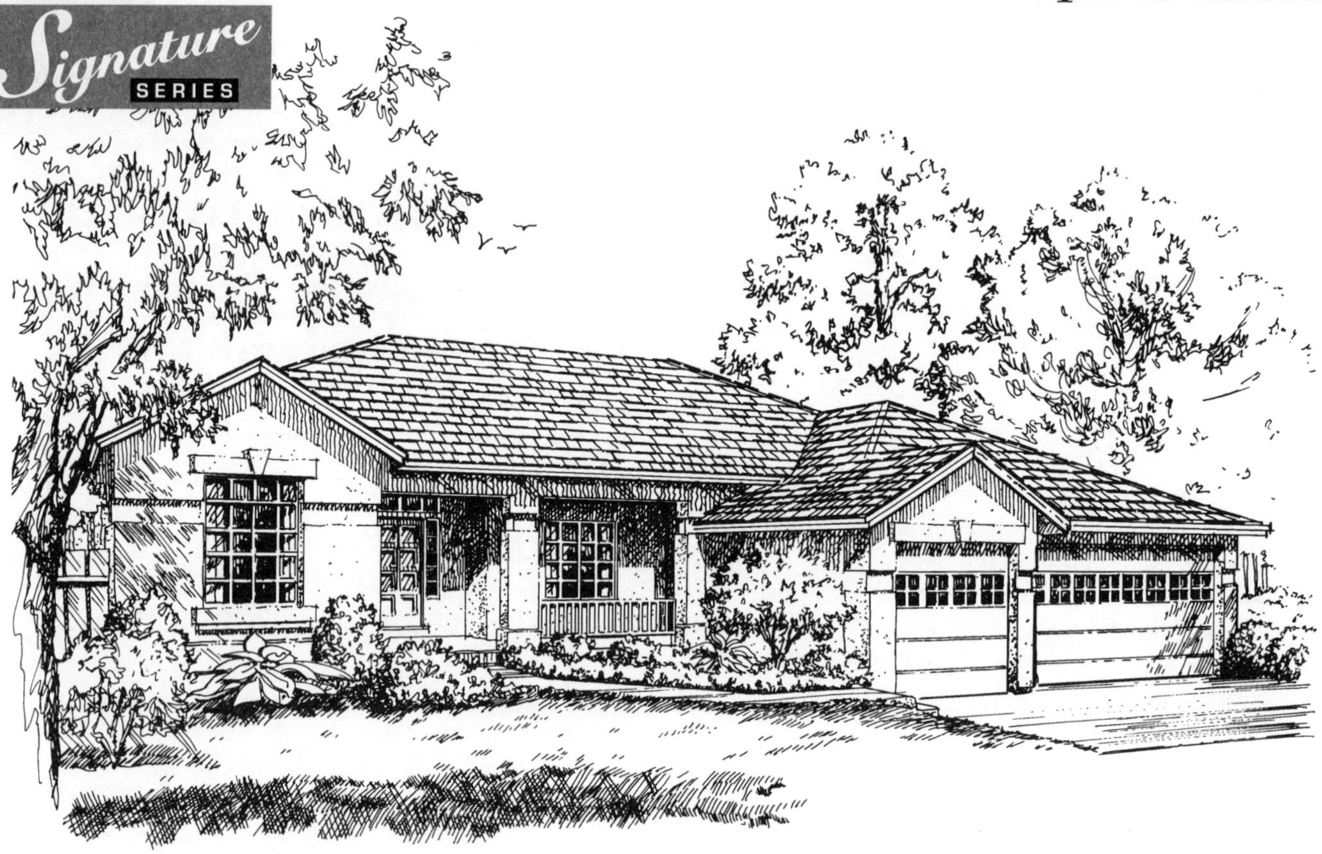

Plan #530-061D-0002

Price Code C

Total Living Area: 1,950 Sq. Ft.

Home has 4 bedrooms, 2 baths, 3-car garage and crawl space foundation.

Special features

- Large corner kitchen with island cooktop opens to the family room
- Master bedroom features a double-door entry, raised ceiling, double-bowl vanity and walk-in closet
- Plant shelf accents hall

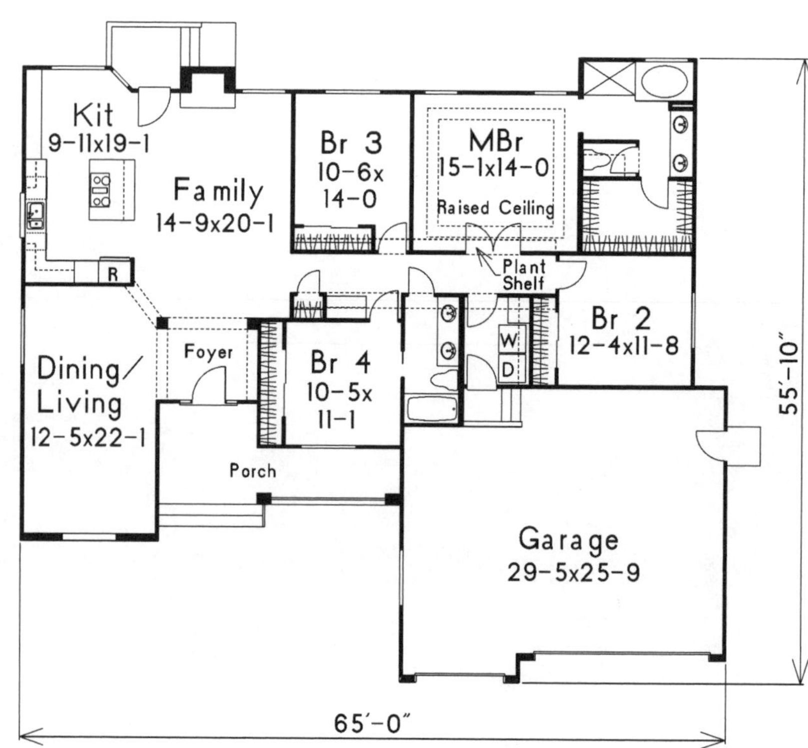

Kit
9-11x19-1
Family
14-9x20-1
Br 3
10-6x
14-0
MBr
15-1x14-0
Raised Ceiling
Plant
Shelf
R
Br 2
12-4x11-8
W
D
Foyer
Dining/
Living
12-5x22-1
Br 4
10-5x
11-1
Porch
Garage
29-5x25-9
55'-10"
65'-0"

LOWE'S

Signature
SERIES

Plan #530-037D-0020

Price Code D

Total Living Area: 1,994 Sq. Ft.

Home has 3 bedrooms, 2 baths, 2-car garage and slab foundation.

Special features

- Convenient entrance from the garage into the main living area through the utility room
- Bedroom #2 features a 12' vaulted ceiling and the dining room boasts a 10' ceiling
- Master bedroom offers a full bath with an oversized tub, separate shower and walk-in closet
- Entry leads to the formal dining room and attractive living room with double French doors and fireplace

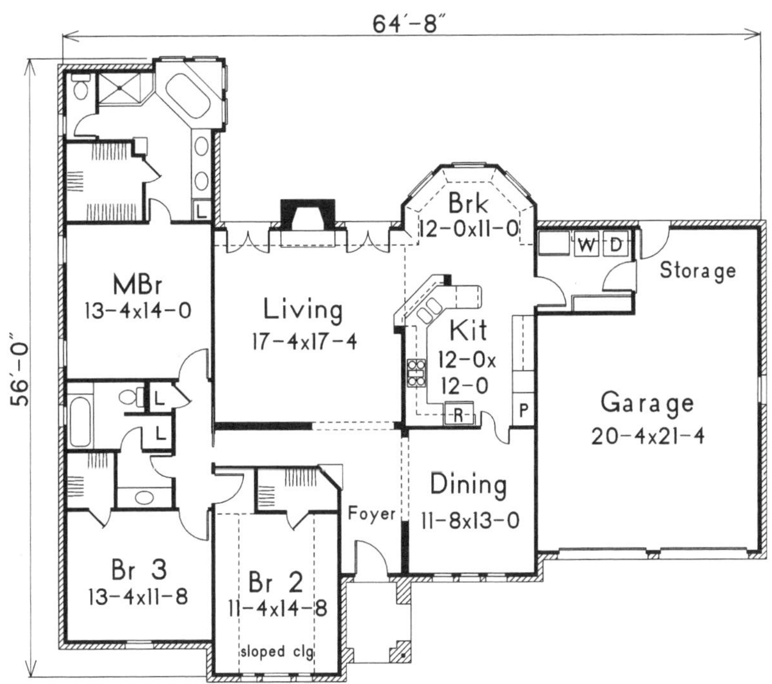
64'-8"
56'-0"
Brk
12-0x11-0
W
D
Storage
MBr
13-4x14-0
Living
17-4x17-4
Kit
12-0x
12-0
R
P
Garage
20-4x21-4
L
L
L
Dining
11-8x13-0
Foyer
Br 3
13-4x11-8
Br 2
11-4x14-8
sloped clg

J.N. HANSEN S.D.G.

Plan #530-007D-0007

Price Code D

Total Living Area: 2,523 Sq. Ft.

Home has 3 bedrooms, 2 baths, 3-car garage and basement foundation.

Special features

- Entry with high ceiling leads to massive vaulted great room with wet bar, plant shelves, pillars and fireplace with a harmonious window trio
- Elaborate kitchen with bay and breakfast bar adjoins morning room with fireplace-in-a-bay
- Vaulted master bedroom features fireplace, book and plant shelves, large walk-in closet and double baths

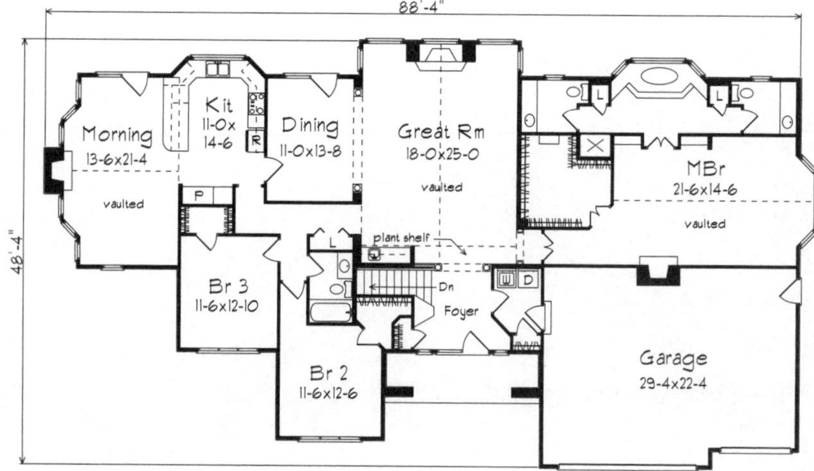
88'-4"
48'-4"
Morning
13-6x21-4
vaulted
Kit
11-0x
14-6
Dining
11-0x13-8
Great Rm
18-0x25-0
vaulted
MBr
21-6x14-6
vaulted
plant shelf
Br 3
11-6x12-10
Br 2
11-6x12-6
Dn
Foyer
Garage
29-4x22-4

TO ORDER BLUEPRINTS USE THE FORM ON PAGE 288 OR CALL TOLL-FREE **1-800-DREAM HOME** (373-2646)

Compact One-Story

LOWE'S

Signature
SERIES

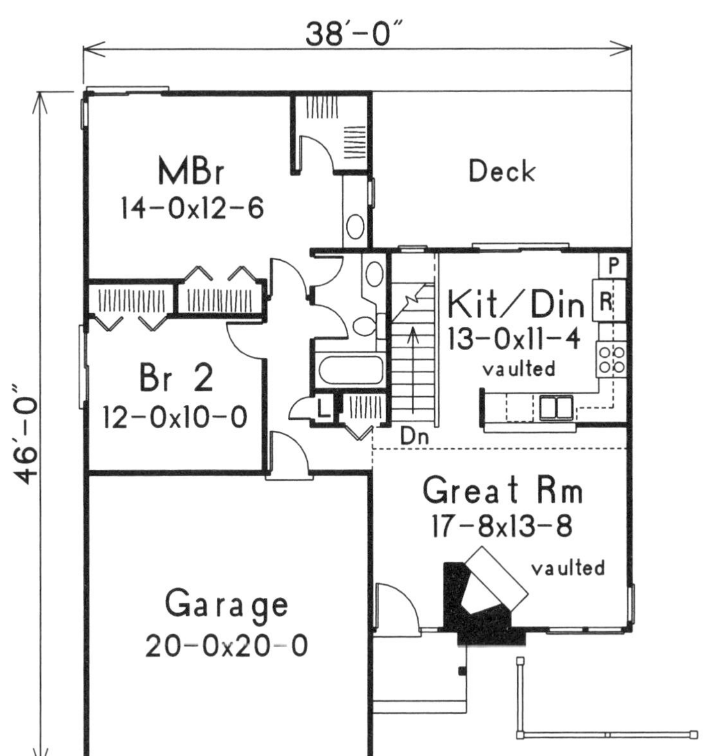
38′-0″
46′-0″
MBr
14-0x12-6
Deck
Kit/Din
13-0x11-4
vaulted
P
R
Br 2
12-0x10-0
L
Dn
Great Rm
17-8x13-8
vaulted
Garage
20-0x20-0

Plan #530-022D-0020

Price Code AA

Total Living Area: 988 Sq. Ft.

Home has 2 bedrooms, 1 bath, 2-car garage and basement foundation.

Special features

- Great room features corner fireplace
- Vaulted ceiling and corner windows add space and light in great room
- Eat-in kitchen with vaulted ceiling accesses deck for outdoor living
- Master bedroom features separate vanities and private access to the bath

Signature SERIES

Plan #530-027D-0009

Price Code F

Total Living Area: 3,808 Sq. Ft.

Home has 3 bedrooms, 3 baths, 2-car garage and basement foundation.

Special features

- Cozy hearth room shares fireplace with great room
- See-through fireplace connects gathering areas
- Master bath features stylish angled glass block walls that frame private toilet and large shower

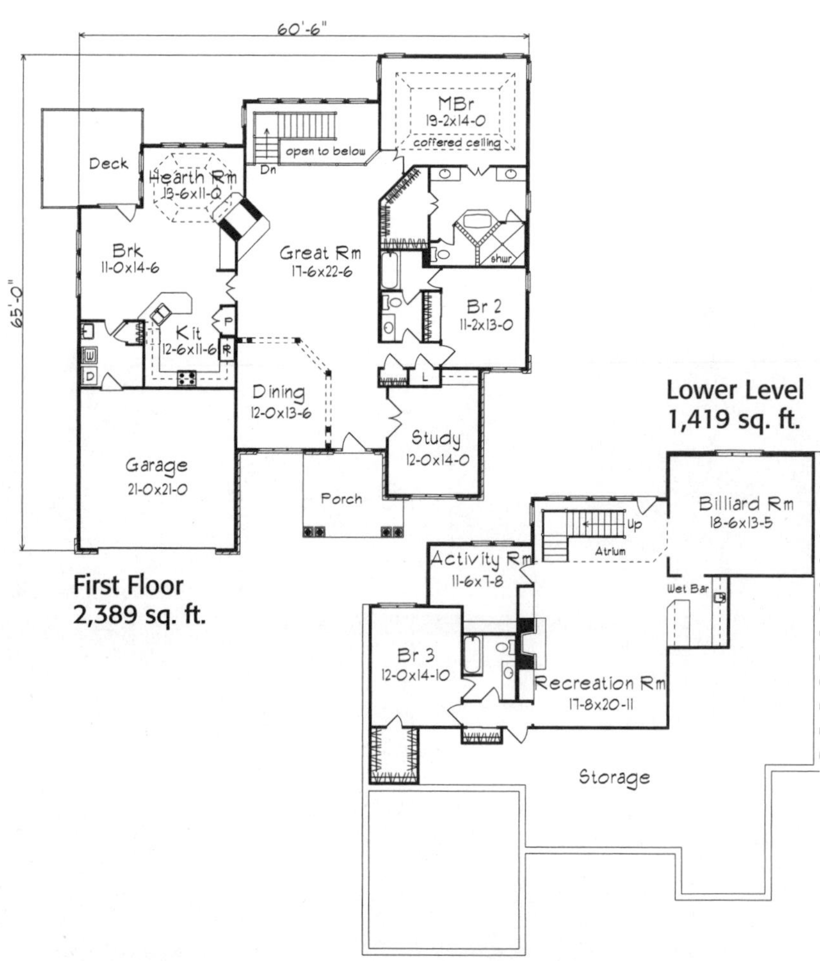
60'-6"
65'-0"
Deck
Hearth Rm
13-6x11-0
open to below
Dn
MBr
19-2x14-0
coffered ceiling
Brk
11-0x14-6
Great Rm
17-6x22-6
shwr
Br 2
11-2x13-0
Kit
12-6x11-6
Dining
12-0x13-6
Study
12-0x14-0
Garage
21-0x21-0
Porch
Billiard Rm
18-6x13-5
Up
Atrium
Activity Rm
11-6x7-8
Wet Bar
Br 3
12-0x14-10
Recreation Rm
17-8x20-11
Storage

First Floor
2,389 sq. ft.

Lower Level
1,419 sq. ft.

TO ORDER BLUEPRINTS USE THE FORM ON PAGE 288 OR CALL TOLL-FREE **1-800-DREAM HOME** (373-2646)

Bold Windows Enhance Front Entry

LOWE'S

Signature
SERIES

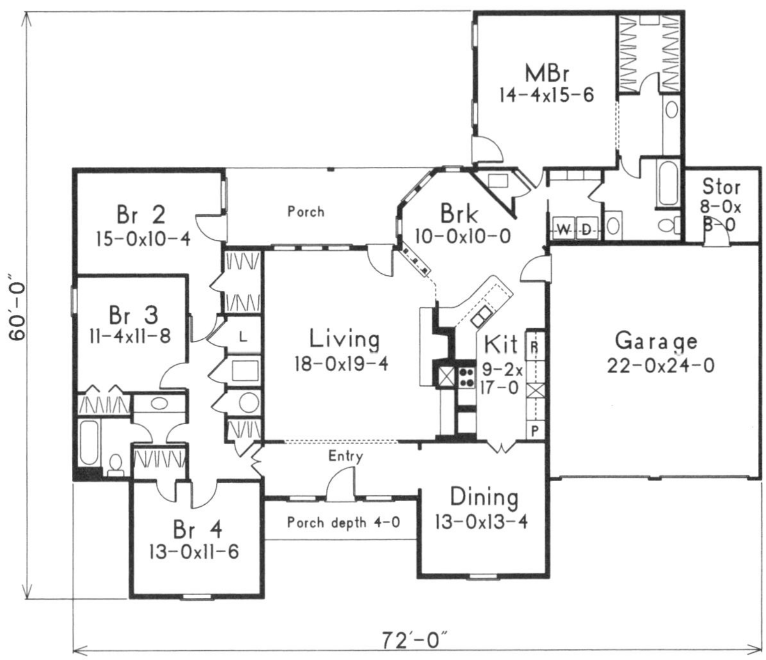
MBr
14-4x15-6
Br 2
15-0x10-4
Porch
Brk
10-0x10-0
Stor
8-0x
8-0
W
D
Br 3
11-4x11-8
L
Living
18-0x19-4
Kit
9-2x
17-0
R
P
Garage
22-0x24-0
Entry
Dining
13-0x13-4
Br 4
13-0x11-6
Porch depth 4-0
60'-0"
72'-0"

Plan #530-021D-0009

Price Code D

Total Living Area: 2,252 Sq. Ft.

Home has 4 bedrooms, 2 baths, 2-car garage and slab foundation, drawings also include basement and crawl space foundations.

Special features

- Central living area
- Private master bedroom with large walk-in closet, dressing area and bath
- Energy efficient home with 2" x 6" exterior walls
- Secondary bedrooms are in a suite arrangement with plenty of closet space
- Sunny breakfast room looks out over the porch and patio
- Large entry area is highlighted by circle-top transoms

Dramatic Vaulted Interior

Plan #530-014D-0009

Price Code A

Total Living Area: 1,428 Sq. Ft.

Home has 3 bedrooms, 2 baths, 2-car garage and basement foundation, drawings also include crawl space foundation.

Special features

- 10' ceiling in entry and hallway
- Vaulted dining room combines a desk area near the see-through fireplace
- Energy efficient home with 2" x 6" exterior walls
- Vaulted secondary bedrooms
- Kitchen is loaded with amenities including an island with salad sink and pantry
- Master bedroom with vaulted ceiling includes a large walk-in closet and private master bath

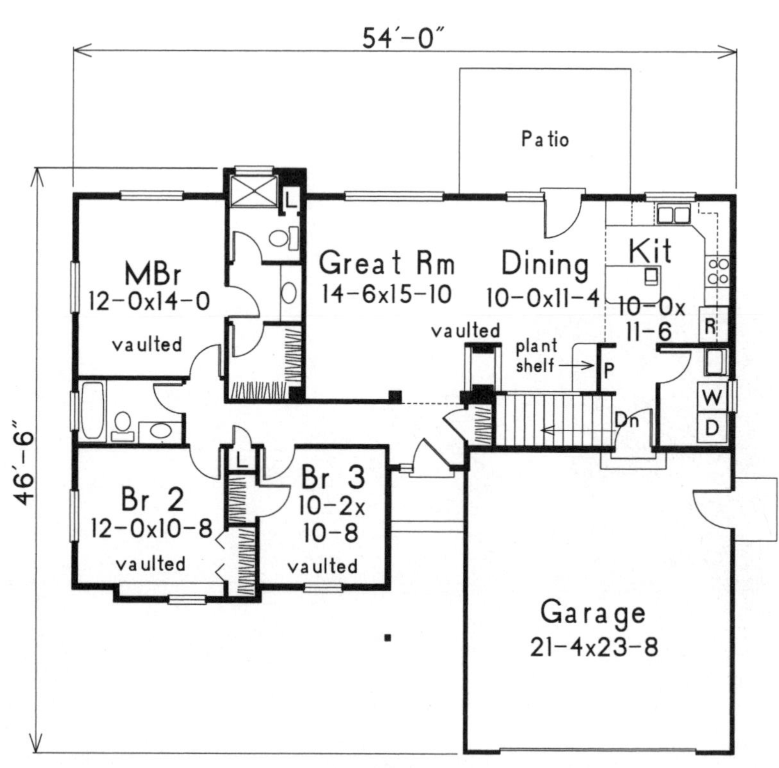

54'-0"
46'-6"
Patio
MBr
12-0x14-0
vaulted
Great Rm
14-6x15-10
Dining
10-0x11-4
vaulted
Kit
10-0x
11-6
plant
shelf
P
R
W
D
Dn
L
Br 2
12-0x10-8
vaulted
Br 3
10-2x
10-8
vaulted
Garage
21-4x23-8

Breakfast Room Provides Casual Dining

LOWE'S

Signature
SERIES

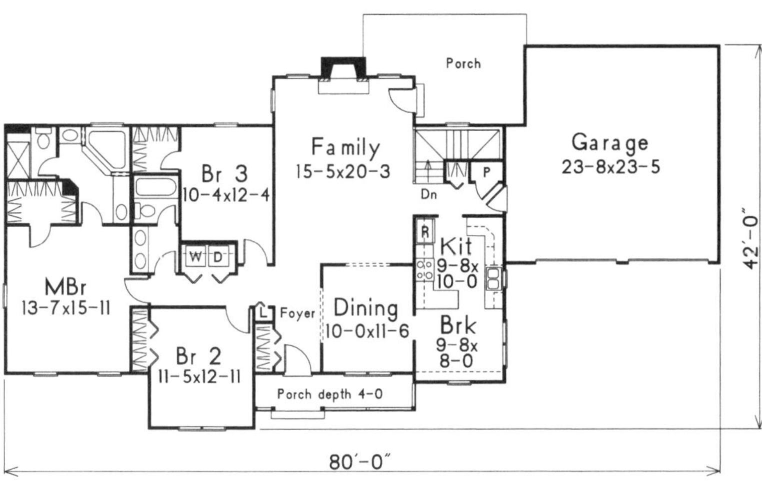
Porch
Family
15-5x20-3
Garage
23-8x23-5
Br 3
10-4x12-4
Dn
P
R
Kit
9-8x
10-0
W D
MBr
13-7x15-11
Foyer
Dining
10-0x11-6
Brk
9-8x
8-0
Br 2
11-5x12-11
Porch depth 4-0
42'-0"
80'-0"

Plan #530-003D-0005

Price Code B

Total Living Area: 1,708 Sq. Ft.

Home has 3 bedrooms, 2 baths, 2-car garage and basement foundation, drawings also include crawl space foundation.

Special features

- Massive family room is enhanced with several windows, a fireplace and access to the porch
- Deluxe master bath is accented by a step-up corner tub flanked by double vanities
- Closets throughout maintain organized living
- Bedrooms are isolated from living areas

SPARR

LOWE'S

Signature
SERIES

Plan #530-045D-0009

Price Code B

Total Living Area: 1,684 Sq. Ft.

Home has 3 bedrooms, 2 1/2 baths, 2-car garage and basement foundation.

Special features

- The bayed dining area boasts convenient double-door access onto the large deck
- The family room features several large windows for brightness
- Bedrooms are separate from living areas for privacy
- Master bedroom offers a bath with walk-in closet, double-bowl vanity and both a shower and a whirlpool tub

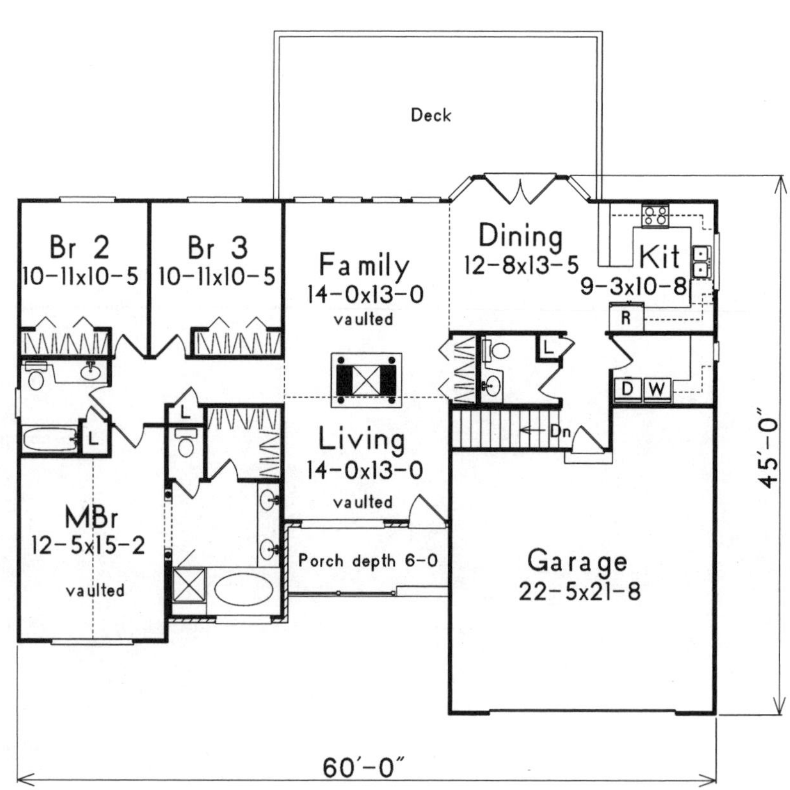
Deck
Br 2
10-11x10-5
Br 3
10-11x10-5
Family
14-0x13-0
vaulted
Dining
12-8x13-5
Kit
9-3x10-8
R
D W
Dn
Living
14-0x13-0
vaulted
MBr
12-5x15-2
vaulted
Porch depth 6-0
Garage
22-5x21-8
45'-0"
60'-0"

 TO ORDER BLUEPRINTS USE THE FORM ON PAGE 288 OR CALL TOLL-FREE **1-800-DREAM HOME** (373-2646)

LOWE'S

Signature
SERIES

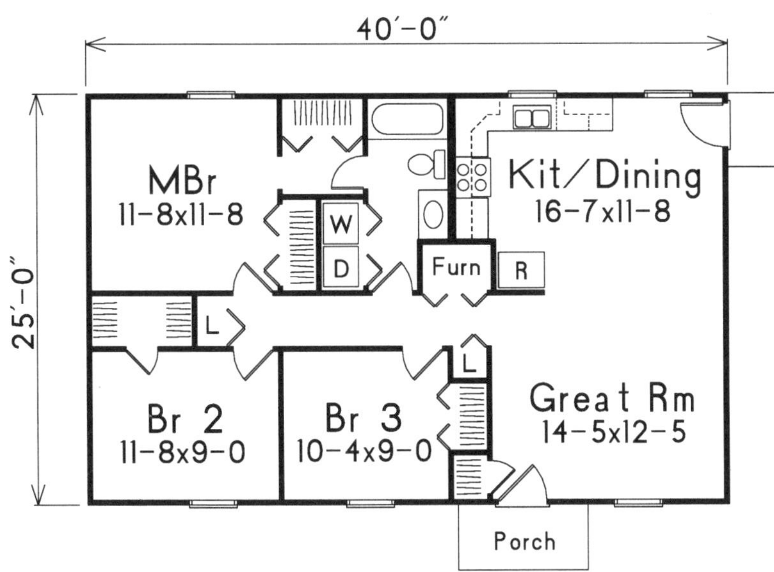
40'-0"
25'-0"
MBr
11-8x11-8
W
D
Kit/Dining
16-7x11-8
Furn
R
L
Br 2
11-8x9-0
Br 3
10-4x9-0
L
Great Rm
14-5x12-5
Porch

Plan #530-001D-0041

Price Code AA

Total Living Area: 1,000 Sq. Ft.

Home has 3 bedrooms, 1 bath and crawl space foundation, drawings also include basement and slab foundations.

Special features

- Bath includes convenient closeted laundry area
- Master bedroom includes double closets and private access to bath
- Foyer features a handy coat closet
- L-shaped kitchen provides easy access outdoors

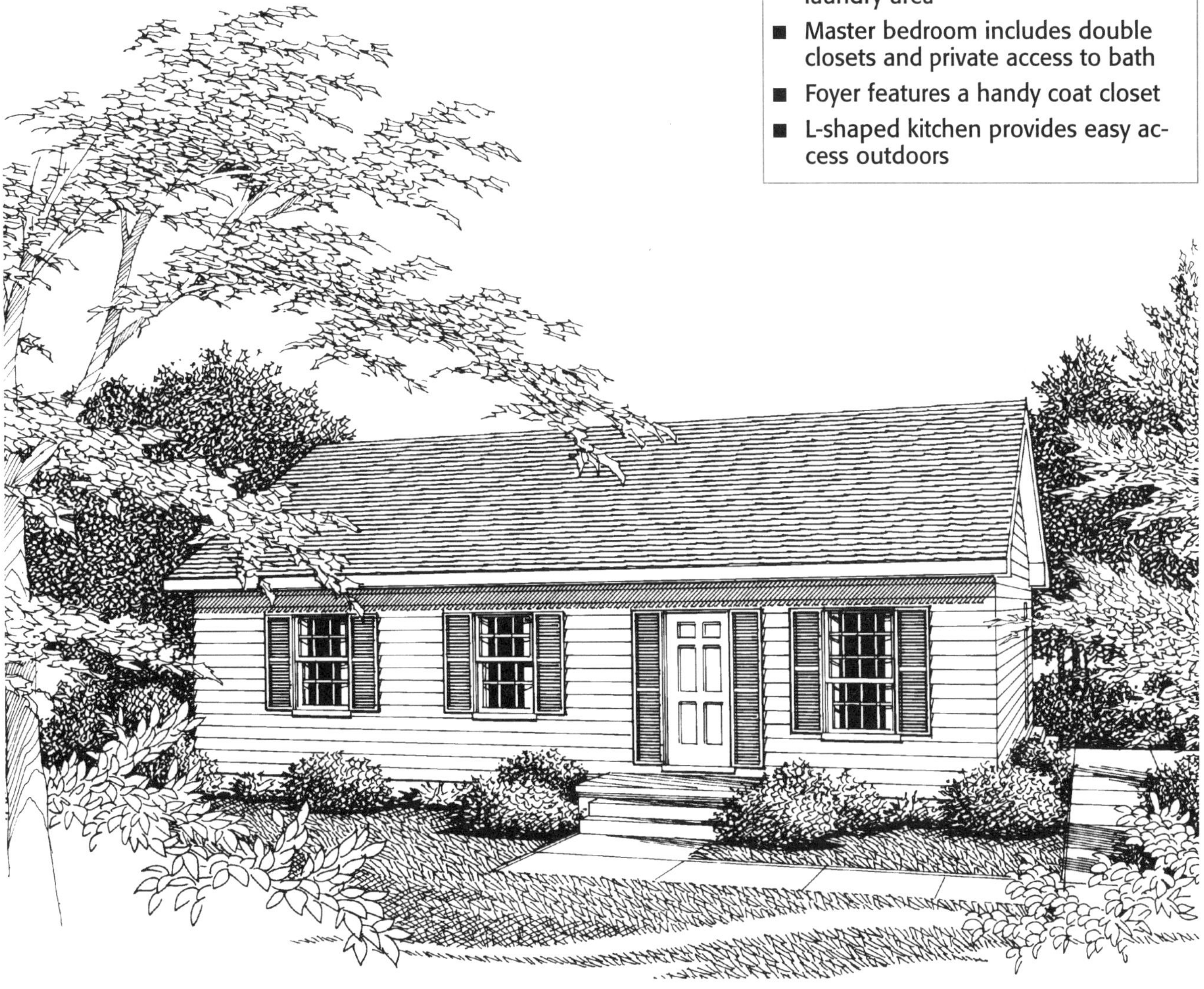

Plan #530-006D-0001

Price Code B

Total Living Area: 1,643 Sq. Ft.

Home has 3 bedrooms, 2 baths, 2-car side entry garage and basement foundation, drawings also include slab and crawl space foundations.

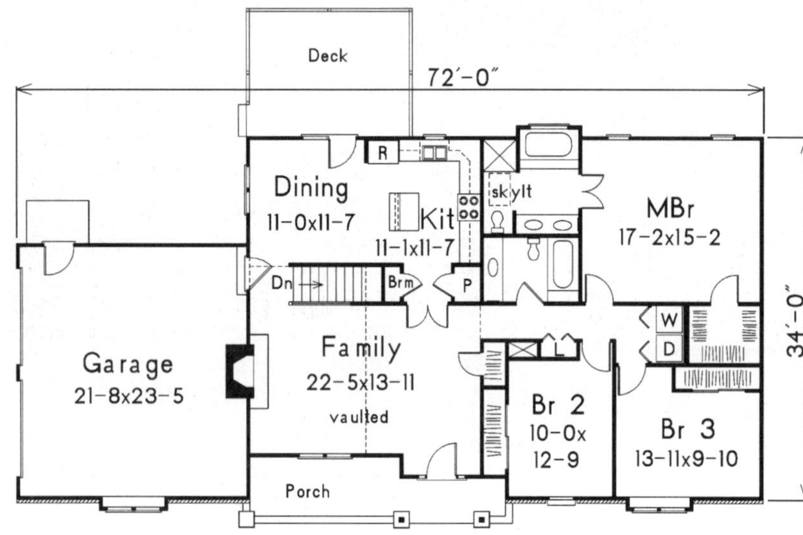
Deck
72'-0"
34'-0"
R
Dining
11-0x11-7
Kit
11-1x11-7
sk ylt
MBr
17-2x15-2
Dn
Brm
P
W
D
Garage
21-8x23-5
Family
22-5x13-11
vaulted
Br 2
10-0x
12-9
Br 3
13-11x9-10
Porch

Special features

- Family room has a vaulted ceiling, open staircase and arched windows allowing for plenty of light
- Kitchen captures full use of space, with a pantry, storage, ample counterspace and work island
- Large closets and storage areas throughout
- Roomy master bath has a skylight for natural lighting plus a separate tub and shower
- Rear of house provides ideal location for future screened-in porch

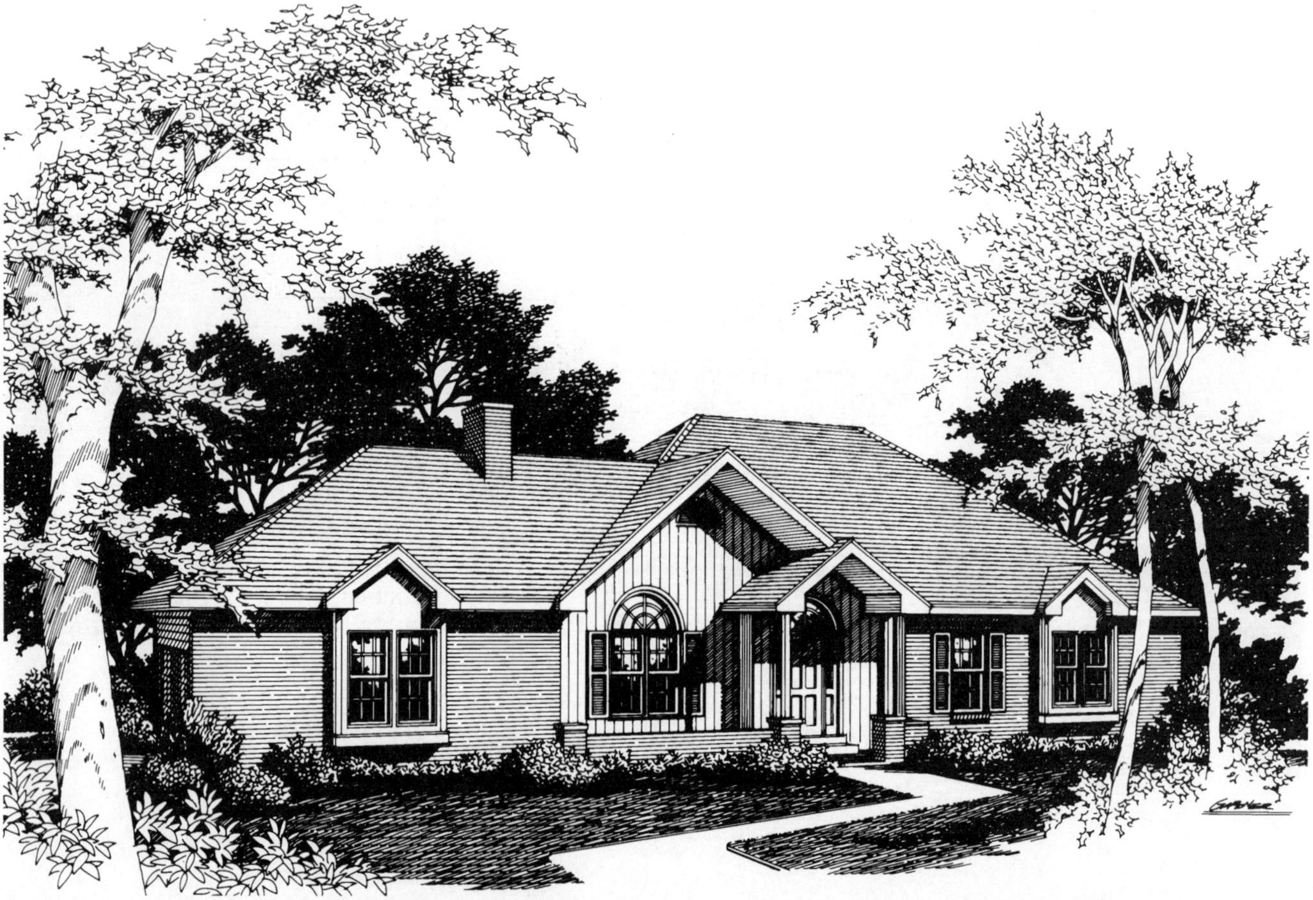

LOWE'S
Signature
SERIES

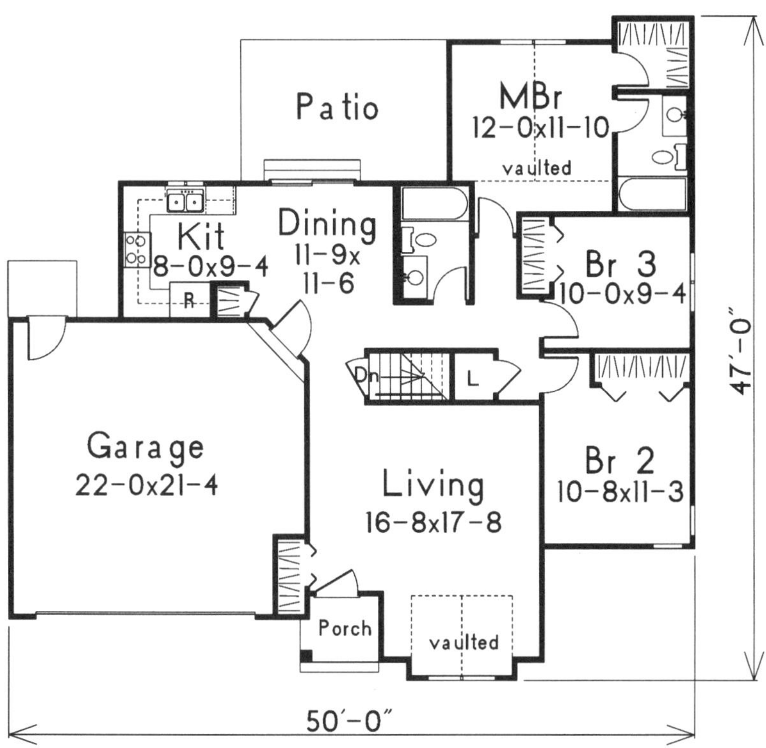
Patio
MBr
12-0x11-10
vaulted
Kit
8-0x9-4
Dining
11-9x
11-6
R
Br 3
10-0x9-4
Dn
L
Garage
22-0x21-4
Living
16-8x17-8
Br 2
10-8x11-3
Porch
vaulted
47'-0"
50'-0"

Plan #530-041D-0004

Price Code AA

Total Living Area: 1,195 Sq. Ft.

Home has 3 bedrooms, 2 baths, 2-car garage and basement foundation.

Special features

- Dining room opens onto the patio
- Master bedroom features a vaulted ceiling, private bath and walk-in closet
- Coat closets are located by both the entrances
- Convenient secondary entrance is located at the back of the garage

Plan #530-018D-0003

Price Code D

Total Living Area: 2,517 Sq. Ft.

Home has 4 bedrooms, 2 1/2 baths, 2-car garage and slab foundation, drawings also include crawl space foundation.

Special features

- Energy efficient home with 2" x 6" exterior walls
- Kitchen with walk-in pantry overlooks large family room with fireplace and unique octagon-shaped breakfast room
- Secluded master bedroom features double-door entry, luxurious bath with separate shower, step-up whirlpool tub, double vanities and walk-in closets
- Varied ceiling heights throughout home
- Central living room with large windows and attractive transoms

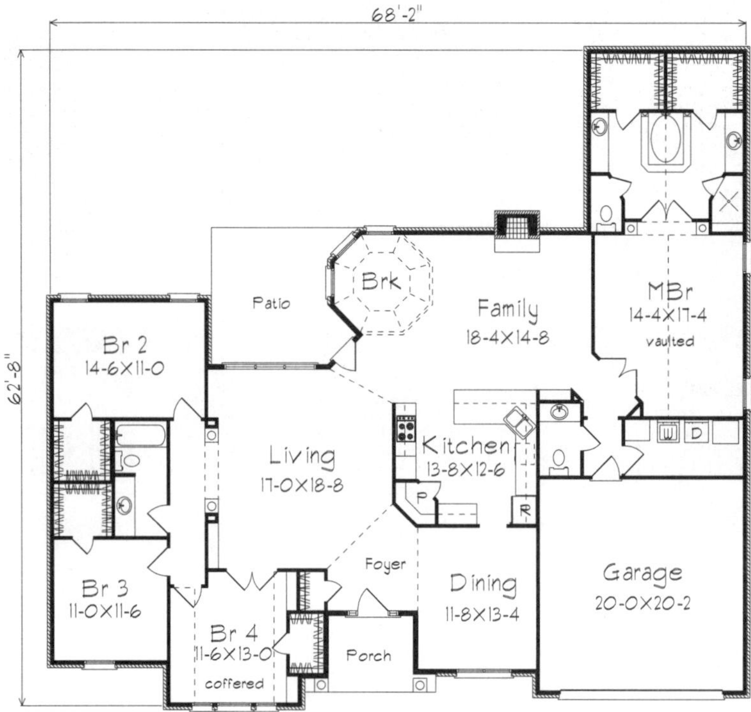
68'-2"
62'-8"
Patio
Brk
Family
18-4X14-8
MBr
14-4X17-4
vaulted
Br 2
14-6X11-0
Living
17-0X18-8
Kitchen
13-8X12-6
P
R
W
D
Foyer
Dining
11-8X13-4
Garage
20-0X20-2
Br 3
11-0X11-6
Br 4
11-6X13-0
coffered
Porch

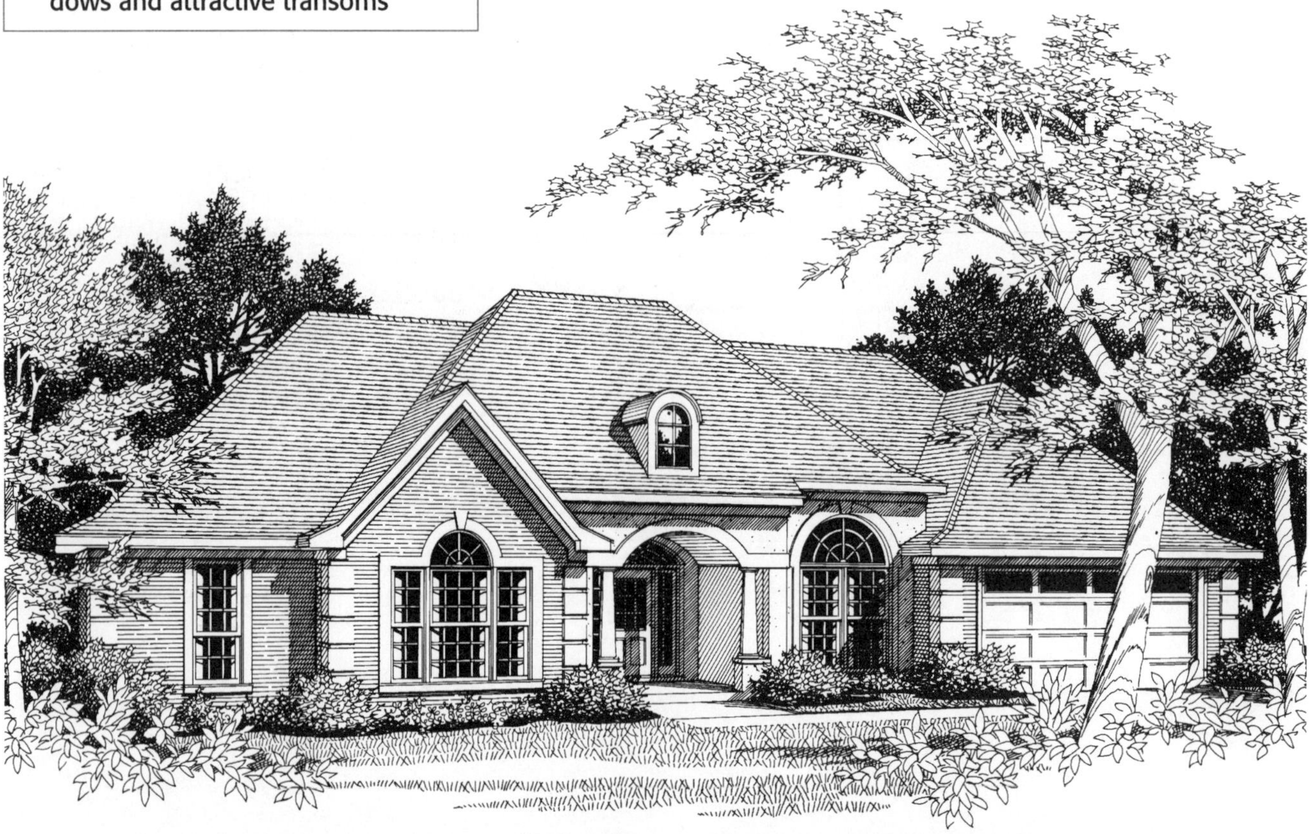

LOWE'S

Signature SERIES

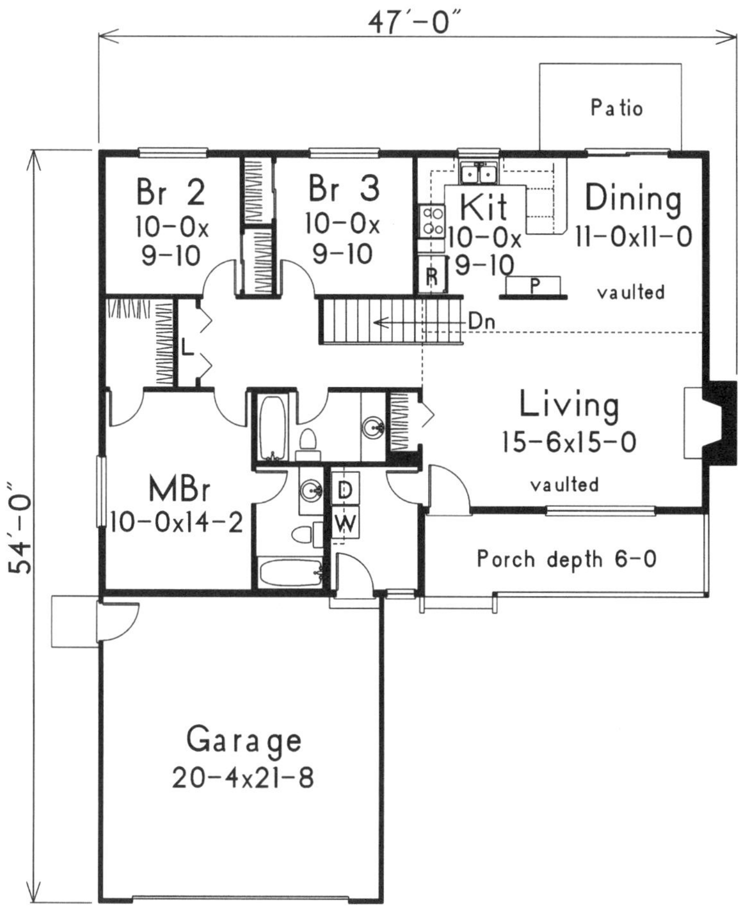
47′-0″
54′-0″
Patio
Br 2
10-0x
9-10
Br 3
10-0x
9-10
Kit
10-0x
9-10
Dining
11-0x11-0
vaulted
R
P
Dn
L
Living
15-6x15-0
vaulted
MBr
10-0x14-2
D
W
Porch depth 6-0
Garage
20-4x21-8

Plan #530-014D-0005

Price Code A

Total Living Area: 1,314 Sq. Ft.

Home has 3 bedrooms, 2 baths, 2-car garage and basement foundation.

Special features

- Energy efficient home with 2" x 6" exterior walls
- Covered porch adds immediate appeal and welcoming charm
- Open floor plan combined with vaulted ceiling offers spacious living
- Functional kitchen complete with pantry and eating bar
- Cozy fireplace in the living room
- Private master bedroom features a large walk-in closet and bath

Signature SERIES

Plan #530-041D-0001

Price Code D

Total Living Area: 2,003 Sq. Ft.

Home has 3 bedrooms, 2 baths, 2-car garage and basement foundation.

Special features

- Octagon-shaped dining room boasts a tray ceiling and deck overlook
- L-shaped island kitchen serves the living and dining rooms
- Master bedroom boasts a luxury bath and walk-in closet
- Living room features columns, elegant fireplace and a 10' ceiling

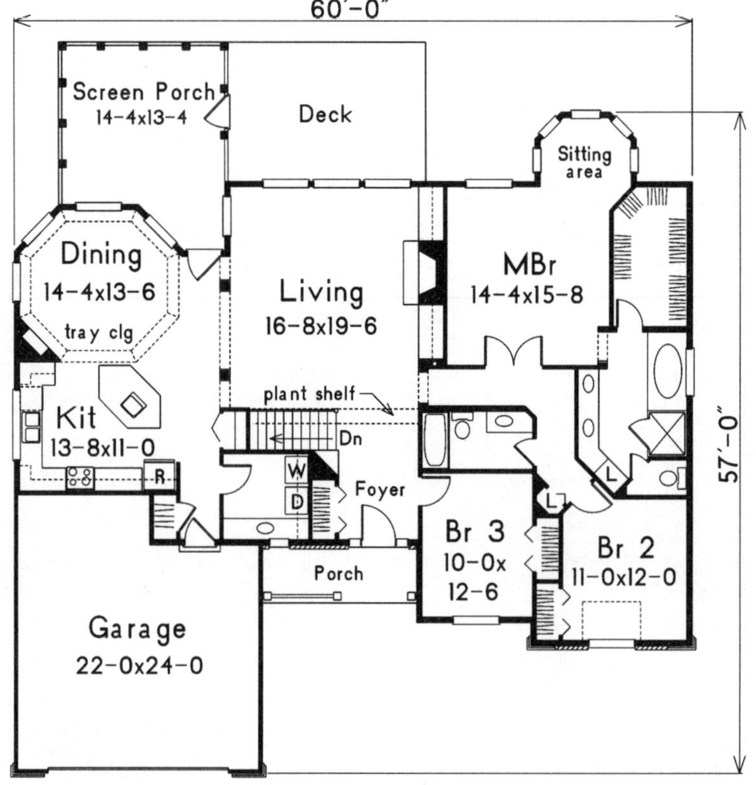
60'-0"
57'-0"
Screen Porch
14-4x13-4
Deck
Sitting area
Dining
14-4x13-6
tray clg
Living
16-8x19-6
MBr
14-4x15-8
plant shelf
Kit
13-8x11-0
R
Dn
W
D
Foyer
Br 3
10-0x
12-6
Br 2
11-0x12-0
L
L
Porch
Garage
22-0x24-0

LOWE'S

Signature
SERIES

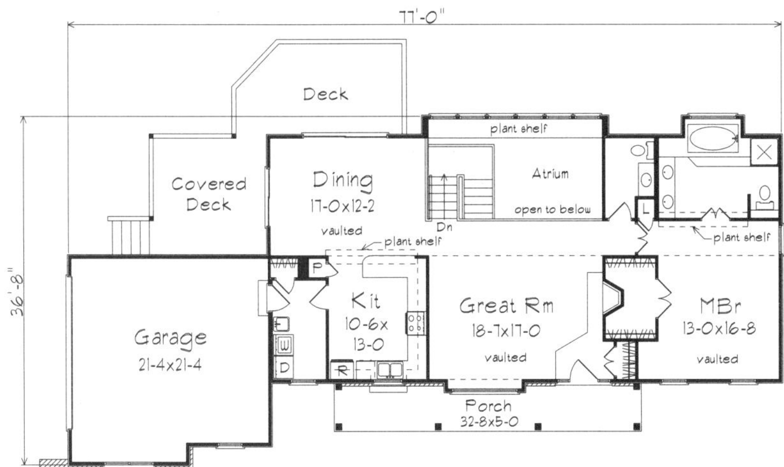
77'-0"
36'-8"
Deck
Covered Deck
Dining
17-0x12-2
vaulted
plant shelf
Atrium
open to below
Dn
plant shelf
plant shelf
Garage
21-4x21-4
Kit
10-6x
13-0
Great Rm
18-7x17-0
vaulted
MBr
13-0x16-8
vaulted
Porch
32-8x5-0

First Floor
1,297 sq. ft.

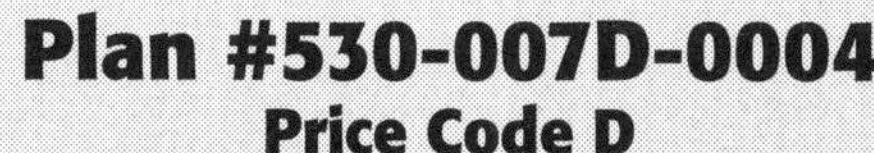

Plan #530-007D-0004

Price Code D

Total Living Area: 2,531 Sq. Ft.

Home has 4 bedrooms, 2 1/2 baths, 2-car side entry garage and walk-out basement foundation.

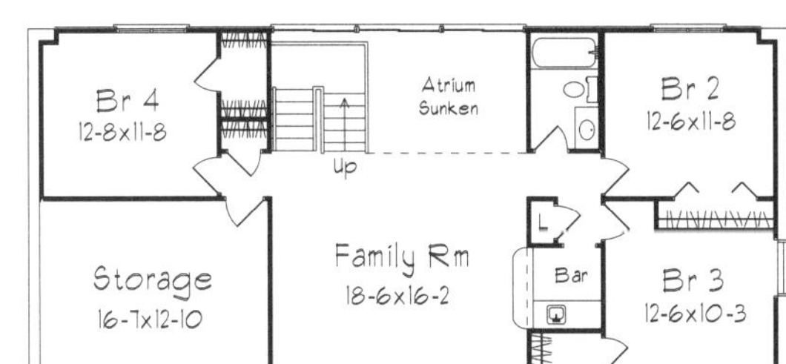
Br 4
12-8x11-8
Atrium
Sunken
Up
Br 2
12-6x11-8
Storage
16-7x12-10
Family Rm
18-6x16-2
Bar
Br 3
12-6x10-3

Lower Level
1,234 sq. ft.

Special features

- Charming porch with dormers leads into vaulted great room with atrium
- Well-designed kitchen and breakfast bar adjoin extra-large laundry/mud room
- Double sinks, tub with window above and plant shelf complete the vaulted master bath

Rear View

LOWE'S

Well-Designed Ranch With Wrap-Around Porch

Signature
SERIES

Plan #530-004D-0002

Price Code C

Total Living Area: 1,823 Sq. Ft.

Home has 3 bedrooms, 2 baths, 2-car garage and basement foundation.

Special features

- Vaulted living room is spacious and easily accesses the dining area
- The master bedroom boasts a tray ceiling, large walk-in closet and a private bath with a corner whirlpool tub
- Cheerful dining area is convenient to the U-shaped kitchen and also enjoys patio access
- Centrally located laundry room connects the garage to the living areas

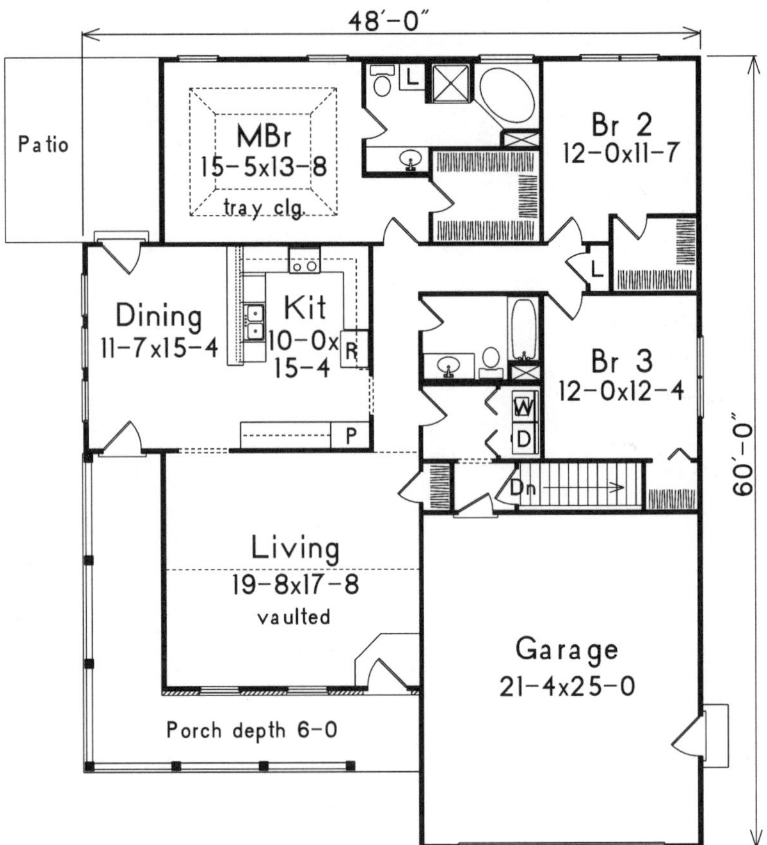
48'-0"
Patio
L
MBr
15-5x13-8
tray clg.
Br 2
12-0x11-7
L
Dining
11-7x15-4
Kit
10-0x
15-4
R
P
Br 3
12-0x12-4
W
D
Dn
60'-0"
Living
19-8x17-8
vaulted
Garage
21-4x25-0
Porch depth 6-0

TO ORDER BLUEPRINTS USE THE FORM ON PAGE 288 OR CALL TOLL-FREE **1-800-DREAM HOME** (373-2646)

LOWE'S

Signature SERIES

Plan #530-021D-0005

Price Code C

Total Living Area: 2,177 Sq. Ft.

Home has 3 bedrooms, 2 baths, 2-car garage and slab foundation, drawings also include basement and crawl space foundations.

Special features

- Master bedroom features a sitting area and double-door entry to an elegant master bath
- Secondary bedrooms are spacious with walk-in closets and a shared bath
- Breakfast room with full windows opens to the rear porch
- Exterior window treatments create a unique style
- Kitchen features an island cooktop, eating bar and wet bar that is accessible to the living room

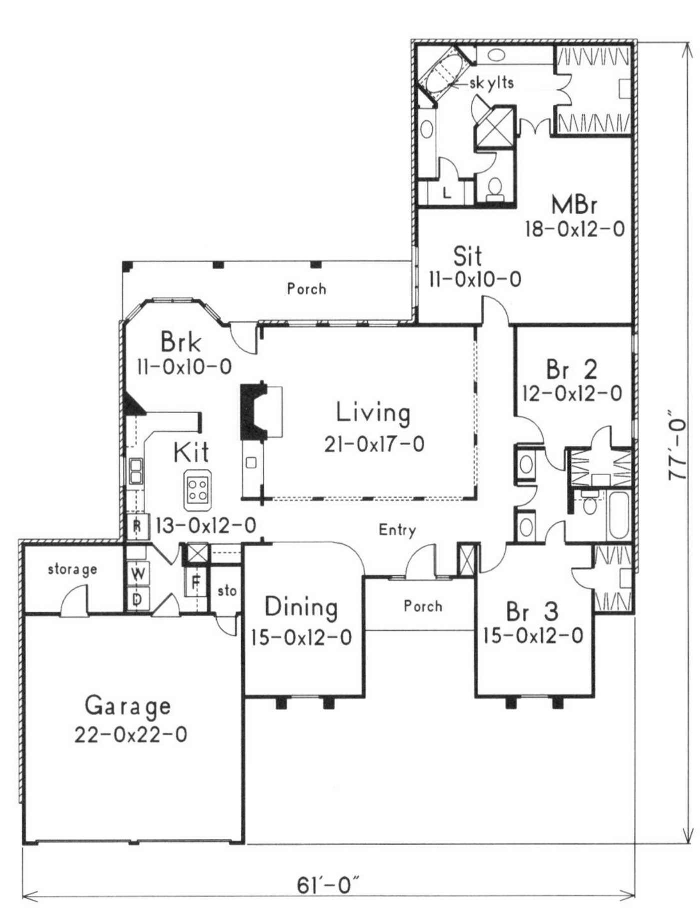
skylts
L
MBr
18-0x12-0
Sit
11-0x10-0
Porch
Brk
11-0x10-0
Living
21-0x17-0
Br 2
12-0x12-0
Kit
13-0x12-0
Entry
storage
W
D
sto
Dining
15-0x12-0
Porch
Br 3
15-0x12-0
Garage
22-0x22-0
77'-0"
61'-0"

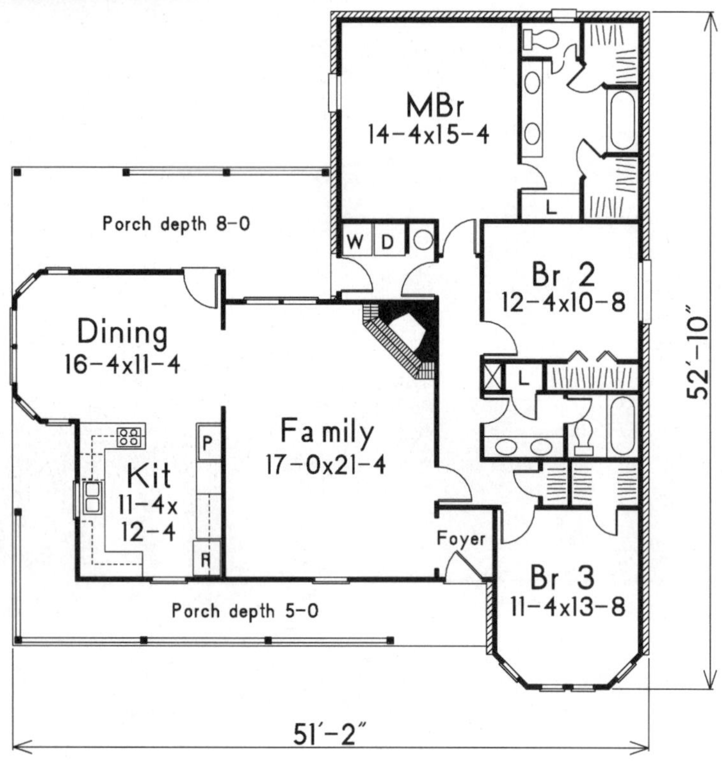
MBr
14-4x15-4
W D
Porch depth 8-0
Br 2
12-4x10-8
Dining
16-4x11-4
L
L
Family
17-0x21-4
P
Kit
11-4x
12-4
R
Foyer
Br 3
11-4x13-8
Porch depth 5-0
52'-10"
51'-2"

Plan #530-037D-0006

Price Code C

Total Living Area: 1,772 Sq. Ft.

Home has 3 bedrooms, 2 baths, 2-car detached garage and slab foundation, drawings also include crawl space foundation.

Special features

- Extended porches in front and rear provide a charming touch
- Large bay windows lend distinction to the dining room and bedroom #3
- Efficient U-shaped kitchen
- Master bedroom includes two walk-in closets
- Full corner fireplace in family room

 TO ORDER BLUEPRINTS USE THE FORM ON PAGE 288 OR CALL TOLL-FREE **1-800-DREAM HOME** (373-2646)

LOWE'S

Signature SERIES

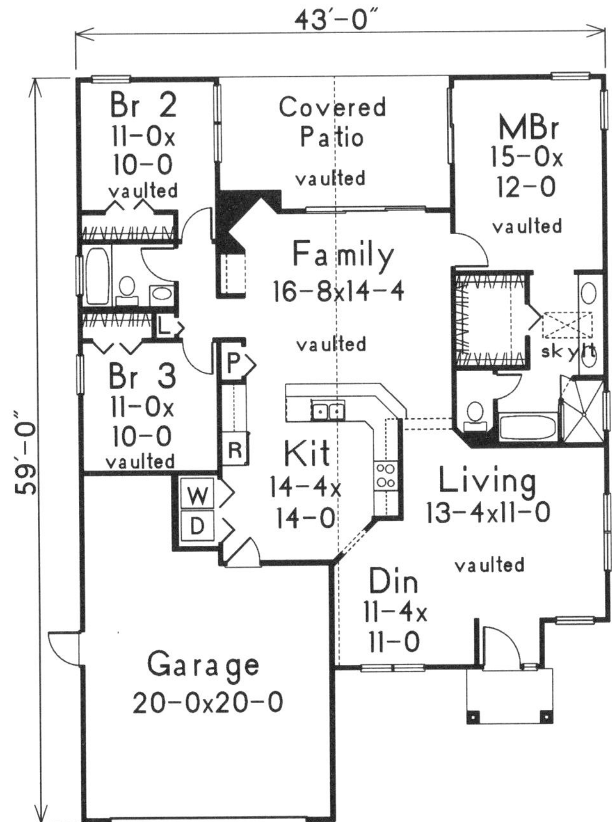
43'-0"
59'-0"
Br 2
11-0x
10-0
vaulted
Covered
Patio
vaulted
MBr
15-0x
12-0
vaulted
Family
16-8x14-4
vaulted
L
P
R
skylt
Br 3
11-0x
10-0
vaulted
Kit
14-4x
14-0
W
D
Living
13-4x11-0
vaulted
Din
11-4x
11-0
Garage
20-0x20-0

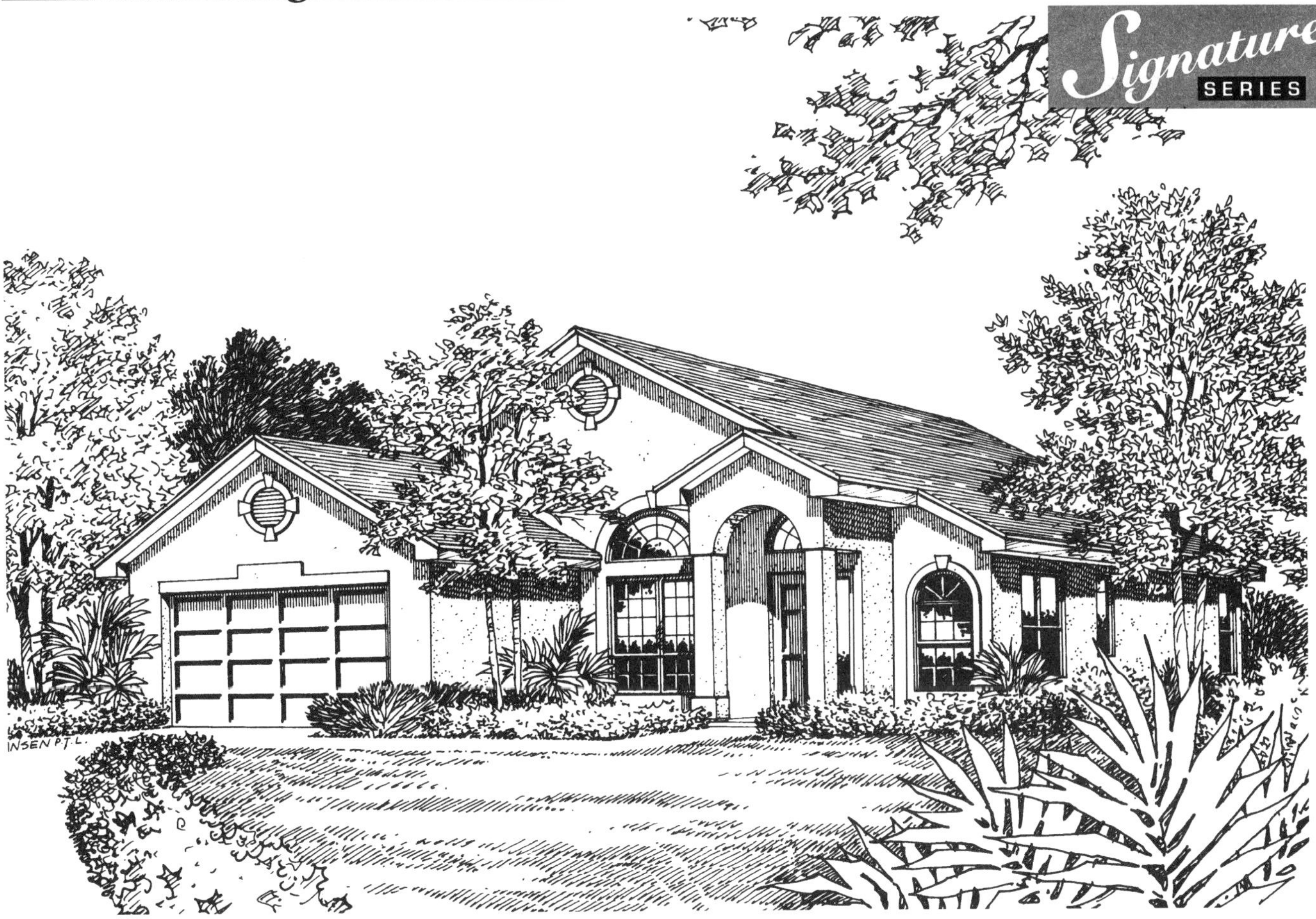

Plan #530-048D-0011

Price Code B

Total Living Area: 1,550 Sq. Ft.

Home has 3 bedrooms, 2 baths, 2-car garage and slab foundation.

Special features

- Cozy corner fireplace provides a focal point in the family room
- Master bedroom features a large walk-in closet, skylight and separate tub and shower
- Convenient laundry closet
- Kitchen with pantry and breakfast bar connects to the family room
- Family room and master bedroom access the covered patio

Plan #530-053D-0051

Price Code E

Total Living Area: 2,731 Sq. Ft.

Home has 4 bedrooms, 3 1/2 baths, 2-car side entry garage and basement foundation.

Special features

- Isolated master bedroom enjoys double walk-in closets, a coffered ceiling and an elegant bath
- Both dining and living rooms feature coffered ceilings and bay windows
- Breakfast room includes a dramatic vaulted ceiling and plenty of windows
- Family room features fireplace flanked by shelves, vaulted ceiling and access to rear deck
- Secondary bedrooms are separate from living areas

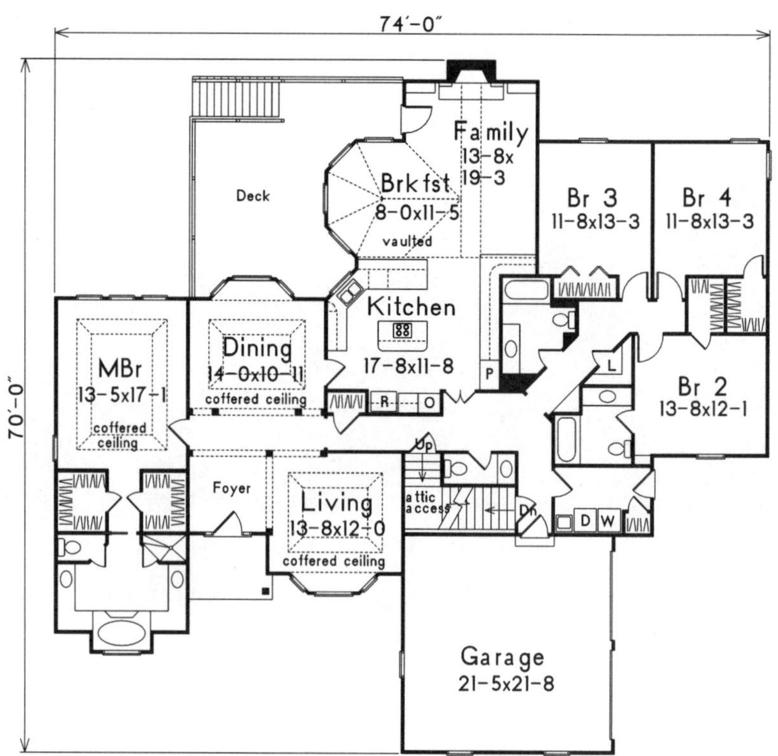

74'-0"
70'-0"
Deck
Family
13-8x
19-3
Brkfst
8-0x11-5
vaulted
Br 3
11-8x13-3
Br 4
11-8x13-3
Kitchen
17-8x11-8
MBr
13-5x17-1
coffered ceiling
Dining
14-0x10-11
coffered ceiling
Br 2
13-8x12-1
Foyer
Living
13-8x12-0
coffered ceiling
attic access
Up
Dn
Garage
21-5x21-8

TO ORDER BLUEPRINTS USE THE FORM ON PAGE 288 OR CALL TOLL-FREE **1-800-DREAM HOME** (373-2646)

Sophisticated Ranch

LOWE'S
Signature
SERIES

Plan #530-007D-0057

Price Code F

Total Living Area: 2,808 Sq. Ft.

Home has 3 bedrooms, 2 1/2 baths, 3-car side entry garage and basement foundation.

Special features

- An impressive front exterior showcases three porches for quiet times
- Large living and dining rooms flank an elegant entry
- Bedroom #3 shares a porch with the living room and a spacious bath with bedroom #2
- Vaulted master bedroom enjoys a secluded screened porch and sumptuous bath with corner tub, double vanities and huge walk-in closet
- Living room can easily convert to an optional fourth bedroom

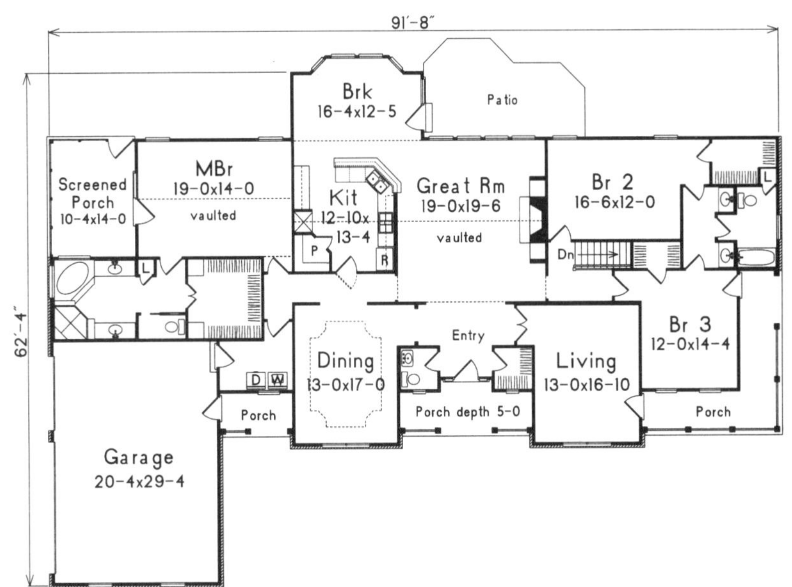
91'-8"
62'-4"
Brk
16-4x12-5
Patio
Screened
Porch
10-4x14-0
MBr
19-0x14-0
vaulted
Kit
12-10x
13-4
Great Rm
19-0x19-6
vaulted
Br 2
16-6x12-0
Dn
Br 3
12-0x14-4
Entry
Dining
13-0x17-0
Living
13-0x16-10
Porch
Porch depth 5-0
Porch
Garage
20-4x29-4

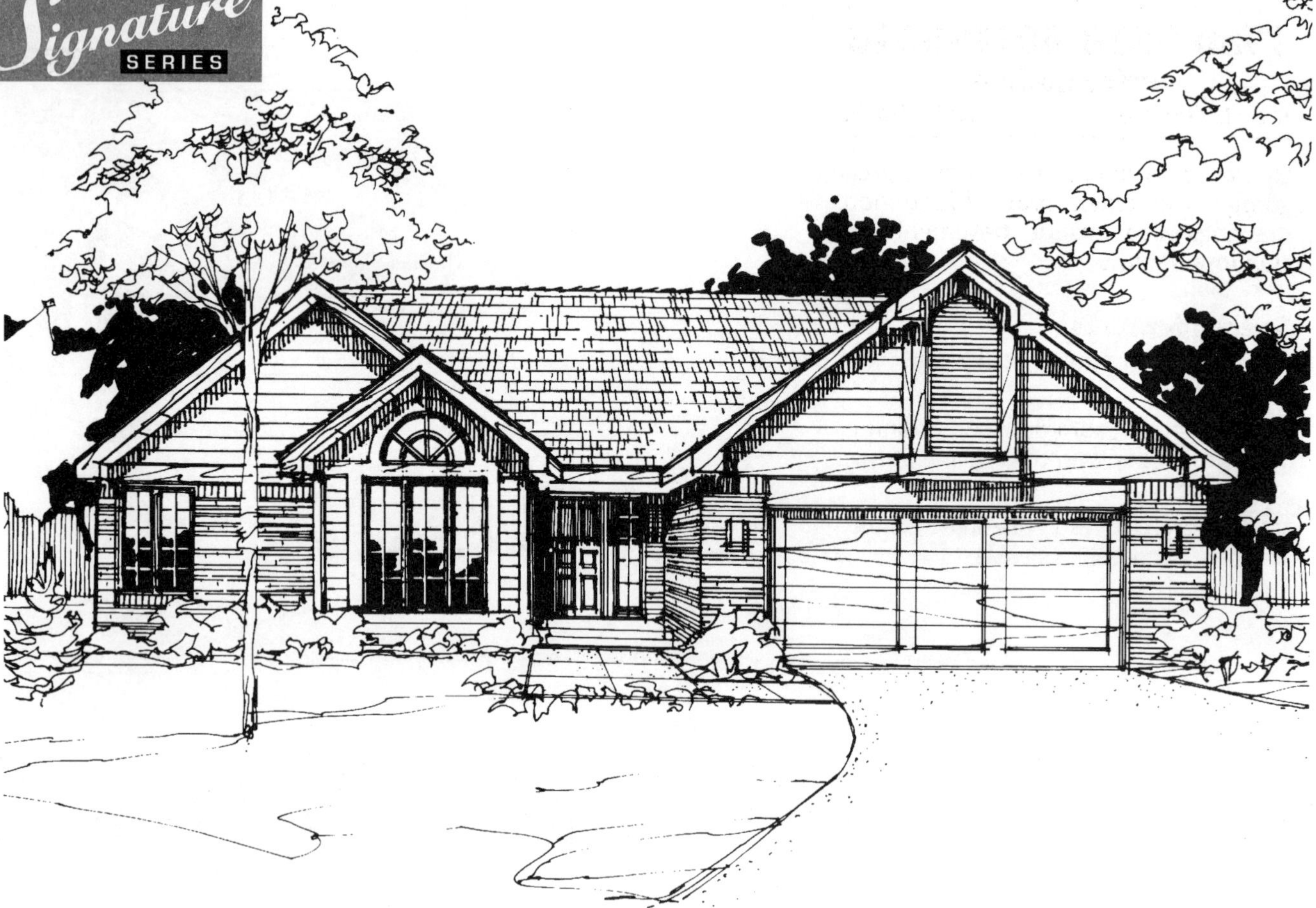

Plan #530-022D-0011

Price Code B

Total Living Area: 1,630 Sq. Ft.

Home has 3 bedrooms, 2 baths, 2-car garage and basement foundation.

Special features

- Crisp facade and full windows front and back offer open viewing
- Wrap-around rear deck is accessible from breakfast room, dining room and master bedroom
- Vaulted ceilings in living room and master bedroom
- Sitting area and large walk-in closet complement master bedroom

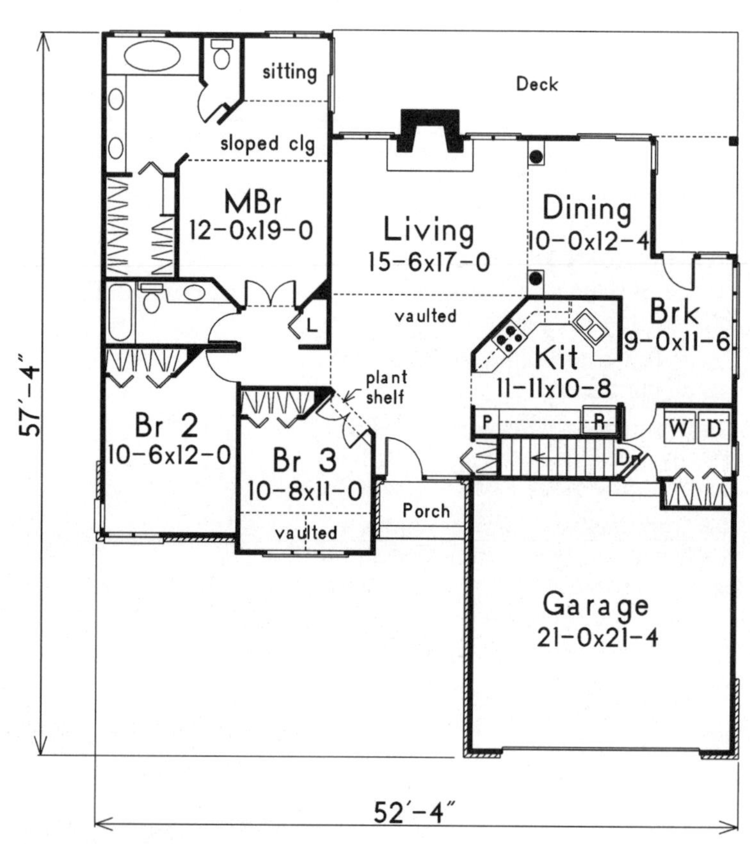

sitting
Deck
sloped clg
MBr
12-0x19-0
Living
15-6x17-0
Dining
10-0x12-4
vaulted
Brk
9-0x11-6
Kit
11-11x10-8
plant shelf
Br 2
10-6x12-0
Br 3
10-8x11-0
vaulted
Porch
Garage
21-0x21-4
57'-4"
52'-4"

LOWE'S

Signature
SERIES

Plan #530-001D-0048

Price Code A

Total Living Area: 1,400 Sq. Ft.

Home has 3 bedrooms, 2 baths, 2-car garage and crawl space foundation, drawings also include basement and slab foundations.

Special features

- Front porch offers warmth and welcome
- Large great room opens into dining room creating an open living atmosphere
- Kitchen features convenient laundry area, pantry and breakfast bar

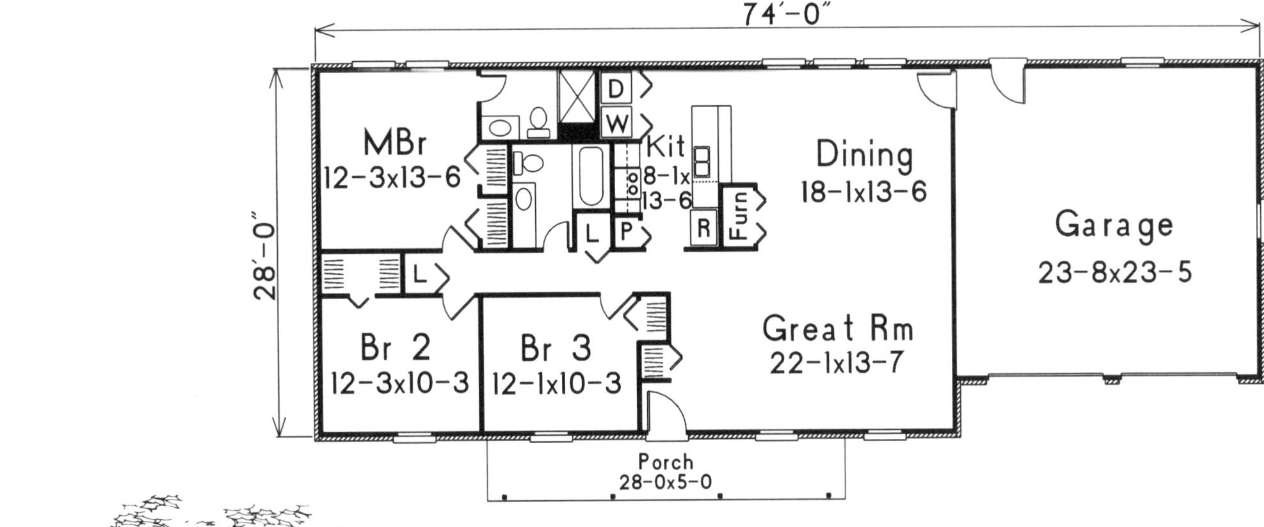
74'-0"
28'-0"
MBr
12-3x13-6
D
W
Kit
8-1x
13-6
Dining
18-1x13-6
Furn
R
L
P
L
Garage
23-8x23-5
Br 2
12-3x10-3
Br 3
12-1x10-3
Great Rm
22-1x13-7
Porch
28-0x5-0

LOWE'S

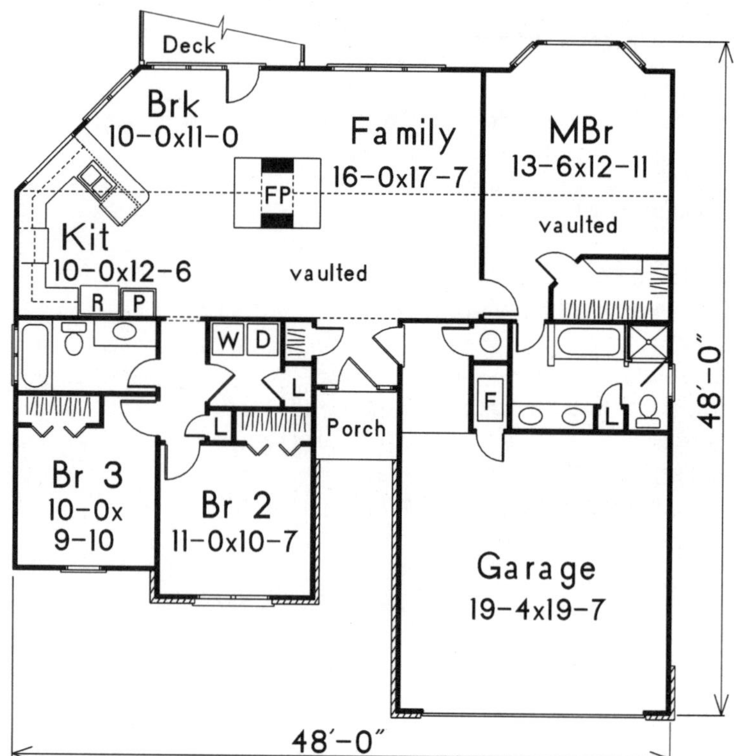

Deck
Brk
10-0x11-0
Family
16-0x17-7
MBr
13-6x12-11
FP
Kit
10-0x12-6
vaulted
vaulted
R
P
W
D
L
L
L
F
Porch
Br 3
10-0x
9-10
Br 2
11-0x10-7
Garage
19-4x19-7
48'-0"
48'-0"

Plan #530-053D-0037

Price Code A

Total Living Area: 1,388 Sq. Ft.

Home has 3 bedrooms, 2 baths, 2-car garage and crawl space foundation, drawings also include slab foundation.

Special features

- Handsome see-through fireplace offers a gathering point for the kitchen, family and breakfast rooms
- Vaulted ceiling and large bay window in the master bedroom add charm to this room
- A dramatic angular wall and large windows add brightness to the kitchen and breakfast room
- Kitchen, breakfast and family rooms have vaulted ceilings, adding to this central living area

TO ORDER BLUEPRINTS USE THE FORM ON PAGE 288 OR CALL TOLL-FREE **1-800-DREAM HOME** (373-2646)

LOWE'S

Signature SERIES

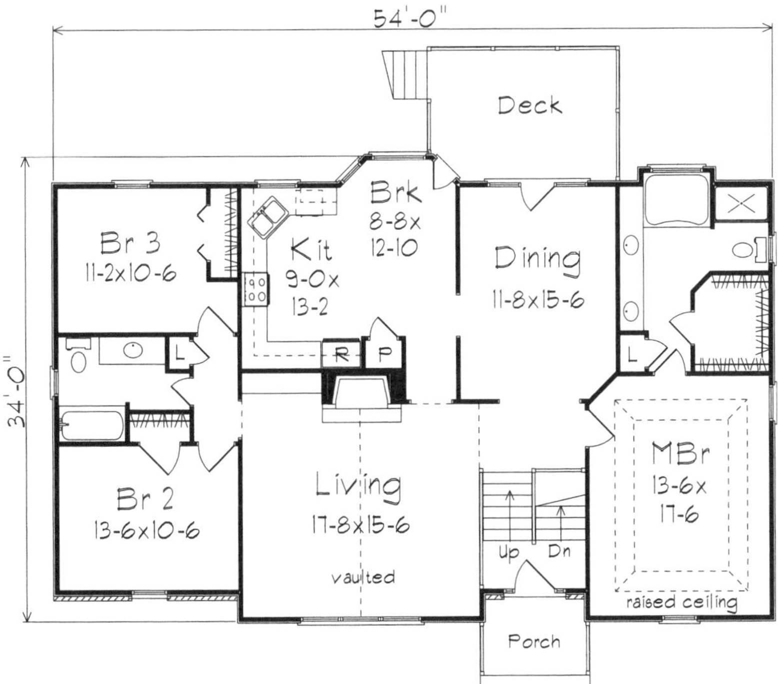
54'-0"
34'-0"
Deck
Brk
8-8x
12-10
Kit
9-0x
13-2
Br 3
11-2x10-6
Dining
11-8x15-6
R
P
L
L
MBr
13-6x
17-6
raised ceiling
Br 2
13-6x10-6
Living
17-8x15-6
vaulted
Up
Dn
Porch

Plan #530-053D-0055

Price Code C

Total Living Area: 1,803 Sq. Ft.

Home has 3 bedrooms, 2 baths, 3-car drive under garage and basement foundation.

Special features

- Master bedroom features a raised ceiling and private bath with a walk-in closet, large double-bowl vanity and separate tub and shower
- U-shaped kitchen includes a corner sink and convenient pantry
- Vaulted living room is complete with a fireplace and built-in cabinet

Dining In A Garden

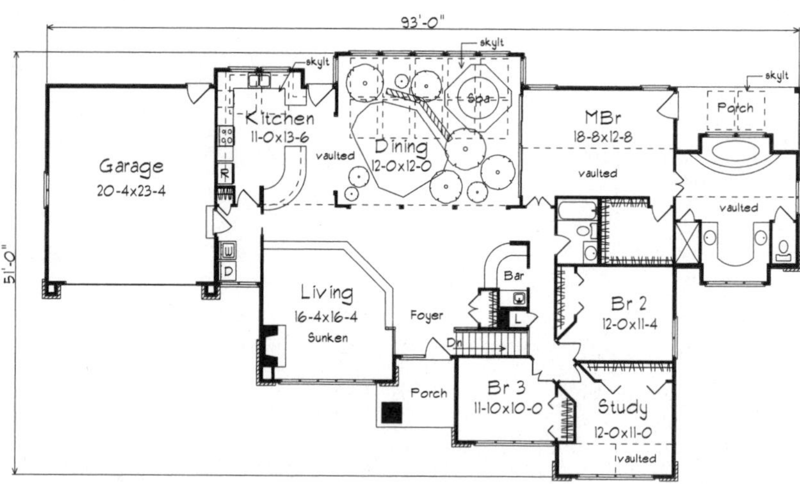
93'-0"
51'-0"
skylt
Spa
Porch
Kitchen
11-0x13-6
vaulted
Dining
12-0x12-0
MBr
18-8x12-8
vaulted
Garage
20-4x23-4
Living
16-4x16-4
Sunken
Foyer
Bar
Dn
Br 2
12-0x11-4
Porch
Br 3
11-10x10-0
Study
12-0x11-0
vaulted

Plan #530-007D-0012

Price Code D

Total Living Area: 2,563 Sq. Ft.

Home has 3 bedrooms, 2 baths, 2-car garage and basement foundation.

Special features

- Contemporary facade with traditional flair
- Impressive 13' high volume ceilings in grand entry and sunken living room
- Breathtaking garden room with dining island features vaulted skylit ceiling, surrounding window wall and hidden whirlpool retreat off the master bedroom
- Vaulted master bedroom includes view of garden and lavish bath

Interior View - Dining Room

TO ORDER BLUEPRINTS USE THE FORM ON PAGE 288 OR CALL TOLL-FREE **1-800-DREAM HOME** (373-2646)

Dramatic Roof Line

LOWE'S

Signature SERIES

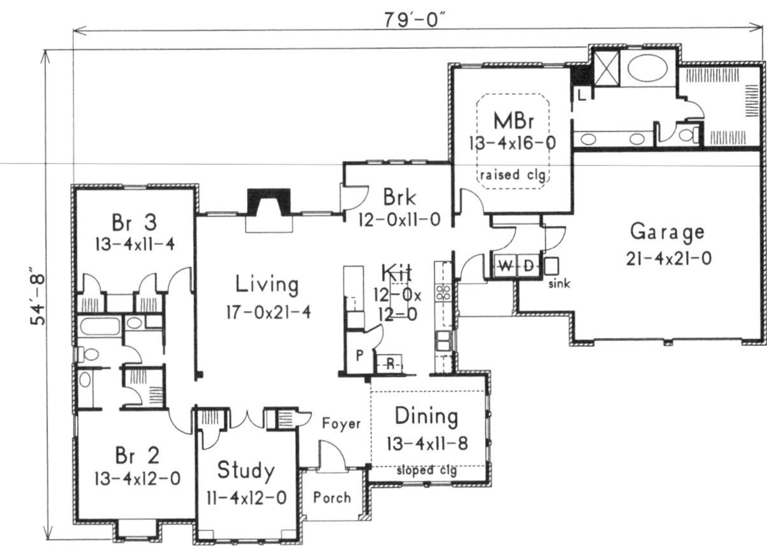
79'-0"
54'-8"
MBr
13-4x16-0
raised clg
Brk
12-0x11-0
Garage
21-4x21-0
Br 3
13-4x11-4
Living
17-0x21-4
Kit
12-0x
12-0
W
D
sink
P
R
Foyer
Dining
13-4x11-8
sloped clg
Br 2
13-4x12-0
Study
11-4x12-0
Porch

Plan #530-037D-0021

Price Code D

Total Living Area: 2,260 Sq. Ft.

Home has 3 bedrooms, 2 baths, 2-car garage and slab foundation.

Special features

- Luxurious master bedroom includes a raised ceiling, bath with oversized tub, separate shower and large walk-in closet
- Convenient kitchen and breakfast area with ample pantry storage
- Formal foyer leads into large living room with warming fireplace
- Convenient secondary entrance for everyday traffic

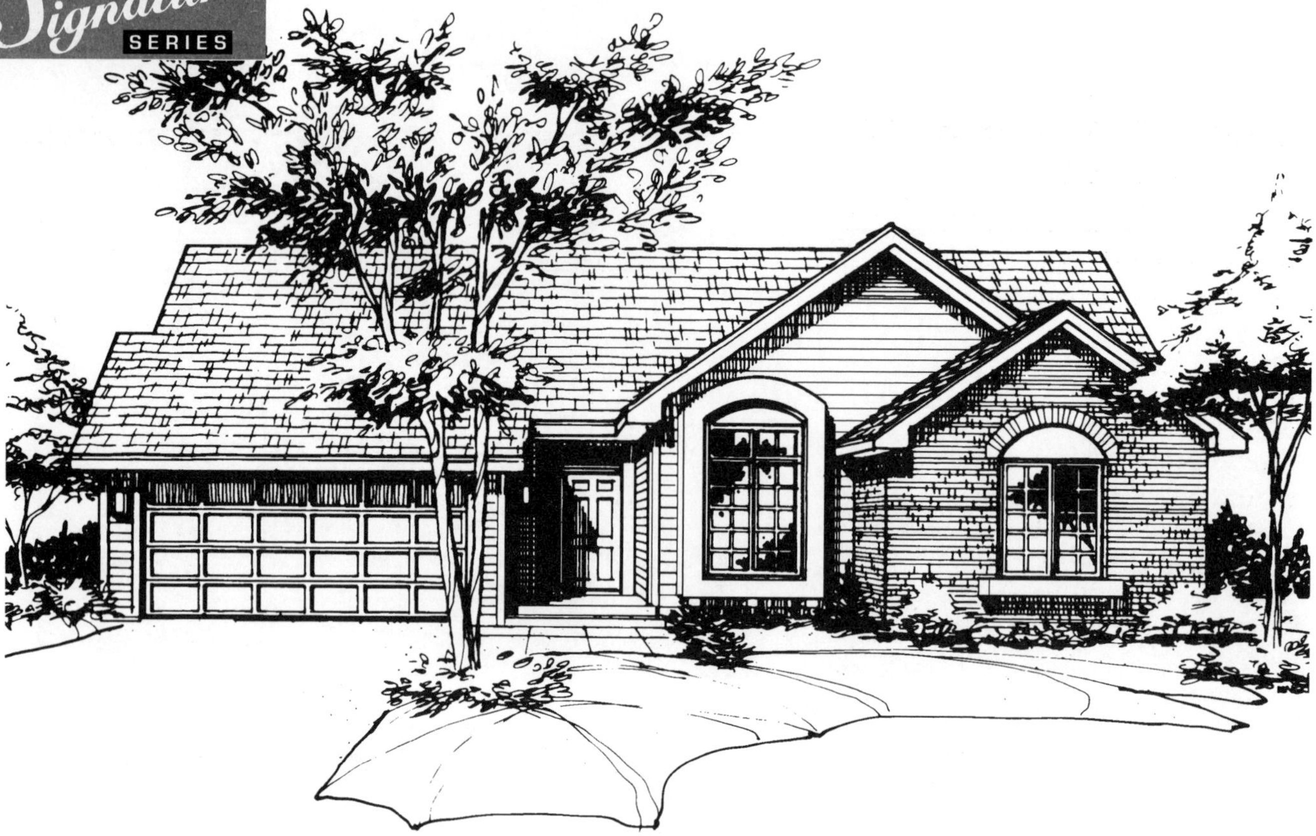

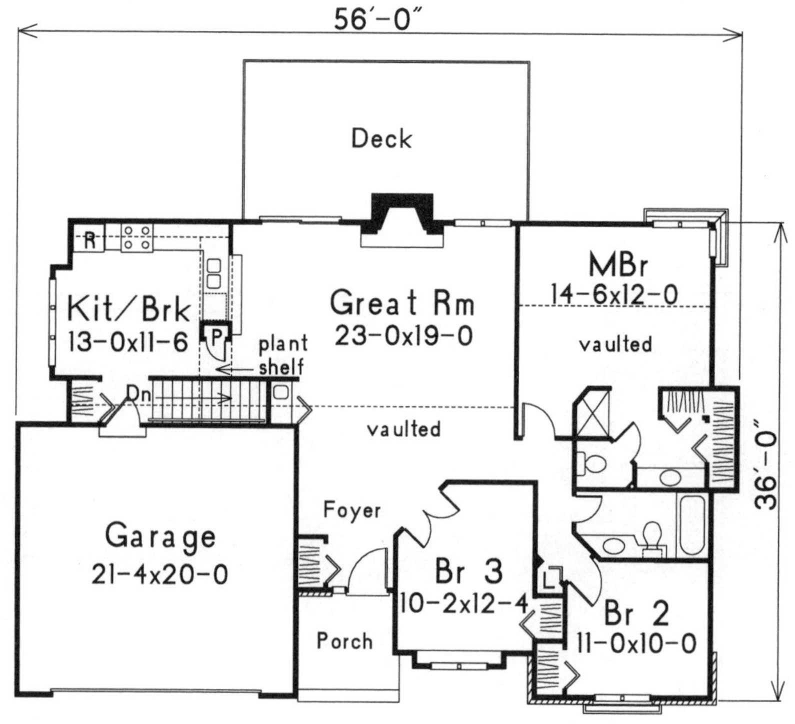
56'-0"
Deck
R
Kit/Brk
13-0x11-6
P
plant shelf
Dn
Great Rm
23-0x19-0
vaulted
MBr
14-6x12-0
vaulted
36'-0"
Garage
21-4x20-0
Foyer
Br 3
10-2x12-4
L
Br 2
11-0x10-0
Porch

Plan #530-022D-0005

Price Code A

Total Living Area: 1,360 Sq. Ft.

Home has 3 bedrooms, 2 baths, 2-car garage and basement foundation.

Special features

- Double-gabled front facade frames large windows
- The foyer opens to the vaulted great room with a fireplace and access to the rear deck
- Vaulted ceiling and large windows add openness to the kitchen/breakfast room
- Bedroom #3 easily converts to a den
- Plan easily adapts to crawl space or slab construction, with the utilities replacing the stairs

LOWE'S

Signature
SERIES

Plan #530-048D-0008

Price Code C

Total Living Area: 2,089 Sq. Ft.

Home has 4 bedrooms, 3 baths, 2-car garage and slab foundation.

Special features

- Family room features a fireplace, built-in bookshelves and triple sliders opening to the covered patio
- Kitchen overlooks the family room and features a pantry and desk
- Separated from the three secondary bedrooms, the master bedroom becomes a quiet retreat with patio access
- Master bedroom features an oversized bath with walk-in closet and corner tub

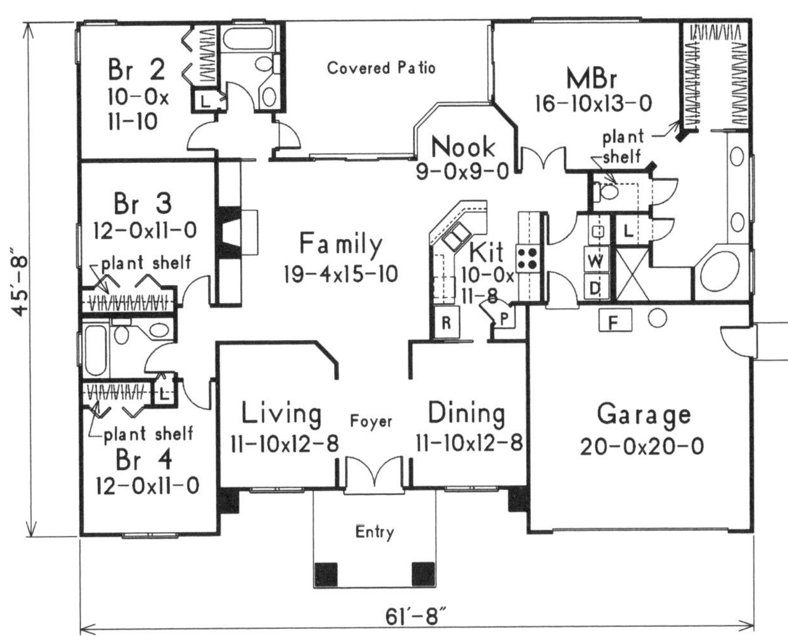
Br 2
10-0x
11-10
Covered Patio
MBr
16-10x13-0
plant shelf
Nook
9-0x9-0
Br 3
12-0x11-0
plant shelf
Family
19-4x15-10
Kit
10-0x
11-8
45'-8"
Living
11-10x12-8
Foyer
Dining
11-10x12-8
Garage
20-0x20-0
plant shelf
Br 4
12-0x11-0
Entry
61'-8"

LOWE'S

Signature SERIES

Plenty Of Bright, Vaulted Spaces

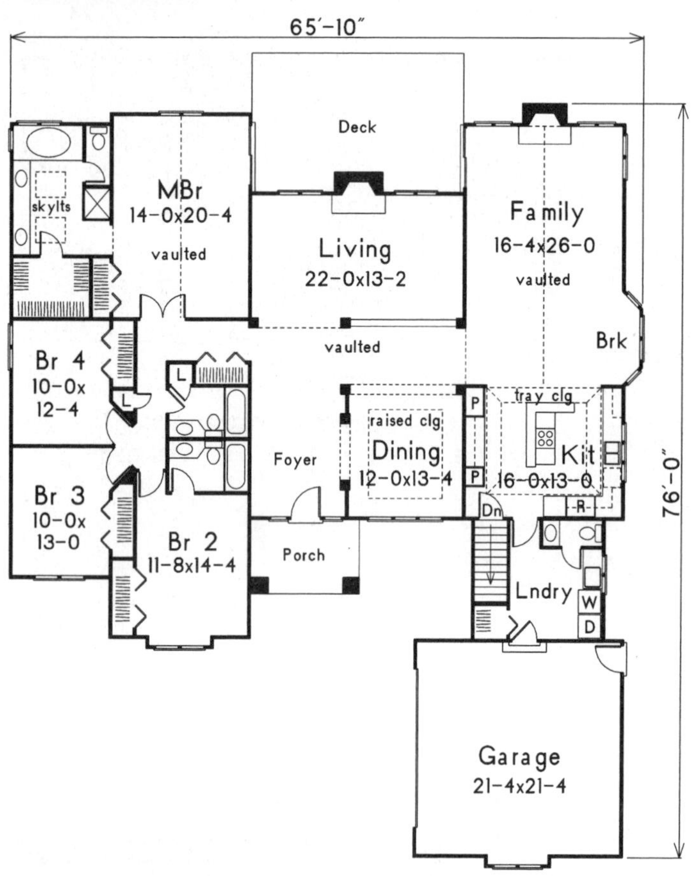
65'-10"
Deck
MBr
14-0x20-4
vaulted
skylts
Living
22-0x13-2
Family
16-4x26-0
vaulted
Brk
vaulted
Br 4
10-0x
12-4
Br 3
10-0x
13-0
Br 2
11-8x14-4
Foyer
Porch
raised clg
Dining
12-0x13-4
tray clg
Kit
16-0x13-0
Dn
Lndry
W
D
Garage
21-4x21-4
76'-0"

Plan #530-022D-0025

Price Code E

Total Living Area: 2,847 Sq. Ft.

Home has 4 bedrooms, 3 1/2 baths, 2-car side entry garage and basement foundation.

Special features

- Master bedroom includes a skylighted bath, deck access and two closets
- Bedroom #2 converts to a guest room with private bath
- Impressive foyer and gallery opens into the large living room with fireplace
- Kitchen features a desk area, center island, adjacent bayed breakfast area and access to the laundry room with half bath

TO ORDER BLUEPRINTS USE THE FORM ON PAGE 288 OR CALL TOLL-FREE **1-800-DREAM HOME** (373-2646)

LOWE'S

Signature SERIES

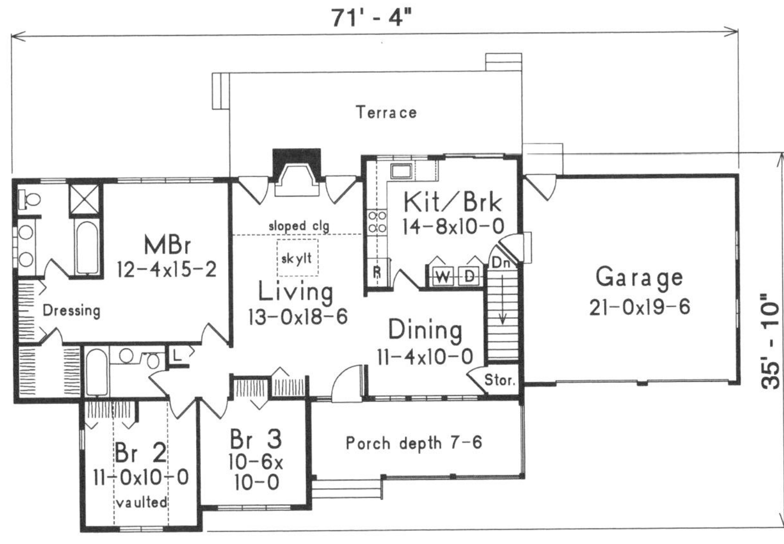
71' - 4"
Terrace
MBr
12-4x15-2
Dressing
sloped clg
skylt
Living
13-0x18-6
Kit/Brk
14-8x10-0
R
W D
Dn
Dining
11-4x10-0
Stor.
Garage
21-0x19-6
35' - 10"
L
Br 2
11-0x10-0
vaulted
Br 3
10-6x
10-0
Porch depth 7-6

Plan #530-017D-0005

Price Code B

Total Living Area: 1,367 Sq. Ft.

Home has 3 bedrooms, 2 baths, 2-car garage and basement foundation, drawings also include slab foundation.

Special features

- Neat front porch shelters the entrance
- Dining room has a full wall of windows and convenient storage area
- Breakfast area leads to the rear terrace through sliding doors
- Large living room with high ceiling, skylight and fireplace

LOWE'S

Plan #530-007D-0018

Price Code C

Total Living Area: 1,941 Sq. Ft.

Home has 4 bedrooms, 2 1/2 baths, 2-car garage and walk-out basement foundation.

Special features

- Dramatic, exciting and spacious interior
- Vaulted great room is brightened by a sunken atrium window wall and skylights
- Vaulted U-shaped gourmet kitchen with plant shelf opens to dining room
- First floor half bath features space for stackable washer and dryer

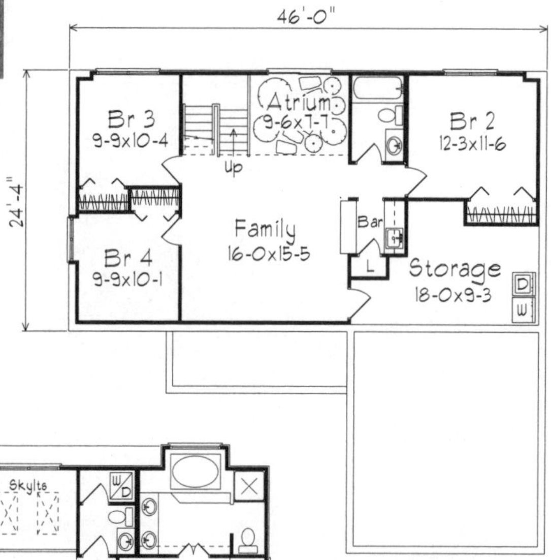

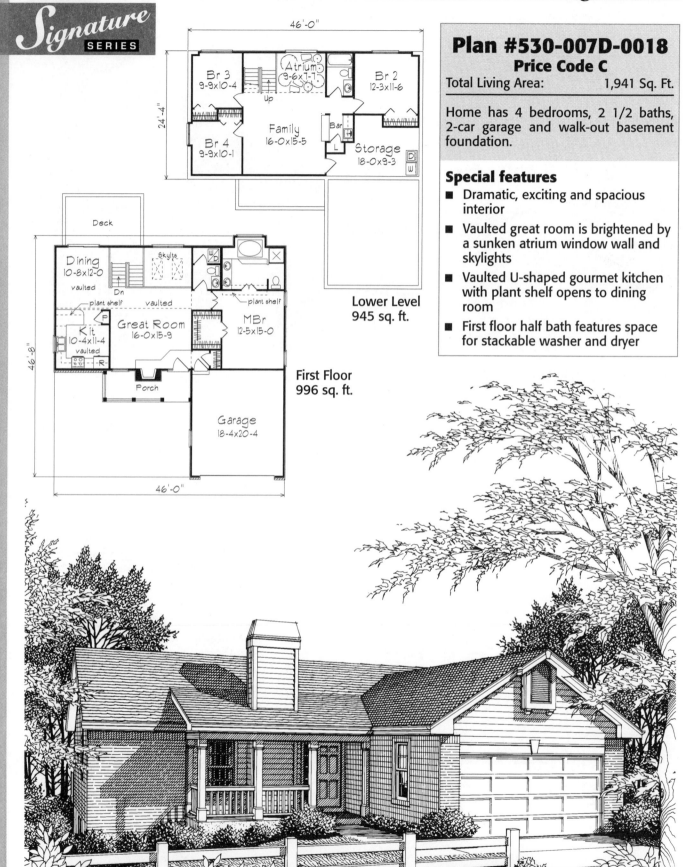

46'-0"
24'-4"
Br 3 9-9x10-4
Atrium 9-6x7-7
Up
Br 2 12-3x11-6
Family 16-0x15-5
Bar
Br 4 9-9x10-1
L
Storage 18-0x9-3
D
W

Lower Level
945 sq. ft.

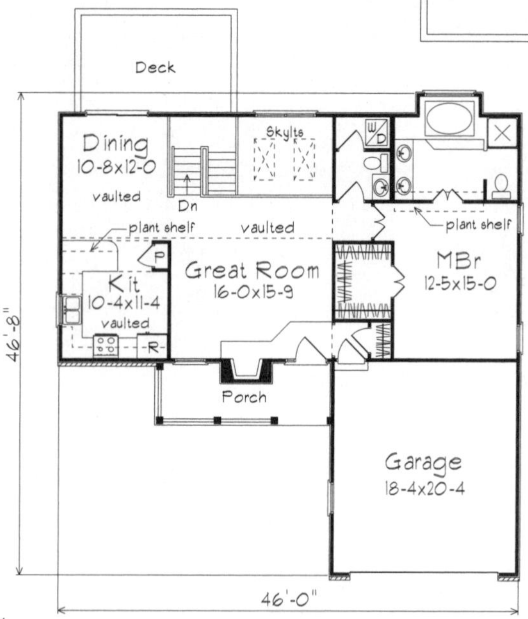

Deck
Dining 10-8x12-0 vaulted
Skylts
Dn
W/D
plant shelf
vaulted
plant shelf
P
Great Room 16-0x15-9
MBr 12-5x15-0
Kit 10-4x11-4 vaulted
R
Porch
Garage 18-4x20-4
46'-8"
46'-0"

First Floor
996 sq. ft.

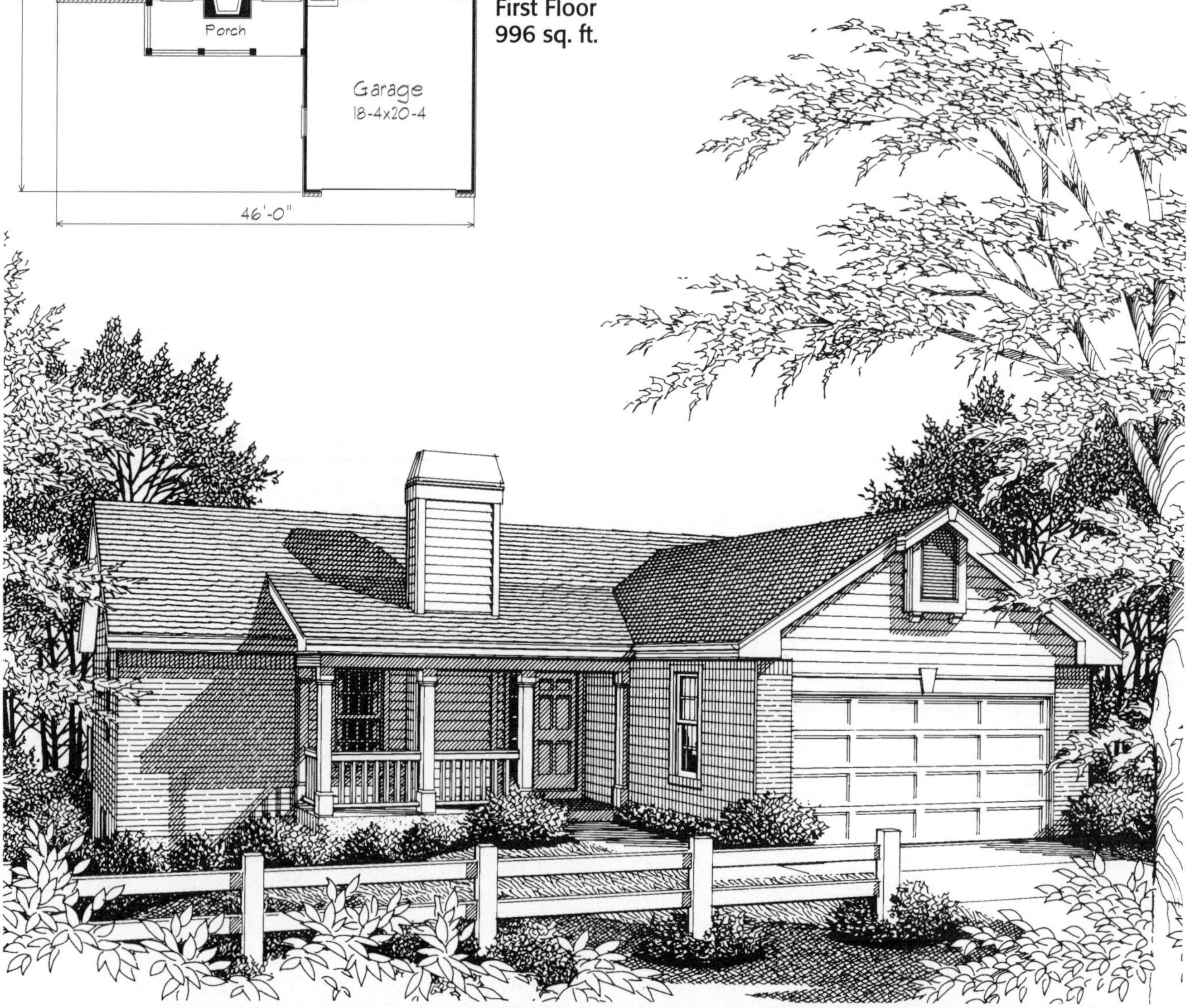

Charming And Functional

LOWE'S

Signature SERIES

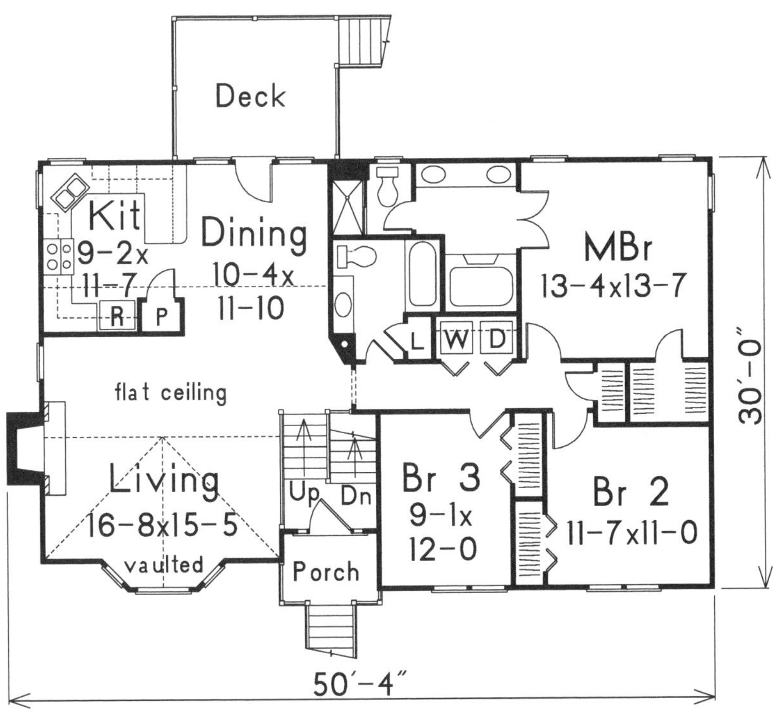
Deck
Kit
9-2x
11-7
R
P
Dining
10-4x
11-10
MBr
13-4x13-7
L
W
D
flat ceiling
Living
16-8x15-5
vaulted
Up
Dn
Porch
Br 3
9-1x
12-0
Br 2
11-7x11-0
30′-0″
50′-4″

Plan #530-053D-0032

Price Code A

Total Living Area: 1,404 Sq. Ft.

Home has 3 bedrooms, 2 baths, 2-car drive under garage and basement foundation, drawings also include partial crawl space foundation.

Special features

- Split-foyer entrance
- Bayed living area features unique vaulted ceiling and fireplace
- Wrap-around kitchen has corner windows for added sunlight and a bar that overlooks dining area
- Master bath features a garden tub with separate shower
- Rear deck provides handy access to dining room and kitchen

LOWE'S

Plan #530-045D-0014

Price Code AA

Total Living Area: 987 Sq. Ft.

Home has 3 bedrooms, 1 bath and basement foundation.

Special features

- Galley kitchen opens into the cozy breakfast room
- Convenient coat closets are located by both entrances
- Dining/living room offers an expansive open area
- Breakfast room has access to the outdoors
- Front porch is great for enjoying outdoor living

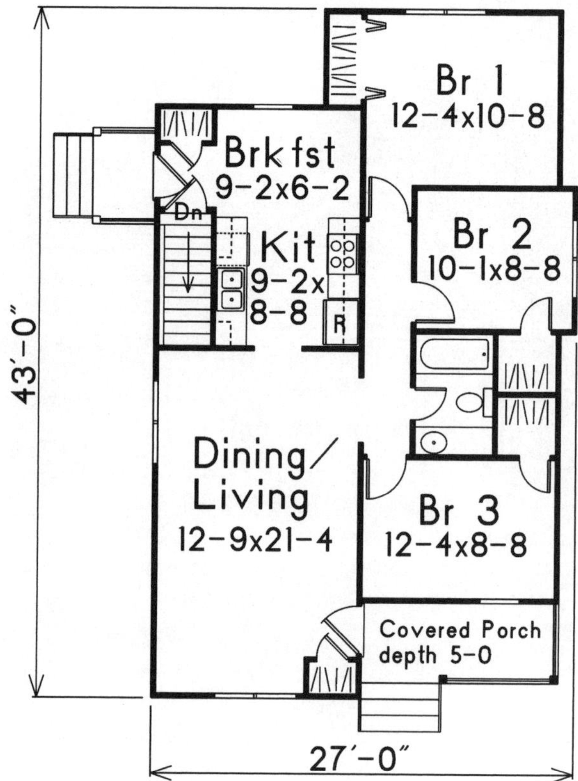
Br 1
12-4x10-8
Brkfst
9-2x6-2
Dn
Kit
9-2x
8-8
R
Br 2
10-1x8-8
Dining/
Living
12-9x21-4
Br 3
12-4x8-8
Covered Porch
depth 5-0
43'-0"
27'-0"

Spacious Floor Plan

LOWE'S

Signature SERIES

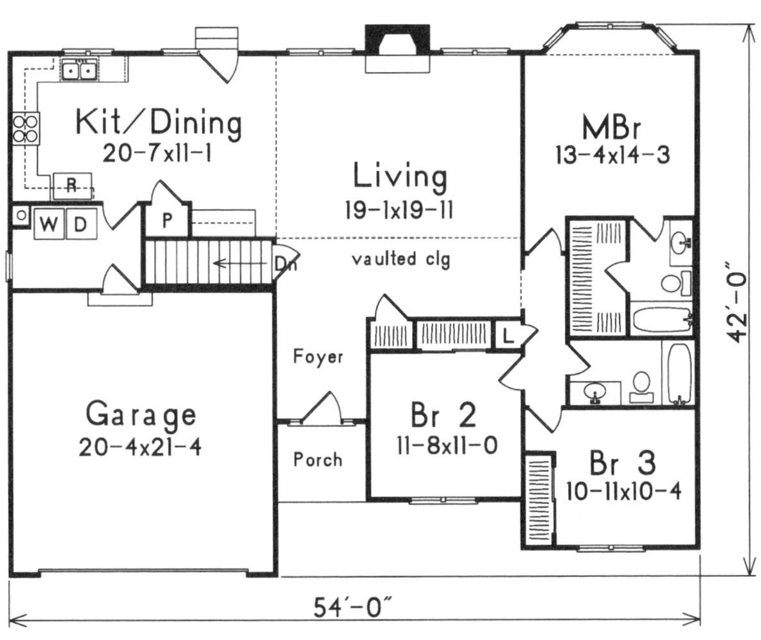
Kit/Dining
20-7x11-1
R
W D
P
Living
19-1x19-11
vaulted clg
Dn
MBr
13-4x14-3
L
Foyer
Garage
20-4x21-4
Porch
Br 2
11-8x11-0
Br 3
10-11x10-4
42'-0"
54'-0"

Plan #530-058D-0016

Price Code B

Total Living Area: 1,558 Sq. Ft.

Home has 3 bedrooms, 2 baths, 2-car garage and basement foundation.

Special features

- The spacious utility room is located conveniently between the garage and kitchen/dining area
- Bedrooms are separated from the living area by a hallway
- Enormous living area with fireplace and vaulted ceiling opens to the kitchen and dining area
- Master bedroom is enhanced with a large bay window, walk-in closet and private bath

Plan #530-021D-0007

Price Code D

Total Living Area: 1,868 Sq. Ft.

Home has 3 bedrooms, 2 baths, 2-car side entry garage and slab foundation, drawings also include crawl space foundation.

Special features

- Luxurious master bath is impressive with an angled quarter-circle tub, separate vanities and large walk-in closet
- Energy efficient home with 2" x 6" exterior walls
- Dining room is surrounded by a series of arched openings which complement the open feeling of this design
- Living room has a 12' ceiling accented by skylights and a large fireplace flanked by sliding doors
- Large storage areas

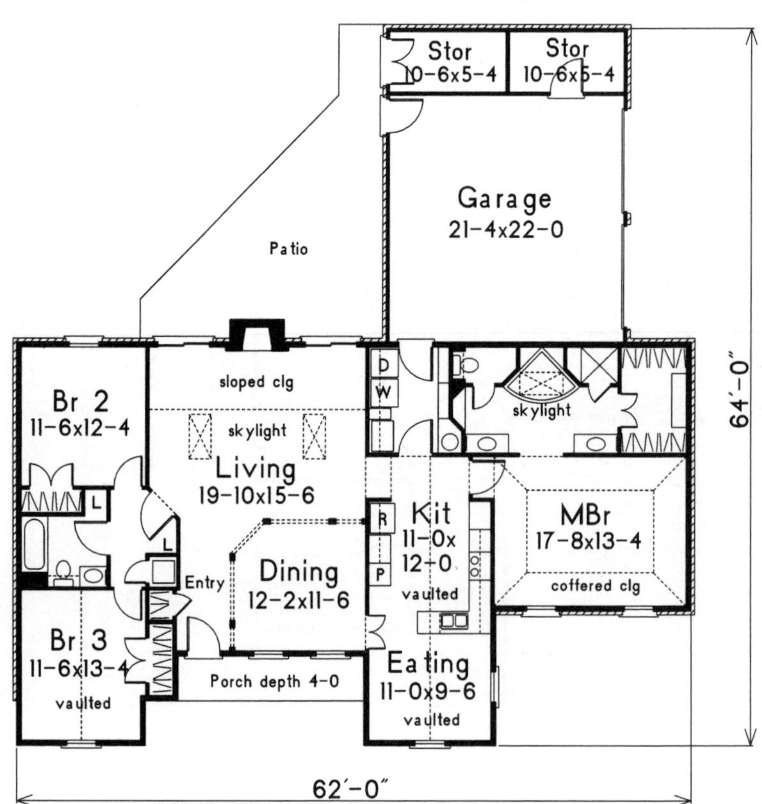
Stor
10-6x5-4
Stor
10-6x5-4
Garage
21-4x22-0
Patio
sloped clg
skylight
Living
19-10x15-6
Br 2
11-6x12-4
Br 3
11-6x13-4
vaulted
Entry
Dining
12-2x11-6
Porch depth 4-0
Kit
11-0x
12-0
vaulted
Eating
11-0x9-6
vaulted
skylight
MBr
17-8x13-4
coffered clg
64'-0"
62'-0"

LOWE'S

Signature
SERIES

Plan #530-007D-0055

Price Code D

Total Living Area: 2,029 Sq. Ft.

Home has 4 bedrooms, 2 baths, 2-car side entry garage and basement foundation, drawings also include crawl space and slab foundations.

Special features

- Stonework, gables, roof dormer and double porches create a country flavor
- Kitchen enjoys extravagant cabinetry and counterspace in a bay, island snack bar, built-in pantry and cheery dining area with multiple tall windows
- Angled stair descends from large entry with wood columns and is open to vaulted great room with corner fireplace
- Master bedroom boasts two walk-in closets, a private bath with double-door entry and a secluded porch

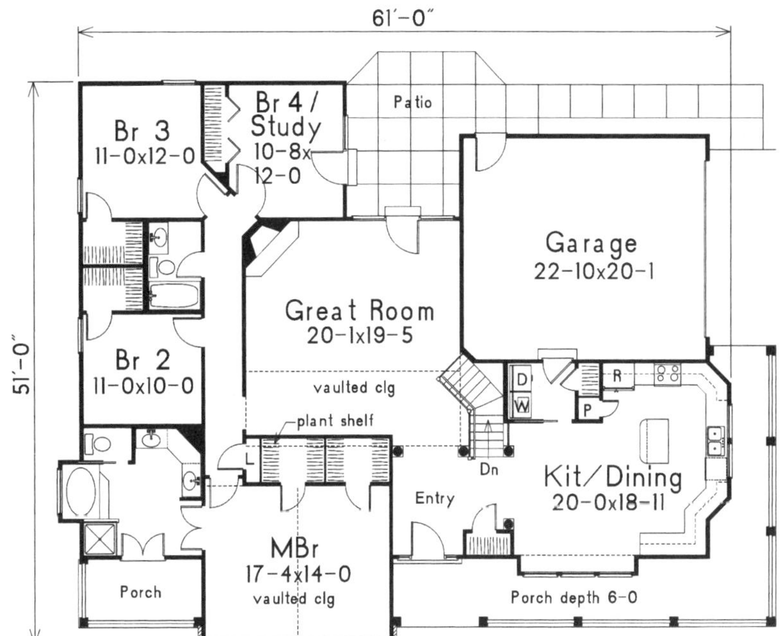
61'-0"
51'-0"
Br 3
11-0x12-0
Br 4 / Study
10-8x
12-0
Patio
Garage
22-10x20-1
Great Room
20-1x19-5
vaulted clg
plant shelf
Br 2
11-0x10-0
D
W
R
P
L
Dn
Entry
Kit/Dining
20-0x18-11
MBr
17-4x14-0
vaulted clg
Porch
Porch depth 6-0

LOWE'S

Signature
SERIES

Cozy Front Porch

Plan #530-040D-0026

Price Code B

Total Living Area: 1,393 Sq. Ft.

Home has 3 bedrooms, 2 baths, 2-car detached garage and crawl space foundation, drawings also include slab foundation.

Special features

- L-shaped kitchen features a walk-in pantry, island cooktop and is convenient to the laundry room and dining area
- Master bedroom features a large walk-in closet and private bath with separate tub and shower
- Convenient storage/coat closet in hall
- View to the patio from the dining area

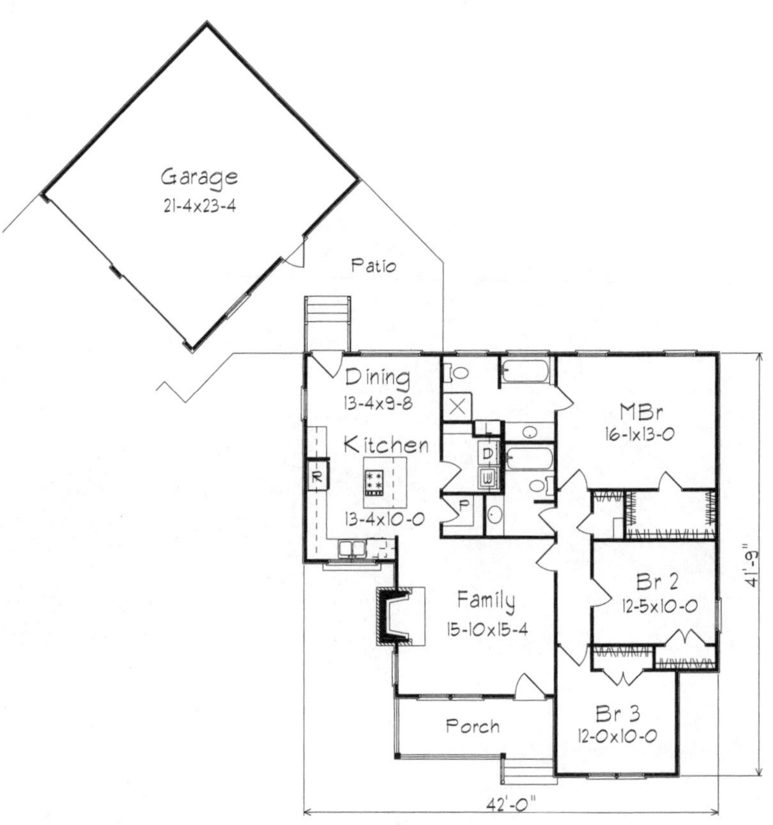
Garage
21-4x23-4
Patio
Dining
13-4x9-8
Kitchen
13-4x10-0
MBr
16-1x13-0
Family
15-10x15-4
Br 2
12-5x10-0
Br 3
12-0x10-0
Porch
42'-0"
41'-9"

LOWE'S

Signature
SERIES

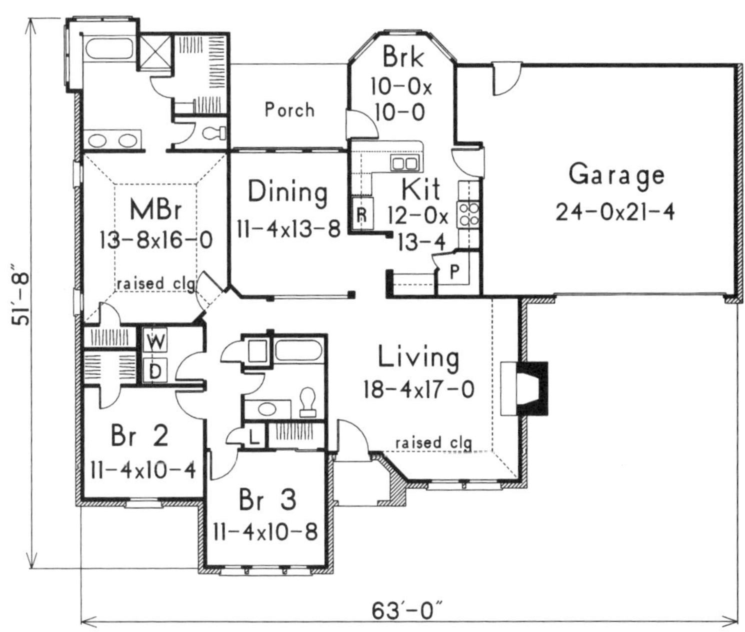
Brk
10-0x
10-0
Porch
Garage
24-0x21-4
Dining
11-4x13-8
Kit
12-0x
13-4
R
P
MBr
13-8x16-0
raised clg
W
D
Living
18-4x17-0
raised clg
L
Br 2
11-4x10-4
Br 3
11-4x10-8
51'-8"
63'-0"

Plan #530-037D-0008

Price Code C

Total Living Area: 1,707 Sq. Ft.

Home has 3 bedrooms, 2 baths, 2-car garage and slab foundation.

Special features

- The formal living room off the entry hall has a high sloping ceiling and prominent fireplace
- Kitchen and breakfast area allow access to an oversized garage and rear porch
- Master bedroom has an impressive vaulted ceiling, luxurious bath, large walk-in closet and separate tub and shower
- Utility room is conveniently located near bedrooms

Plan #530-007D-0044

Price Code B

Total Living Area: 1,516 Sq. Ft.

Home has 3 bedrooms, 2 baths, 2-car garage and basement foundation.

Special features

- Spacious great room is open to dining area with a bay and unique stair location
- Attractive and well-planned kitchen offers breakfast bar and built-in pantry
- Smartly designed master bedroom enjoys patio view

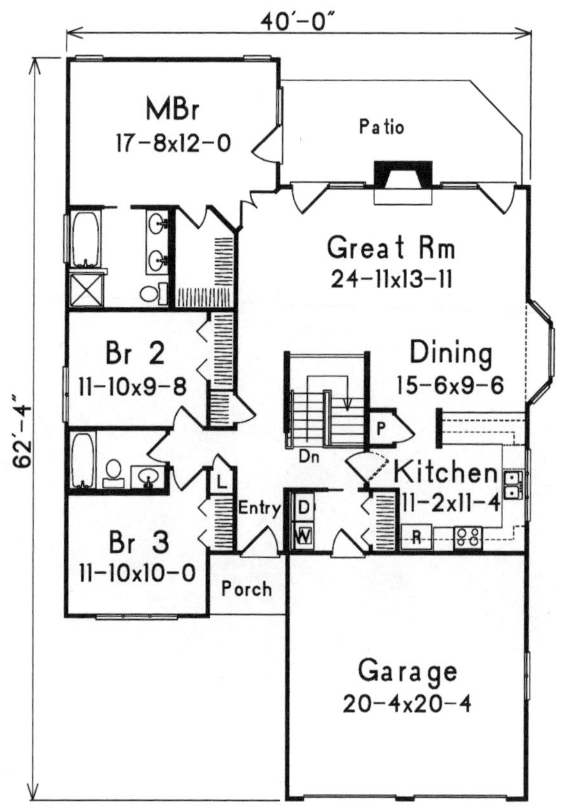
40'-0"
62'-4"
MBr
17-8x12-0
Patio
Great Rm
24-11x13-11
Br 2
11-10x9-8
Dining
15-6x9-6
P
Dn
Kitchen
11-2x11-4
L
Entry
D
W
R
Br 3
11-10x10-0
Porch
Garage
20-4x20-4

TO ORDER BLUEPRINTS USE THE FORM ON PAGE 288 OR CALL TOLL-FREE **1-800-DREAM HOME** (373-2646)

LOWE'S

Signature
SERIES

Plan #530-001D-0030

Price Code A

Total Living Area: 1,416 Sq. Ft.

Home has 3 bedrooms, 2 baths, 2-car garage and basement foundation, drawings also include crawl space and slab foundations.

Special features

- Family room includes fireplace, elevated plant shelf and vaulted ceiling
- Patio is accessible from dining area and garage
- Centrally located laundry area
- Oversized walk-in pantry

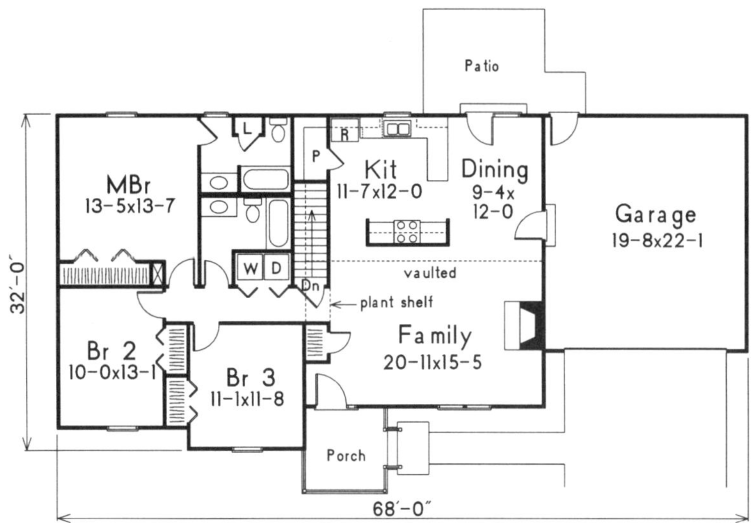
Patio
MBr
13-5x13-7
L
P
R
Kit
11-7x12-0
Dining
9-4x
12-0
Garage
19-8x22-1
W
D
Dn
vaulted
plant shelf
Family
20-11x15-5
Br 2
10-0x13-1
Br 3
11-1x11-8
Porch
32'-0"
68'-0"

Plan #530-007D-0045

Price Code A

Total Living Area: 1,321 Sq. Ft.

Home has 3 bedrooms, 2 baths, 1-car rear entry garage and basement foundation.

Special features

- Rear entry garage and elongated brick wall add to appealing facade
- Dramatic vaulted living room includes corner fireplace and towering feature windows
- Breakfast room is immersed in light from two large windows and glass sliding doors

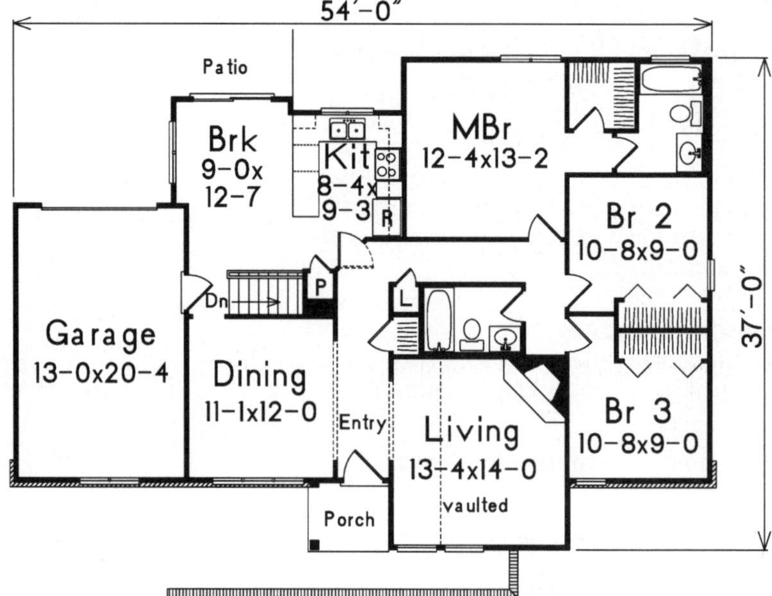
54'-0"
Patio
Brk
9-0x
12-7
Kit
8-4x
9-3
R
MBr
12-4x13-2
Br 2
10-8x9-0
37'-0"
Garage
13-0x20-4
Dn
P
L
Dining
11-1x12-0
Entry
Living
13-4x14-0
vaulted
Br 3
10-8x9-0
Porch

Front Porch And Center Gable

LOWE'S

Signature
SERIES

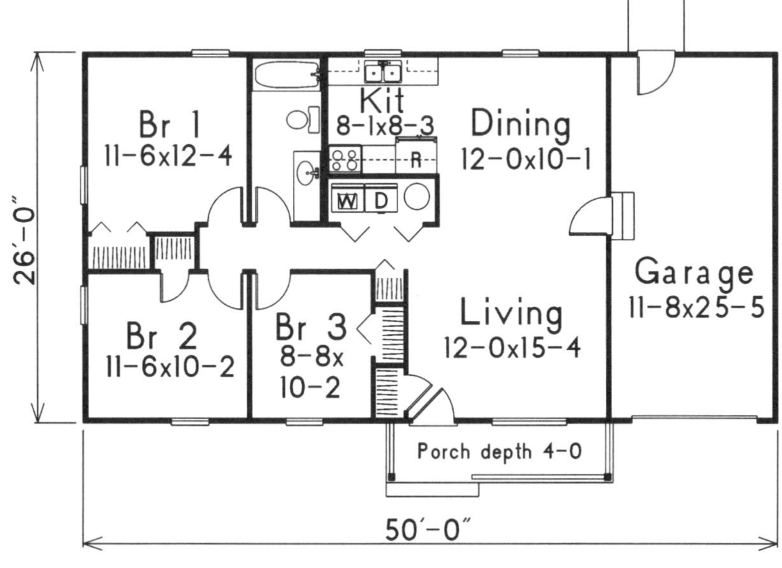
26'-0"
Br 1
11-6x12-4
Kit
8-1x8-3
R
W D
Dining
12-0x10-1
Garage
11-8x25-5
Br 2
11-6x10-2
Br 3
8-8x
10-2
Living
12-0x15-4
Porch depth 4-0
50'-0"

Plan #530-001D-0018

Price Code AA

Total Living Area: 988 Sq. Ft.

Home has 3 bedrooms, 1 bath, 1-car garage and basement foundation, drawings also include crawl space foundation.

Special features

- Pleasant covered porch entry
- The kitchen, living and dining areas are combined to maximize space
- Entry has convenient coat closet
- Laundry closet is located adjacent to bedrooms

LOWE'S

Signature SERIES

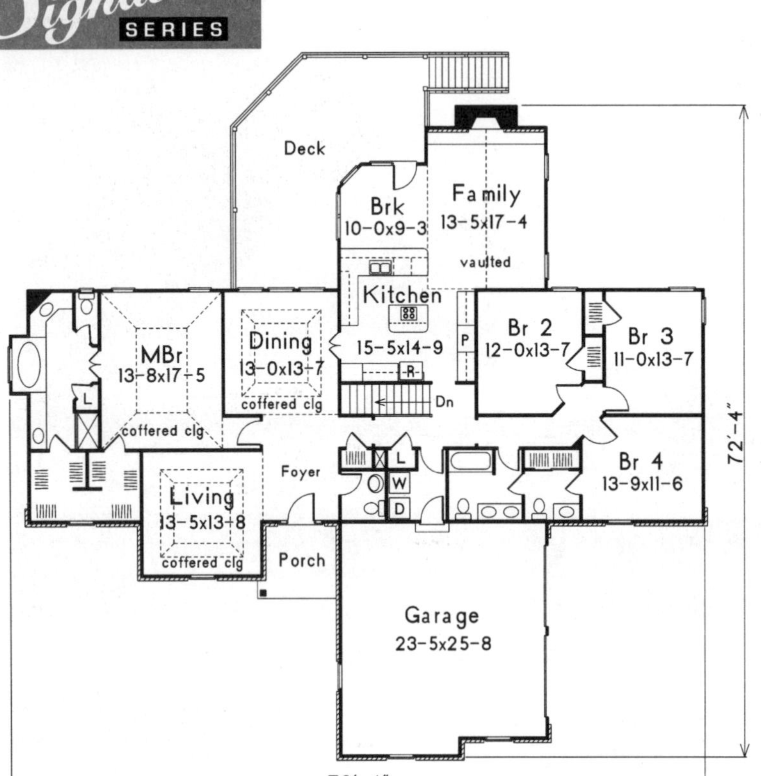
Deck
Brk
10-0x9-3
Family
13-5x17-4
vaulted
Kitchen
15-5x14-9
Br 2
12-0x13-7
Br 3
11-0x13-7
MBr
13-8x17-5
coffered clg
Dining
13-0x13-7
coffered clg
Dn
Foyer
Br 4
13-9x11-6
Living
13-5x13-8
coffered clg
Porch
Garage
23-5x25-8
72'-4"
79'-4"

Plan #530-053D-0052

Price Code D

Total Living Area: 2,513 Sq. Ft.

Home has 4 bedrooms, 2 full baths, 2 half baths, 2-car side entry garage and basement foundation.

Special features

- Coffered ceilings in master bedroom, living and dining rooms
- Kitchen features island cooktop and built-in desk
- Dramatic vaulted ceiling in the breakfast room is framed by plenty of windows
- Covered entry porch leads into spacious foyer
- Family room features an impressive fireplace and vaulted ceiling that joins the breakfast room creating a spacious entertainment area

TO ORDER BLUEPRINTS USE THE FORM ON PAGE 288 OR CALL TOLL-FREE **1-800-DREAM HOME** (373-2646)

LOWE'S

Signature SERIES

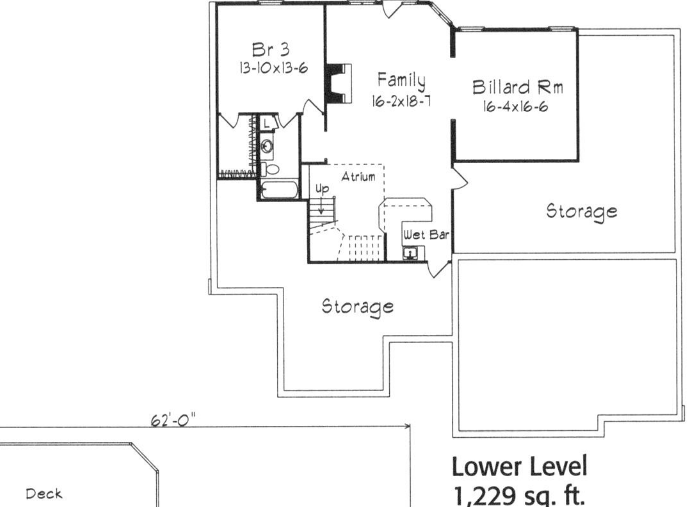
Br 3
13-10x13-6
Family
16-2x18-7
Billard Rm
16-4x16-6
Atrium
Up
Wet Bar
Storage
Storage

Lower Level
1,229 sq. ft.

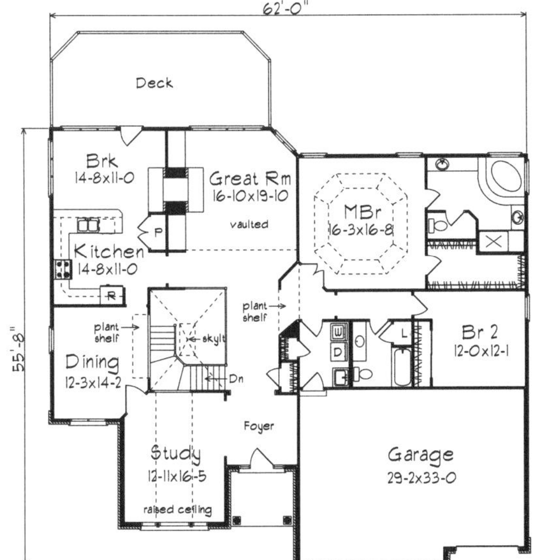
62'-0"
Deck
Brk
14-8x11-0
Great Rm
16-10x19-10
vaulted
MBr
16-3x16-8
Kitchen
14-8x11-0
plant shelf
skylt
plant shelf
Dining
12-3x14-2
Dn
Br 2
12-0x12-1
Foyer
Study
12-11x16-5
raised ceiling
Garage
29-2x33-0
55'-8"

First Floor
2,182 sq. ft.

Plan #530-027D-0008

Price Code F

Total Living Area: 3,411 Sq. Ft.

Home has 3 bedrooms, 3 baths, 3-car garage and basement foundation.

Special features

- Foyer opens to a large study with raised ceiling
- Master bedroom features an octagon-shaped raised ceiling and private bath with double vanities and corner whirlpool tub
- Expansive windows and a two-way fireplace enhance the great room

LOWE'S

Signature SERIES

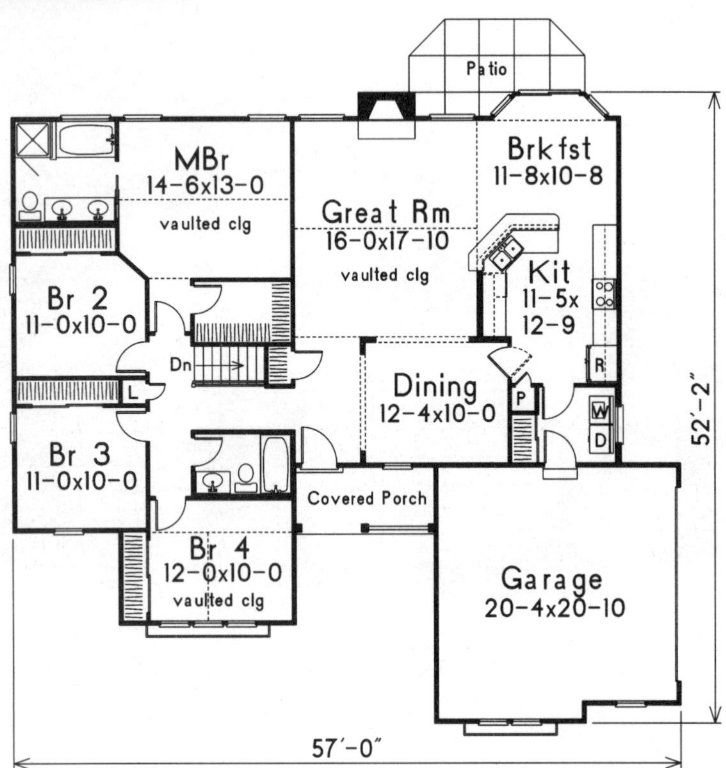
Patio
MBr
14-6x13-0
vaulted clg
Brkfst
11-8x10-8
Great Rm
16-0x17-10
vaulted clg
Kit
11-5x
12-9
Br 2
11-0x10-0
Dn
L
R
P
W
D
Dining
12-4x10-0
Br 3
11-0x10-0
Covered Porch
Br 4
12-0x10-0
vaulted clg
Garage
20-4x20-10
52'-2"
57'-0"

Plan #530-007D-0067

Price Code B

Total Living Area: 1,761 Sq. Ft.

Home has 4 bedrooms, 2 baths, 2-car side entry garage and basement foundation.

Special features

- Exterior window dressing, roof dormers and planter boxes provide visual warmth and charm
- Great room boasts a vaulted ceiling, fireplace and opens to a pass-through kitchen
- The vaulted master bedroom includes a luxury bath and walk-in closet
- Home features eight separate closets with an abundance of storage

Distinctive Garden Courtyard

LOWE'S

Signature
SERIES

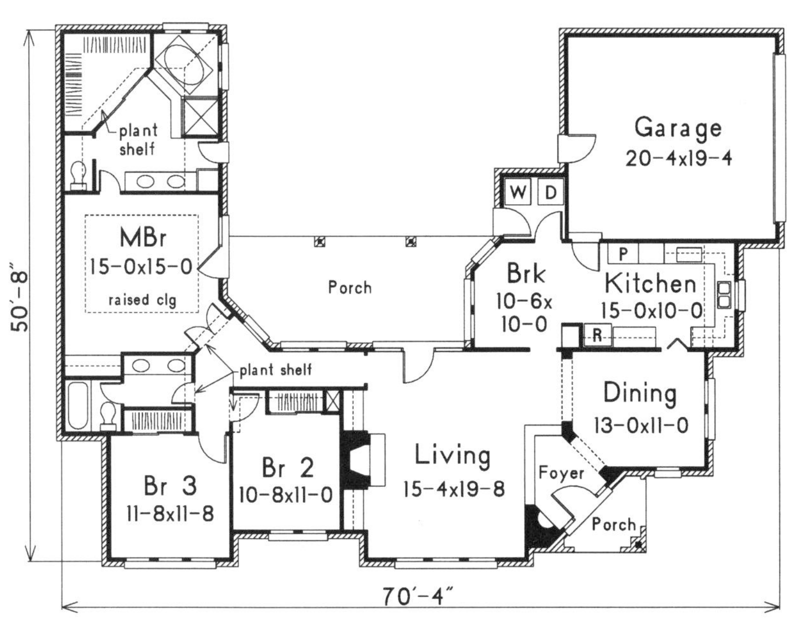
plant shelf
MBr
15-0x15-0
raised clg
Porch
plant shelf
Br 3
11-8x11-8
Br 2
10-8x11-0
Living
15-4x19-8
Foyer
Porch
Garage
20-4x19-4
W
D
Brk
10-6x
10-0
P
Kitchen
15-0x10-0
R
Dining
13-0x11-0
50'-8"
70'-4"

Plan #530-037D-0003

Price Code D

Total Living Area: 1,996 Sq. Ft.

Home has 3 bedrooms, 2 baths, 2-car side entry garage and slab foundation, drawings also include crawl space foundation.

Special features

- Garden courtyard comes with large porch and direct access to master bedroom, breakfast room and garage
- Sculptured entrance has artful plant shelves and special niche in foyer
- Master bedroom boasts French doors, garden tub, desk with book-shelves and generous storage
- Plant shelves and a high ceiling grace the hallway

Plan #530-001D-0021

Price Code A

Total Living Area 1,416 Sq. Ft.

Home has 3 bedrooms, 2 baths, 2-car garage and crawl space foundation, drawings also include basement foundation.

Special features

- Excellent floor plan eases traffic
- Master bedroom features private bath
- Foyer opens to both formal living room and informal great room
- Great room has access to the outdoors through sliding doors

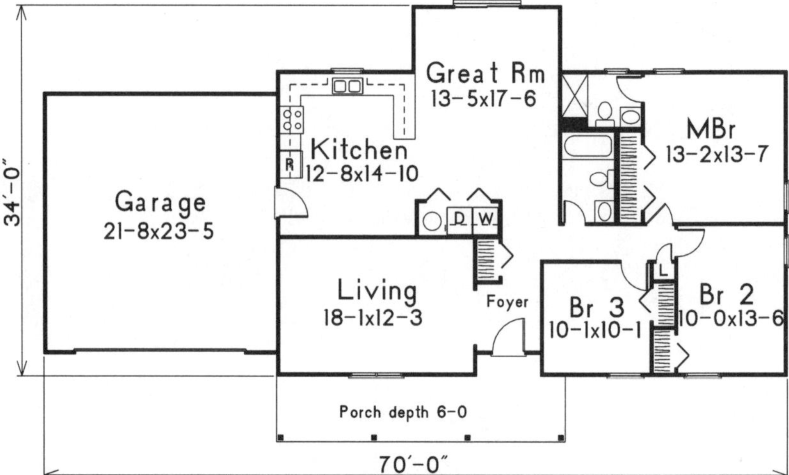
Great Rm
13-5x17-6
Kitchen
12-8x14-10
MBr
13-2x13-7
Garage
21-8x23-5
Living
18-1x12-3
Foyer
Br 3
10-1x10-1
Br 2
10-0x13-6
Porch depth 6-0
34'-0"
70'-0"

Distinctive Home For Sloping Terrain

LOWE'S

Signature SERIES

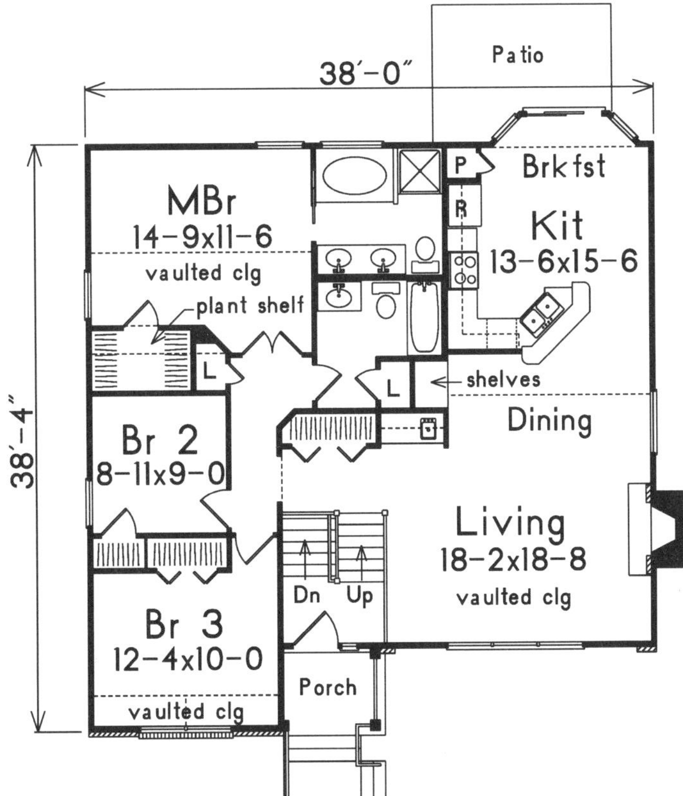

Patio
38′-0″
38′-4″
MBr
14-9x11-6
vaulted clg
plant shelf
P
R
Brkfst
Kit
13-6x15-6
L
L
shelves
Dining
Br 2
8-11x9-0
Living
18-2x18-8
vaulted clg
Dn
Up
Br 3
12-4x10-0
vaulted clg
Porch

Plan #530-007D-0061

Price Code A

Total Living Area: 1,340 Sq. Ft.

Home has 3 bedrooms, 2 baths, 2-car drive under garage and basement foundation.

Special features

- Grand-sized vaulted living and dining rooms offer fireplace, wet bar and breakfast counter open to spacious kitchen
- Vaulted master bedroom features a double-door entry, walk-in closet and an elegant bath
- Basement includes a huge two-car garage and space for a bedroom/bath expansion

Trim Arrangement Of Living Areas

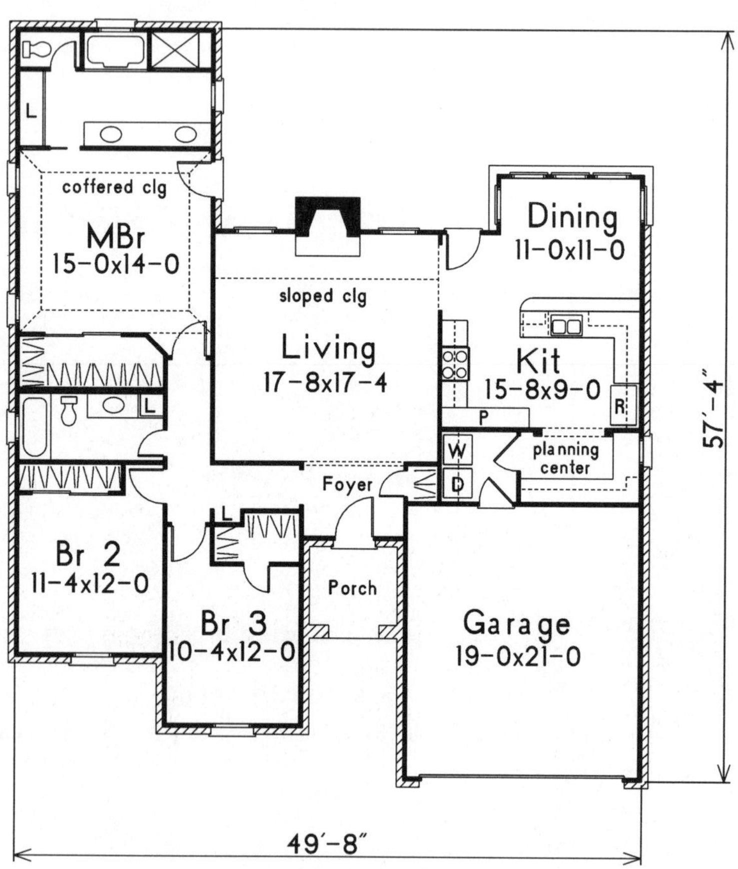
coffered clg
MBr
15-0x14-0
sloped clg
Living
17-8x17-4
Dining
11-0x11-0
Kit
15-8x9-0
P
R
W
D
planning center
Foyer
L
Br 2
11-4x12-0
Br 3
10-4x12-0
Porch
Garage
19-0x21-0
57'-4"
49'-8"

Plan #530-037D-0010

Price Code B

Total Living Area: 1,770 Sq. Ft.

Home has 3 bedrooms, 2 baths, 2-car garage and slab foundation.

Special features

- Distinctive covered entrance leads into spacious foyer
- Master bedroom, living and dining rooms feature large windows for plenty of light
- Oversized living room has a high ceiling and large windows that flank the fireplace
- Kitchen includes a pantry and large planning center
- Master bedroom has a high vaulted ceiling, deluxe bath, and private access outdoors

Inviting Covered Corner Entry

LOWE'S

Signature
SERIES

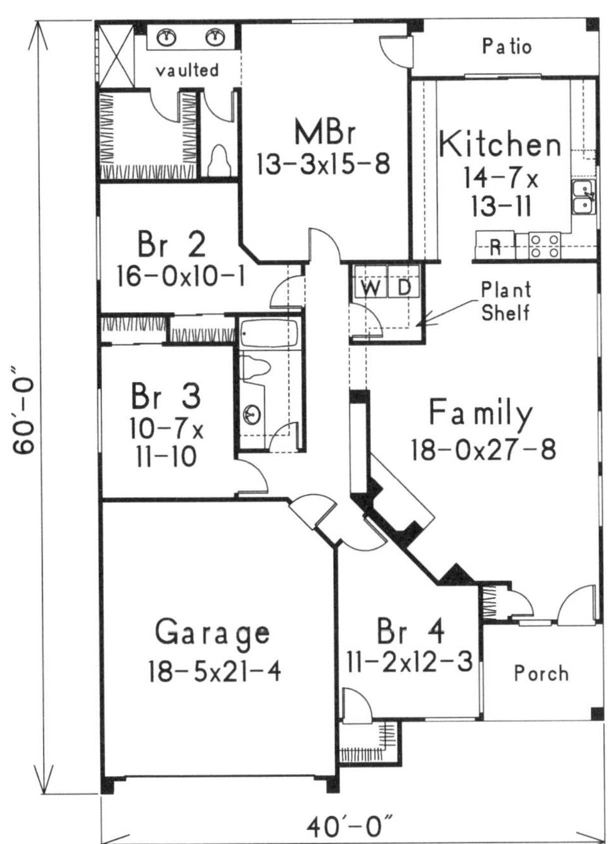
Patio
vaulted
MBr
13-3x15-8
Kitchen
14-7x
13-11
R
Br 2
16-0x10-1
W D
Plant
Shelf
Br 3
10-7x
11-10
Family
18-0x27-8
Garage
18-5x21-4
Br 4
11-2x12-3
Porch
60'-0"
40'-0"

Plan #530-061D-0001

Price Code B

Total Living Area: 1,747 Sq. Ft.

Home has 4 bedrooms, 2 baths, 2-car garage and slab foundation.

Special features

- Entry opens into large family room with coat closet, angled fireplace and attractive plant shelf
- Kitchen and master bedroom access covered patio
- Functional kitchen includes ample workspace

First Floor
2,070 sq. ft.

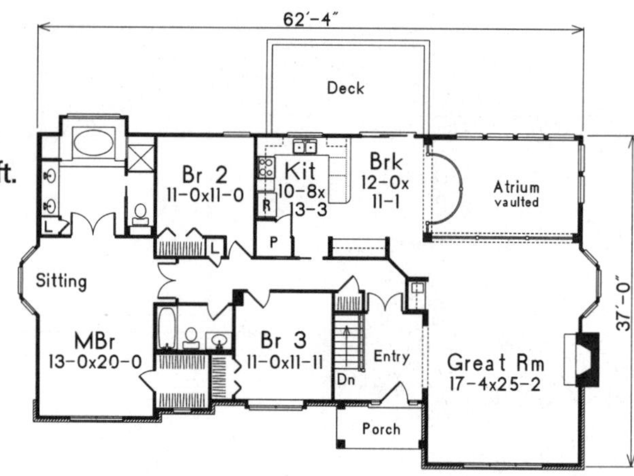

62'-4"
Deck
Br 2
11-0x11-0
Kit
10-8x
13-3
Brk
12-0x
11-1
Atrium
vaulted
P
Sitting
MBr
13-0x20-0
Br 3
11-0x11-11
Entry
Dn
Great Rm
17-4x25-2
Porch
37'-0"

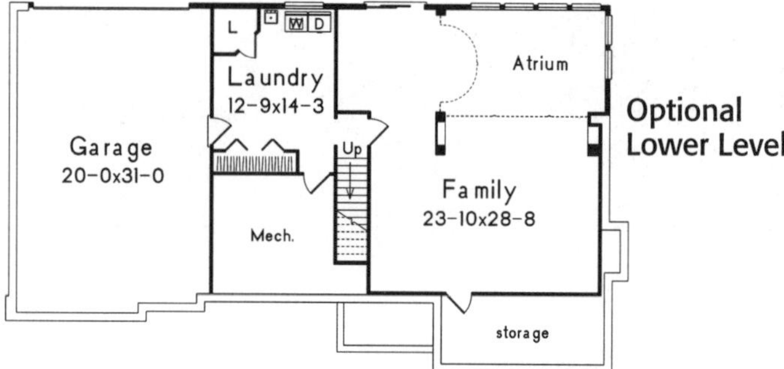

Laundry
12-9x14-3
Atrium
Garage
20-0x31-0
Up
Family
23-10x28-8
Mech.
storage
Optional
Lower Level

Plan #530-007D-0069

Price Code C

Total Living Area: 2,070 Sq. Ft.

Home has 3 bedrooms, 2 baths, 2-car drive under garage and walk-out basement foundation.

Special features

- Great room enjoys a fireplace, wet bar and rear views through two-story vaulted atrium
- The U-shaped kitchen opens to the breakfast area and features a walk-in pantry, computer center and atrium overlook
- Master bath has a Roman whirlpool tub, TV alcove, separate shower/toilet area and linen closet
- Extra storage in garage
- Atrium opens to 1,062 square feet of optional living area below

Rear View

Family Room With Fireplace

LOWE'S

Signature SERIES

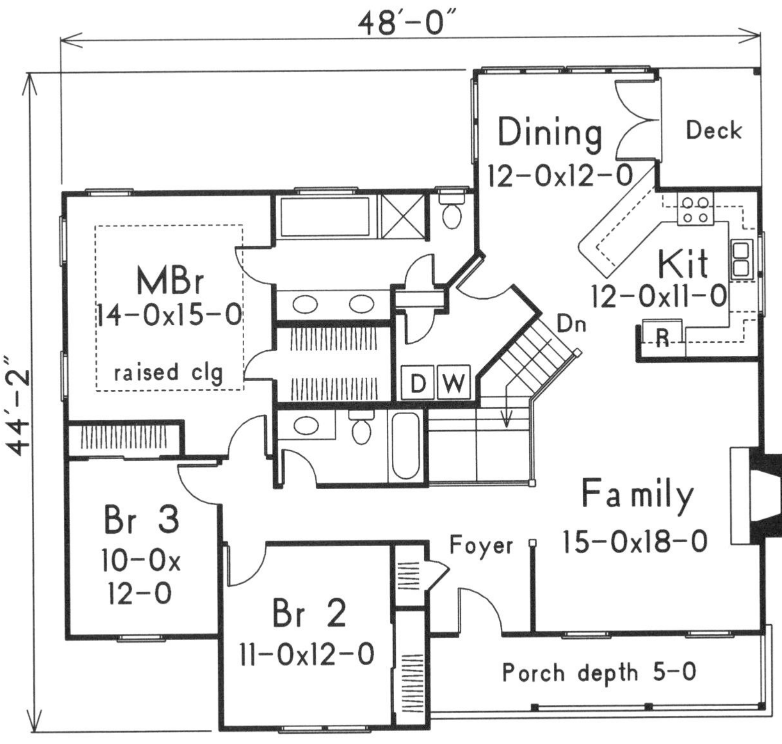

48'-0"
44'-2"
Dining
12-0x12-0
Deck
Kit
12-0x11-0
R
Dn
MBr
14-0x15-0
raised clg
D W
Family
15-0x18-0
Br 3
10-0x
12-0
Foyer
Br 2
11-0x12-0
Porch depth 5-0

Plan #530-040D-0008

Price Code B

Total Living Area: 1,631 Sq. Ft.

Home has 3 bedrooms, 2 baths, 2-car drive under garage and basement foundation.

Special features

- 9' ceilings throughout this home
- Utility room is conveniently located near the kitchen
- Roomy kitchen and dining area boast a breakfast bar and deck access
- Raised ceiling accents master bedroom

LOWE'S

High-Style Vaulted Ranch

Plan #530-014D-0007

Price Code A

Total Living Area: 1,453 Sq. Ft.

Home has 3 bedrooms, 2 baths, 2-car garage and basement foundation, drawings also include crawl space foundation.

Special features

- Decorative vents, window trim, shutters and brick blend to create dramatic curb appeal
- Energy efficient home with 2" x 6" exterior walls
- Kitchen opens to the living area and includes a salad sink in the island as well as a pantry and handy laundry room
- Exquisite master bedroom is highlighted by a vaulted ceiling, dressing area with walk-in closet, private bath and spa tub/shower

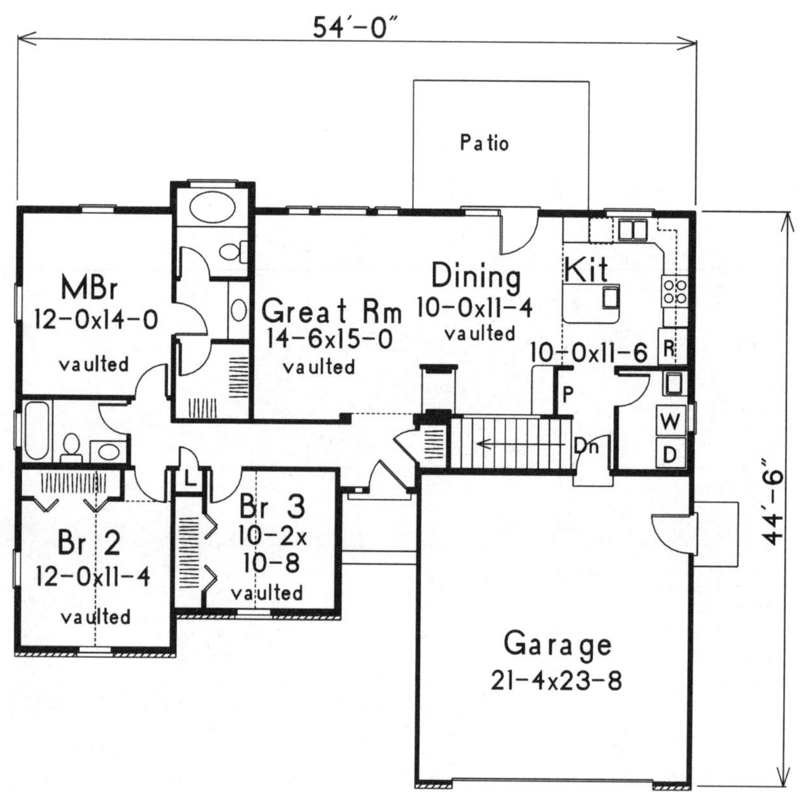
54'-0"
Patio
MBr
12-0x14-0
vaulted
Great Rm
14-6x15-0
vaulted
Dining
10-0x11-4
vaulted
Kit
10-0x11-6
R
P
W
D
Dn
L
Br 2
12-0x11-4
vaulted
Br 3
10-2x
10-8
vaulted
Garage
21-4x23-8
44'-6"

 TO ORDER BLUEPRINTS USE THE FORM ON PAGE 288 OR CALL TOLL-FREE **1-800-DREAM HOME** (373-2646)

LOWE'S

Signature
SERIES

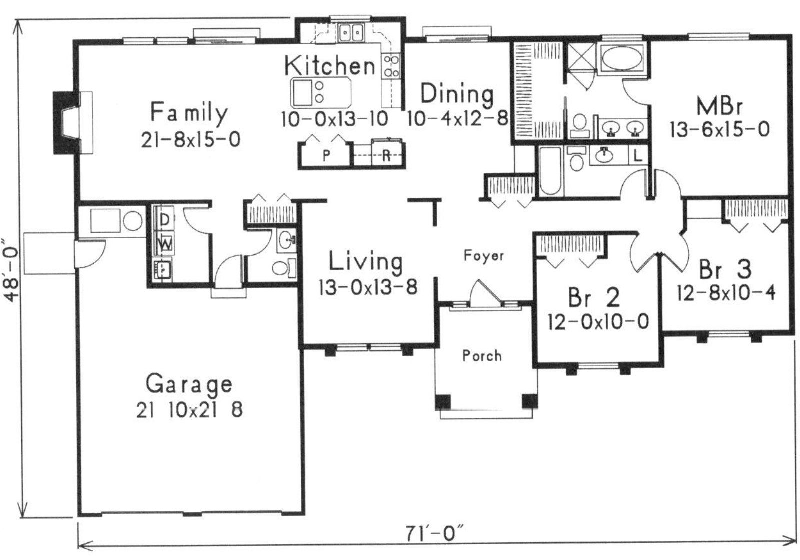
Kitchen
10-0x13-10
Family
21-8x15-0
Dining
10-4x12-8
MBr
13-6x15-0
P
R
L
D
W
Living
13-0x13-8
Foyer
Br 3
12-8x10-4
Br 2
12-0x10-0
Porch
Garage
21 10x21 8
48'-0"
71'-0"

Plan #530-014D-0015

Price Code C

Total Living Area: 1,941 Sq. Ft.

Home has 3 bedrooms, 2 1/2 baths, 2-car garage and crawl space foundation.

Special features

- Kitchen incorporates a cooktop island, a handy pantry and adjoins the dining and family rooms
- Formal living room, to the left of the foyer, lends a touch of privacy
- Raised ceilings enhance the foyer, kitchen, dining and living areas
- Laundry room, half bath and closet are all located near the garage
- Both the dining and family rooms have access outdoors through sliding doors

Plan #530-021D-0001

Price Code D

Total Living Area: 2,396 Sq. Ft.

Home has 4 bedrooms, 2 baths, 2-car garage and slab foundation, drawings also include basement and crawl space foundations.

Special features

- Generously wide entry welcomes guests
- Central living area with a 12' ceiling and large fireplace serves as a convenient traffic hub
- Kitchen is secluded, yet has easy access to the living, dining and breakfast areas
- Deluxe master bath has a walk-in closet, oversized tub, shower and other amenities
- Energy efficient home with 2" x 6" exterior walls

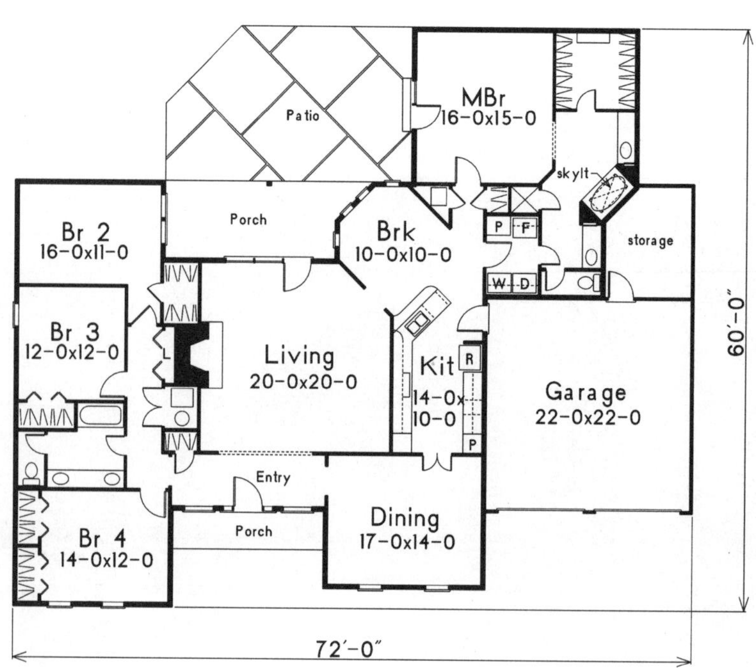

Patio
MBr
16-0x15-0
skylt
Br 2
16-0x11-0
Porch
Brk
10-0x10-0
storage
P
F
W
D
Br 3
12-0x12-0
L
Living
20-0x20-0
Kit
14-0x
10-0
R
P
Garage
22-0x22-0
60'-0"
Entry
Br 4
14-0x12-0
Porch
Dining
17-0x14-0
72'-0"

LOWE'S

Signature
SERIES

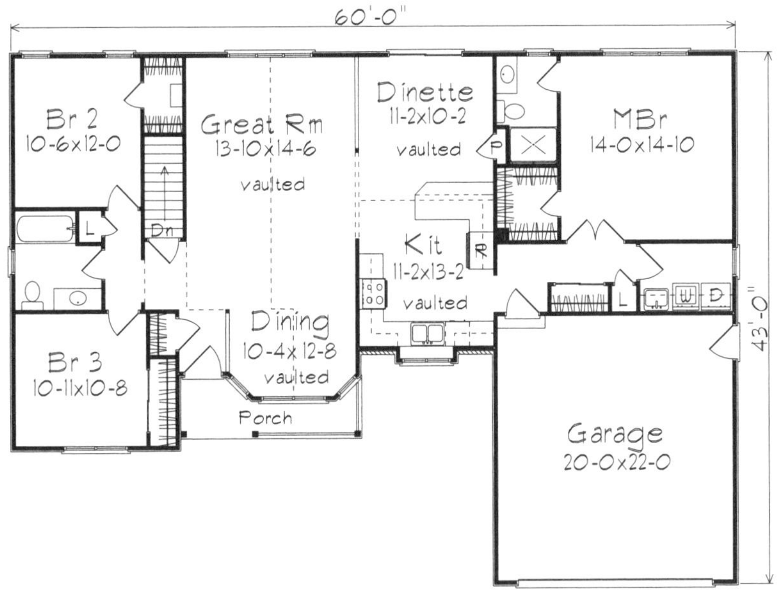
60'-0"
43'-0"
Br 2
10-6x12-0
Great Rm
13-10x14-6
vaulted
Dinette
11-2x10-2
vaulted
MBr
14-0x14-10
Dn
Kit
11-2x13-2
vaulted
Dining
10-4x12-8
vaulted
Br 3
10-11x10-8
Porch
Garage
20-0x22-0

Plan #530-033D-0012

Price Code C

Total Living Area: 1,546 Sq. Ft.

Home has 3 bedrooms, 2 baths, 2-car garage and basement foundation.

Special features

- Spacious, open rooms create a casual atmosphere
- Master bedroom is secluded for privacy
- Dining room features a large bay window
- Kitchen and dinette combine for added space and include access to the outdoors
- Large laundry room includes a convenient sink

LOWE'S

Signature SERIES

Graciously Designed Atrium Ranch

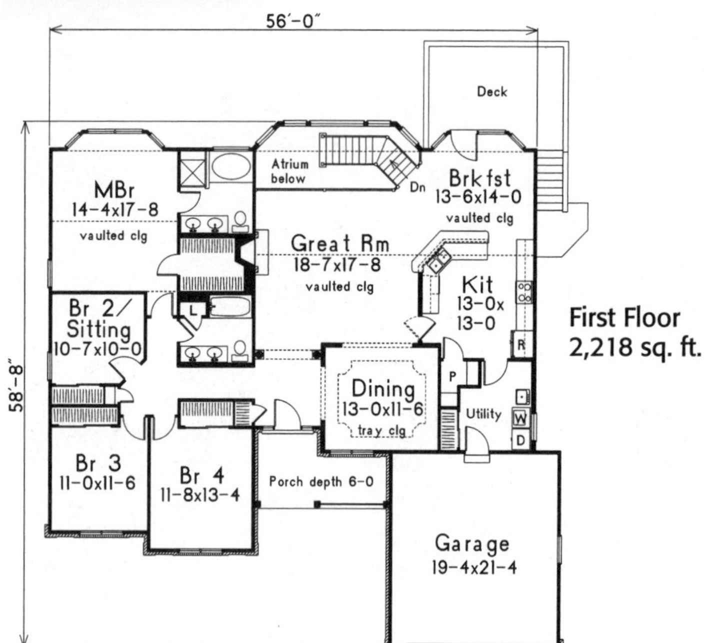
56'-0"
58'-8"
Deck
Atrium below
Dn
Brkfst
13-6x14-0
vaulted clg
MBr
14-4x17-8
vaulted clg
Great Rm
18-7x17-8
vaulted clg
Kit
13-0x
13-0
Br 2/
Sitting
10-7x10-0
Dining
13-0x11-6
tray clg
Utility
Br 3
11-0x11-6
Br 4
11-8x13-4
Porch depth 6-0
Garage
19-4x21-4

First Floor
2,218 sq. ft.

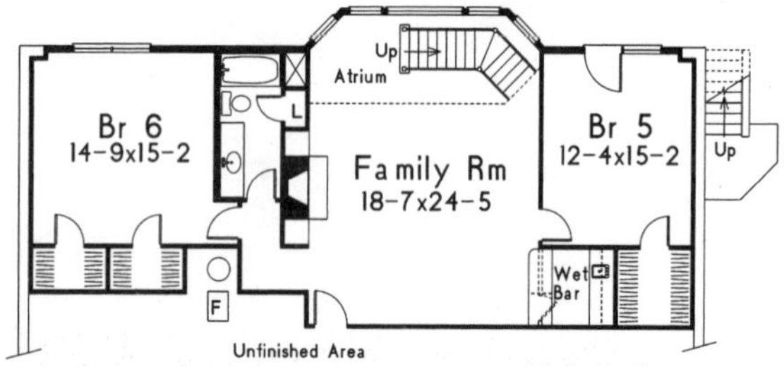

Plan #530-007D-0065

Price Code D

Total Living Area: 2,218 Sq. Ft.

Home has 4 bedrooms, 2 baths, 2-car garage and walk-out basement foundation.

Special features

- Vaulted great room has an arched colonnade entry, bay windowed atrium with staircase and a fireplace
- Vaulted kitchen enjoys bay doors to deck, pass-through breakfast bar and walk-in pantry
- Breakfast room offers bay window and snack bar open to kitchen with laundry nearby
- Atrium opens to 1,217 square feet of optional living area below

Optional Lower Level

Rear View

Striking Front Facade

LOWE'S

Signature SERIES

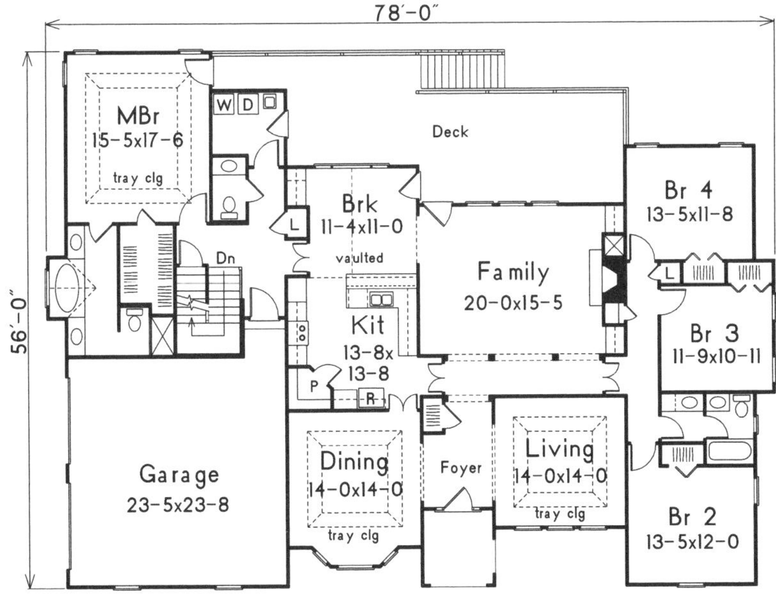
78'-0"
56'-0"
MBr
15-5x17-6
tray clg
W D
Deck
Br 4
13-5x11-8
Brk
11-4x11-0
vaulted
L
Dn
Family
20-0x15-5
Kit
13-8x
13-8
Br 3
11-9x10-11
P
R
Garage
23-5x23-8
Dining
14-0x14-0
tray clg
Foyer
Living
14-0x14-0
tray clg
Br 2
13-5x12-0

Plan #530-053D-0050

Price Code E

Total Living Area: 2,718 Sq. Ft.

Home has 4 bedrooms, 2 1/2 baths, 2-car side entry garage and basement foundation.

Special features

- Master bedroom has a tray ceiling, access to the rear deck, walk-in closet and an impressive private bath
- Dining and living rooms flank the foyer and both feature tray ceilings
- Spacious family room features a 12' ceiling, fireplace and access to the rear deck
- Kitchen has a 9' ceiling, large pantry and bar overlooking the breakfast room

LOWE'S

Signature SERIES

Rambling Country Bungalow

Plan #530-040D-0003

Price Code B

Total Living Area: 1,475 Sq. Ft.

Home has 3 bedrooms, 2 baths, 2-car detached side entry garage and slab foundation, drawings also include crawl space foundation.

Special features

- Family room features a high ceiling and prominent corner fireplace
- Kitchen with island counter and garden window makes a convenient connection between the family and dining rooms
- Hallway leads to three bedrooms all with large walk-in closets
- Covered breezeway joins main house and garage
- Full-width covered porch entry lends a country touch

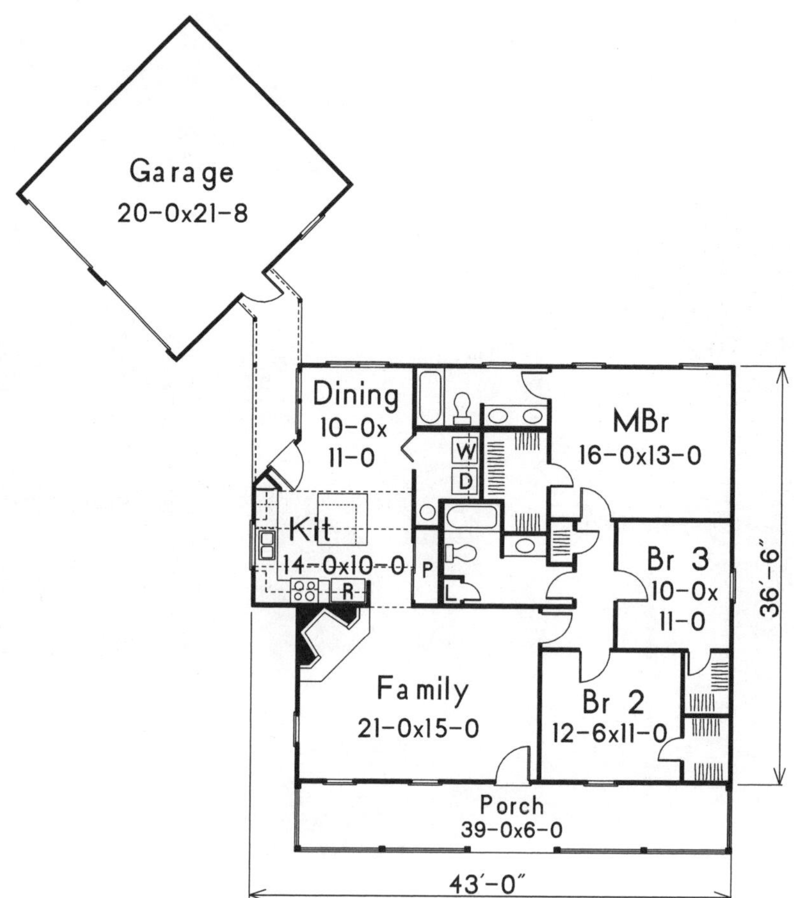
Garage
20-0x21-8
Dining
10-0x
11-0
W
D
MBr
16-0x13-0
Kit
14-0x10-0
P
R
L
Br 3
10-0x
11-0
36′-6″
Family
21-0x15-0
Br 2
12-6x11-0
Porch
39-0x6-0
43′-0″

TO ORDER BLUEPRINTS USE THE FORM ON PAGE 288 OR CALL TOLL-FREE **1-800-DREAM HOME** (373-2646)

Great Room Forms Core Of This Home

LOWE'S

Signature SERIES

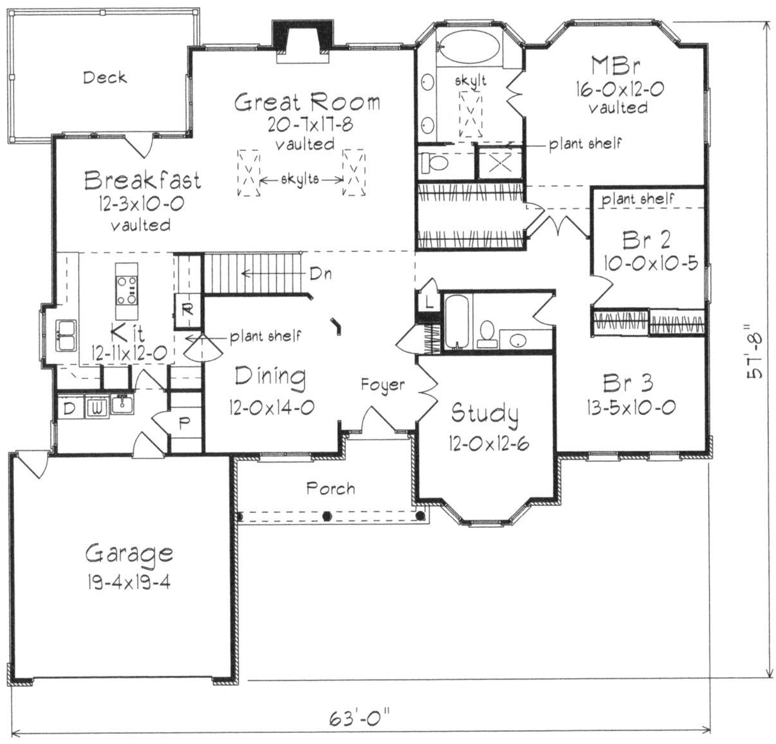

Deck
Great Room
20-7x17-8
vaulted
skylts
Breakfast
12-3x10-0
vaulted
MBr
16-0x12-0
vaulted
skylt
plant shelf
plant shelf
Br 2
10-0x10-5
Dn
R
L
Kit
12-11x12-0
plant shelf
Dining
12-0x14-0
Foyer
Study
12-0x12-6
Br 3
13-5x10-0
D
W
P
Porch
Garage
19-4x19-4
57'-8"
63'-0"

Plan #530-027D-0006

Price Code C

Total Living Area: 2,076 Sq. Ft.

Home has 3 bedrooms, 2 baths, 2-car garage and basement foundation.

Special features

- Vaulted great room has a fireplace flanked by windows and skylights that welcome the sun
- Kitchen leads to the vaulted breakfast room and rear deck
- Study located off the foyer provides a great location for a home office
- Large bay windows grace the master bedroom and bath

Signature SERIES

Summer Home Or Year-Round

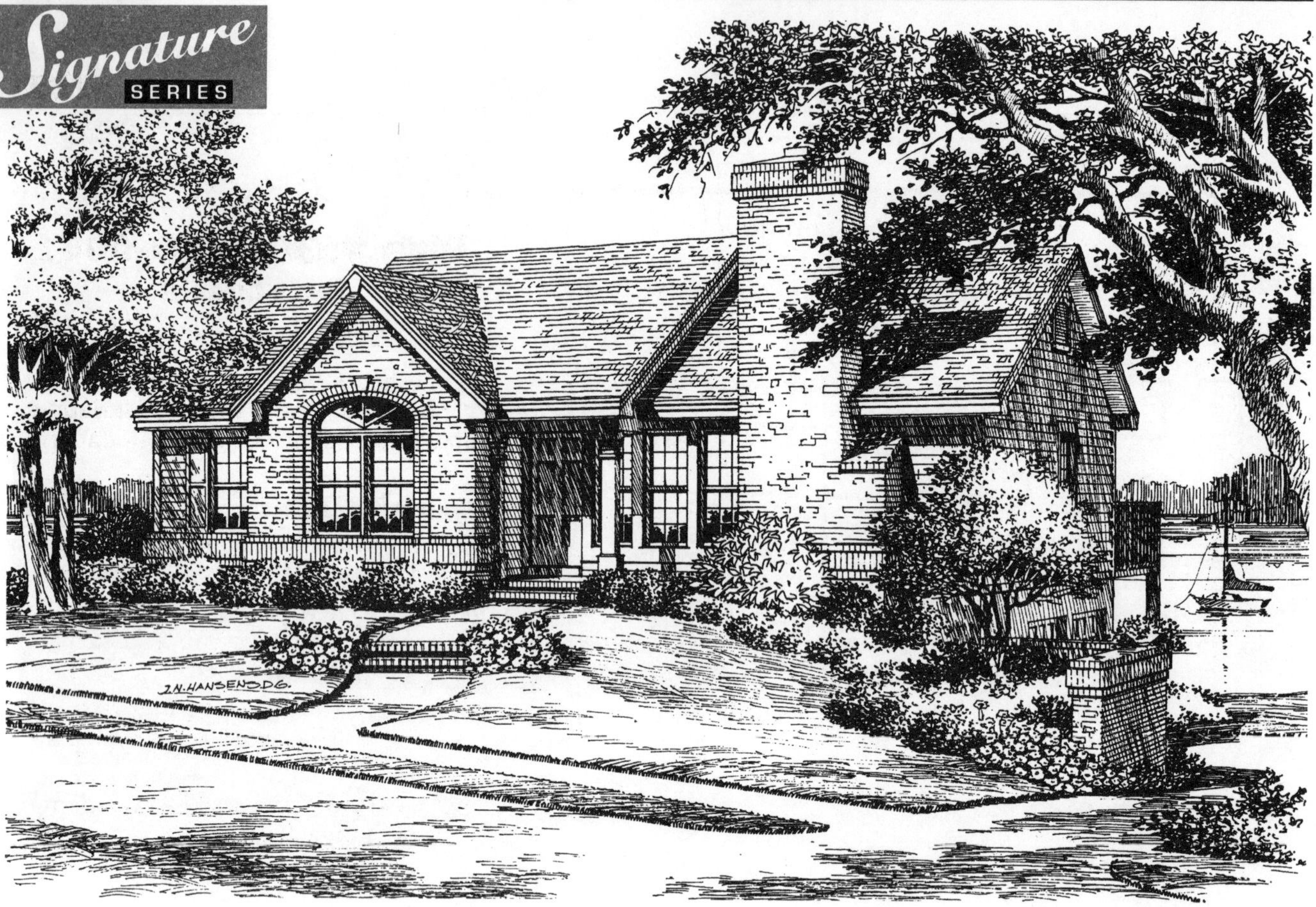

Plan #530-007D-0037

Price Code A

Total Living Area: 1,403 Sq. Ft.

Home has 3 bedrooms, 2 baths, 2-car drive under garage with second bath on lower level and basement foundation.

Special features

- Impressive living areas for a modest-sized home
- Special master/hall bath has linen storage, step-up tub and lots of window light
- Spacious closets everywhere you look

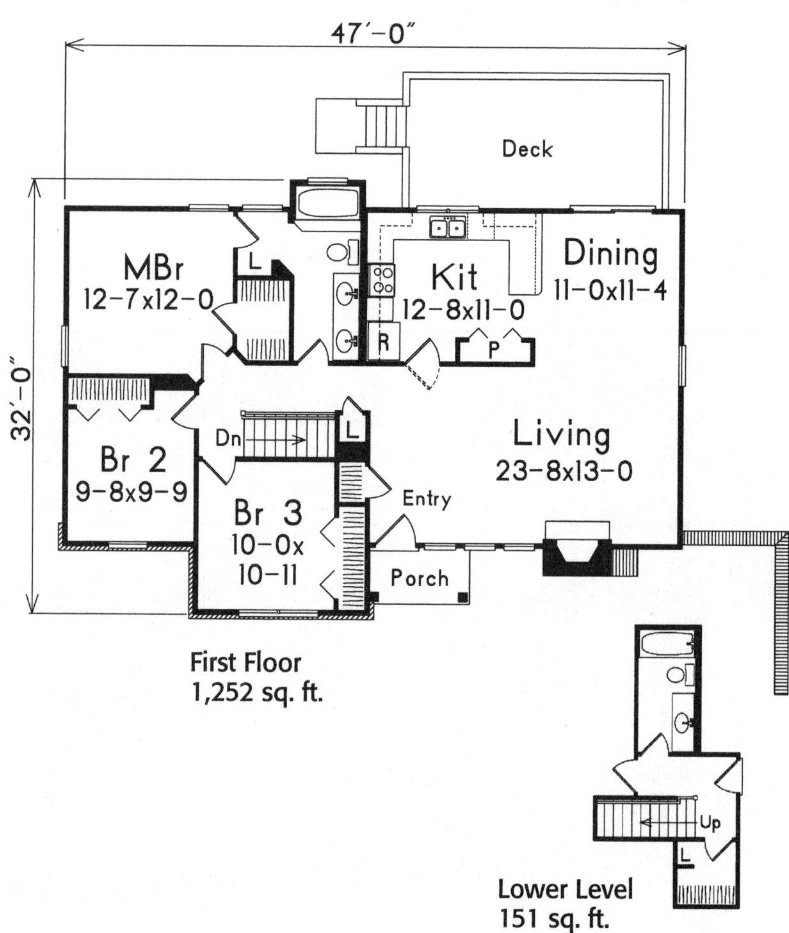

47'-0"
Deck
MBr
12-7x12-0
L
Kit
12-8x11-0
Dining
11-0x11-4
R
P
32'-0"
Dn
L
Br 2
9-8x9-9
Living
23-8x13-0
Entry
Br 3
10-0x
10-11
Porch
Up
L

First Floor
1,252 sq. ft.

Lower Level
151 sq. ft.

LOWE'S

Signature
SERIES

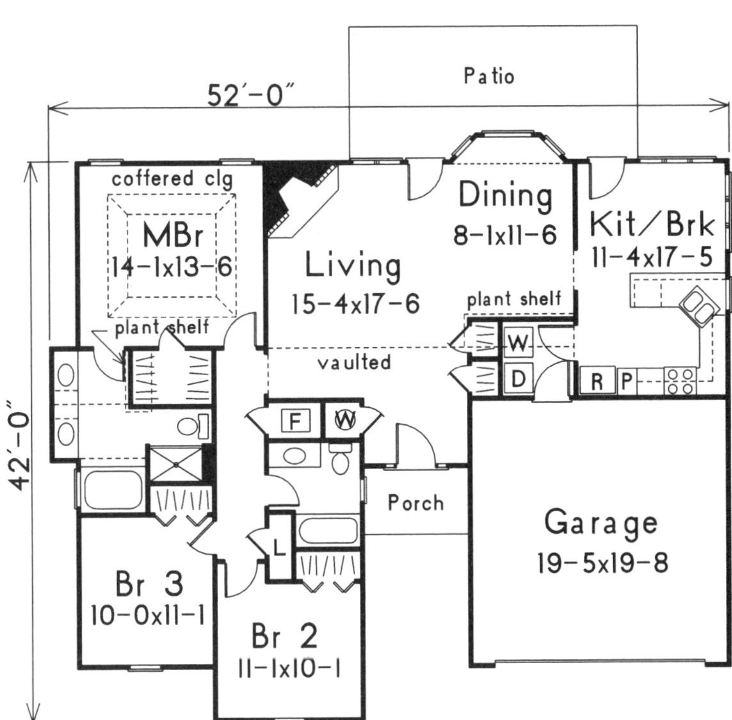
Patio
52'-0"
42'-0"
coffered clg
MBr
14-1x13-6
plant shelf
Dining
8-1x11-6
Kit/Brk
11-4x17-5
Living
15-4x17-6
plant shelf
vaulted
W
D
R
P
F
Porch
Garage
19-5x19-8
L
Br 3
10-0x11-1
Br 2
11-1x10-1

Plan #530-053D-0042

Price Code A

Total Living Area: 1,458 Sq. Ft.

Home has 3 bedrooms, 2 baths, 2-car garage and crawl space foundation, drawings also include slab foundation.

Special features

- Convenient snack bar joins kitchen with breakfast room
- Large living room has a fireplace, plenty of windows, vaulted ceiling and nearby plant shelf
- Master bedroom offers a private bath, walk-in closet, plant shelf and coffered ceiling
- Corner windows provide abundant light in breakfast room

Grand Master Bath

Plan #530-021D-0014

Price Code C

Total Living Area: 1,856 Sq. Ft.

Home has 3 bedrooms, 2 baths, 2-car side entry garage and slab foundation, drawings also include crawl space foundation.

Special features

- Living room features include fireplace, 12' ceiling and skylights
- Energy efficient home with 2" x 6" exterior walls
- Common vaulted ceiling creates an open atmosphere in the kitchen and breakfast room
- Garage with storage areas conveniently accesses home through handy utility room
- Private hall separates secondary bedrooms from living areas

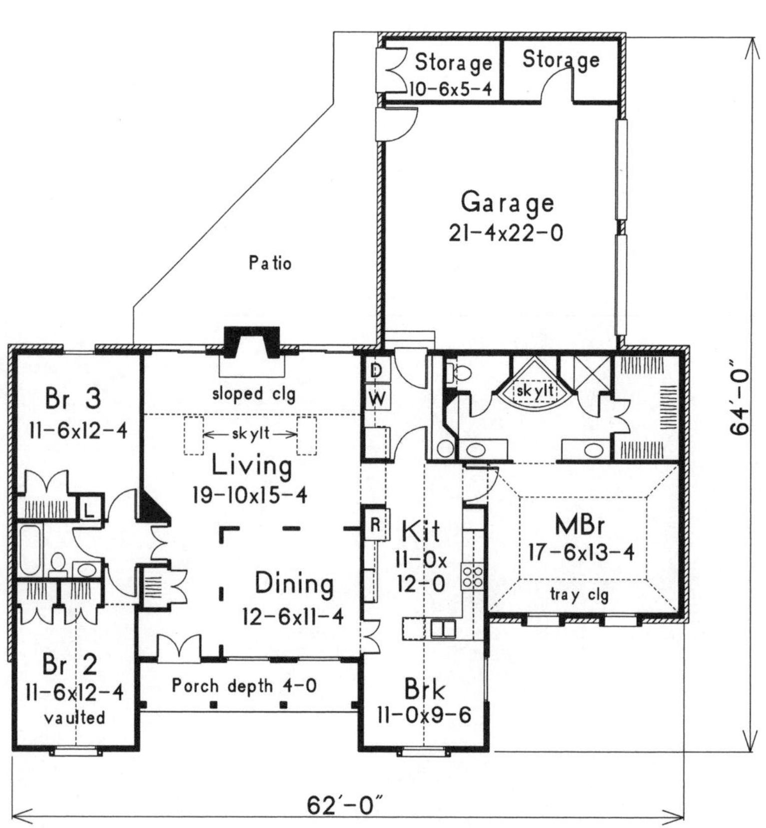
Storage
10-6x5-4
Storage
Garage
21-4x22-0
Patio
Br 3
11-6x12-4
sloped clg
skylt
Living
19-10x15-4
D
W
skylt
L
R
Kit
11-0x
12-0
MBr
17-6x13-4
tray clg
Dining
12-6x11-4
Br 2
11-6x12-4
vaulted
Porch depth 4-0
Brk
11-0x9-6
64'-0"
62'-0"

LOWE'S

Signature
SERIES

Plan #530-045D-0003

Price Code C

Total Living Area: 1,958 Sq. Ft.

Home has 3 bedrooms, 2 baths, 2-car garage and basement foundation.

Special features

- Large wrap-around kitchen opens to a bright and cheerful breakfast area with access to large covered deck and open stairway to basement
- Kitchen is nestled between the dining and breakfast rooms
- Master bedroom includes large walk-in closet, double-bowl vanity, garden tub and separate shower
- Foyer features an attractive plant shelf and opens into the living room that includes a lovely central fireplace

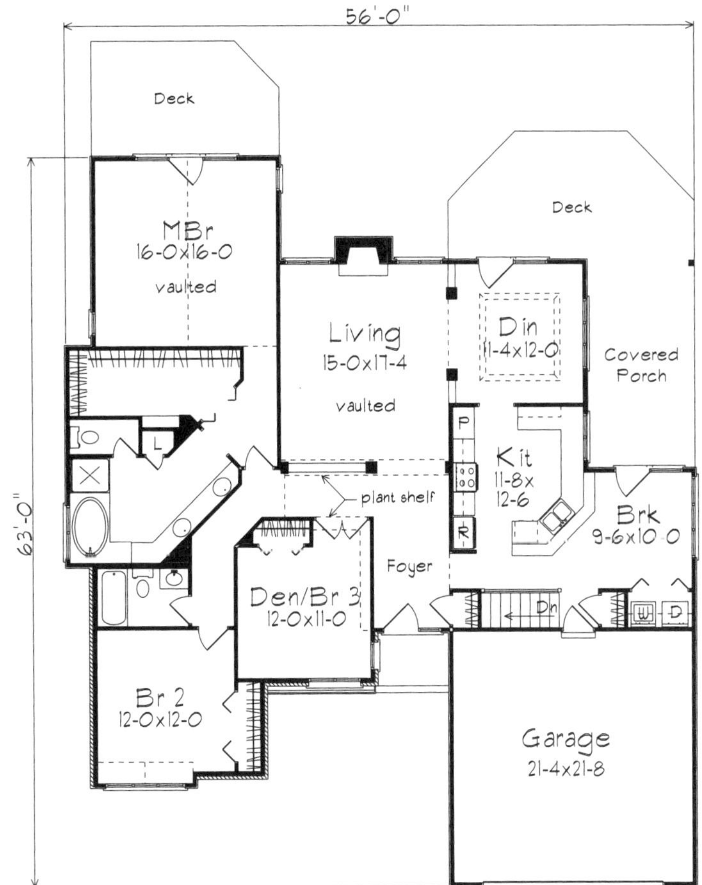
56'-0"
63'-0"
Deck
Deck
MBr
16-0x16-0
vaulted
Living
15-0x17-4
vaulted
Din
11-4x12-0
Covered Porch
Kit
11-8x
12-6
Brk
9-6x10-0
plant shelf
Foyer
Den/Br 3
12-0x11-0
Dn
Br 2
12-0x12-0
Garage
21-4x21-8

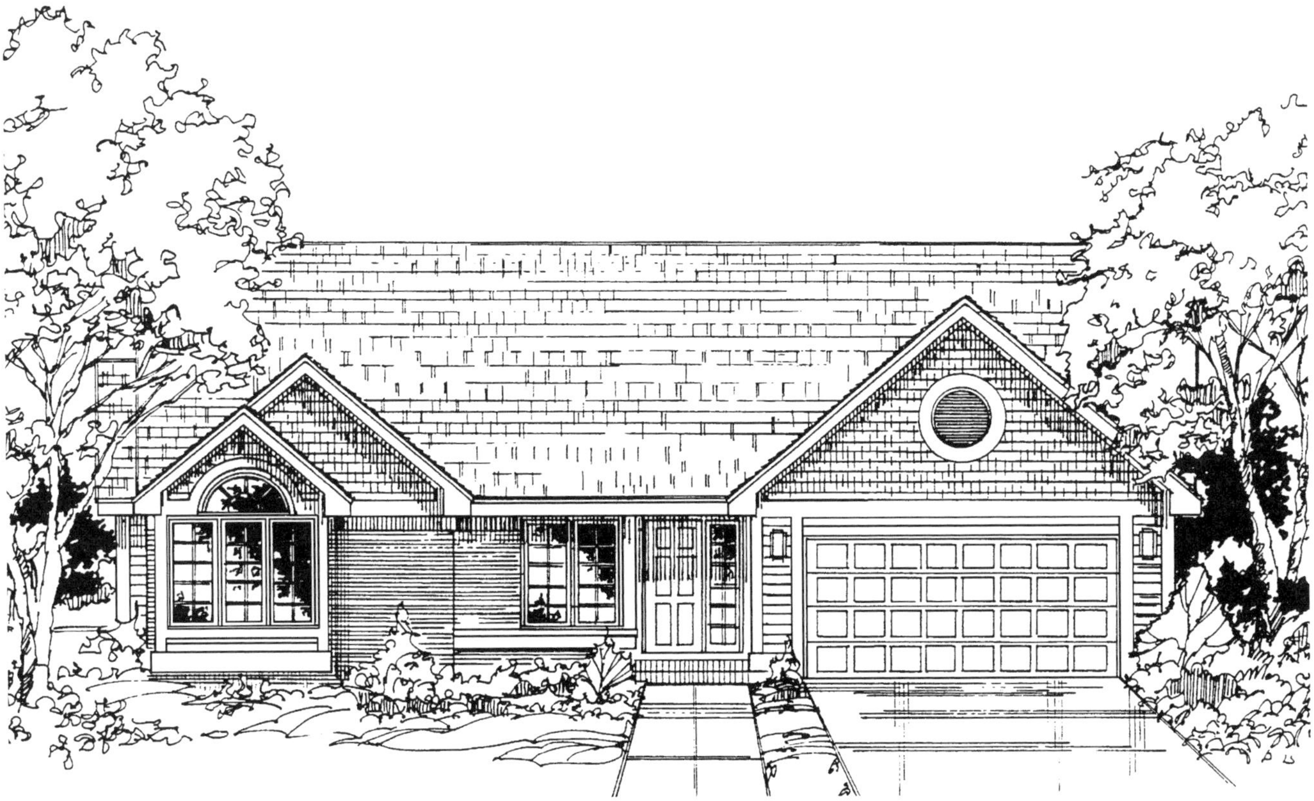

LOWE'S

Elegant Entrance

Plan #530-014D-0010

Price Code D

Total Living Area: 2,563 Sq. Ft.

Home has 4 bedrooms, 2 baths, 2-car garage and basement foundation.

Special features

- Energy efficient home with 2" x 6" exterior walls
- Remote master bedroom features a bath with double sinks, spa tub and separate room with toilet
- Arched columns separate the foyer from the great room which includes a fireplace and accesses the nook
- Well-designed kitchen provides plenty of workspace and storage plus room for extra cooks

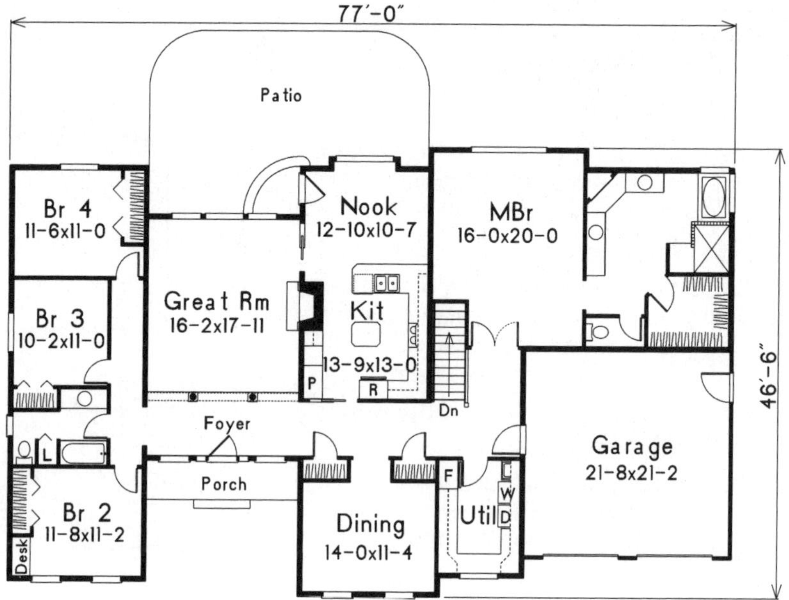
77'-0"
Patio
Br 4
11-6x11-0
Nook
12-10x10-7
MBr
16-0x20-0
Great Rm
16-2x17-11
Kit
13-9x13-0
Br 3
10-2x11-0
Dn
Foyer
Porch
Dining
14-0x11-4
Util
Garage
21-8x21-2
Br 2
11-8x11-2
Desk
46'-6"

Atrium Cottage

LOWE'S

Signature SERIES

Rear View

Plan #530-007D-0068

Price Code B

Total Living Area: 1,384 Sq. Ft.

Home has 2 bedrooms, 2 baths, 1-car side entry garage and walk-out basement foundation.

Special features

- Wrap-around country porch for peaceful evenings
- Vaulted great room enjoys a large bay window, stone fireplace, pass-through kitchen and awesome rear views through atrium window wall
- Master bedroom features a double-door entry, walk-in closet and a fabulous bath
- Atrium opens to 611 square feet of optional living area below

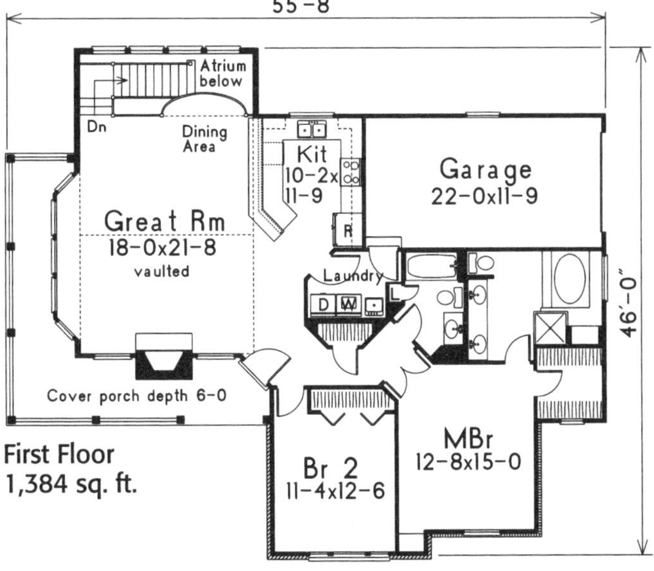

55'-8"
46'-0"
Atrium below
Dn
Dining Area
Kit 10-2x 11-9
Garage 22-0x11-9
Great Rm 18-0x21-8 vaulted
R
Laundry
D W
Cover porch depth 6-0
MBr 12-8x15-0
Br 2 11-4x12-6

First Floor
1,384 sq. ft.

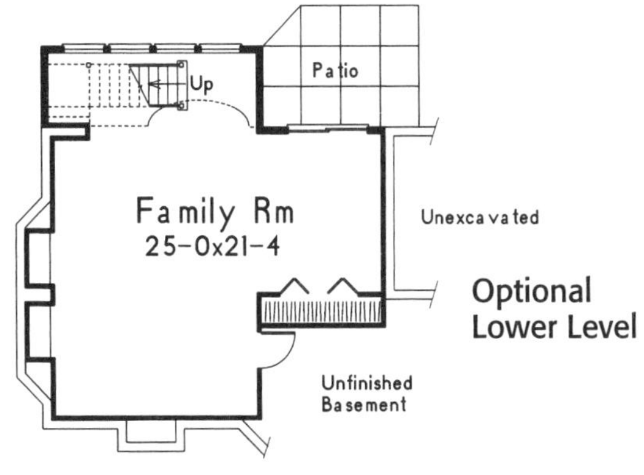

Up
Patio
Family Rm 25-0x21-4
Unexcavated
Unfinished Basement

Optional
Lower Level

LOWE'S

Signature SERIES

Plan #530-053D-0044

Price Code A

Total Living Area: 1,340 Sq. Ft.

Home has 3 bedrooms, 2 baths, 2-car side entry garage and slab foundation, drawings also include crawl space foundation.

Special features

- Master bedroom has a private bath and walk-in closet
- Recessed entry leads to the vaulted family room that shares a see-through fireplace with the kitchen/ dining area
- Garage includes a handy storage area
- Convenient laundry closet is located in the kitchen

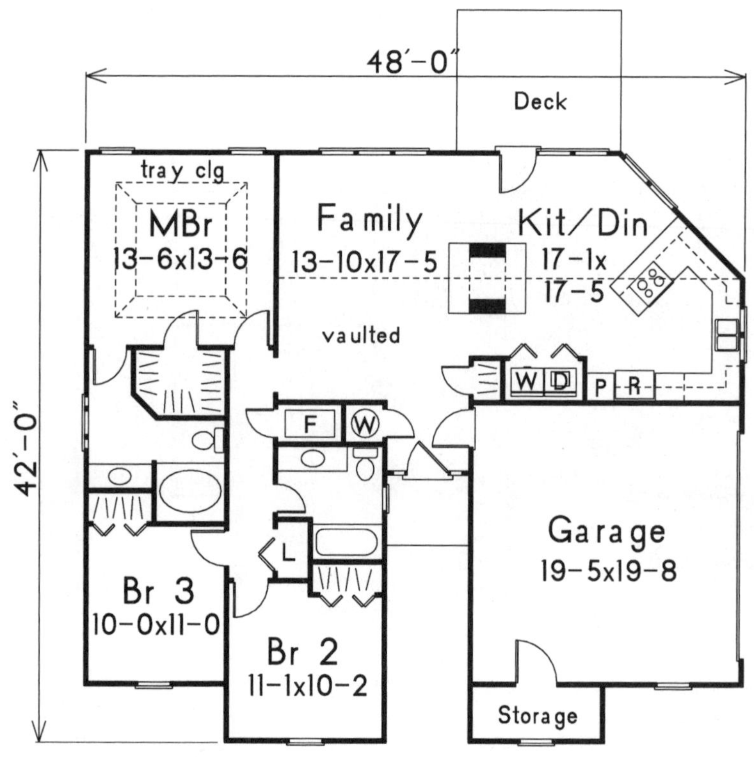
48'-0"
Deck
tray clg
MBr
13-6x13-6
Family
13-10x17-5
Kit/Din
17-1x
17-5
vaulted
W D
P R
F
W
L
42'-0"
Garage
19-5x19-8
Br 3
10-0x11-0
Br 2
11-1x10-2
Storage

 TO ORDER BLUEPRINTS USE THE FORM ON PAGE 288 OR CALL TOLL-FREE **1-800-DREAM HOME** (373-2646)

LOWE'S

Signature
SERIES

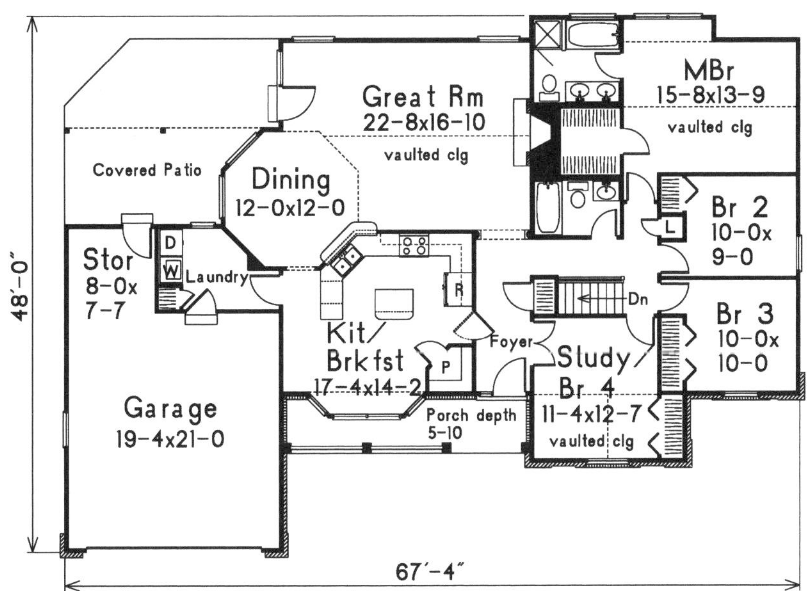
Great Rm
22-8x16-10
vaulted clg
MBr
15-8x13-9
vaulted clg
Covered Patio
Dining
12-0x12-0
Br 2
10-0x
9-0
L
Stor
8-0x
7-7
D
W
Laundry
R
Dn
Br 3
10-0x
10-0
Kit/
Brkfst
17-4x14-2
P
Foyer
Study
Br 4
11-4x12-7
vaulted clg
Porch depth
5-10
Garage
19-4x21-0
48'-0"
67'-4"

Plan #530-007D-0049

Price Code C

Total Living Area: 1,791 Sq. Ft.

Home has 4 bedrooms, 2 baths, 2-car garage and basement foundation, drawings also include crawl space and slab foundations.

Special features

- Vaulted great room and octagon-shaped dining area enjoy a spectacular view of the covered patio
- Kitchen features a pass-through to dining area, center island, large walk-in pantry and breakfast room with large bay window
- Master bedroom is vaulted with sitting area
- The garage includes extra storage space

Spacious Plan With Many Features

Plan #530-058D-0015

Price Code D

Total Living Area: 2,308 Sq. Ft.

Home has 3 bedrooms, 2 baths, 2-car side entry garage and walk-out basement foundation.

Special features

- Efficient kitchen designed with many cabinets and large walk-in pantry adjoins family/breakfast area featuring a beautiful fireplace
- Dining area has architectural colonnades that separate it from the living area while maintaining spaciousness
- A double-door entry leads into the luxurious master bedroom which features two walk-in closets and a beautiful bath
- Living room includes a vaulted ceiling, fireplace and a sunny atrium window wall creating a dramatic atmosphere

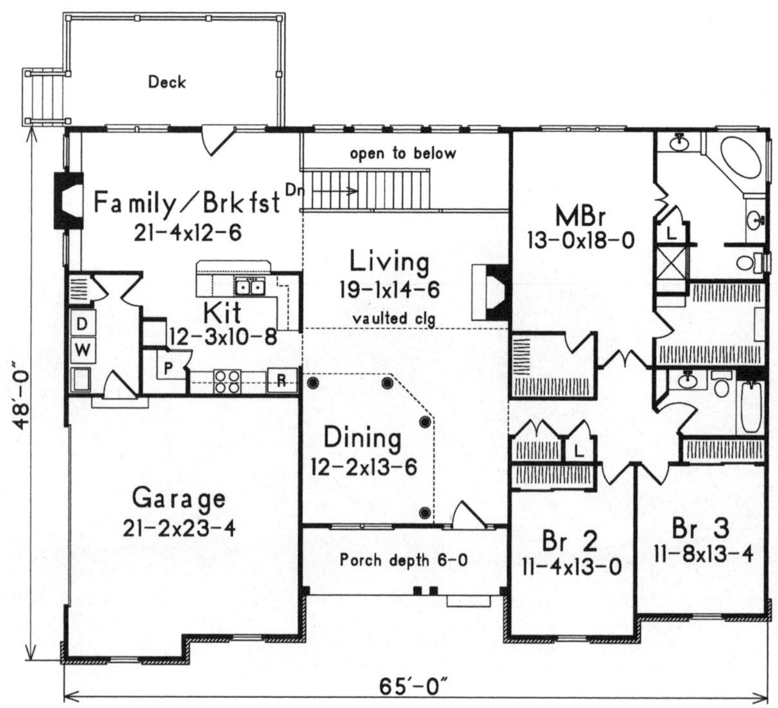
Deck
open to below
Family/Brkfst
21-4x12-6
Dn
Living
19-1x14-6
vaulted clg
MBr
13-0x18-0
Kit
12-3x10-8
D
W
P
R
L
Dining
12-2x13-6
Garage
21-2x23-4
Porch depth 6-0
Br 2
11-4x13-0
Br 3
11-8x13-4
48'-0"
65'-0"

LOWE'S

Signature
SERIES

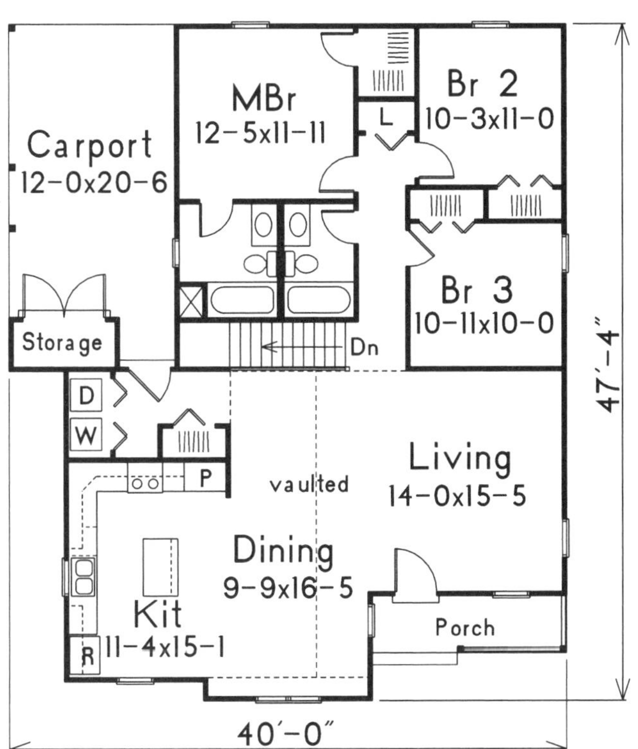
MBr
12-5x11-11
Br 2
10-3x11-0
L
Carport
12-0x20-6
Br 3
10-11x10-0
Storage
Dn
D
W
P
Living
14-0x15-5
vaulted
Dining
9-9x16-5
Kit
11-4x15-1
R
Porch
47'-4"
40'-0"

Plan #530-001D-0035

Price Code A

Total Living Area: 1,396 Sq. Ft.

Home has 3 bedrooms, 2 baths, 1-car carport and basement foundation, drawings also include crawl space foundation.

Special features

- Gabled front adds interest to facade
- Living and dining rooms share a vaulted ceiling
- Master bedroom features a walk-in closet and private bath
- Functional kitchen boasts a center work island and convenient pantry

Irresistible Paradise Retreat

Rear View

Plan #530-007D-0039
Price Code B

Total Living Area: 1,563 Sq. Ft.

Home has 2 bedrooms, 1 1/2 baths and basement foundation.

Special features

- Enjoyable wrap-around porch and lower sundeck
- Vaulted entry is adorned with a palladian window, plant shelves, stone floor and fireplace
- Huge vaulted great room has a magnificent view through a two-story atrium window wall

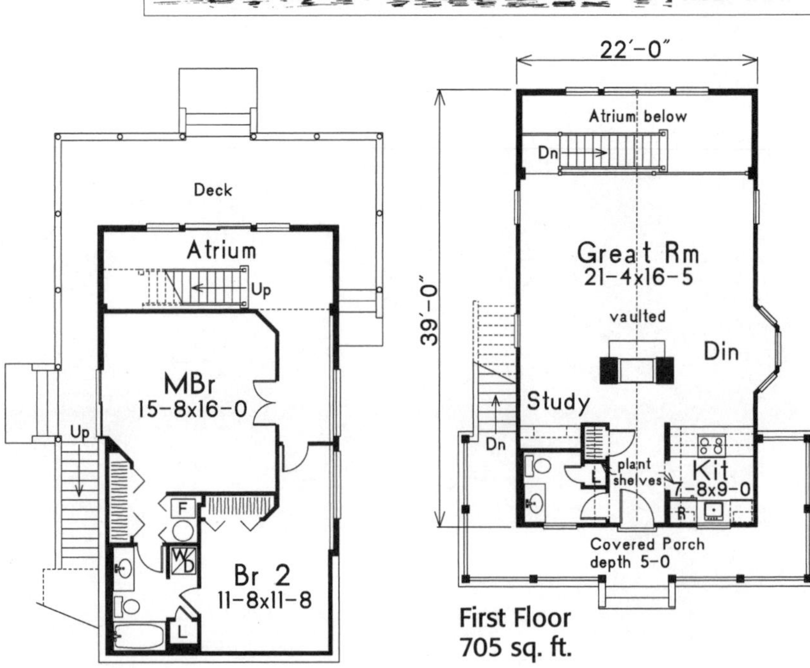

Deck
Atrium
Up
MBr
15-8x16-0
Up
F
W/D
Br 2
11-8x11-8
L
22′-0″
39′-0″
Atrium below
Dn
Great Rm
21-4x16-5
vaulted
Din
Study
Dn
plant shelves
Kit
7-8x9-0
R
Covered Porch
depth 5-0

Lower Level
858 sq. ft.

First Floor
705 sq. ft.

TO ORDER BLUEPRINTS USE THE FORM ON PAGE 288 OR CALL TOLL-FREE **1-800-DREAM HOME** (373-2646)

Spectacular View From The Great Room

LOWE'S

Signature
SERIES

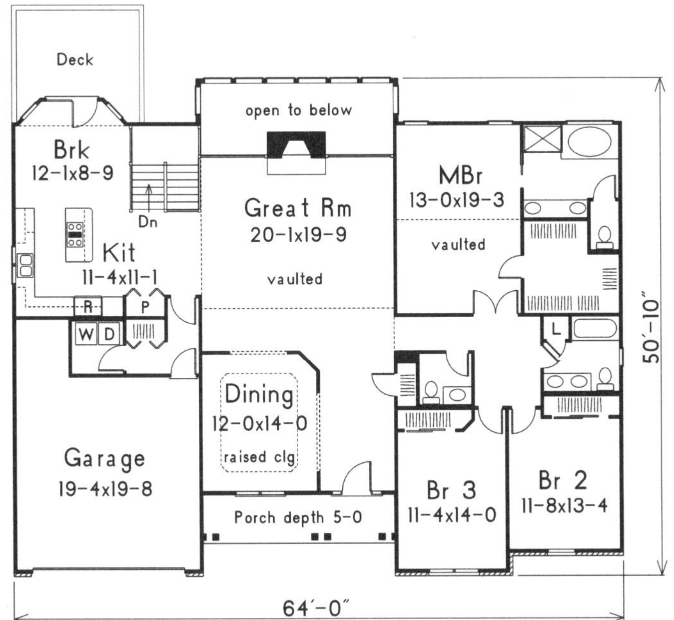
Deck
open to below
Brk
12-1x8-9
Dn
Kit
11-4x11-1
R
P
W D
Great Rm
20-1x19-9
vaulted
MBr
13-0x19-3
vaulted
L
Dining
12-0x14-0
raised clg
Garage
19-4x19-8
Porch depth 5-0
Br 3
11-4x14-0
Br 2
11-8x13-4
50'-10"
64'-0"

First Floor
2,436 sq. ft.

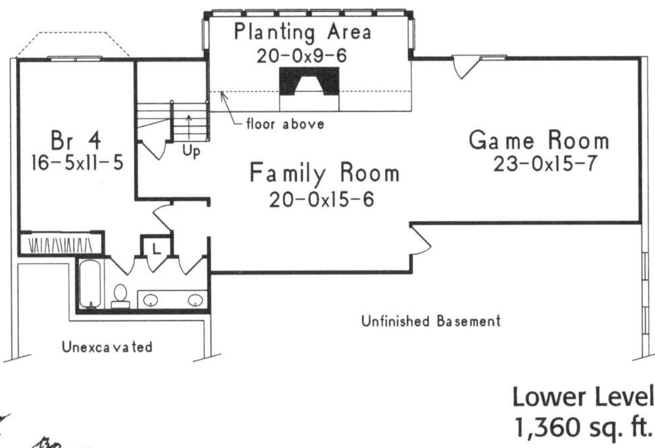
Planting Area
20-0x9-6
floor above
Br 4
16-5x11-5
Up
Family Room
20-0x15-6
Game Room
23-0x15-7
L
Unfinished Basement
Unexcavated

Lower Level
1,360 sq. ft.

Plan #530-027D-0002

Price Code F

Total Living Area: 3,796 Sq. Ft.

Home has 4 bedrooms, 3 1/2 baths, 2-car garage and basement foundation.

Special features

- Entry foyer leads directly to the great room with a fireplace and wonderful view through a wall of windows
- Kitchen and breakfast area feature a large island cooktop, pantry and easy access outdoors
- Master bedroom includes a vaulted ceiling and pocket door entrance into the master bath that features a double-bowl vanity and large tub

LOWE'S

Signature SERIES

Rustic Stone Exterior

Plan #530-017D-0008

Price Code B

Total Living Area: 1,466 Sq. Ft.

Home has 3 bedrooms, 2 baths, 2-car garage and basement foundation, drawings also include slab foundation.

Special features

- Energy efficient home with 2" x 6" exterior walls
- Foyer separates the living room from the dining room and contains a generous coat closet
- Large living room features a corner fireplace, bay window and pass-through to the kitchen
- Informal breakfast area opens to a large terrace through sliding glass doors which brighten area
- Master bedroom has a large walk-in closet and private bath

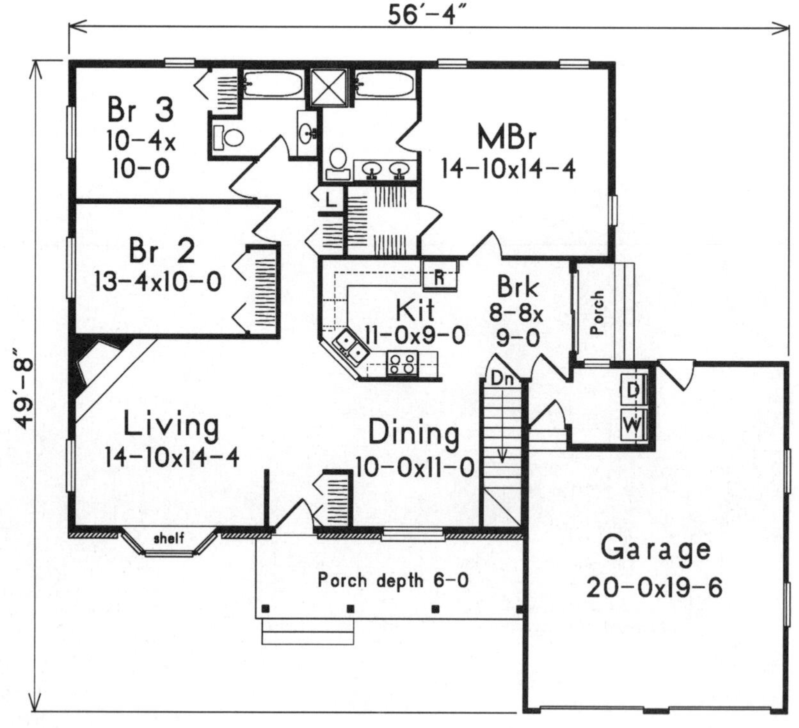
56'-4"
49'-8"
Br 3
10-4x
10-0
MBr
14-10x14-4
L
Br 2
13-4x10-0
R
Kit
11-0x9-0
Brk
8-8x
9-0
Porch
Dn
D
W
Living
14-10x14-4
Dining
10-0x11-0
shelf
Porch depth 6-0
Garage
20-0x19-6

Impressive Front Entry

LOWE'S

Signature
SERIES

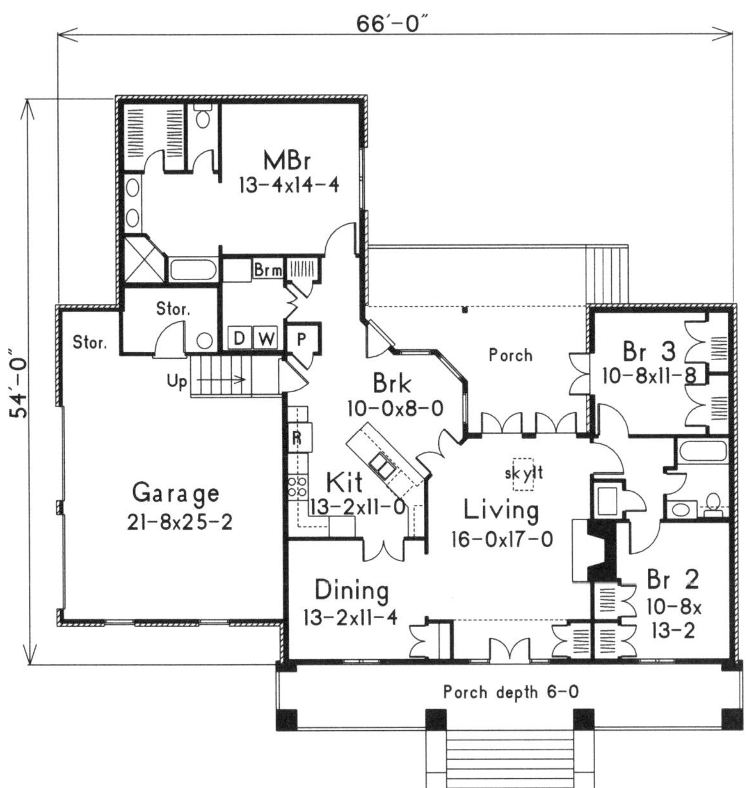
66'-0"
54'-0"
MBr
13-4x14-4
Brm
Stor.
Stor.
D W
P
Up
Brk
10-0x8-0
Porch
Br 3
10-8x11-8
R
Kit
13-2x11-0
sky lt
Living
16-0x17-0
Garage
21-8x25-2
Dining
13-2x11-4
Br 2
10-8x
13-2
Porch depth 6-0

Plan #530-021D-0011

Price Code D

Total Living Area: 1,800 Sq. Ft.

Home has 3 bedrooms, 2 baths, 2-car side entry garage and crawl space foundation, drawings also include slab foundation.

Special features

- Energy efficient home with 2" x 6" exterior walls
- Covered front and rear porches add outdoor living area
- 12' ceilings in the kitchen, breakfast area, dining and living rooms
- Private master bedroom features an expansive bath
- Pillared styling with brick and stucco exterior finish

LOWE'S

Signature
SERIES

Plan #530-058D-0017

Price Code D

Total Living Area: 2,412 Sq. Ft.

Home has 4 bedrooms, 2 baths, 3-car side entry garage and walk-out basement foundation.

Special features

- Coffered ceiling in dining room adds character and spaciousness
- Great room is enhanced by a vaulted ceiling and atrium window wall
- Spacious and well-planned kitchen includes counterspace dining and overlooks breakfast room and beyond to the deck
- Luxurious master bedroom features an enormous walk-in closet, private bath and easy access to the laundry area

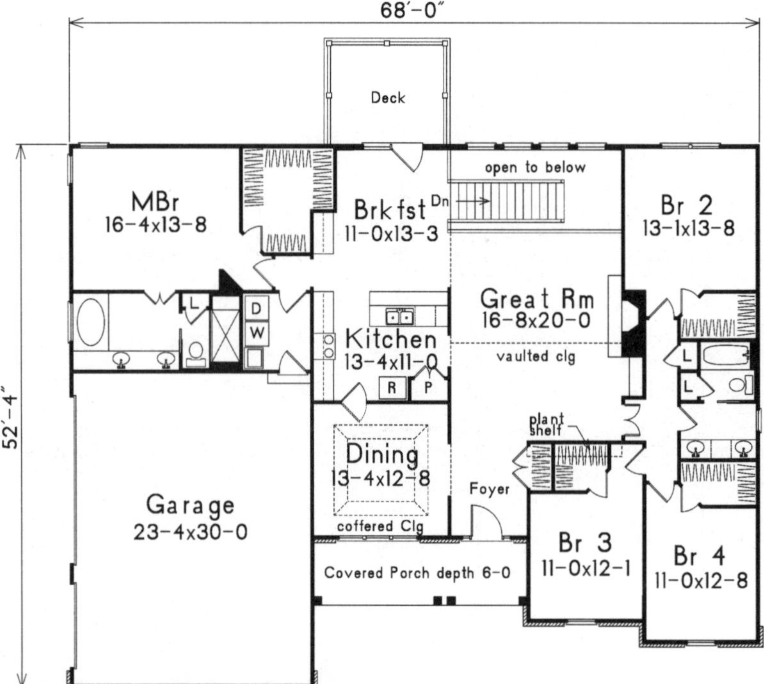
68'-0"
52'-4"
Deck
open to below
MBr
16-4x13-8
Brk fst
11-0x13-3
Dn
Br 2
13-1x13-8
Great Rm
16-8x20-0
vaulted clg
Kitchen
13-4x11-0
D
W
R
P
L
plant shelf
Dining
13-4x12-8
coffered Clg
Foyer
Garage
23-4x30-0
Covered Porch depth 6-0
Br 3
11-0x12-1
Br 4
11-0x12-8

Cozy Corner Patio

LOWE'S

Signature SERIES

Plan #530-007D-0031

Price Code AA

Total Living Area: 1,092 Sq. Ft.

Home has 3 bedrooms, 1 1/2 baths, 1-car garage and basement foundation.

Special features

- Box window and inviting porch with dormers create a charming facade
- Eat-in kitchen offers a pass-through breakfast bar, corner window wall to patio, pantry and convenient laundry with half bath
- Master bedroom features a double-door entry and walk-in closet

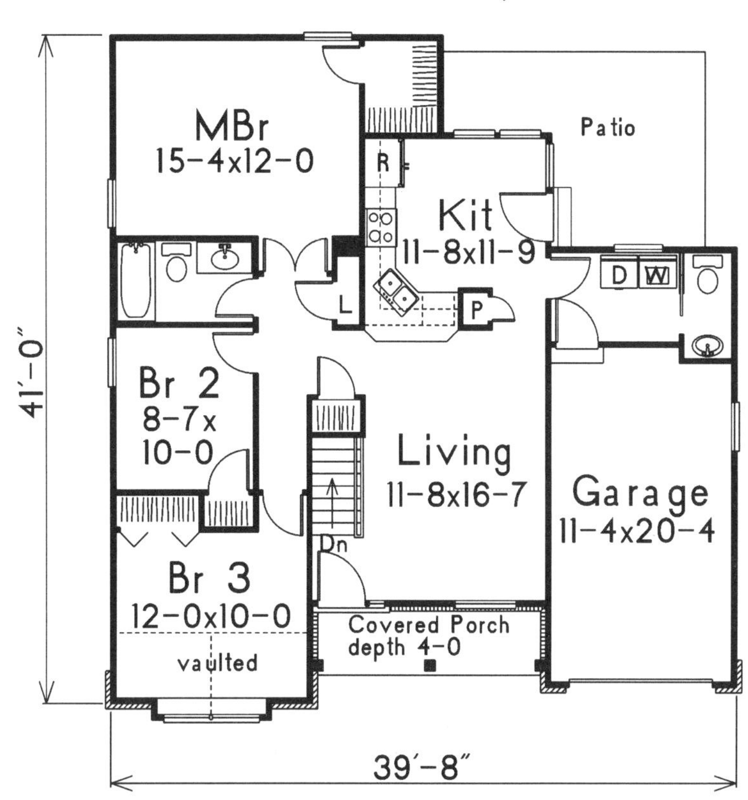

MBr
15-4x12-0
Patio
R
Kit
11-8x11-9
L
P
D
W
Br 2
8-7x
10-0
Living
11-8x16-7
Garage
11-4x20-4
Dn
Br 3
12-0x10-0
vaulted
Covered Porch
depth 4-0
41'-0"
39'-8"

Signature SERIES

Plan #530-007D-0017

Price Code C

Total Living Area: 1,882 Sq. Ft.

Home has 4 bedrooms, 2 baths, 2-car side entry garage and basement foundation.

Special features

- Handsome brick facade
- Spacious great room and dining area combination is brightened by unique corner windows and patio access
- Well-designed kitchen incorporates a breakfast bar peninsula, sweeping casement window above sink and a walk-in pantry island
- Master bedroom features a large walk-in closet and private bath with bay window

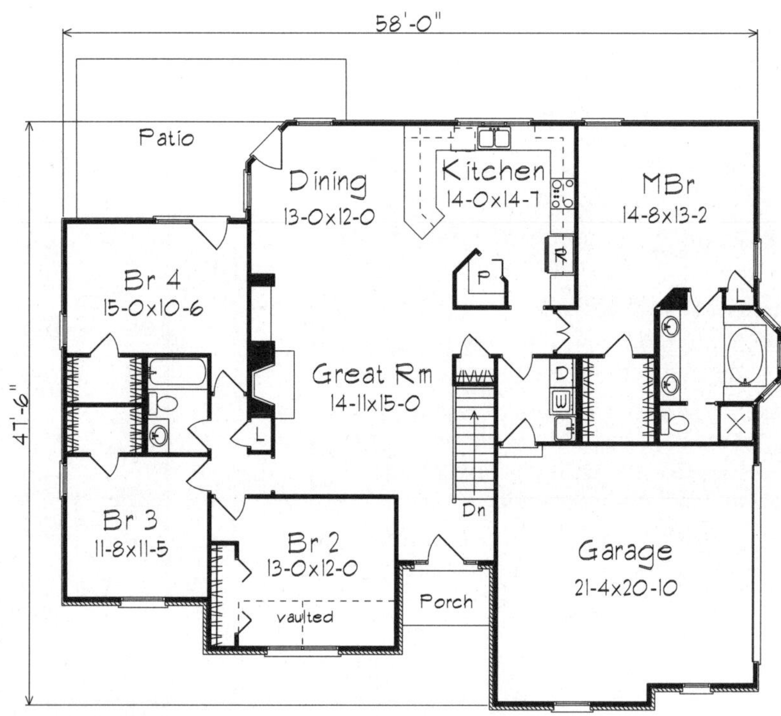
58'-0"
47'-6"
Patio
Dining
13-0x12-0
Kitchen
14-0x14-7
MBr
14-8x13-2
Br 4
15-0x10-6
Great Rm
14-11x15-0
Br 3
11-8x11-5
Br 2
13-0x12-0
vaulted
Porch
Garage
21-4x20-10
Dn

TO ORDER BLUEPRINTS USE THE FORM ON PAGE 288 OR CALL TOLL-FREE **1-800-DREAM HOME** (373-2646)

LOWE'S

Signature
SERIES

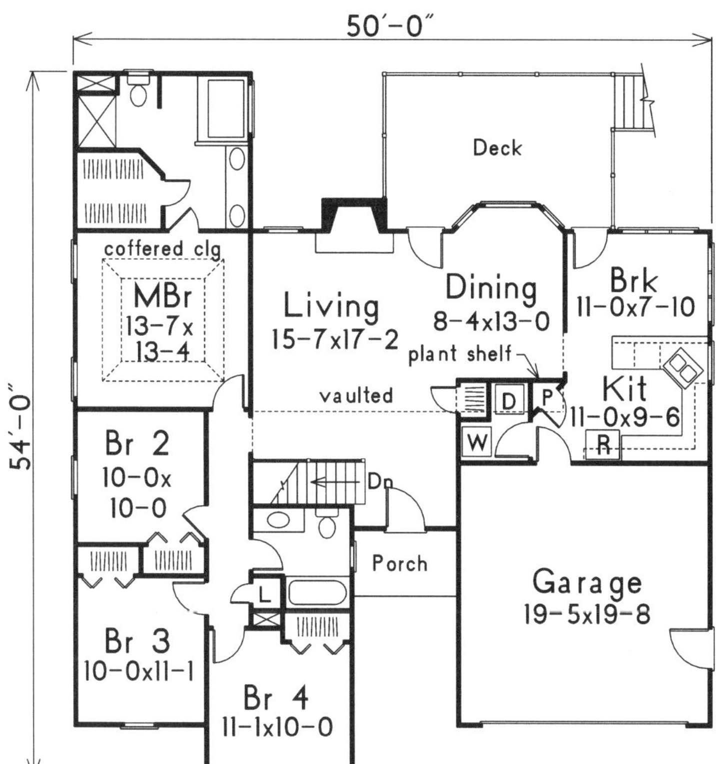
50'-0"
54'-0"
Deck
coffered clg
MBr
13-7x
13-4
Living
15-7x17-2
Dining
8-4x13-0
plant shelf
Brk
11-0x7-10
Kit
11-0x9-6
vaulted
D
P
W
R
Dn
Br 2
10-0x
10-0
Porch
Garage
19-5x19-8
L
Br 3
10-0x11-1
Br 4
11-1x10-0

Plan #530-053D-0053

Price Code B

Total Living Area: 1,609 Sq. Ft.

Home has 4 bedrooms, 2 baths, 2-car garage and basement foundation.

Special features

- Efficient kitchen includes a corner pantry and adjacent laundry room
- Breakfast room boasts plenty of windows and opens onto rear deck
- Master bedroom features a tray ceiling and private deluxe bath
- Entry opens into large living area with fireplace

LOWE'S

Signature
SERIES

Plan #530-048D-0004

Price Code E

Total Living Area: 2,397 Sq. Ft.

Home has 3 bedrooms, 2 1/2 baths, 2-car garage and slab foundation.

Special features

- Covered entrance with fountain leads to the double-door entry and foyer
- Kitchen features two pantries and opens into the breakfast and family rooms
- Master bath features a huge walk-in closet, electric clothes carousel, double-bowl vanity and corner tub

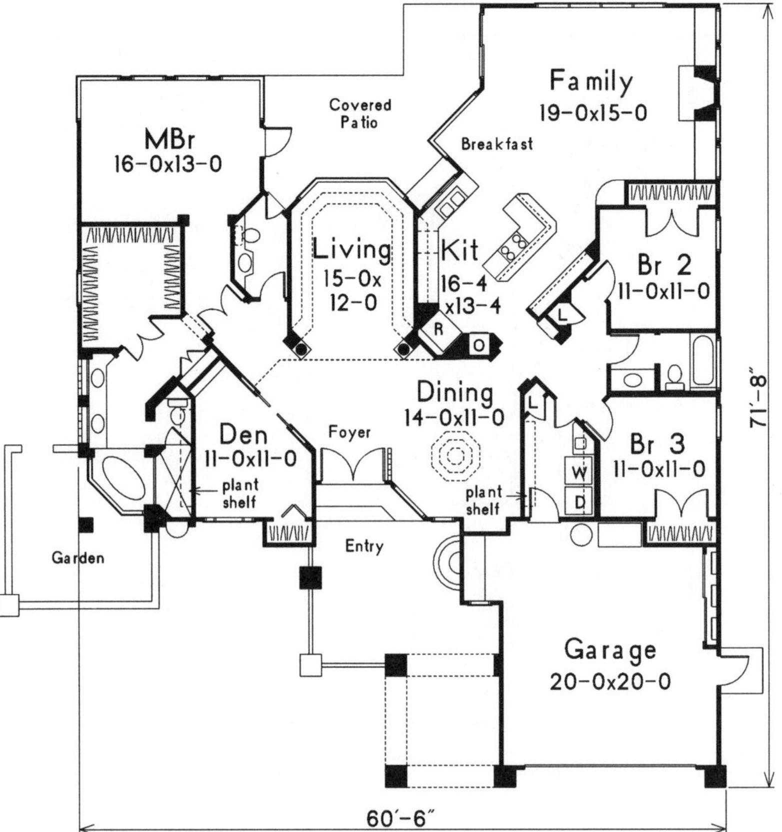
Family
19-0x15-0
Covered
Patio
Breakfast
MBr
16-0x13-0
Living
15-0x
12-0
Kit
16-4
x13-4
R
O
L
Br 2
11-0x11-0
Dining
14-0x11-0
Den
11-0x11-0
Foyer
plant
shelf
L
W
D
Br 3
11-0x11-0
plant
shelf
Garden
Entry
Garage
20-0x20-0
71'-8"
60'-6"

Excellent Ranch For Country Setting

LOWE'S

Signature
SERIES

Plan #530-007D-0048

Price Code E

Total Living Area: 2,758 Sq. Ft.

Home has 4 bedrooms, 2 1/2 baths, 3-car side entry garage and basement foundation.

Special features

- Vaulted great room excels with fireplace, wet bar, plant shelves and skylights
- Fabulous master bedroom enjoys a fireplace, large bath, walk-in closet and vaulted ceiling
- Trendsetting kitchen and breakfast area adjoins the spacious screened porch
- Convenient office near kitchen is perfect for computer room, hobby enthusiast or fifth bedroom

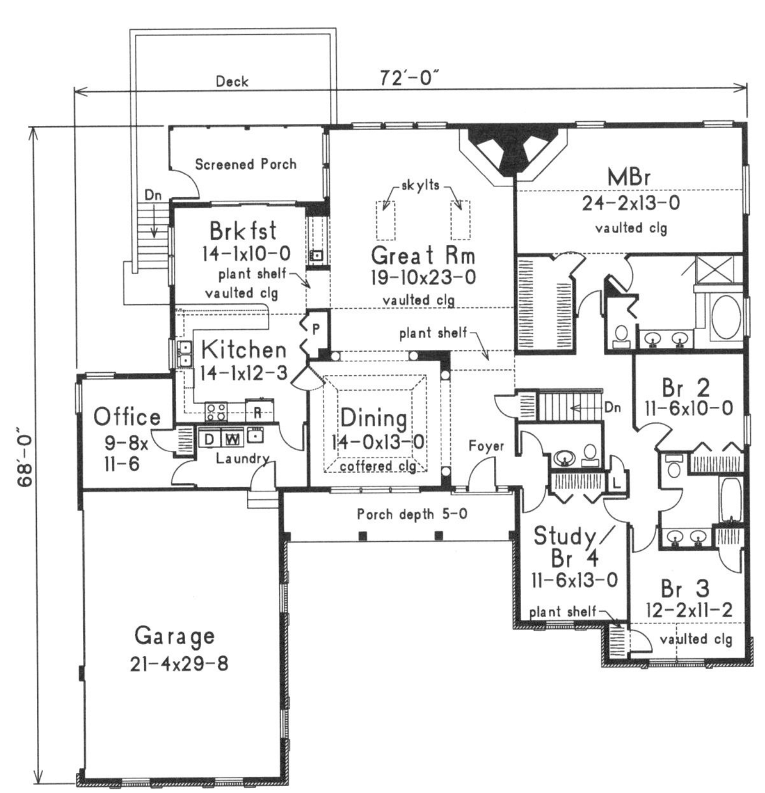
Deck
72'-0"
68'-0"
Screened Porch
Dn
Brkfst
14-1x10-0
plant shelf
vaulted clg
skylts
Great Rm
19-10x23-0
vaulted clg
plant shelf
MBr
24-2x13-0
vaulted clg
Kitchen
14-1x12-3
P
Office
9-8x
11-6
D W
R
Laundry
Dining
14-0x13-0
coffered clg
Foyer
Dn
Br 2
11-6x10-0
L
Porch depth 5-0
Study/
Br 4
11-6x13-0
plant shelf
Br 3
12-2x11-2
vaulted clg
Garage
21-4x29-8

Signature SERIES

First Floor
3,050 sq. ft.

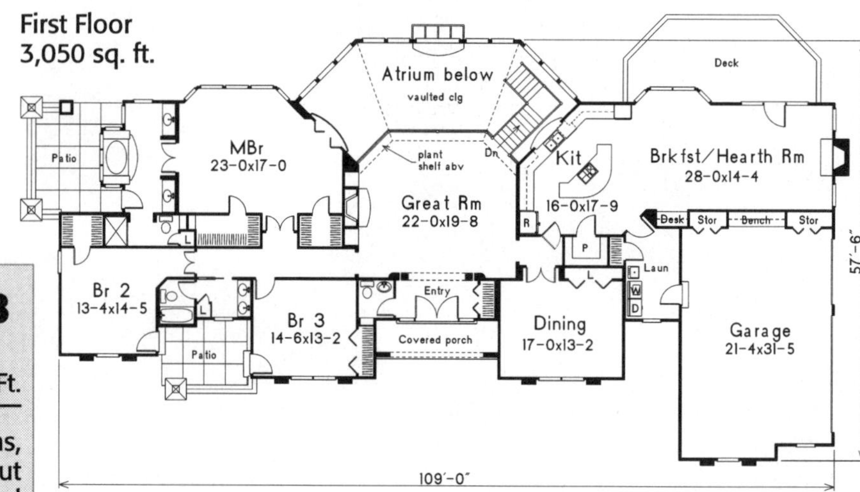
Atrium below
vaulted clg
Deck
Patio
MBr
23-0x17-0
plant shelf abv
Dn
Kit
16-0x17-9
Brkfst/Hearth Rm
28-0x14-4
Great Rm
22-0x19-8
R
Desk
Stor
Bench
Stor
P
L
Laun
W
D
57'-6"
Br 2
13-4x14-5
L
Br 3
14-6x13-2
Entry
Covered porch
Dining
17-0x13-2
Garage
21-4x31-5
Patio
109'-0"

Plan #530-007D-0058

Price Code G

Total Living Area: 4,826 Sq. Ft.

Home has 4 bedrooms, 3 1/2 baths, 3-car side entry garage and walk-out basement foundation with lawn and garden workroom.

Special features

- Brightly lit entry connects to great room with balcony and massive bay-shaped atrium
- Kitchen has island/snack bar, walk-in pantry, computer area and an atrium overlook
- Master bedroom has sitting area, walk-in closets, atrium overlook and luxury bath with private courtyard
- Family room/atrium, home theater area with wet bar, game room and guest bedroom comprise the lower level

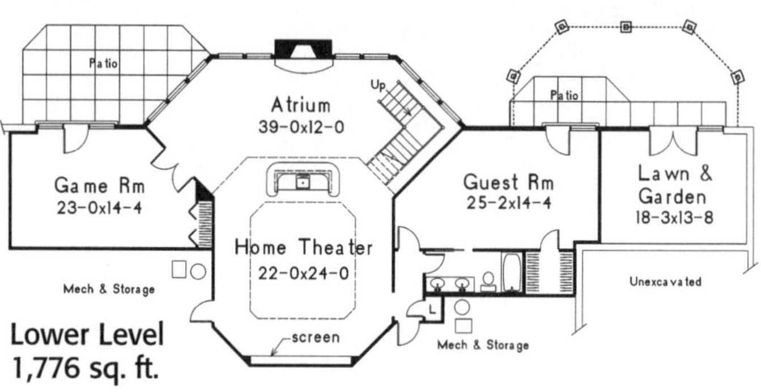
Patio
Atrium
39-0x12-0
Up
Patio
Game Rm
23-0x14-4
Guest Rm
25-2x14-4
Lawn &
Garden
18-3x13-8
Home Theater
22-0x24-0
Mech & Storage
Unexcavated
L
screen
Mech & Storage

Lower Level
1,776 sq. ft.

Great Room/Atrium Interior View

TO ORDER BLUEPRINTS USE THE FORM ON PAGE 288 OR CALL TOLL-FREE **1-800-DREAM HOME** (373-2646)

Ranch Offers Country Elegance

LOWE'S

Signature SERIES

Plan #530-007D-0085

Price Code B

Total Living Area: 1,787 Sq. Ft.

Home has 3 bedrooms, 2 baths, 2-car drive under garage and walk-out basement foundation.

Special features

- Large great room with fireplace and vaulted ceiling features three large skylights and windows galore
- Cooking is sure to be a pleasure in this L-shaped well-appointed kitchen which includes a bayed breakfast area with access to the rear deck
- Every bedroom offers a spacious walk-in closet with a convenient laundry room just steps away
- 415 square feet of optional living area available on the lower level

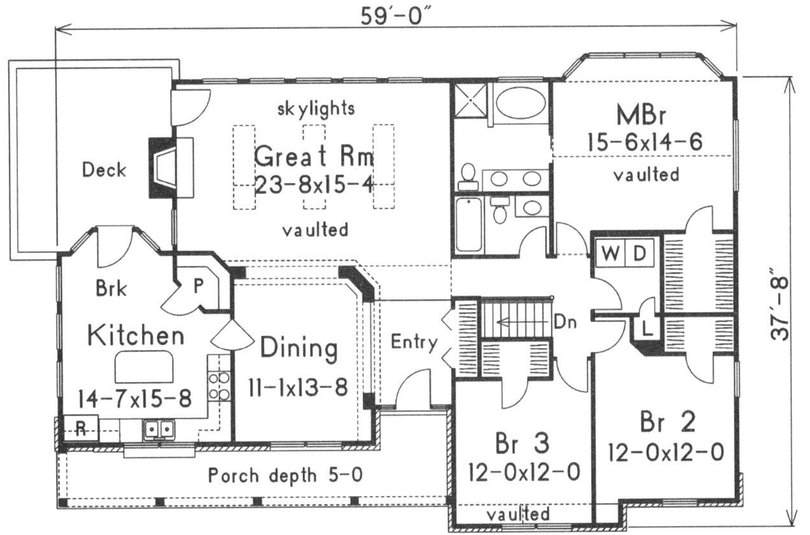
59′-0″
37′-8″
Deck
skylights
Great Rm
23-8x15-4
vaulted
MBr
15-6x14-6
vaulted
W D
Brk
P
Kitchen
14-7x15-8
Dining
11-1x13-8
Entry
Dn
L
R
Br 3
12-0x12-0
Br 2
12-0x12-0
Porch depth 5-0
vaulted

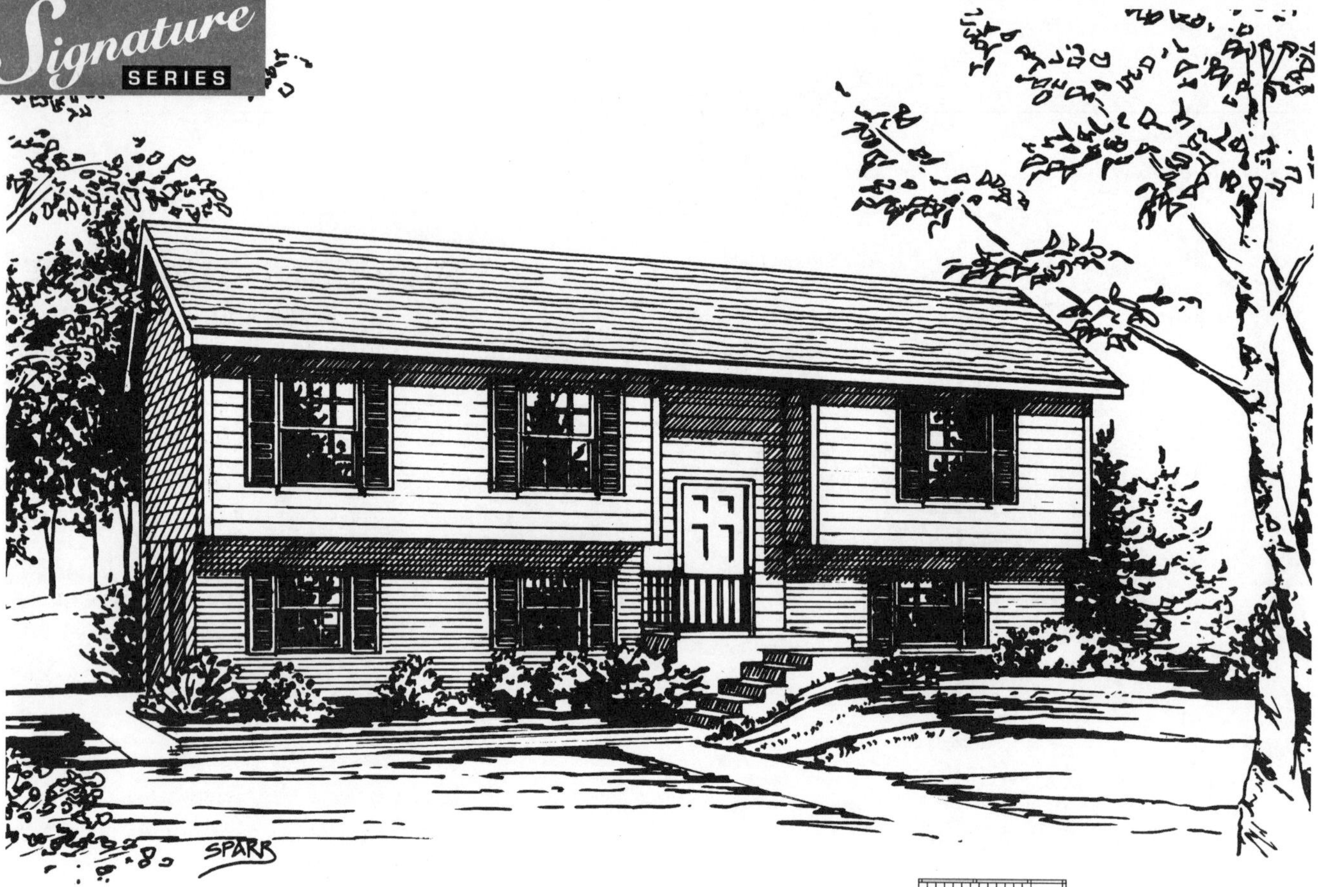

SPARR

Plan #530-001D-0058

Price Code B

Total Living Area: 1,720 Sq. Ft.

Home has 3 bedrooms, 1 full bath, 2 half baths, 2-car drive under garage and basement foundation.

Special features

- Lower level includes large family room with laundry area and half bath
- L-shaped kitchen has a convenient serving bar and pass-through to dining area
- Private half bath in master bedroom

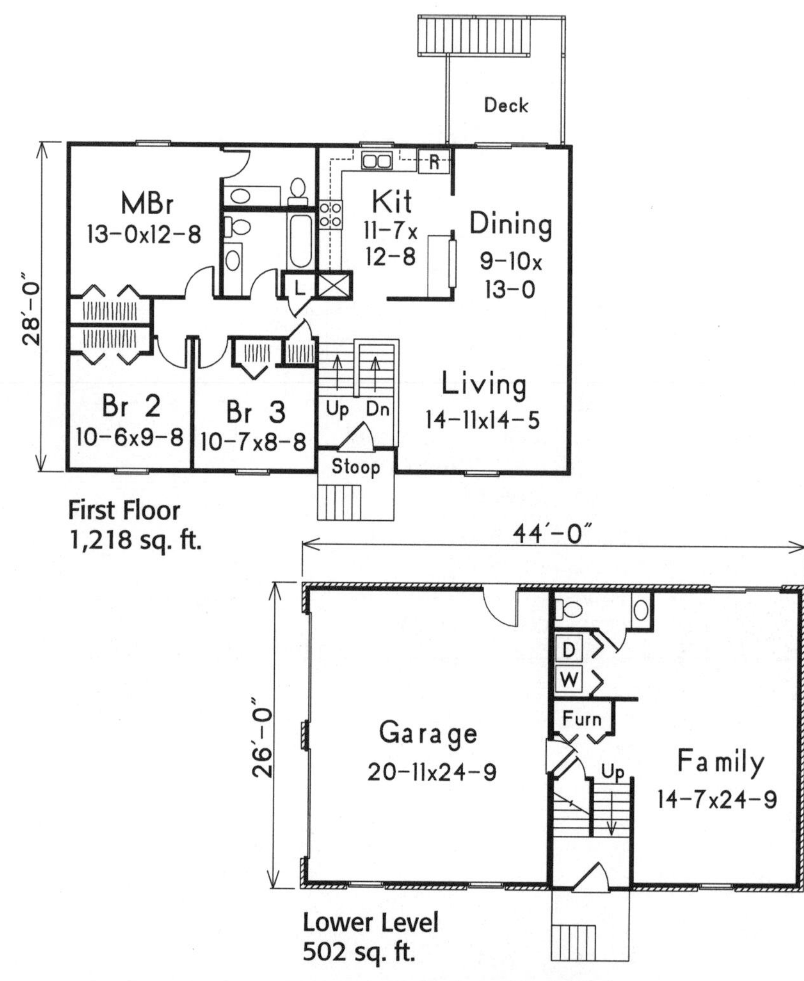
Deck
MBr
13-0x12-8
Kit
11-7x
12-8
R
L
Dining
9-10x
13-0
Living
14-11x14-5
Br 2
10-6x9-8
Br 3
10-7x8-8
Up
Dn
Stoop
28'-0"
44'-0"
26'-0"
D
W
Furn
Garage
20-11x24-9
Up
Family
14-7x24-9

First Floor
1,218 sq. ft.

Lower Level
502 sq. ft.

Columns Accent This Home

LOWE'S

Signature
SERIES

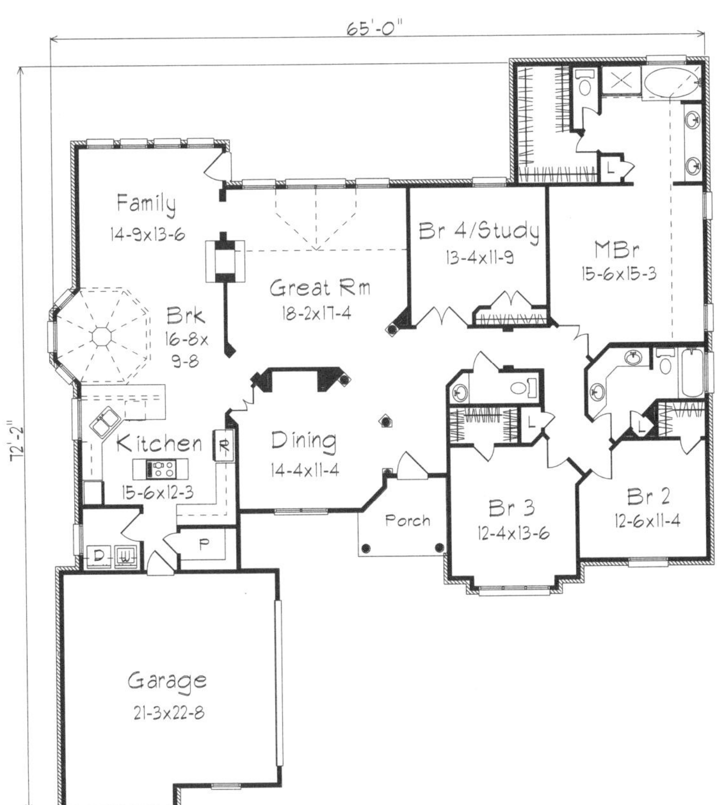
65'-0"
72'-2"
Family
14-9x13-6
Great Rm
18-2x17-4
Br 4/Study
13-4x11-9
MBr
15-6x15-3
Brk
16-8x
9-8
Kitchen
15-6x12-3
Dining
14-4x11-4
Porch
Br 3
12-4x13-6
Br 2
12-6x11-4
Garage
21-3x22-8

Plan #530-018D-0005

Price Code D

Total Living Area: 2,598 Sq. Ft.

Home has 4 bedrooms, 2 1/2 baths, 2-car side entry garage and slab foundation, drawings also include crawl space foundation.

Special features

- Varied ceiling heights throughout home
- Stylish see-through fireplace is shared by the great room and family room
- Walk-in pantry and laundry room are located near the kitchen
- An abundance of windows provides natural light

Plan #530-001D-0091

Price Code A

Total Living Area: 1,344 Sq. Ft.

Home has 3 bedrooms, 2 baths and crawl space foundation, drawings also include basement and slab foundations.

Special features

- Kitchen has side entry, laundry area, pantry and joins family/dining area
- Master bedroom includes a private bath
- Linen and storage closets in hall
- Covered porch opens to the spacious living room with a handy coat closet

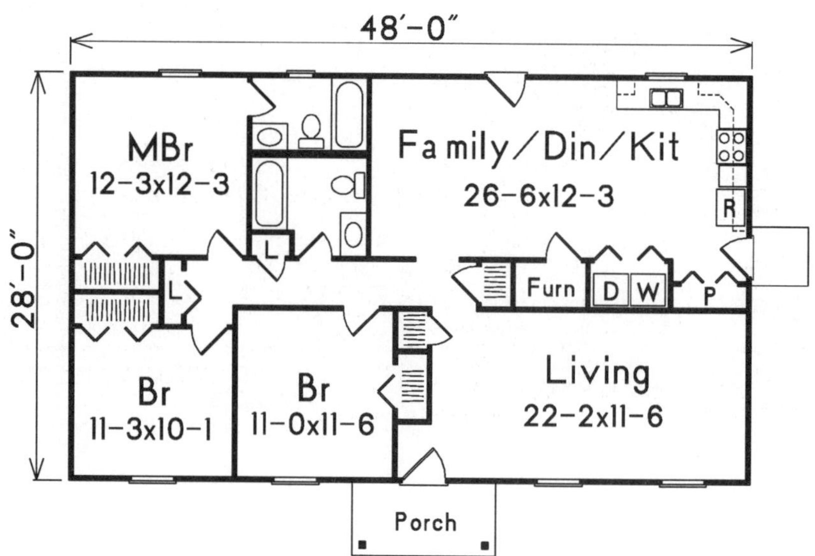

48′-0″
28′-0″
MBr
12-3x12-3
Family/Din/Kit
26-6x12-3
R
L
L
Furn
D
W
P
Br
11-3x10-1
Br
11-0x11-6
Living
22-2x11-6
Porch

Circle-Top Windows Grace The Facade

LOWE'S

Signature SERIES

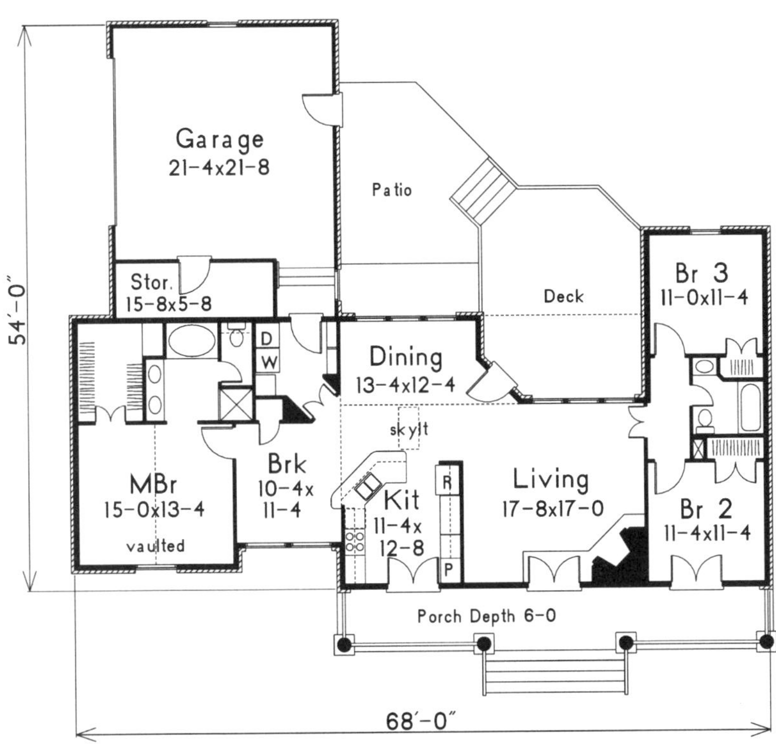
Garage
21-4x21-8
Patio
Deck
Stor.
15-8x5-8
Br 3
11-0x11-4
D
W
Dining
13-4x12-4
skylt
MBr
15-0x13-4
vaulted
Brk
10-4x
11-4
Kit
11-4x
12-8
R
P
Living
17-8x17-0
Br 2
11-4x11-4
Porch Depth 6-0
54'-0"
68'-0"

Plan #530-021D-0012

Price Code C

Total Living Area: 1,672 Sq. Ft.

Home has 3 bedrooms, 2 baths, 2-car side entry garage and crawl space foundation, drawings also include basement and slab foundations.

Special features

- Vaulted master bedroom features a walk-in closet and adjoining bath with separate tub and shower
- Energy efficient home with 2" x 6" exterior walls
- Covered front and rear porches
- 12' ceilings in living room, kitchen and bedroom #2
- Kitchen is complete with a pantry, angled bar and adjacent eating area
- Sloped ceiling in the dining room

LOWE'S

Signature SERIES

Plan #530-007D-0053

Price Code D

Total Living Area: 2,334 Sq. Ft.

Home has 3 bedrooms, 2 baths, 2-car garage and walk-out basement foundation.

Special features

- Roomy front porch gives home a country flavor
- Vaulted great room boasts a fireplace, TV alcove, pass-through snack bar to kitchen and atrium featuring bayed window wall and an ascending stair to family room
- Oversized master bedroom features a vaulted ceiling, double-door entry and large walk-in closet

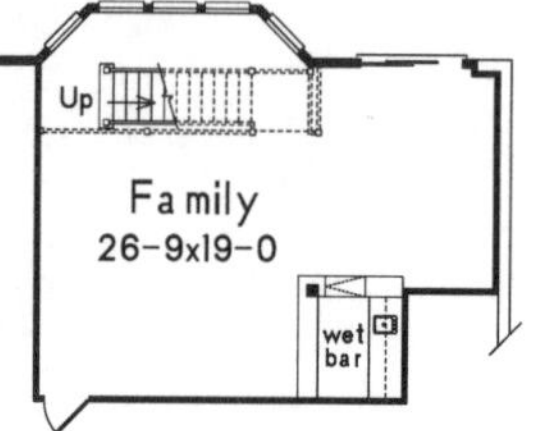
Up
Family
26-9x19-0
wet bar

Lower Level
557 sq. ft.

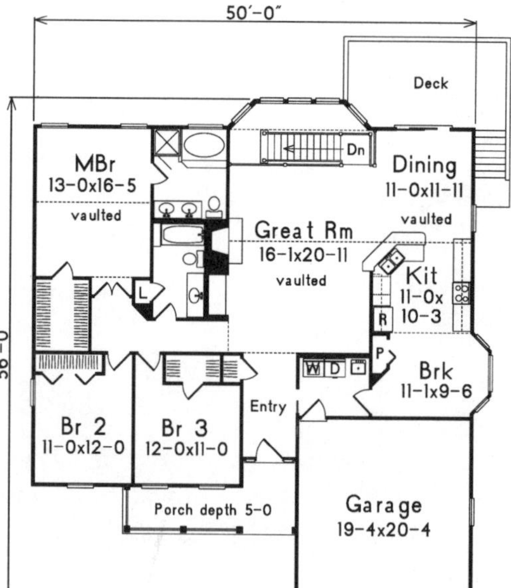
50'-0"
56'-0"
Deck
MBr
13-0x16-5
vaulted
Dn
Dining
11-0x11-11
vaulted
Great Rm
16-1x20-11
vaulted
Kit
11-0x
10-3
R
P
W D
Brk
11-1x9-6
Br 2
11-0x12-0
Br 3
12-0x11-0
Entry
Porch depth 5-0
Garage
19-4x20-4

First Floor
1,777 sq. ft.

Rear View

Front Entrance Flanked By Windows

LOWE'S

Signature SERIES

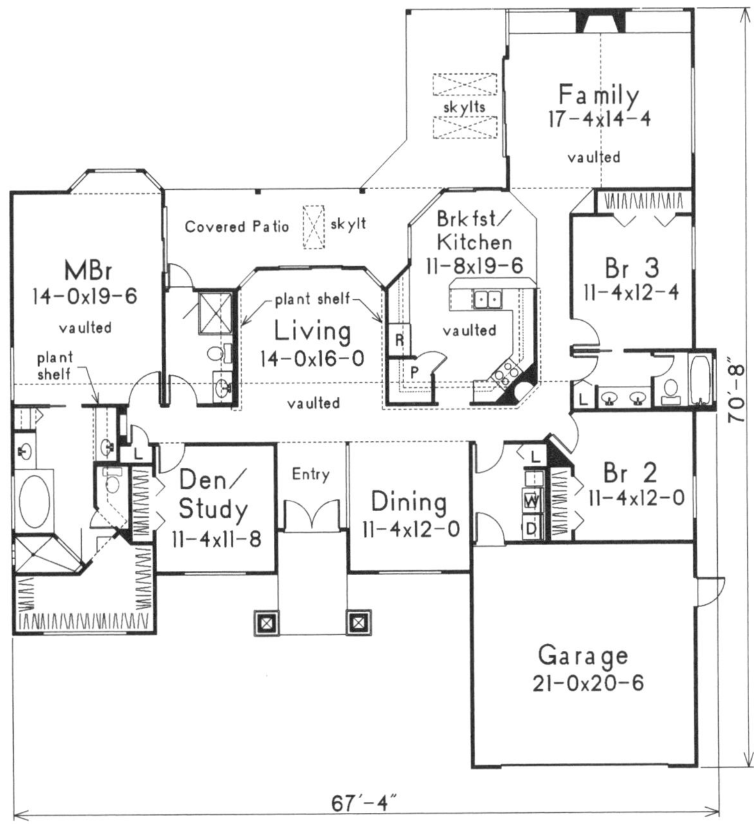
Family
17-4x14-4
vaulted
skylts
Covered Patio
skylt
MBr
14-0x19-6
vaulted
plant shelf
Brk fst/ Kitchen
11-8x19-6
vaulted
plant shelf
Living
14-0x16-0
vaulted
Br 3
11-4x12-4
Den/ Study
11-4x11-8
Entry
Dining
11-4x12-0
Br 2
11-4x12-0
Garage
21-0x20-6
70'-8"
67'-4"

Plan #530-048D-0002

Price Code D

Total Living Area: 2,467 Sq. Ft.

Home has 3 bedrooms, 3 baths, 2-car garage and slab foundation.

Special features

- Tiled foyer leads into the living room with vaulted ceiling and large bay window
- Kitchen features a walk-in pantry and adjacent breakfast nook
- Master bedroom includes a bay window and bath with large walk-in closet
- Varied ceiling heights throughout

LOWE'S

Stylish Ranch With Rustic Charm

Signature
SERIES

Plan #530-001D-0053

Price Code A

Total Living Area: 1,344 Sq. Ft.

Home has 3 bedrooms, 2 baths, 2-car garage and crawl space foundation, drawings also include basement and slab foundations.

Special features

- Family/dining room has sliding glass doors to the outdoors
- Master bedroom features a private bath
- Hall bath includes a double-bowl vanity for added convenience
- U-shaped kitchen features a large pantry and laundry area

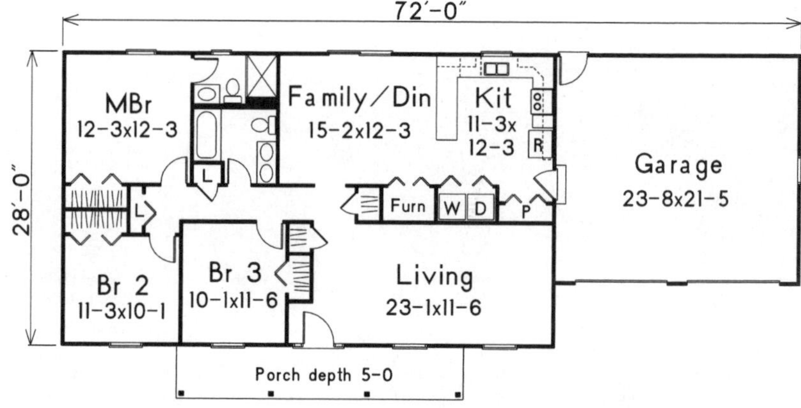
72'-0"
28'-0"
MBr
12-3x12-3
Family/Din
15-2x12-3
Kit
11-3x
12-3
R
L
L
Furn
W
D
P
Garage
23-8x21-5
Br 2
11-3x10-1
Br 3
10-1x11-6
Living
23-1x11-6
Porch depth 5-0

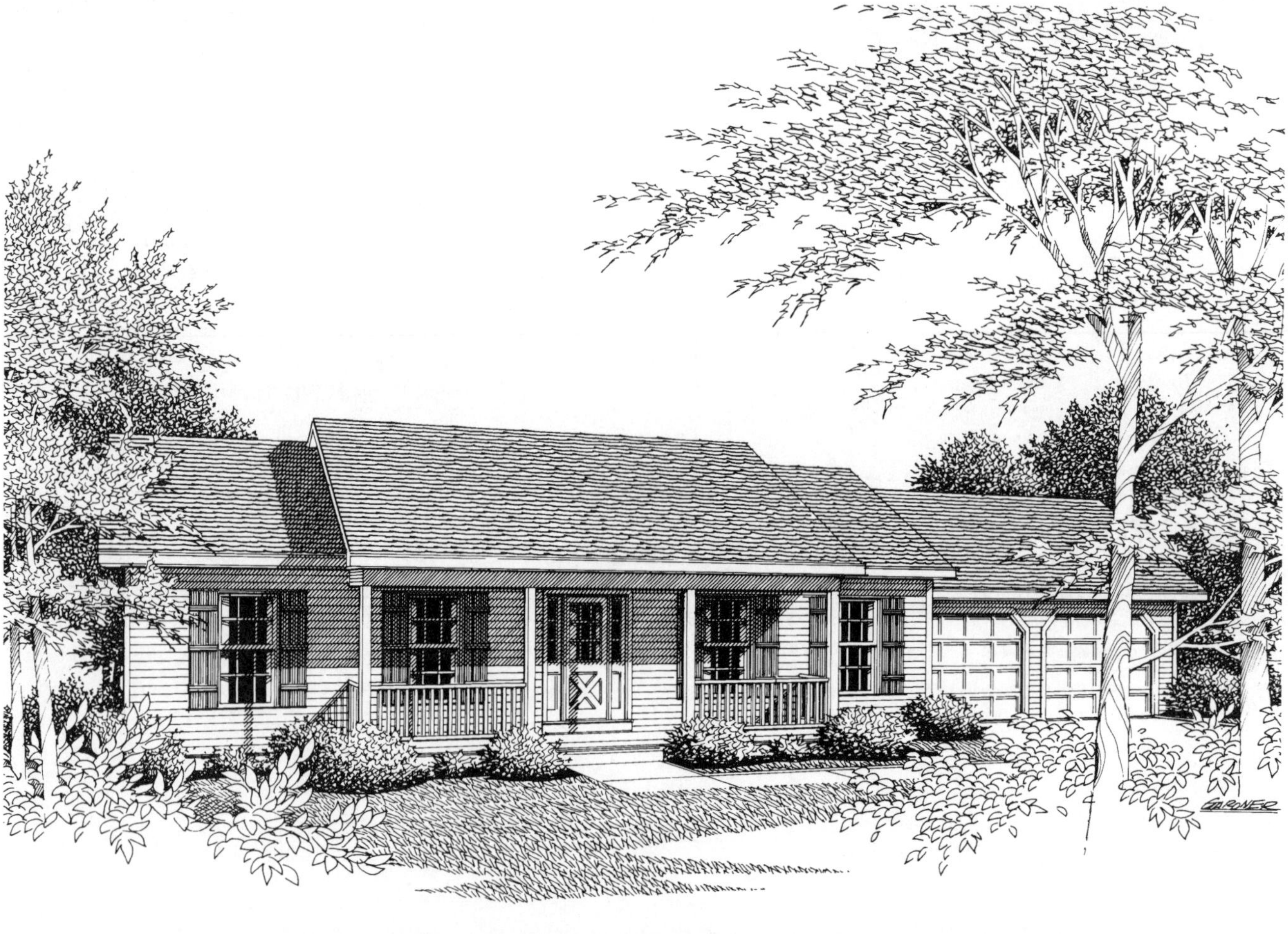

LOWE'S

Signature SERIES

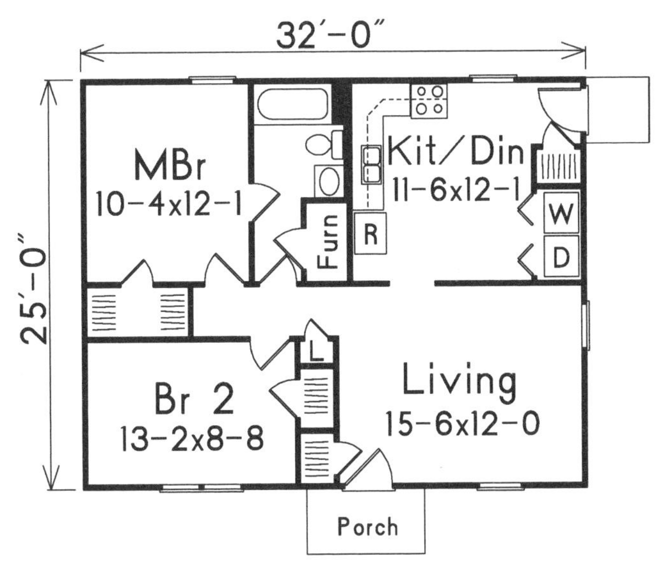
32′–0″
25′–0″
MBr
10–4x12–1
Kit/Din
11–6x12–1
R
W
D
Furn
L
Br 2
13–2x8–8
Living
15–6x12–0
Porch

Plan #530-001D-0088

Price Code AAA

Total Living Area: 800 Sq. Ft.

Home has 2 bedrooms, 1 bath and crawl space foundation, drawings also include basement foundation.

Special features

- Master bedroom has a walk-in closet and private access to the bath
- Large living room features a handy coat closet
- Kitchen includes side entrance, closet and convenient laundry area

LOWE'S

Distinguished Styling For A Small Lot

Plan #530-007D-0060

Price Code B

Total Living Area: 1,268 Sq. Ft.

Home has 3 bedrooms, 2 baths, 2-car garage and basement foundation, drawings also include crawl space and slab foundations.

Special features

- Multiple gables, large porch and arched windows create a classy exterior
- Innovative design provides openness in great room, kitchen and breakfast room
- Secondary bedrooms have private hall with bath

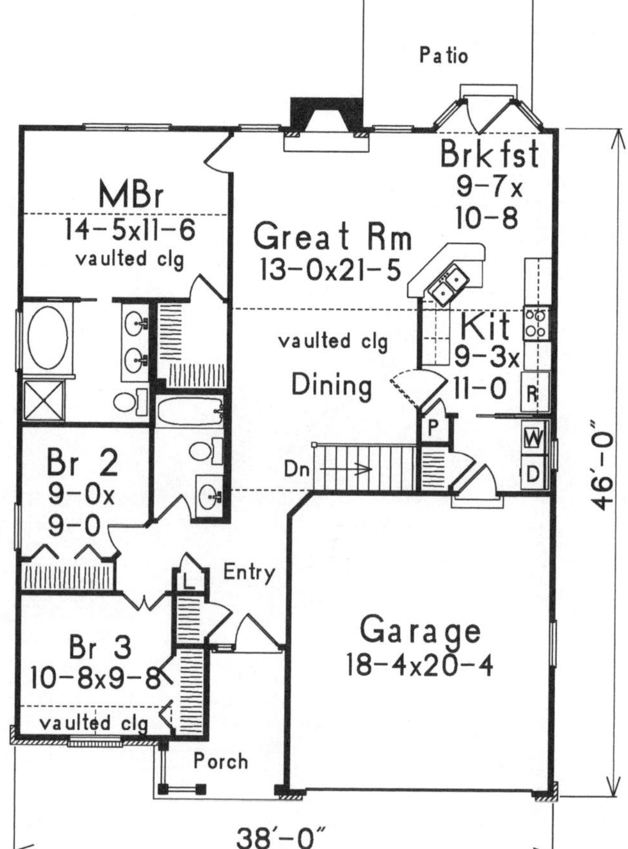
Patio
MBr
14-5x11-6
vaulted clg
Brkfst
9-7x
10-8
Great Rm
13-0x21-5
vaulted clg
Dining
Kit
9-3x
11-0
R
P
W
D
Dn
Br 2
9-0x
9-0
Entry
L
Br 3
10-8x9-8
vaulted clg
Garage
18-4x20-4
Porch
46'-0"
38'-0"

 TO ORDER BLUEPRINTS USE THE FORM ON PAGE 288 OR CALL TOLL-FREE **1-800-DREAM HOME** (373-2646)

LOWE'S

Signature SERIES

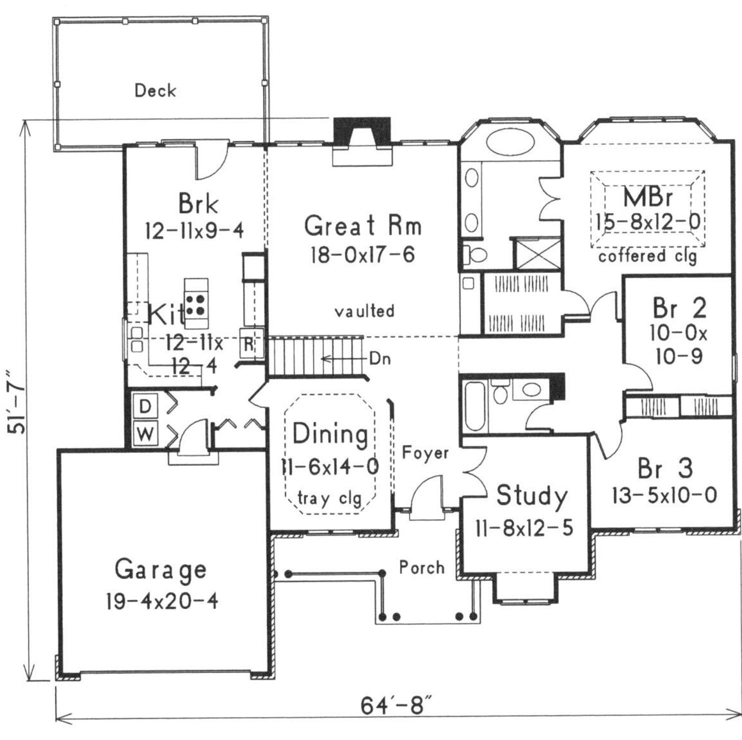
Deck
Brk
12-11x9-4
Great Rm
18-0x17-6
vaulted
MBr
15-8x12-0
coffered clg
Br 2
10-0x
10-9
Kit
12-11x
12-4
R
Dn
D
W
Dining
11-6x14-0
tray clg
Foyer
Study
11-8x12-5
Br 3
13-5x10-0
Porch
Garage
19-4x20-4
51'-7"
64'-8"

Plan #530-027D-0003

Price Code D

Total Living Area: 2,061 Sq. Ft.

Home has 3 bedrooms, 2 baths, 2-car garage and basement foundation.

Special features

- Convenient entrance from garage into home through laundry room
- Master bedroom features a walk-in closet and double-door entrance into master bath with an oversized tub
- Formal dining room enjoys a tray ceiling
- Kitchen features an island cooktop and adjacent breakfast room

LOWE'S
Signature
SERIES

Graciously Designed Ranch

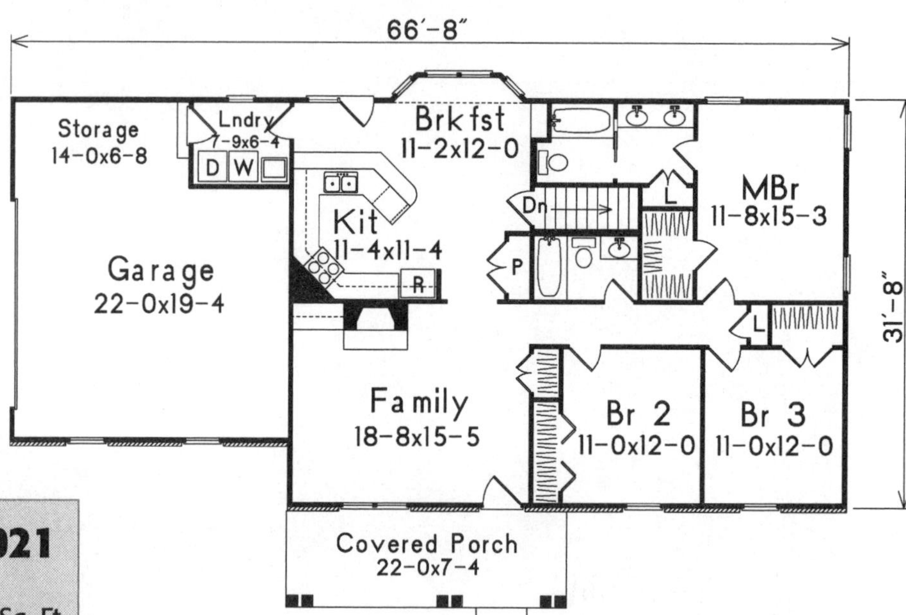
66'-8"
31'-8"
Storage
14-0x6-8
Lndry
7-9x6-4
D
W
Brkfst
11-2x12-0
Kit
11-4x11-4
R
Dn
P
L
MBr
11-8x15-3
Garage
22-0x19-4
Family
18-8x15-5
Br 2
11-0x12-0
Br 3
11-0x12-0
Covered Porch
22-0x7-4

Plan #530-058D-0021

Price Code A

Total Living Area: 1,477 Sq. Ft.

Home has 3 bedrooms, 2 baths, 2-car side entry garage and basement foundation.

Special features

- Oversized porch provides protection from the elements
- Innovative kitchen employs step-saving design
- Kitchen has snack bar which opens to the breakfast room with bay window
- Extra storage in garage

 TO ORDER BLUEPRINTS USE THE FORM ON PAGE 288 OR CALL TOLL-FREE **1-800-DREAM HOME** (373-2646)

Large Open Living Area

LOWE'S

Signature SERIES

Plan #530-001D-0067

Price Code B

Total Living Area: 1,285 Sq. Ft.

Home has 3 bedrooms, 2 baths and crawl space foundation, drawings also include basement and slab foundations.

Special features

- Accommodating home with ranch-style porch
- Large storage area on back of home
- Master bedroom includes dressing area, private bath and built-in bookcase
- Kitchen features pantry, breakfast bar and complete view to the dining room

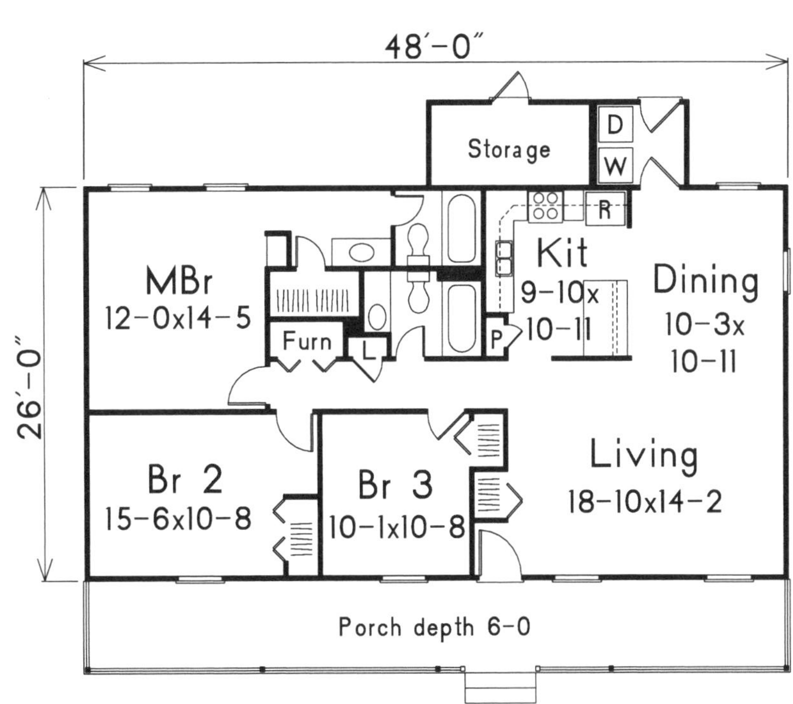

48'-0"
26'-0"
Storage
D
W
R
MBr
12-0x14-5
Furn
L
P
Kit
9-10x
10-11
Dining
10-3x
10-11
Living
18-10x14-2
Br 2
15-6x10-8
Br 3
10-1x10-8
Porch depth 6-0

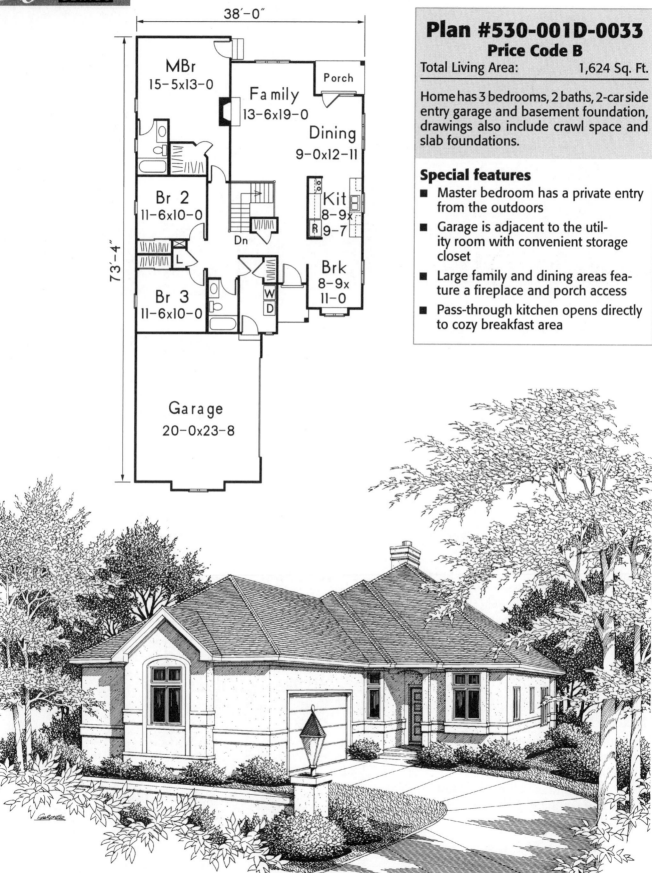

LOWE'S

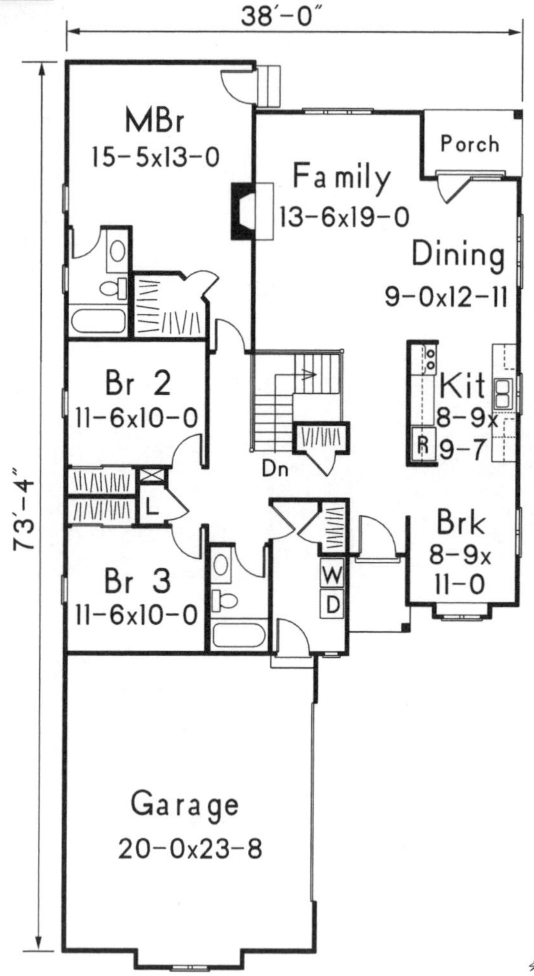

38′-0″

73′-4″

MBr
15-5x13-0

Family
13-6x19-0

Porch

Dining
9-0x12-11

Kit
8-9x
9-7

Br 2
11-6x10-0

Dn

L

Brk
8-9x
11-0

Br 3
11-6x10-0

W
D

Garage
20-0x23-8

Plan #530-001D-0033

Price Code B

Total Living Area: 1,624 Sq. Ft.

Home has 3 bedrooms, 2 baths, 2-car side entry garage and basement foundation, drawings also include crawl space and slab foundations.

Special features

- Master bedroom has a private entry from the outdoors
- Garage is adjacent to the utility room with convenient storage closet
- Large family and dining areas feature a fireplace and porch access
- Pass-through kitchen opens directly to cozy breakfast area

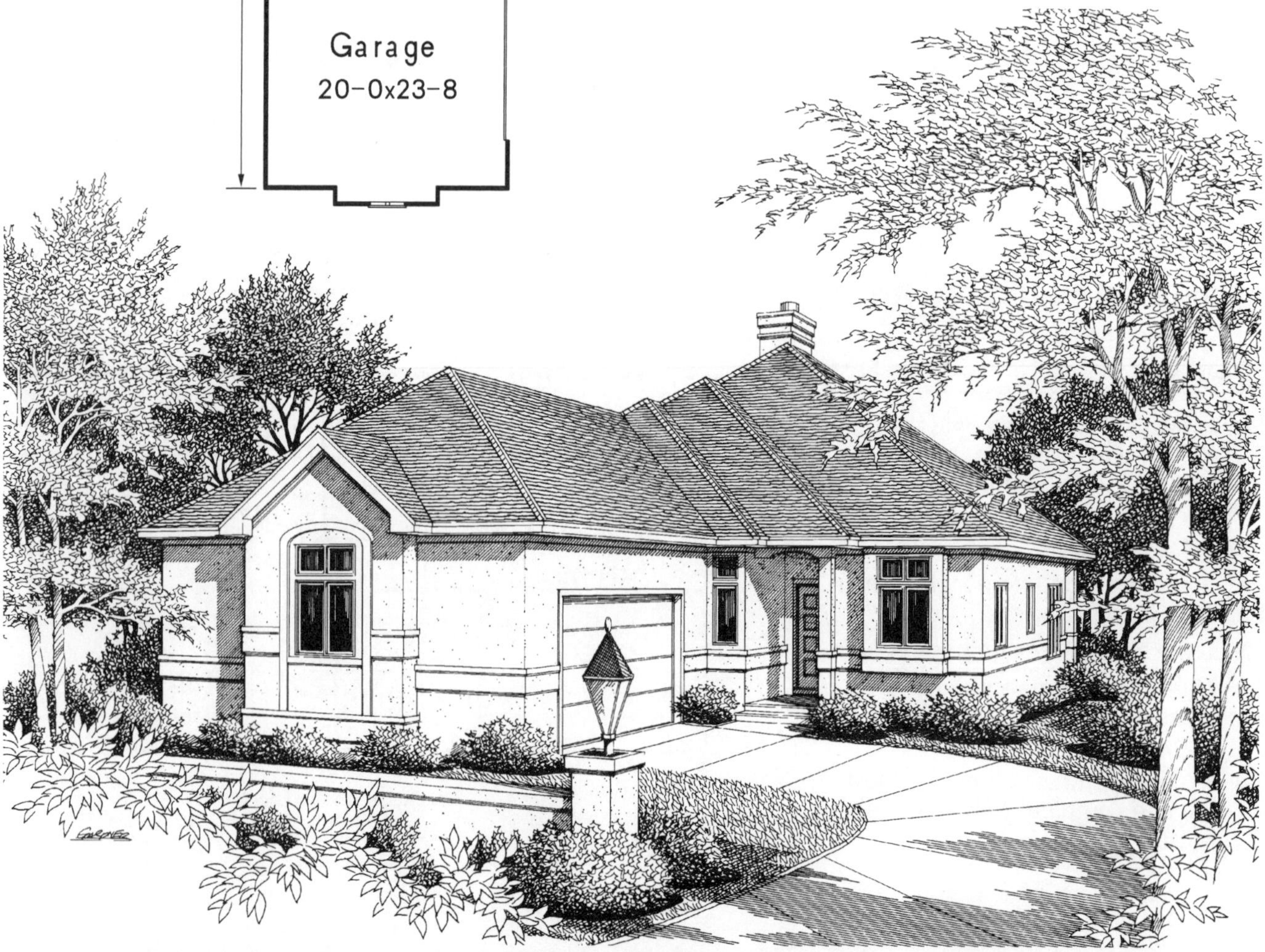

LOWE'S

Signature SERIES

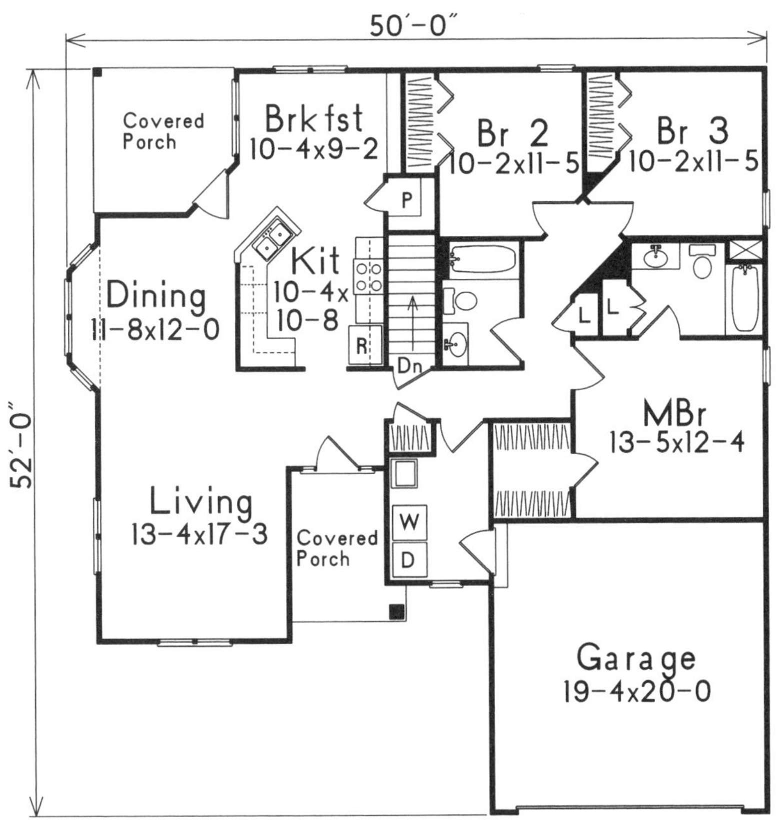
50'-0"
52'-0"
Covered Porch
Brkfst 10-4x9-2
Br 2 10-2x11-5
Br 3 10-2x11-5
P
Kit 10-4x 10-8
Dining 11-8x12-0
R
Dn
L
L
MBr 13-5x12-4
Living 13-4x17-3
Covered Porch
W
D
Garage 19-4x20-0

Plan #530-058D-0022

Price Code B

Total Living Area: 1,578 Sq. Ft.

Home has 3 bedrooms, 2 baths, 2-car garage and basement foundation.

Special features

- Plenty of closet, linen and storage space
- Covered porches in the front and rear of home add charm to this design
- Open floor plan has a unique angled layout

Secluded Master Bedroom

Plan #530-058D-0026

Price Code C

Total Living Area: 1,819 Sq. Ft.

Home has 3 bedrooms, 2 baths, 2-car side entry garage and basement foundation.

Special features

- Master bedroom features access to the outdoors, large walk-in closet and private bath
- 9' ceilings throughout
- Formal foyer with coat closet opens into the vaulted great room with fireplace and formal dining room
- Kitchen and breakfast room create a cozy and casual area

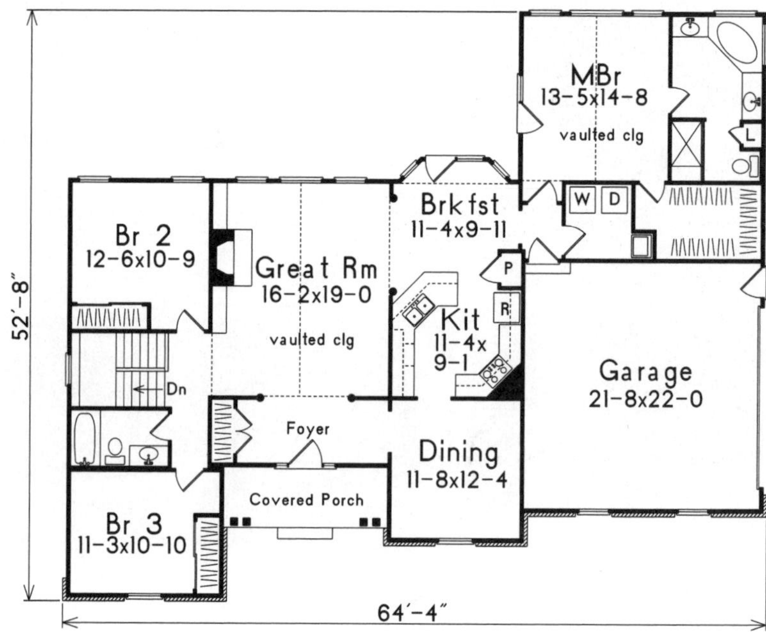

MBr
13-5x14-8
vaulted clg
Brk fst
11-4x9-11
W
D
P
R
L
Br 2
12-6x10-9
Great Rm
16-2x19-0
vaulted clg
Kit
11-4x
9-1
Garage
21-8x22-0
Dn
Foyer
Dining
11-8x12-4
Covered Porch
Br 3
11-3x10-10
52'-8"
64'-4"

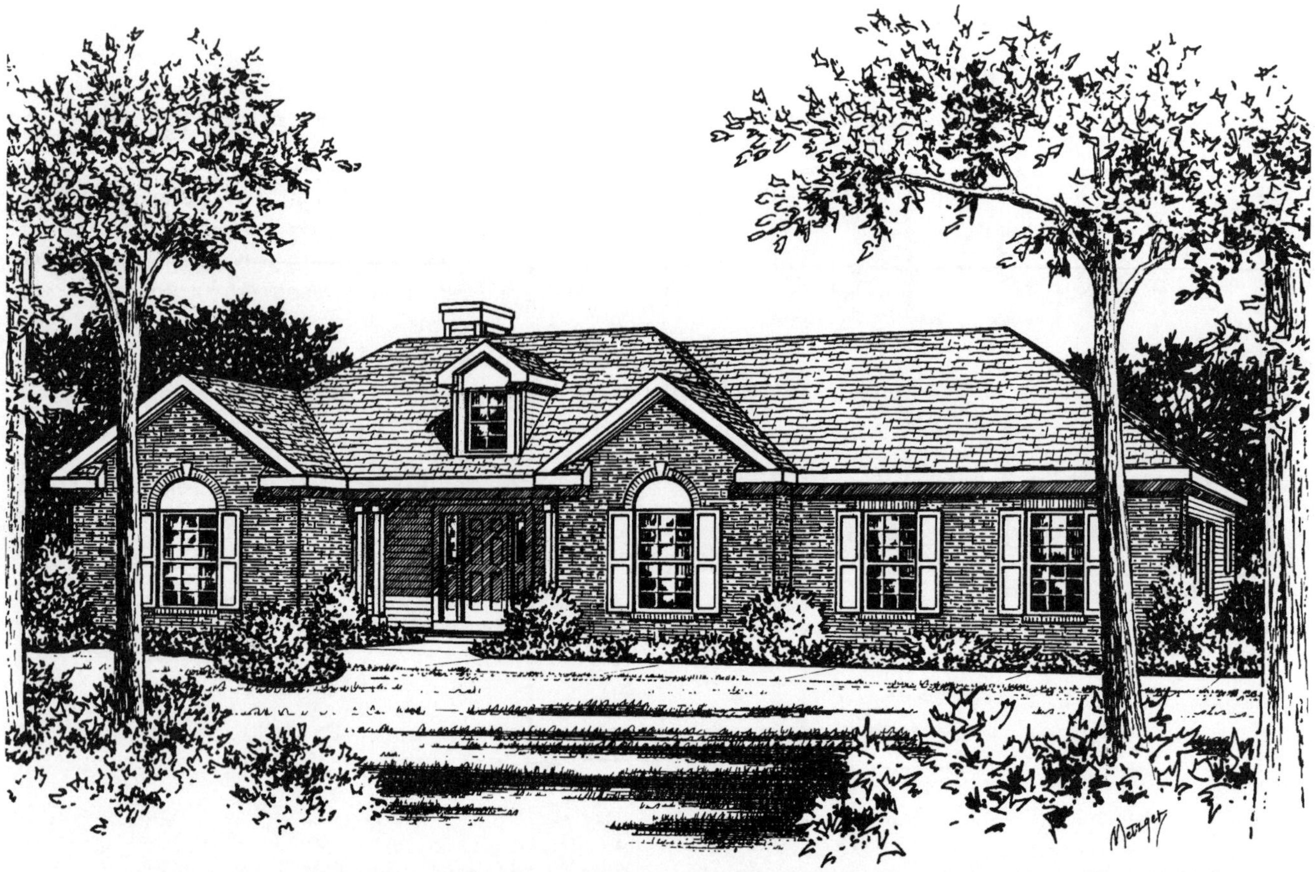

Practical Layout

LOWE'S

Signature SERIES

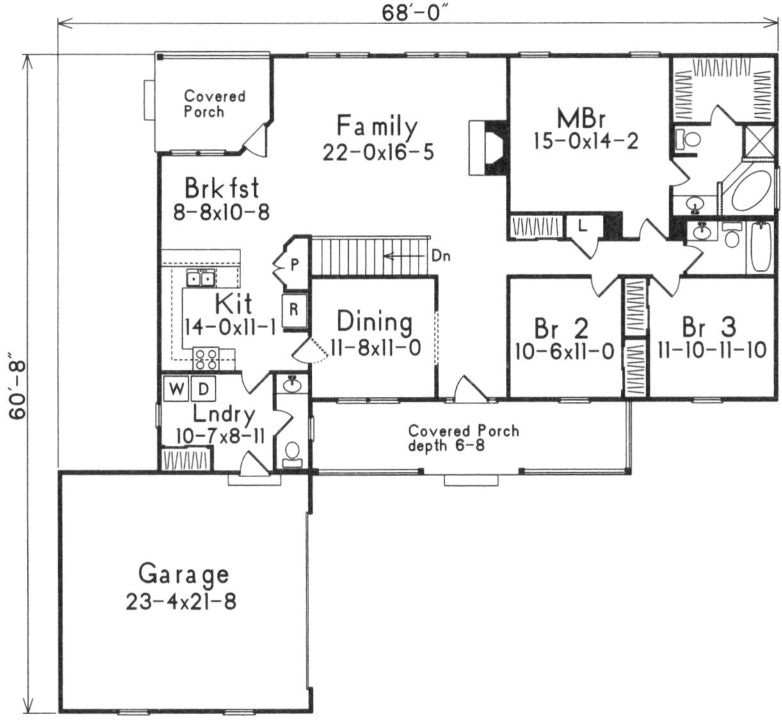
68'-0"
60'-8"
Covered Porch
Family
22-0x16-5
MBr
15-0x14-2
Brkfst
8-8x10-8
L
P
Dn
Kit
14-0x11-1
R
Dining
11-8x11-0
Br 2
10-6x11-0
Br 3
11-10-11-10
W D
Lndry
10-7x8-11
Covered Porch
depth 6-8
Garage
23-4x21-8

Plan #530-058D-0023

Price Code C

Total Living Area: 1,883 Sq. Ft.

Home has 3 bedrooms, 2 1/2 baths, 2-car side entry garage and basement foundation.

Special features

- Large laundry room located off the garage has a coat closet and half bath
- Large family room with fireplace and access to the covered porch is a great central gathering room
- U-shaped kitchen has breakfast bar, large pantry and swing door to dining room for convenient serving

LOWE'S

Signature
SERIES

Open Floor Plan Makes Home Feel Larger

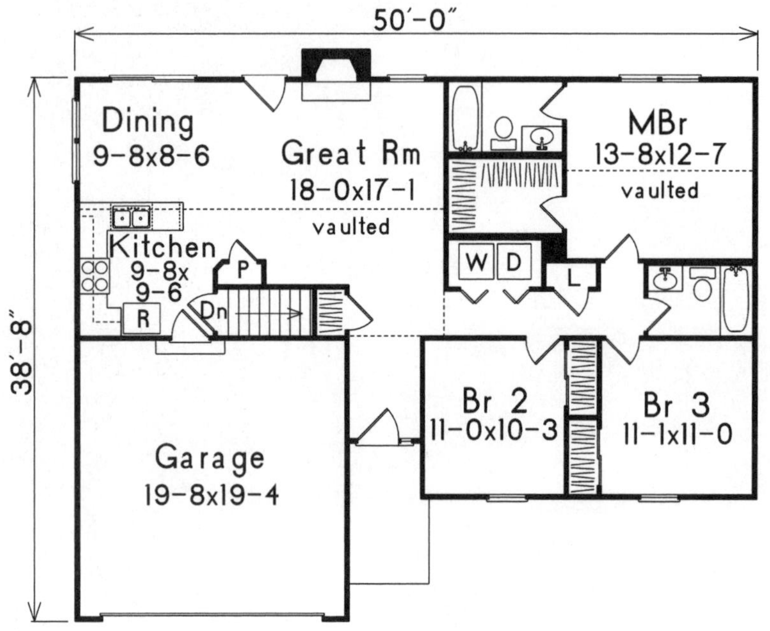
50'-0"
38'-8"
Dining
9-8x8-6
Great Rm
18-0x17-1
vaulted
MBr
13-8x12-7
vaulted
Kitchen
9-8x
9-6
P
R
Dn
W
D
L
Br 2
11-0x10-3
Br 3
11-1x11-0
Garage
19-8x19-4

Plan #530-058D-0043

Price Code A

Total Living Area: 1,277 Sq. Ft.

Home has 3 bedrooms, 2 baths, 2-car garage and basement foundation.

Special features

- Vaulted ceilings grace the master bedroom, great room, kitchen and dining room
- Laundry closet is located near the bedrooms for convenience
- Compact, yet efficient kitchen

LOWE'S

Signature SERIES

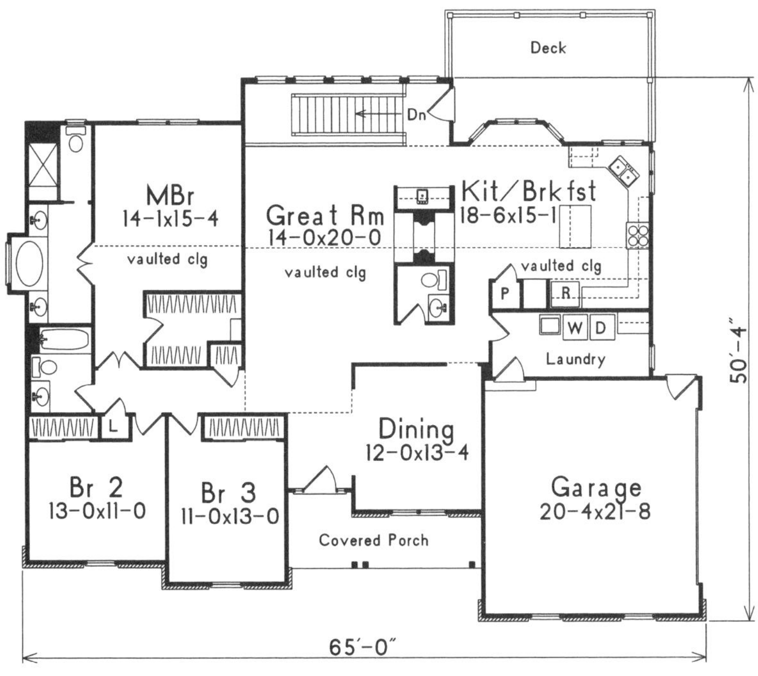
Deck
Dn
MBr
14-1x15-4
vaulted clg
Great Rm
14-0x20-0
vaulted clg
Kit/Brkfst
18-6x15-1
vaulted clg
P
R
W
D
Laundry
L
Dining
12-0x13-4
Br 2
13-0x11-0
Br 3
11-0x13-0
Covered Porch
Garage
20-4x21-8
50'-4"
65'-0"

Plan #530-058D-0025

Price Code C

Total Living Area: 2,164 Sq. Ft.

Home has 3 bedrooms, 2 1/2 baths, 2-car side entry garage and basement foundation.

Special features

- Great design for entertaining with a wet bar and see-through fireplace in the great room
- Plenty of closet space
- Vaulted ceilings enlarge the master bedroom, great room and kitchen/breakfast area
- Great room features great view to the rear of the home

LOWE'S Signature SERIES

Classic Atrium Ranch With Rooms To Spare

Plan #530-007D-0077

Price Code C

Total Living Area: 1,977 Sq. Ft.

Home has 4 bedrooms, 2 1/2 baths, 3-car side entry garage and walk-out basement foundation.

Special features

- Classic traditional exterior is always in style
- Spacious great room boasts a vaulted ceiling, dining area, atrium with elegant staircase and feature windows
- Atrium opens to 1,416 square feet of optional living area below which consists of a family room, two bedrooms, two baths and a study

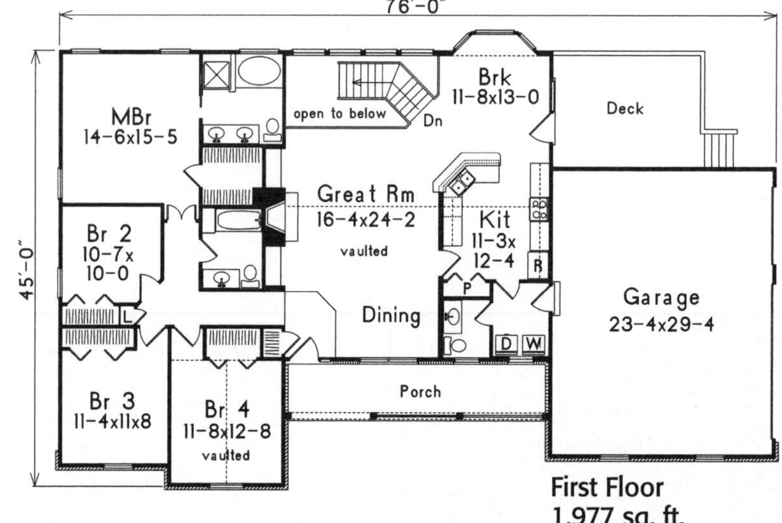
76'-0"
45'-0"
MBr
14-6x15-5
open to below
Dn
Brk
11-8x13-0
Deck
Great Rm
16-4x24-2
vaulted
Kit
11-3x
12-4
R
P
Br 2
10-7x
10-0
L
Dining
D
W
Garage
23-4x29-4
Porch
Br 3
11-4x11x8
Br 4
11-8x12-8
vaulted

First Floor
1,977 sq. ft.

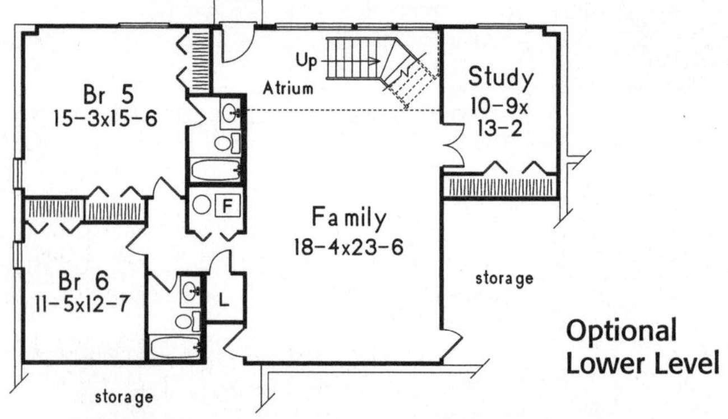
Up
Atrium
Br 5
15-3x15-6
Study
10-9x
13-2
F
Family
18-4x23-6
storage
Br 6
11-5x12-7
L
storage

Optional
Lower Level

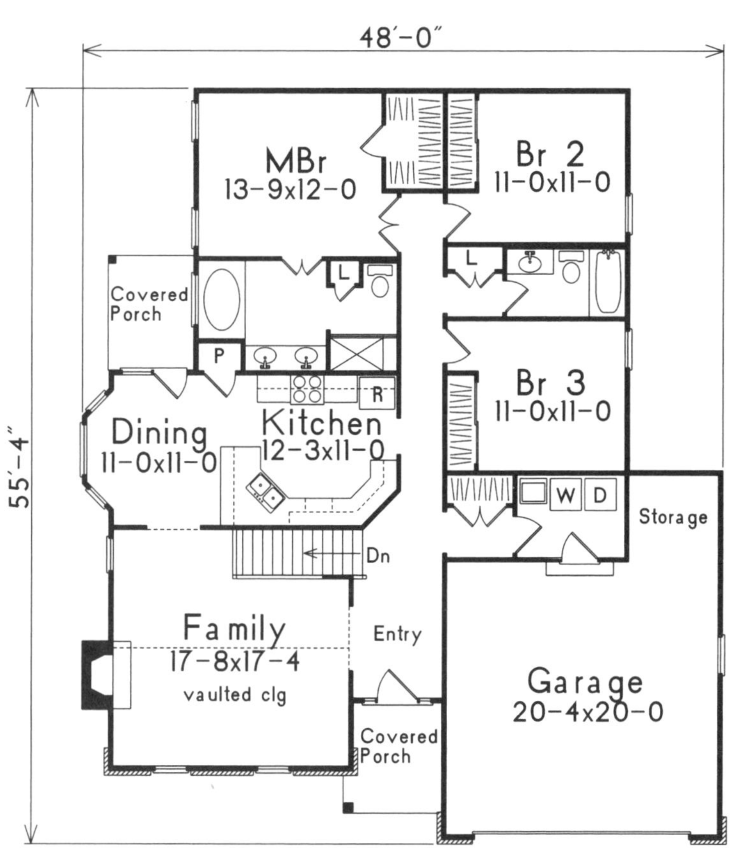
48'-0"
55'-4"
MBr
13-9x12-0
Br 2
11-0x11-0
Covered Porch
P
L
L
R
Dining
11-0x11-0
Kitchen
12-3x11-0
Br 3
11-0x11-0
W
D
Storage
Dn
Family
17-8x17-4
vaulted clg
Entry
Covered Porch
Garage
20-4x20-0

Plan #530-058D-0024

Price Code B

Total Living Area: 1,598 Sq. Ft.

Home has 3 bedrooms, 2 baths, 2-car garage and basement foundation.

Special features

- Double-door entry into master bedroom with luxurious master bath
- Entry opens into large family room with vaulted ceiling and open stairway to basement
- Additional storage area in garage

LOWE'S

Signature
SERIES

Plan #530-007D-0078

Price Code D

Total Living Area: 2,514 Sq. Ft.

Home has 3 bedrooms, 2 baths, 3-car side entry garage and walk-out basement foundation.

Special features

- Expansive porch welcomes you to the foyer, spacious dining area with bay and a gallery-sized hall with plant shelf above
- A highly functional U-shaped kitchen is open to a bayed breakfast room, study and family room with a 46' vista
- Vaulted rear sunroom has fireplace
- 1,509 square feet of optional living area on the lower level with recreation room, bedroom #4 with bath and an office with storage closet
- Extra storage in garage

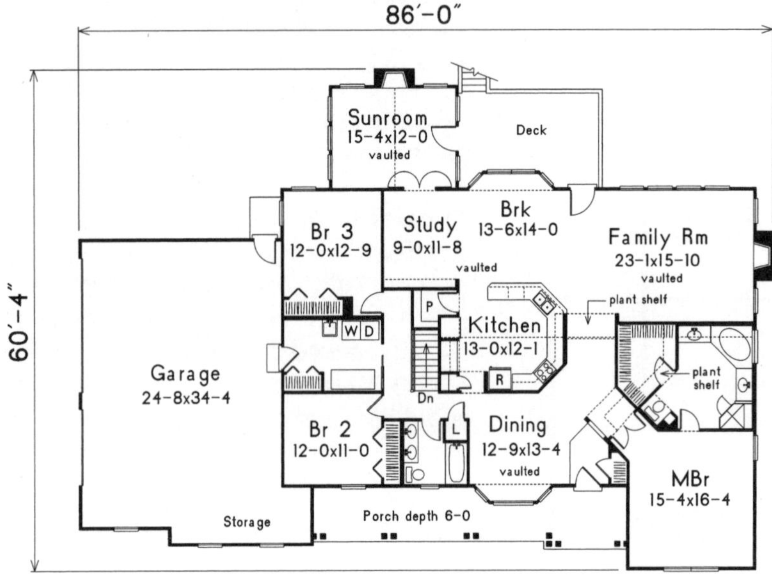
86'-0"
60'-4"
Sunroom
15-4x12-0
vaulted
Deck
Brk
13-6x14-0
Study
9-0x11-8
vaulted
Br 3
12-0x12-9
Family Rm
23-1x15-10
vaulted
plant shelf
Kitchen
13-0x12-1
W D
P
R
plant shelf
Garage
24-8x34-4
Dn
Br 2
12-0x11-0
L
Dining
12-9x13-4
vaulted
MBr
15-4x16-4
Storage
Porch depth 6-0

LOWE'S

Signature SERIES

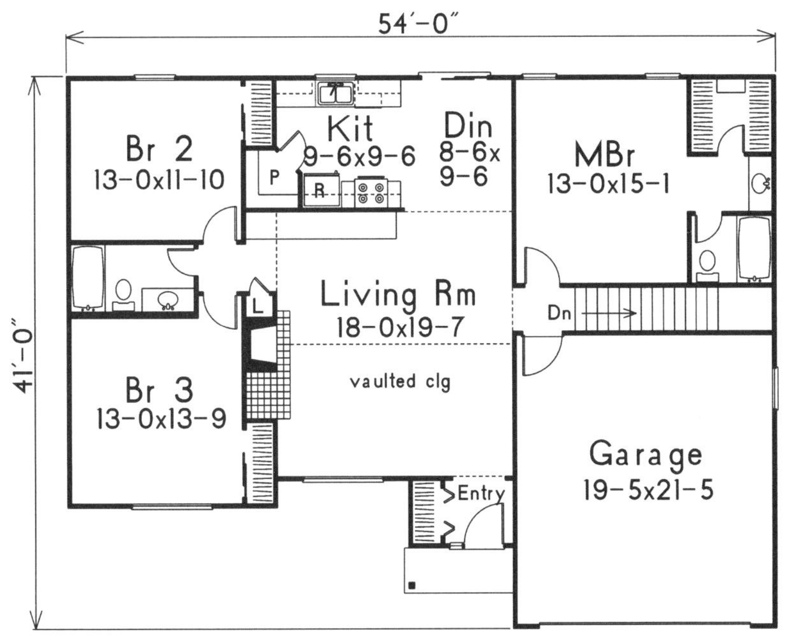
54'-0"
41'-0"
Br 2
13-0x11-10
Kit
9-6x9-6
Din
8-6x
9-6
MBr
13-0x15-1
P
R
L
Living Rm
18-0x19-7
vaulted clg
Dn
Br 3
13-0x13-9
Garage
19-5x21-5
Entry

Plan #530-068D-0005

Price Code A

Total Living Area: 1,433 Sq. Ft.

Home has 3 bedrooms, 2 baths, 2-car garage and basement foundation, drawings also include crawl space and slab foundations.

Special features

- Vaulted living room includes a cozy fireplace and an oversized entertainment center
- Bedrooms #2 and #3 share a full bath
- Master bedroom has a full bath and large walk-in closet

LOWE'S

Signature SERIES

Four Bedroom Living For A Narrow Lot

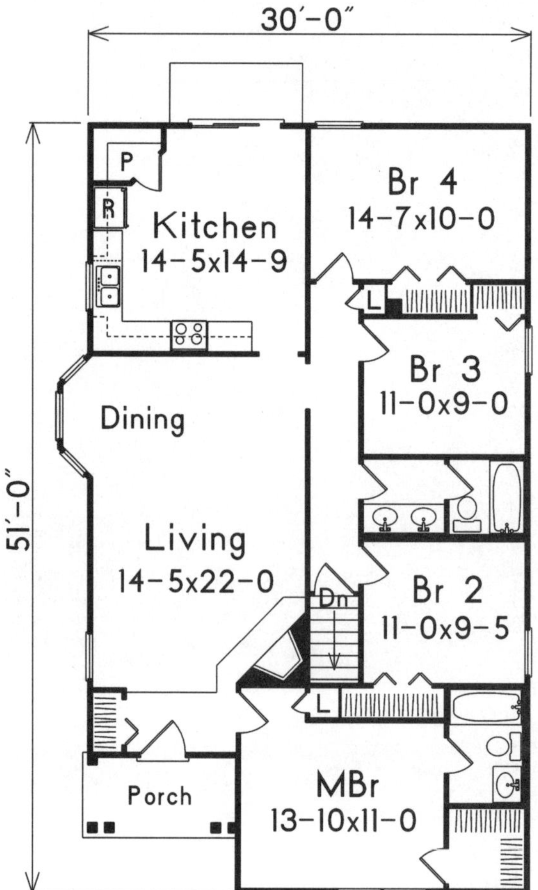
30'-0"
51'-0"
P
R
Kitchen
14-5x14-9
Br 4
14-7x10-0
L
Br 3
11-0x9-0
Dining
Living
14-5x22-0
Dn
Br 2
11-0x9-5
L
Porch
MBr
13-10x11-0

Plan #530-007D-0102

Price Code A

Total Living Area: 1,452 Sq. Ft.

Home has 4 bedrooms, 2 baths and basement foundation.

Special features

- Large living room features a cozy corner fireplace, bayed dining area and access from entry with guest closet
- Forward master bedroom enjoys having its own bath and linen closet
- Three additional bedrooms share a bath with a double-bowl vanity

Dormers Add Southern Accent

LOWE'S

Signature SERIES

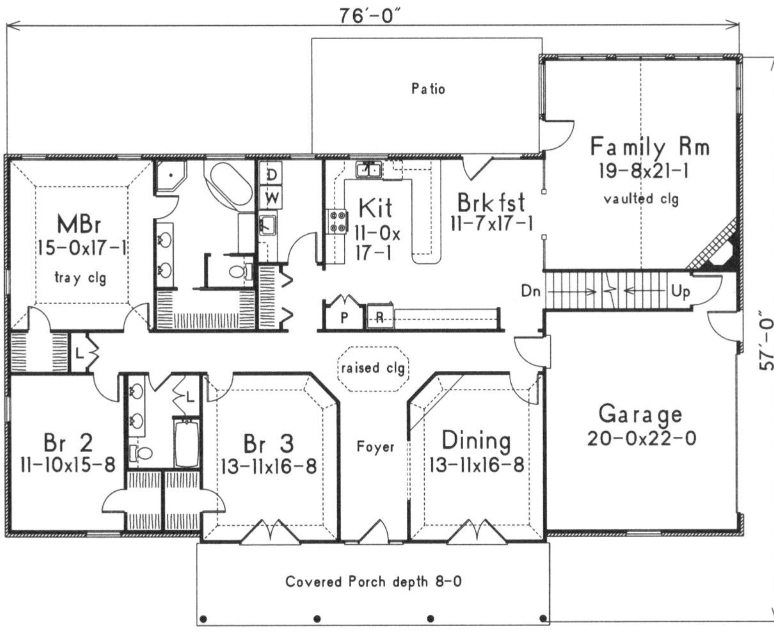

76'-0"
57'-0"
Patio
Family Rm
19-8x21-1
vaulted clg
Brk fst
11-7x17-1
Kit
11-0x
17-1
MBr
15-0x17-1
tray clg
D
W
Dn
Up
P
R
L
raised clg
Br 2
11-10x15-8
Br 3
13-11x16-8
Foyer
Dining
13-11x16-8
Garage
20-0x22-0
Covered Porch depth 8-0

Plan #530-068D-0008

Price Code E

Total Living Area: 2,651 Sq. Ft.

Home has 3 bedrooms, 2 baths, 2-car side entry garage and basement foundation, drawings also include crawl space and slab foundations.

Special features

- Vaulted family room has a corner fireplace and access to the breakfast room and outdoor patio
- Dining room has a double-door entry from the covered front porch and a beautiful built-in corner display area
- Master bedroom has a 10' tray ceiling, private bath and two walk-in closets
- Kitchen has an enormous amount of counterspace with plenty of eating area and overlooks a cheerful breakfast room

Exciting Living For A Narrow Sloping Lot

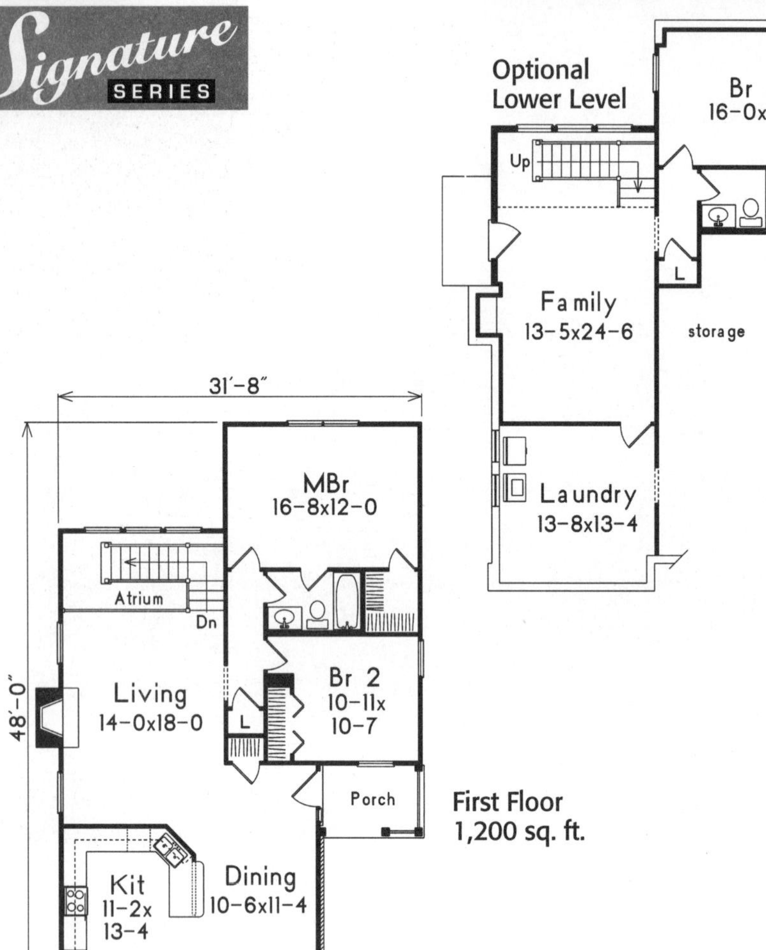
Optional
Lower Level
Br 3
16-0x11-4
Up
L
Family
13-5x24-6
storage
Laundry
13-8x13-4
31'-8"
48'-0"
MBr
16-8x12-0
Atrium
Dn
Living
14-0x18-0
L
Br 2
10-11x
10-7
Porch
Kit
11-2x
13-4
Dining
10-6x11-4
R
P
First Floor
1,200 sq. ft.

Plan #530-007D-0106

Price Code A

Total Living Area: 1,200 Sq. Ft.

Home has 2 bedrooms, 1 bath and walk-out basement foundation.

Special features

- Entry leads to a large dining area which opens to the kitchen and sun-drenched living room
- An expansive window wall in the two-story atrium lends space and light to living room with fireplace
- The large kitchen features a breakfast bar, built-in pantry and storage galore
- 697 square feet of optional living area on the lower level includes a family room, bedroom #3 and a bath

LOWE'S

Signature SERIES

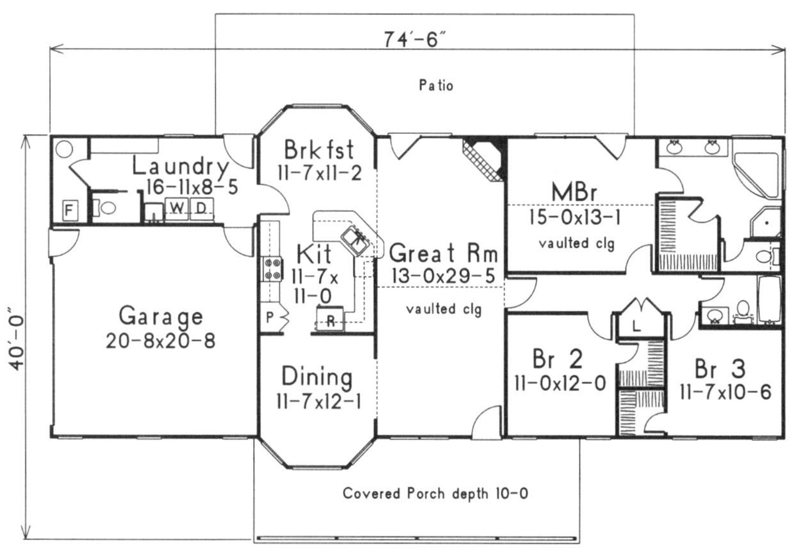
74'-6"
Patio
Laundry
16-11x8-5
W D
F
Brkfst
11-7x11-2
Kit
11-7x
11-0
P
R
Great Rm
13-0x29-5
vaulted clg
MBr
15-0x13-1
vaulted clg
Garage
20-8x20-8
Dining
11-7x12-1
Br 2
11-0x12-0
L
Br 3
11-7x10-6
40'-0"
Covered Porch depth 10-0

Plan #530-068D-0010

Price Code C

Total Living Area: 1,849 Sq. Ft.

Home has 3 bedrooms, 2 1/2 baths, 2-car side entry garage and slab foundation, drawings also include crawl space foundation.

Special features

- Enormous laundry/mud room has many extras including a storage area and half bath
- Lavish master bath has a corner jacuzzi tub, double sinks, separate shower and walk-in closet
- Secondary bedrooms include walk-in closets
- Kitchen has a wrap-around eating counter and is positioned between the formal dining area and breakfast room for convenience

LOWE'S

Signature
SERIES

Three Bedroom Luxury In A Small Home

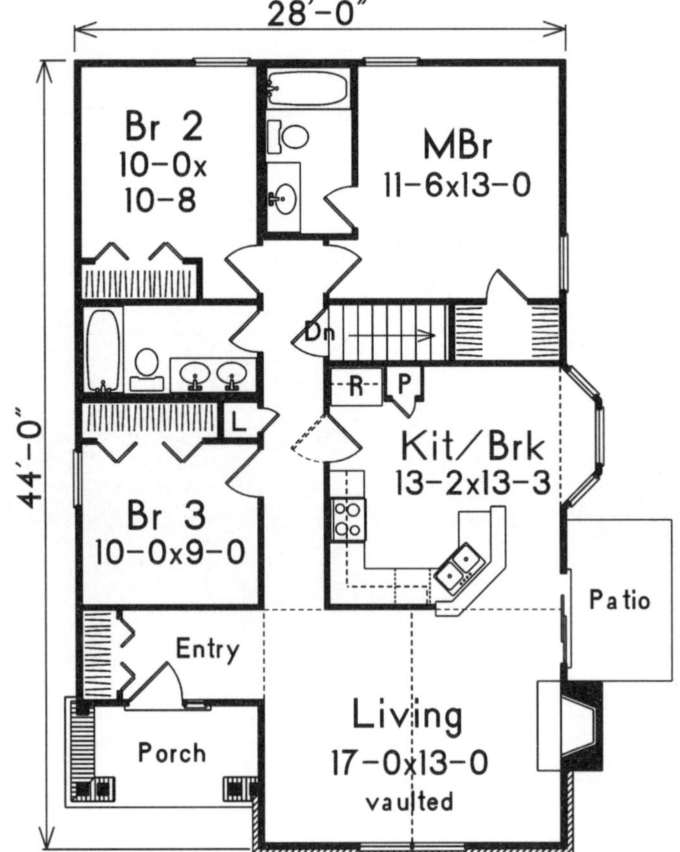
28'-0"
44'-0"
Br 2
10-0x
10-8
MBr
11-6x13-0
Dn
R
P
L
Kit/Brk
13-2x13-3
Br 3
10-0x9-0
Patio
Entry
Porch
Living
17-0x13-0
vaulted

Plan #530-007D-0107

Price Code AA

Total Living Area: 1,161 Sq. Ft.

Home has 3 bedrooms, 2 baths and basement foundation.

Special features

- Brickwork and feature window add elegance to this home for a narrow lot
- Living room enjoys a vaulted ceiling, fireplace and opens to kitchen
- U-shaped kitchen offers a breakfast area with bay window, snack bar and built-in pantry

Colossal Great Room

LOWE'S

Signature SERIES

Plan #530-068D-0007

Price Code B

Total Living Area: 1,599 Sq. Ft.

Home has 4 bedrooms, 2 baths, 2-car garage and basement foundation, drawings also include crawl space and slab foundations.

Special features

- Efficiently designed kitchen includes a large pantry and easy access to the laundry room
- Bedroom #3 has a charming window seat
- Master bedroom has a full bath and large walk-in closet

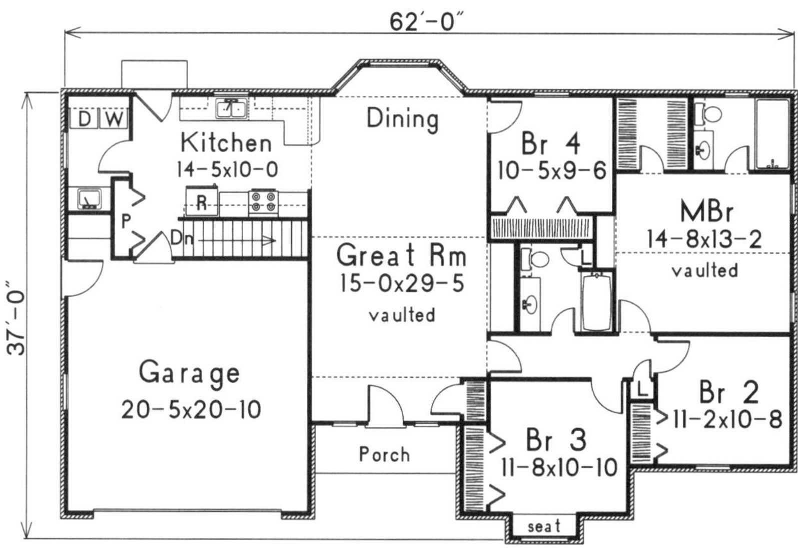
62'-0"
37'-0"
D W
Kitchen
14-5x10-0
R
P
Dn
Dining
Great Rm
15-0x29-5
vaulted
Br 4
10-5x9-6
MBr
14-8x13-2
vaulted
Garage
20-5x20-10
Porch
Br 3
11-8x10-10
seat
Br 2
11-2x10-8
L

LOWE'S

Signature SERIES

Stylish Retreat For A Narrow Lot

Plan #530-007D-0105

Price Code AA

Total Living Area: 1,084 Sq. Ft.

Home has 2 bedrooms, 2 baths and basement foundation.

Special features

- Delightful country porch for quiet evenings
- The living room offers a front feature window which invites the sun and includes a fireplace and dining area with private patio
- The U-shaped kitchen features lots of cabinets and bayed breakfast room with built-in pantry
- Both bedrooms have walk-in closets and access to their own bath

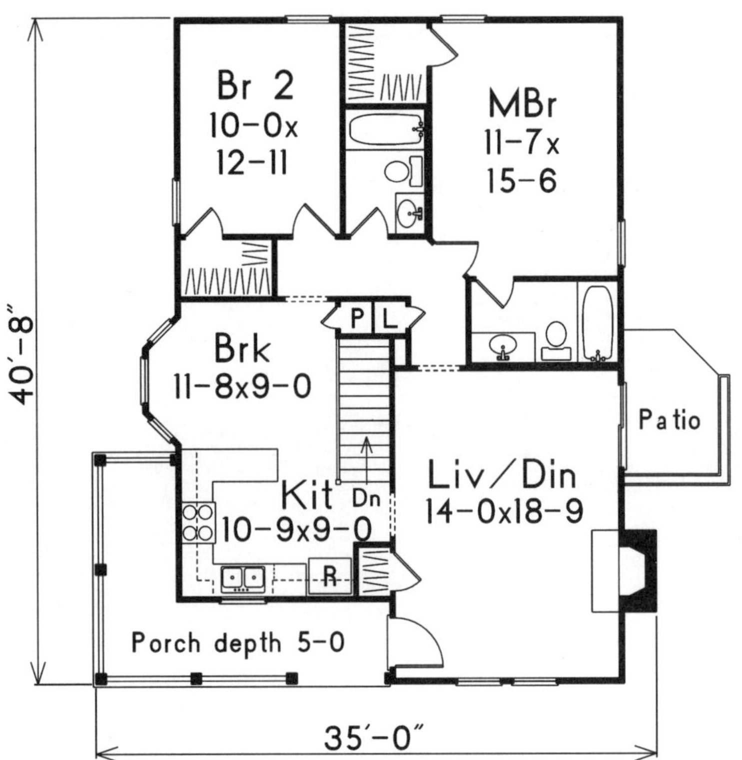
Br 2
10-0x
12-11
MBr
11-7x
15-6
Brk
11-8x9-0
P
L
Patio
Kit
10-9x9-0
Dn
R
Liv/Din
14-0x18-9
Porch depth 5-0
40'-8"
35'-0"

TO ORDER BLUEPRINTS USE THE FORM ON PAGE 288 OR CALL TOLL-FREE **1-800-DREAM HOME** (373-2646)

LOWE'S

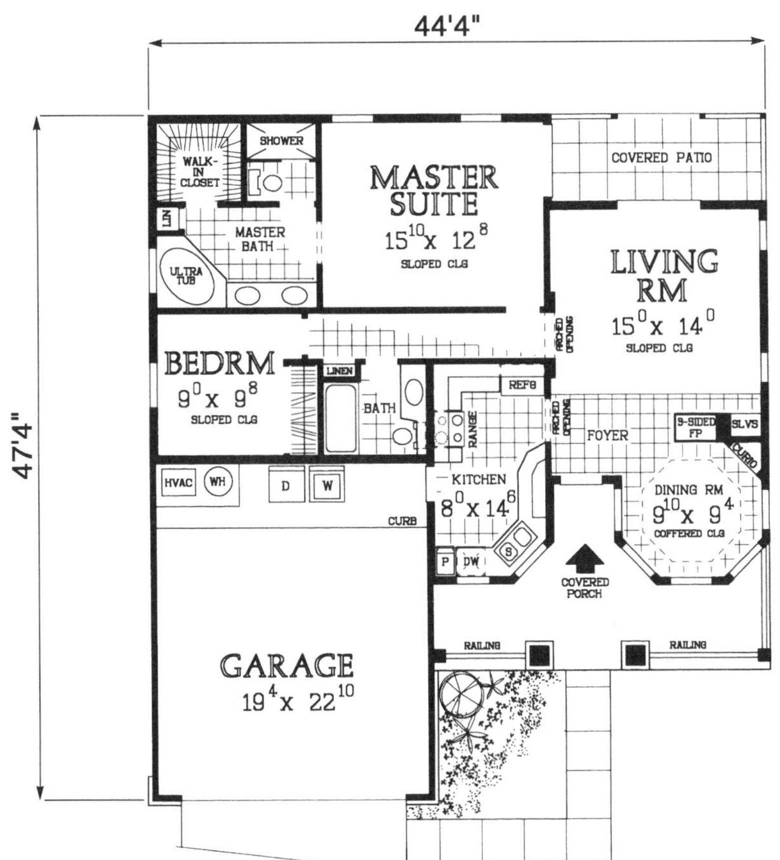
44'4"
47'4"
WALK-IN CLOSET
SHOWER
LIN
MASTER BATH
ULTRA TUB
MASTER SUITE
15^10 x 12^8
SLOPED CLG
COVERED PATIO
LIVING RM
15^0 x 14^0
SLOPED CLG
ARCHED OPENING
BEDRM
9^0 x 9^8
SLOPED CLG
LINEN
BATH
REFG
RANGE
FOYER
9-SIDED FP
SLVS
CURIO
HVAC
WH
D
W
KITCHEN
8^0 x 14^6
DINING RM
9^10 x 9^4
COFFERED CLG
CURB
P
DW
S
COVERED PORCH
RAILING
RAILING
GARAGE
19^4 x 22^10

Plan #530-049D-0007

Price Code AA

Total Living Area: 1,118 Sq. Ft.

Home has 2 bedrooms, 2 baths, 2-car garage and slab foundation.

Special features

- Convenient kitchen has direct access into garage and looks out onto front covered porch
- The covered patio is enjoyed by both the living room and master suite
- Octagon-shaped dining room adds interest to the front exterior while the interior is sunny and bright

Trio Of Dormers Adds Appeal

Plan #530-031D-0011

Price Code C

Total Living Area: 2,164 Sq. Ft.

Home has 4 bedrooms, 2 1/2 baths, 2-car side entry garage and slab foundation.

Special features

- Country-styled front porch adds charm
- Plenty of counterspace in the kitchen
- Large utility area meets big families' laundry needs
- French doors lead to the covered rear porch

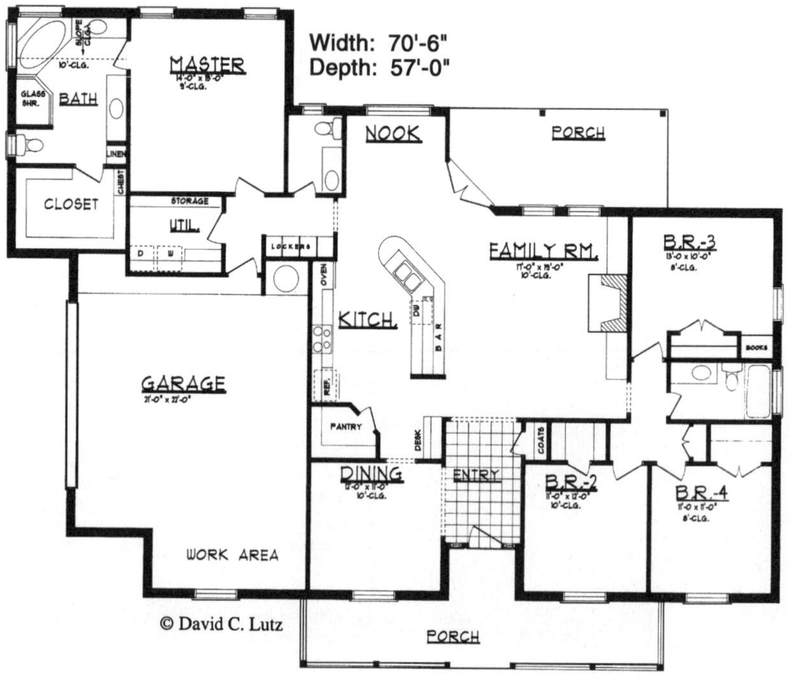
Width: 70'-6"
Depth: 57'-0"
MASTER
BATH
GLASS SHR.
CLOSET
STORAGE
UTIL.
LOCKERS
NOOK
PORCH
FAMILY RM.
KITCH.
B.R.-3
GARAGE
PANTRY
DINING
ENTRY
B.R.-2
B.R.-4
WORK AREA
PORCH

© David C. Lutz

LOWE'S

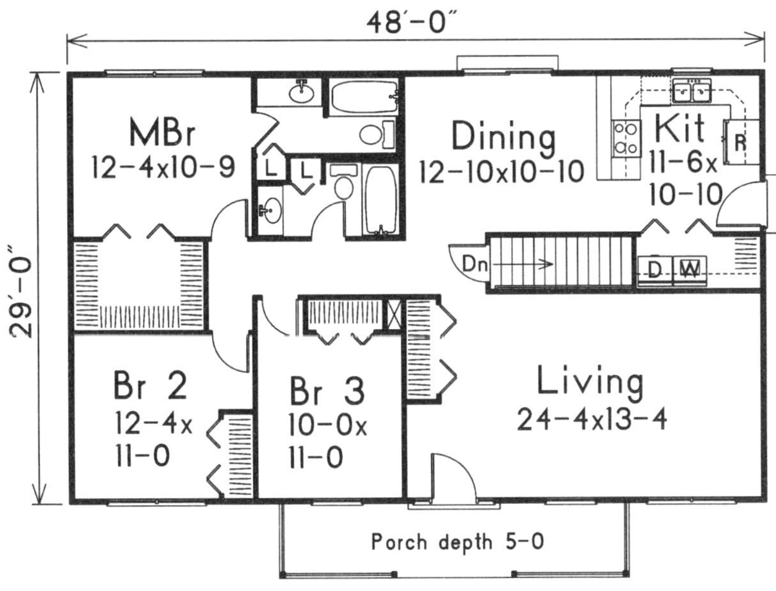
48'-0"
29'-0"
MBr
12-4x10-9
Dining
12-10x10-10
Kit
11-6x
10-10
R
L
L
Dn
D
W
Br 2
12-4x
11-0
Br 3
10-0x
11-0
Living
24-4x13-4
Porch depth 5-0

Plan #530-008D-0094

Price Code A

Total Living Area: 1,364 Sq. Ft.

Home has 3 bedrooms, 2 baths, optional 2-car garage and basement foundation, drawings also include crawl space foundation.

Special features

- Master bedroom features a spacious walk-in closet and private bath
- Living room is highlighted with several windows
- Kitchen with snack bar is adjacent to the dining area
- Plenty of storage space throughout

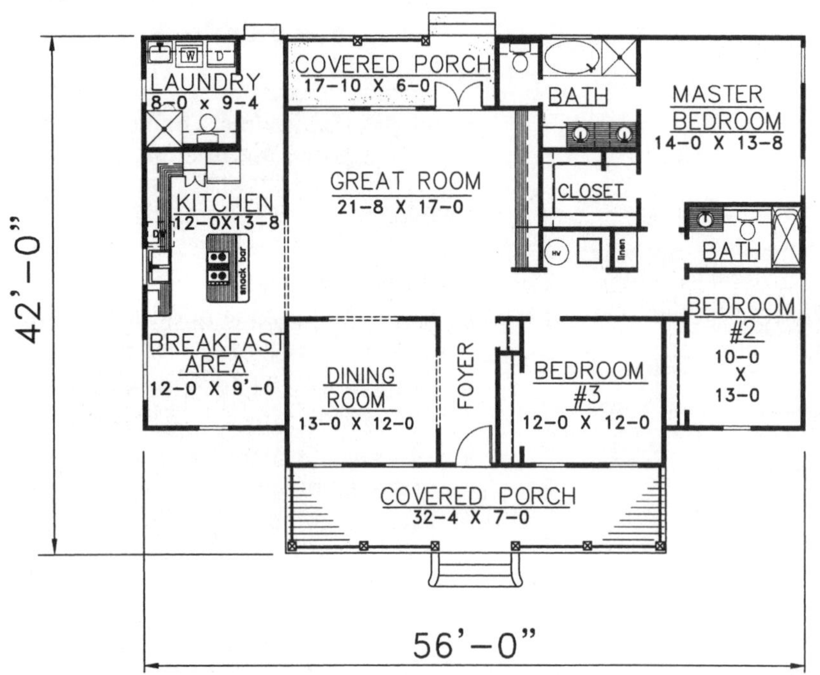
COVERED PORCH
17-10 X 6-0
LAUNDRY
8-0 x 9-4
BATH
MASTER
BEDROOM
14-0 X 13-8
GREAT ROOM
21-8 X 17-0
CLOSET
KITCHEN
12-0X13-8
snack bar
linen
BATH
BEDROOM
#2
10-0
X
13-0
BREAKFAST
AREA
12-0 X 9'-0
DINING
ROOM
13-0 X 12-0
FOYER
BEDROOM
#3
12-0 X 12-0
COVERED PORCH
32-4 X 7-0
42'-0"
56'-0"

Plan #530-028D-0004

Price Code B

Total Living Area: 1,785 Sq. Ft.

Home has 3 bedrooms, 3 baths, 2-car detached garage and basement, crawl space or slab foundation, please specify when ordering.

Special features

- 9' ceilings throughout home
- Luxurious master bath includes a whirlpool tub and separate shower
- Cozy breakfast area is convenient to the kitchen

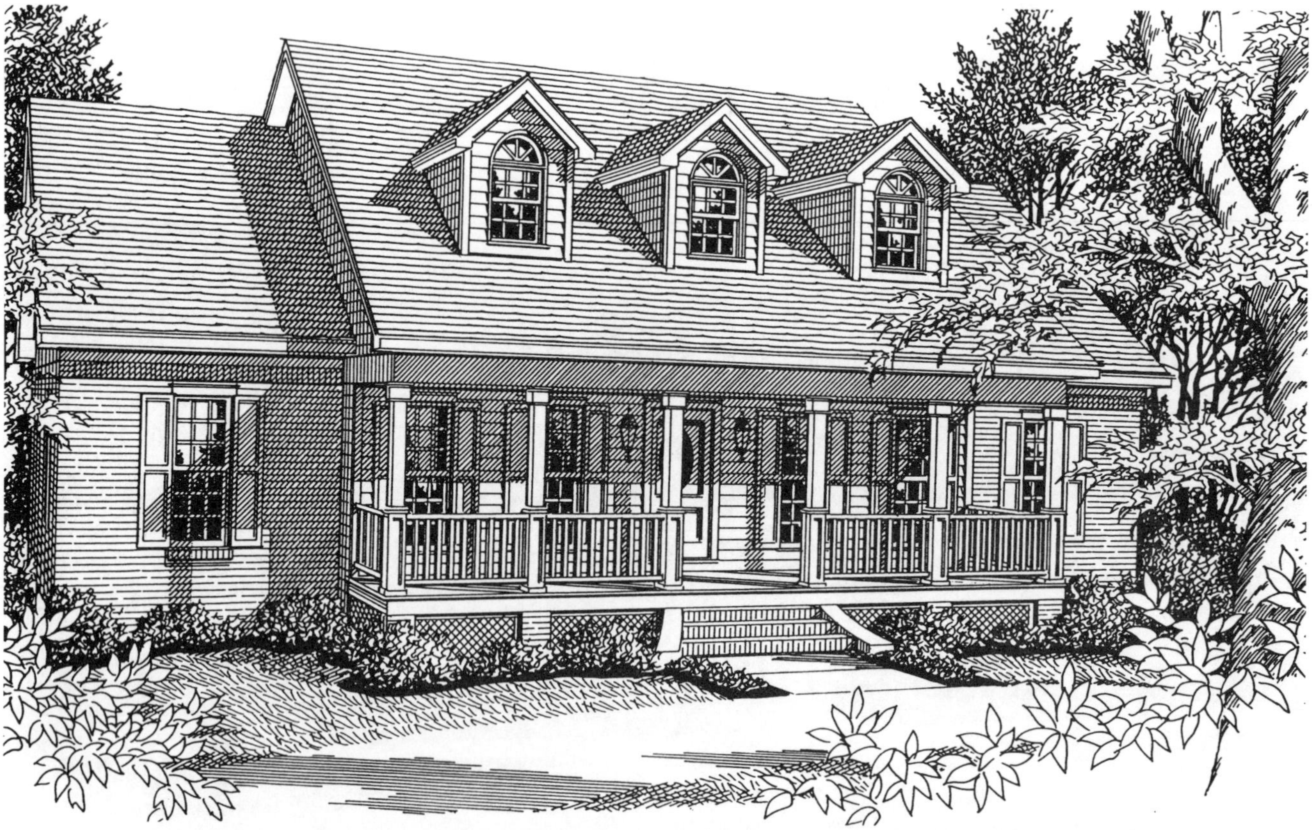

Corner Window Wall

LOWE'S

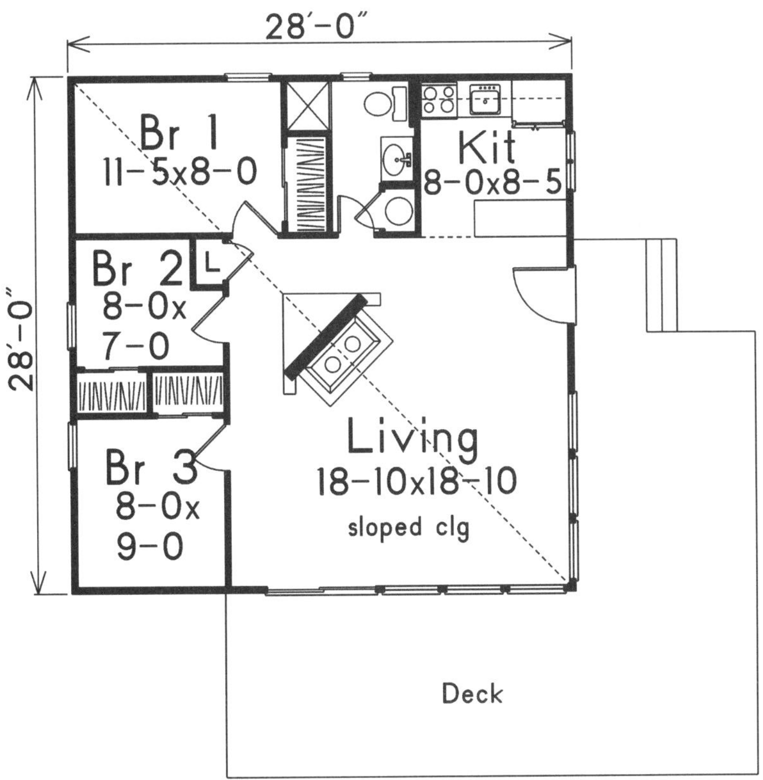
28'-0"
28'-0"
Br 1
11-5x8-0
Kit
8-0x8-5
Br 2
8-0x
7-0
Br 3
8-0x
9-0
Living
18-10x18-10
sloped clg
Deck

Plan #530-008D-0148

Price Code AAA

Total Living Area: 784 Sq. Ft.

Home has 3 bedrooms, 1 bath and a pier foundation.

Special features

- Outdoor relaxation will be enjoyed with this home's huge wrap-around wood deck
- Upon entering the spacious living area, a cozy free-standing fireplace, sloped ceiling and corner window wall catch the eye
- Charming kitchen features pass-through peninsula to dining area

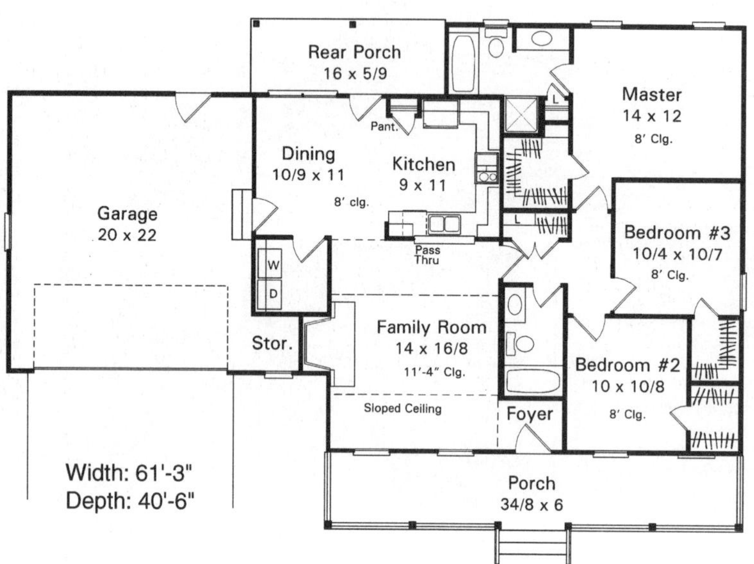
Rear Porch
16 x 5/9
Master
14 x 12
8' Clg.
Dining
10/9 x 11
8' clg.
Pant.
Kitchen
9 x 11
Garage
20 x 22
Bedroom #3
10/4 x 10/7
8' Clg.
Pass Thru
W
D
Family Room
14 x 16/8
11'-4" Clg.
Stor.
Bedroom #2
10 x 10/8
8' Clg.
Sloped Ceiling
Foyer
Width: 61'-3"
Depth: 40'-6"
Porch
34/8 x 6

Plan #530-039D-0001

Price Code A

Total Living Area: 1,253 Sq. Ft.

Home has 3 bedrooms, 2 baths, 2-car garage and crawl space or slab foundation, please specify when ordering.

Special features

- Sloped ceiling and fireplace in family room add drama
- U-shaped kitchen is efficiently designed
- Large walk-in closets are found in all the bedrooms

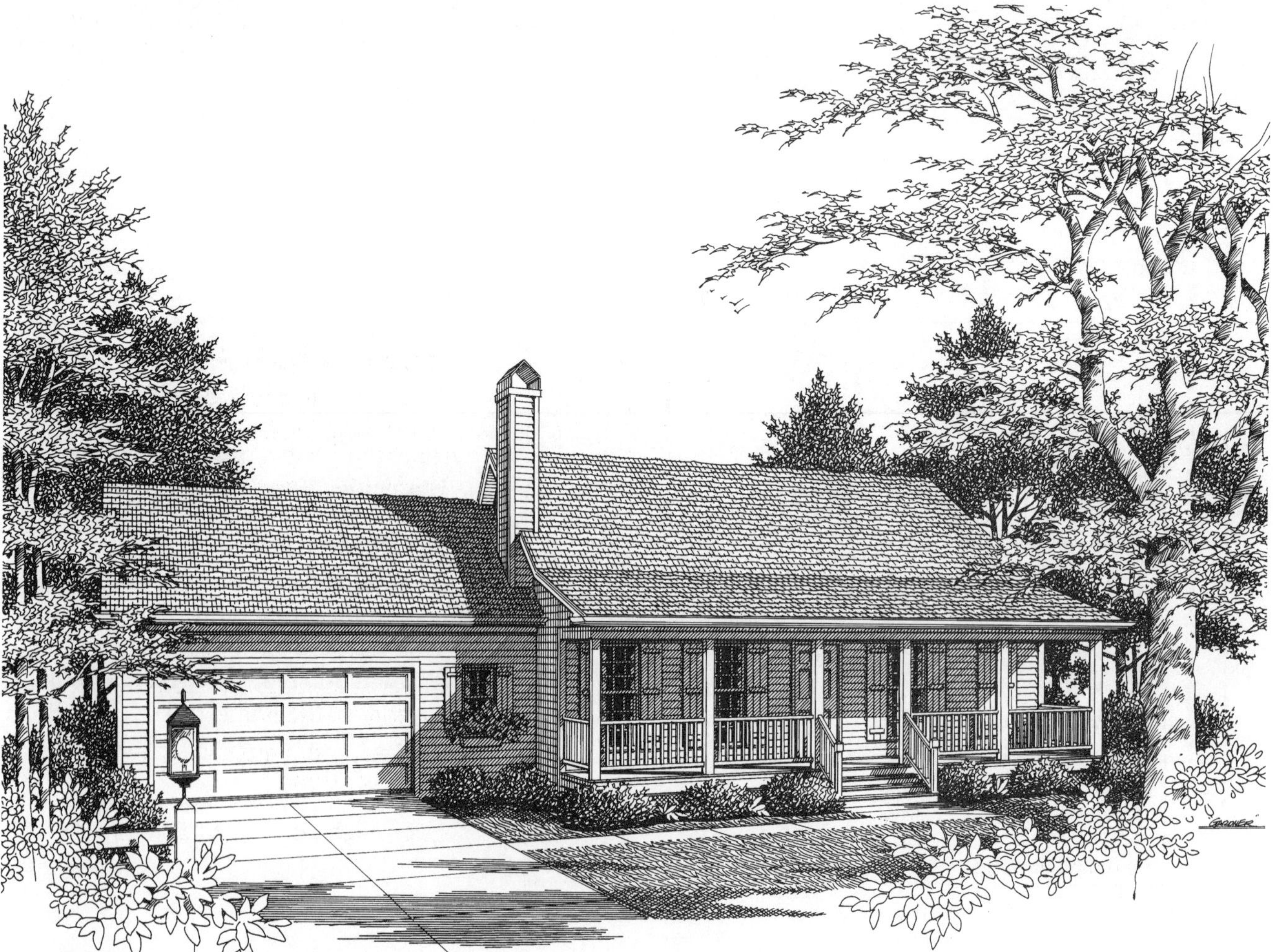

LOWE'S

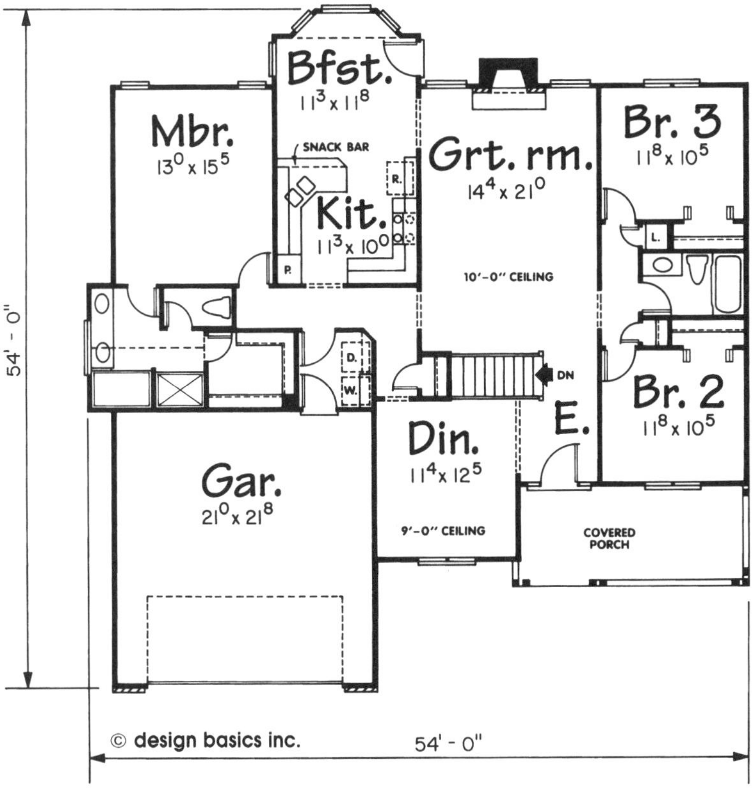

Plan #530-026D-0155

Price Code B

Total Living Area: 1,691 Sq. Ft.

Home has 3 bedrooms, 2 baths, 2-car garage and basement foundation.

Special features

- Bay windowed breakfast room allows for plenty of sunlight
- Large inviting covered porch in the front of the home
- Great room fireplace is surrounded by windows

Plan #530-020D-0015

Price Code AA

Total Living Area: 1,191 Sq. Ft.

Home has 3 bedrooms, 2 baths, 2-car side entry garage and slab foundation, drawings also include crawl space foundation.

Special features

- Energy efficient home with 2" x 6" exterior walls
- Master bedroom is located near living areas for maximum convenience
- Living room has a cathedral ceiling and stone fireplace

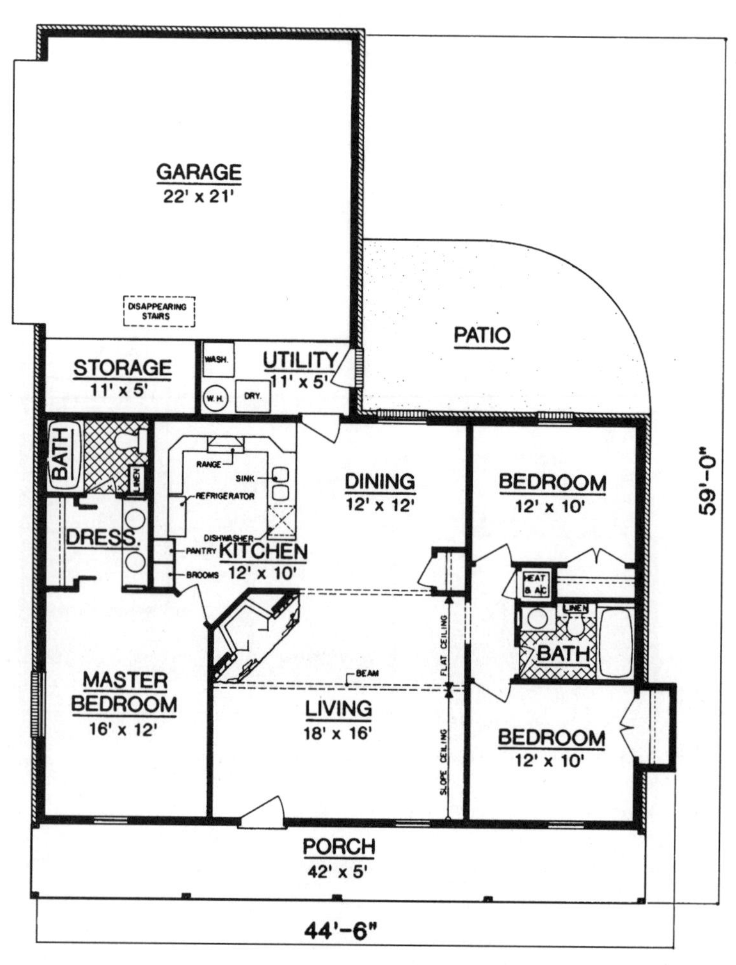
GARAGE
22' x 21'
DISAPPEARING STAIRS
STORAGE
11' x 5'
WASH.
UTILITY
11' x 5'
W.H.
DRY.
PATIO
BATH
DRESS.
RANGE
SINK
REFRIGERATOR
DISHWASHER
PANTRY
BROOMS
KITCHEN
12' x 10'
DINING
12' x 12'
BEDROOM
12' x 10'
HEAT & A/C
BATH
BEAM
FLAT CEILING
SLOPE CEILING
MASTER BEDROOM
16' x 12'
LIVING
18' x 16'
BEDROOM
12' x 10'
PORCH
42' x 5'
59'-0"
44'-6"

LOWE'S

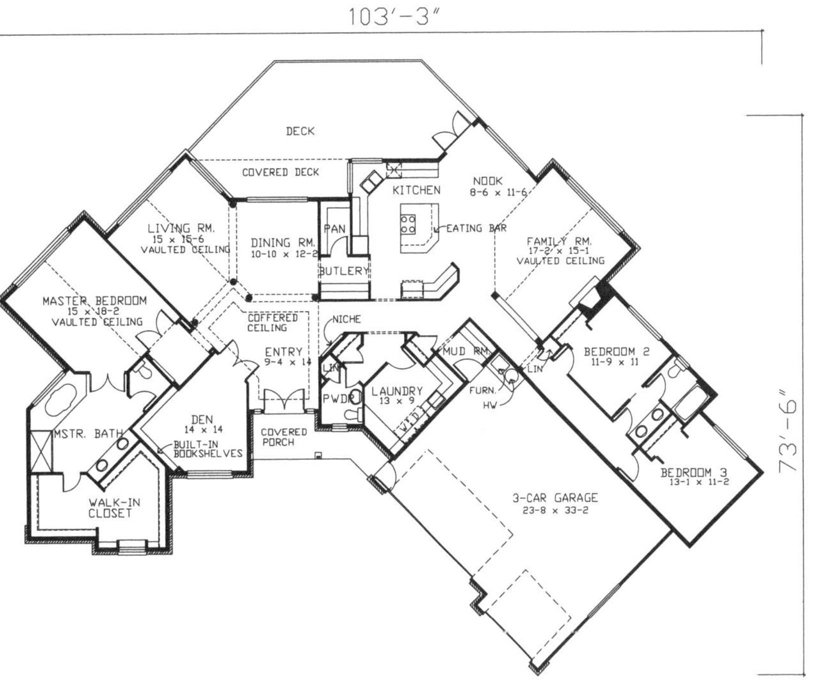
103'-3"
73'-6"
DECK
COVERED DECK
KITCHEN
NOOK
8-6 x 11-6
LIVING RM.
15 x 16-6
VAULTED CEILING
DINING RM.
10-10 x 12-2
PAN
EATING BAR
FAMILY RM.
17-2 x 15-1
VAULTED CEILING
BUTLERY
MASTER BEDROOM
15 x 18-2
VAULTED CEILING
COFFERED CEILING
NICHE
ENTRY
9-4 x 14
MUD RM.
BEDROOM 2
11-9 x 11
LIN
LAUNDRY
13 x 9
PWDR
FURN.
HW
MSTR. BATH
DEN
14 x 14
BUILT-IN BOOKSHELVES
COVERED PORCH
BEDROOM 3
13-1 x 11-2
3-CAR GARAGE
23-8 x 33-2
WALK-IN CLOSET

Plan #530-043D-0001

Price Code E

Total Living Area: 3,158 Sq. Ft.

Home has 3 bedrooms, 2 1/2 baths, 3-car garage and crawl space foundation.

Special features

- Coffered ceiling in entry
- Vaulted ceilings grace the living room, master bedroom and family room
- Interior columns accent the entry, living and dining areas
- Kitchen island has an eating bar adding extra seating
- Master bath has a garden tub and a separate shower

Plan #530-025D-0003

Price Code A

Total Living Area: 1,379 Sq. Ft.

Home has 3 bedrooms, 2 baths, 2-car garage and slab foundation.

Special features

- Vaulted great room makes a lasting impression with corner fireplace and windows
- Formal dining room easily connects to kitchen making entertaining easy
- Master bath includes all the luxuries such as a spacious walk-in closet, oversized tub and separate shower

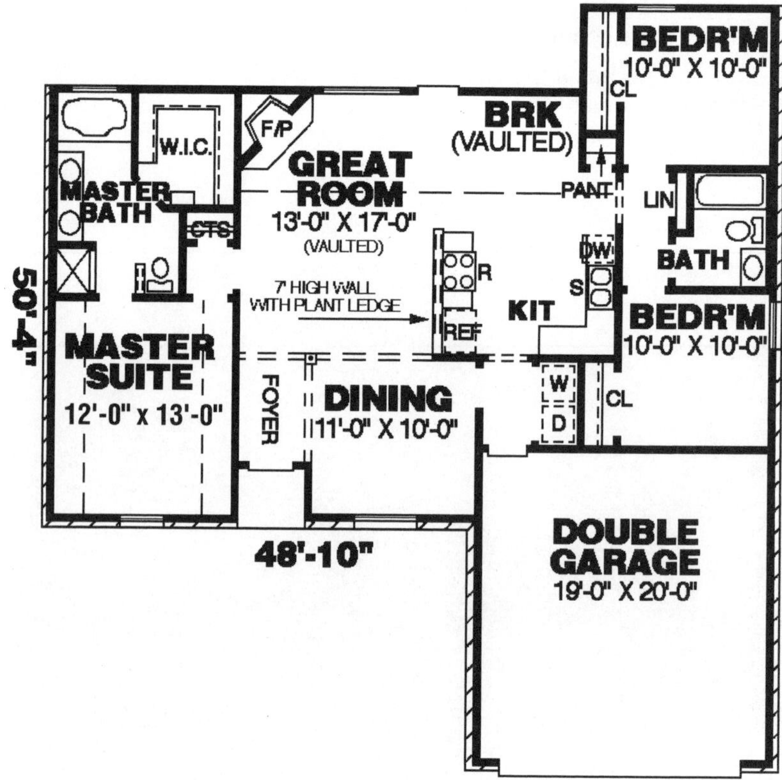
BEDR'M
10'-0" X 10'-0"
CL
BRK
(VAULTED)
F/P
W.I.C.
GREAT ROOM
13'-0" X 17'-0"
(VAULTED)
MASTER BATH
CTS
PANT
LIN
BATH
DW
R
S
7' HIGH WALL WITH PLANT LEDGE
KIT
REF
BEDR'M
10'-0" X 10'-0"
50'-4"
MASTER SUITE
12'-0" x 13'-0"
FOYER
DINING
11'-0" X 10'-0"
W
D
CL
48'-10"
DOUBLE GARAGE
19'-0" X 20'-0"

 TO ORDER BLUEPRINTS USE THE FORM ON PAGE 288 OR CALL TOLL-FREE **1-800-DREAM HOME** (373-2646)

Riverside Views From Covered Deck

LOWE'S

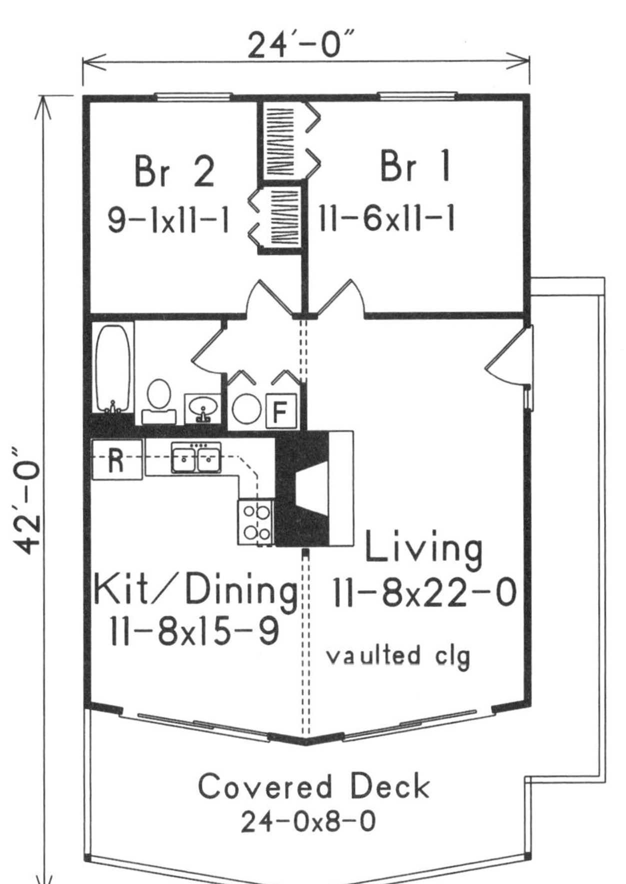
24'-0"
42'-0"
Br 2
9-1x11-1
Br 1
11-6x11-1
R
F
Living
11-8x22-0
Kit/Dining
11-8x15-9
vaulted clg
Covered Deck
24-0x8-0

Plan #530-008D-0153

Price Code AAA

Total Living Area: 792 Sq. Ft.

Home has 2 bedrooms, 1 bath and crawl space foundation, drawings also include slab foundation.

Special features

- Attractive exterior features wood posts and beams, wrap-around deck with railing and glass sliding doors with transoms
- Kitchen, living and dining areas enjoy sloped ceilings, a cozy fireplace and views over the deck
- Two bedrooms share a bath just off the hall

LOWE'S

Plan #530-008D-0110

Price Code B

Total Living Area: 1,500 Sq. Ft.

Home has 3 bedrooms, 2 baths, 2-car garage and basement foundation.

Special features

- Living room features a cathedral ceiling and opens to the breakfast room
- Breakfast room has a spectacular bay window and adjoins a well-appointed kitchen with generous storage
- Laundry is convenient to the kitchen and includes a large closet
- Large walk-in closet gives the master bedroom abundant storage

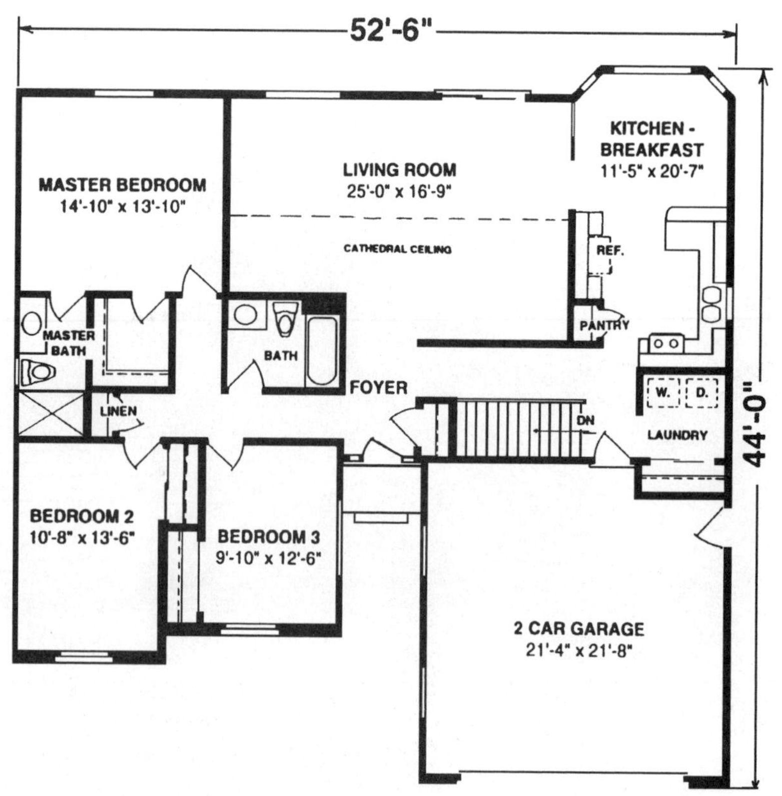
52'-6"
44'-0"
KITCHEN - BREAKFAST
11'-5" x 20'-7"
LIVING ROOM
25'-0" x 16'-9"
MASTER BEDROOM
14'-10" x 13'-10"
CATHEDRAL CEILING
REF.
PANTRY
MASTER BATH
BATH
FOYER
W.
D.
LINEN
DN
LAUNDRY
BEDROOM 2
10'-8" x 13'-6"
BEDROOM 3
9'-10" x 12'-6"
2 CAR GARAGE
21'-4" x 21'-8"

 TO ORDER BLUEPRINTS USE THE FORM ON PAGE 288 OR CALL TOLL-FREE **1-800-DREAM HOME** (373-2646)

LOWE'S

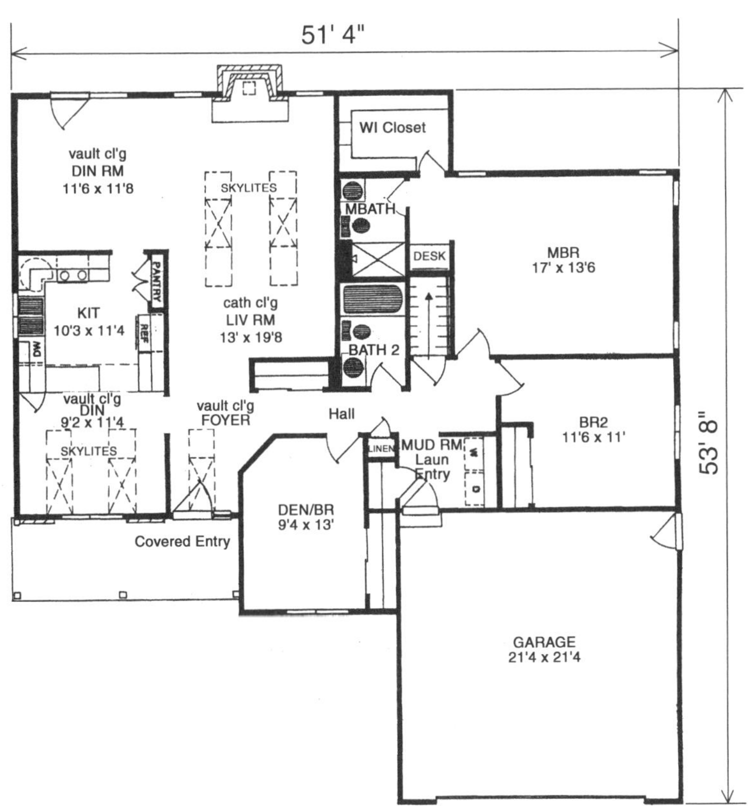
51' 4"
53' 8"
WI Closet
vault cl'g
DIN RM
11'6 x 11'8
SKYLITES
MBATH
DESK
MBR
17' x 13'6
KIT
10'3 x 11'4
PANTRY
REF
DW
cath cl'g
LIV RM
13' x 19'8
BATH 2
vault cl'g
DIN
9'2 x 11'4
SKYLITES
vault cl'g
FOYER
Hall
BR2
11'6 x 11'
LINEN
MUD RM
Laun
Entry
DEN/BR
9'4 x 13'
Covered Entry
GARAGE
21'4 x 21'4

Plan #530-034D-0003

Price Code B

Total Living Area: 1,629 Sq. Ft.

Home has 3 bedrooms, 2 baths, 2-car garage and basement foundation.

Special features

- A fireplace and cathedral ceiling in living room add drama
- Skylights in dining room and foyer brighten the entry and entertaining areas
- Efficiently designed kitchen is positioned between front and back dining areas

LOWE'S

Charming Country Facade

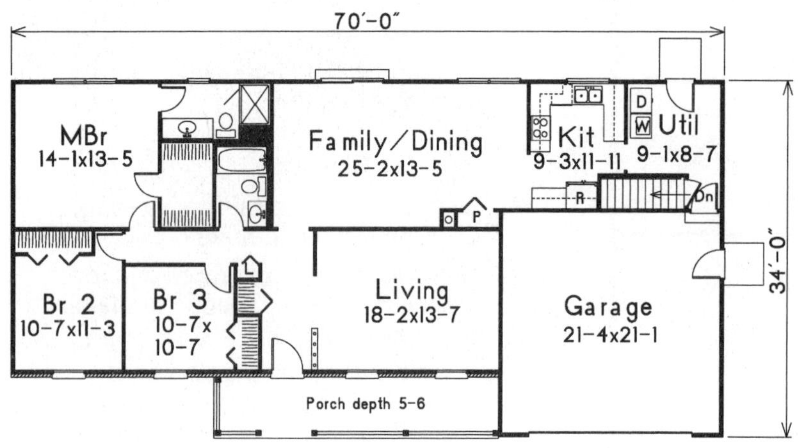
70'-0"
34'-0"
MBr
14-1x13-5
Family/Dining
25-2x13-5
Kit
9-3x11-11
D
W
Util
9-1x8-7
R
Dn
P
Br 2
10-7x11-3
Br 3
10-7x
10-7
Living
18-2x13-7
Garage
21-4x21-1
Porch depth 5-6

Plan #530-008D-0004

Price Code B

Total Living Area: 1,643 Sq. Ft.

Home has 3 bedrooms, 2 baths, 2-car garage and basement foundation, drawings also include crawl space and slab foundations.

Special features

- An attractive front entry porch gives this ranch a country accent
- Spacious family/dining room is the focal point of this design
- Kitchen and utility room are conveniently located near gathering areas
- Formal living room in the front of the home provides area for quiet and privacy
- Master bedroom has view to the rear of the home and a generous walk-in closet

TO ORDER BLUEPRINTS USE THE FORM ON PAGE 288 OR CALL TOLL-FREE **1-800-DREAM HOME** (373-2646)

LOWE'S

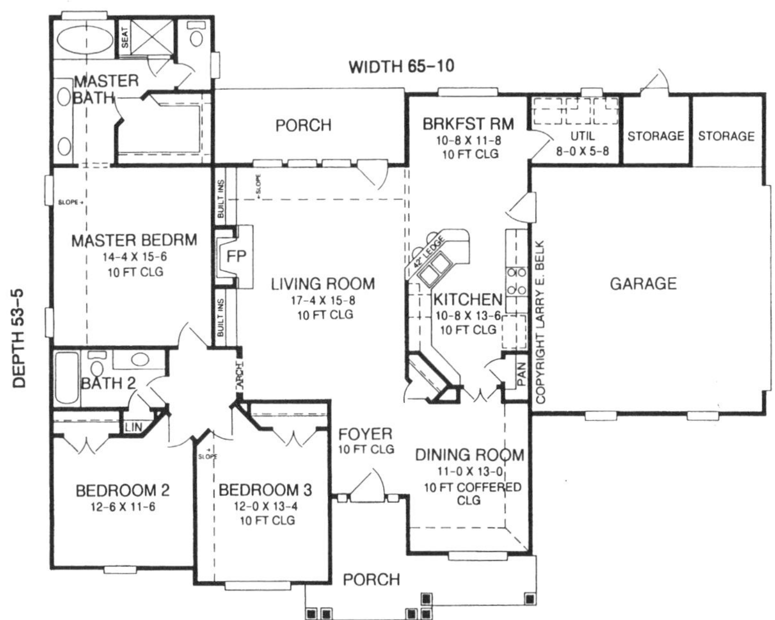
WIDTH 65–10
DEPTH 53–5
MASTER BATH
PORCH
BRKFST RM
10–8 X 11–8
10 FT CLG
UTIL
8–0 X 5–8
STORAGE
STORAGE
MASTER BEDRM
14–4 X 15–6
10 FT CLG
FP
BUILT INS
LIVING ROOM
17–4 X 15–8
10 FT CLG
KITCHEN
10–8 X 13–6
10 FT CLG
COPYRIGHT LARRY E. BELK
PAN
GARAGE
BATH 2
LIN
ARCH
FOYER
10 FT CLG
DINING ROOM
11–0 X 13–0
10 FT COFFERED CLG
BEDROOM 2
12–6 X 11–6
BEDROOM 3
12–0 X 13–4
10 FT CLG
PORCH

Plan #530-019D-0010

Price Code C

Total Living Area: 1,890 Sq. Ft.

Home has 3 bedrooms, 2 baths, 2-car side entry garage and crawl space foundation, drawings also include slab foundation.

Special features

- 10' ceilings give this home a spacious feel
- Efficient kitchen has a breakfast bar which overlooks the living room
- Master bedroom has a private bath with walk-in closet

LOWE'S

Arched Elegance

Plan #530-015D-0018

Price Code E

Total Living Area: 2,710 Sq. Ft.

Home has 3 bedrooms, 2 1/2 baths, 2-car garage and basement, crawl space or slab foundation, please specify when ordering.

Special features

- Private master suite is secluded on the left side of the home and boasts a 10' ceiling, double closets and vanity
- Peninsula kitchen with walk-in pantry and counterspace galore overlooks nook and family room with fireplace
- Den or optional fourth bedroom/ guest quarters offers flexibility in living space

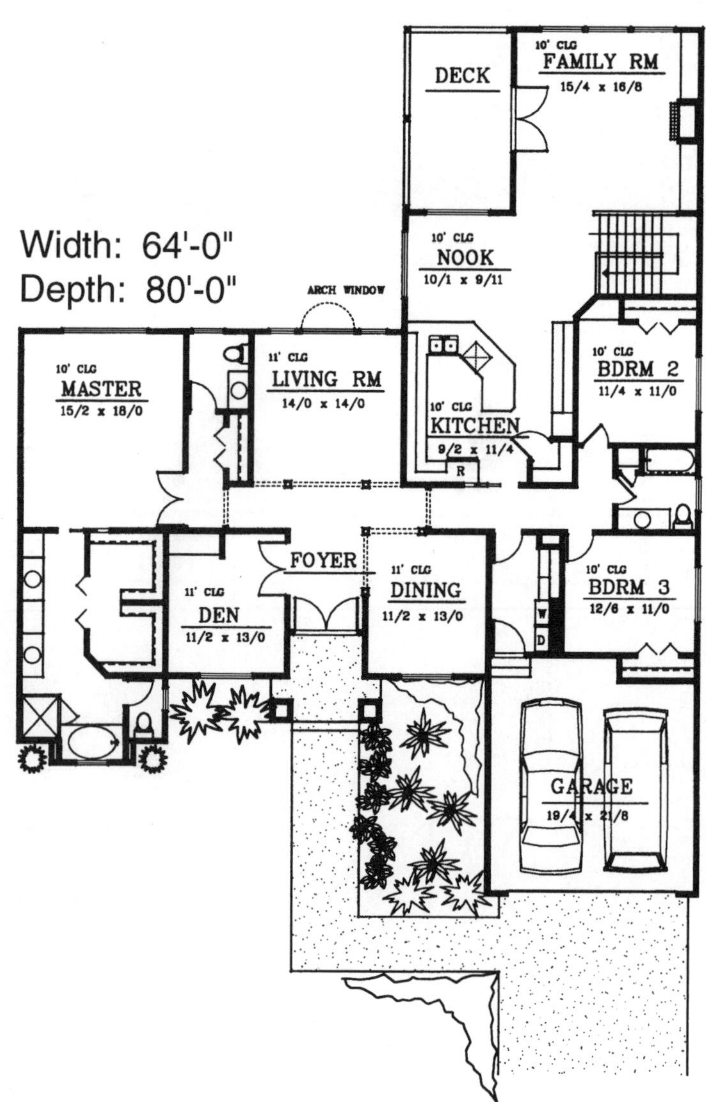
Width: 64'-0"
Depth: 80'-0"
DECK
10' CLG FAMILY RM 15/4 x 16/8
10' CLG NOOK 10/1 x 9/11
ARCH WINDOW
10' CLG MASTER 15/2 x 18/0
11' CLG LIVING RM 14/0 x 14/0
10' CLG KITCHEN 9/2 x 11/4
10' CLG BDRM 2 11/4 x 11/0
FOYER
11' CLG DEN 11/2 x 13/0
11' CLG DINING 11/2 x 13/0
10' CLG BDRM 3 12/6 x 11/0
GARAGE 19/4 x 21/8

LOWE'S

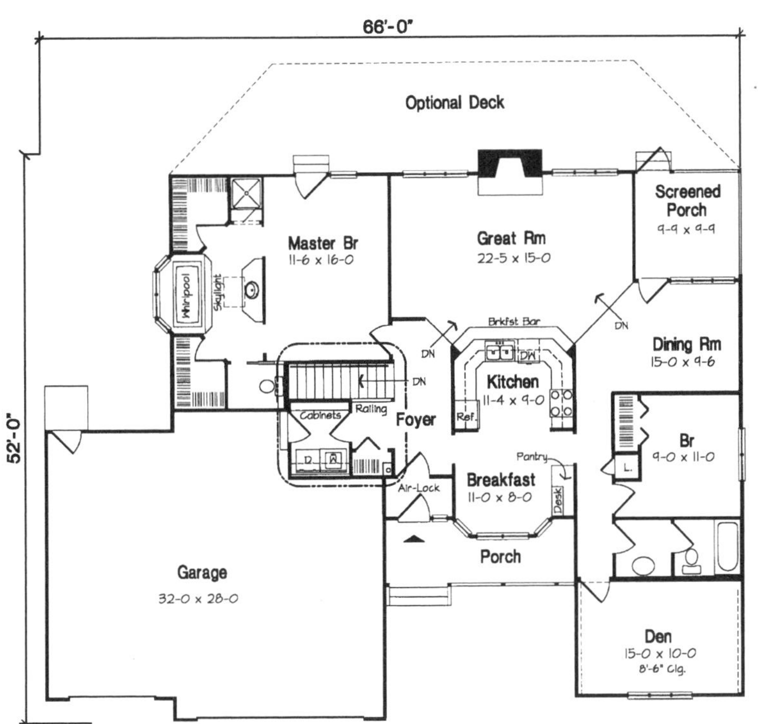
66'-0"
52'-0"
Optional Deck
Screened Porch
9-9 x 9-9
Master Br
11-6 x 16-0
Great Rm
22-5 x 15-0
Whirlpool
Skylight
Brkfst Bar
DN
Dining Rm
15-0 x 9-6
Kitchen
11-4 x 9-0
DW
Ref.
Cabinets
Railing
Foyer
Br
9-0 x 11-0
Pantry
Breakfast
11-0 x 8-0
Desk
Air-Lock
Porch
Garage
32-0 x 28-0
Den
15-0 x 10-0
8'-6" Clg.

Furn.

WH

Crawl Space Access

Crawl / Slab Option

Plan #530-038D-0008

Price Code B

Total Living Area: 1,738 Sq. Ft.

Home has 2 bedrooms, 2 baths, 3-car garage and basement, crawl space or slab foundation, please specify when ordering.

Special features

- A den in the front of the home can easily be converted to a third bedroom
- Kitchen includes an eating nook for family gatherings
- Master bedroom has an unforgettable bath with a super skylight
- Large sunken great room is centralized with a cozy fireplace

Rear View

Country Ranch With Spacious Wrap-Around Porch

Plan #530-062D-0041

Price Code B

Total Living Area: 1,541 Sq. Ft.

Home has 3 bedrooms, 2 baths, 2-car garage and basement or crawl space foundation, please specify when ordering.

Special features

- Dining area offers access to a screened porch for outdoor dining and entertaining
- Country kitchen features a center island and a breakfast bay for casual meals
- Great room is warmed by a wood-stove

Width: 87'-0"
Depth: 39'-0"

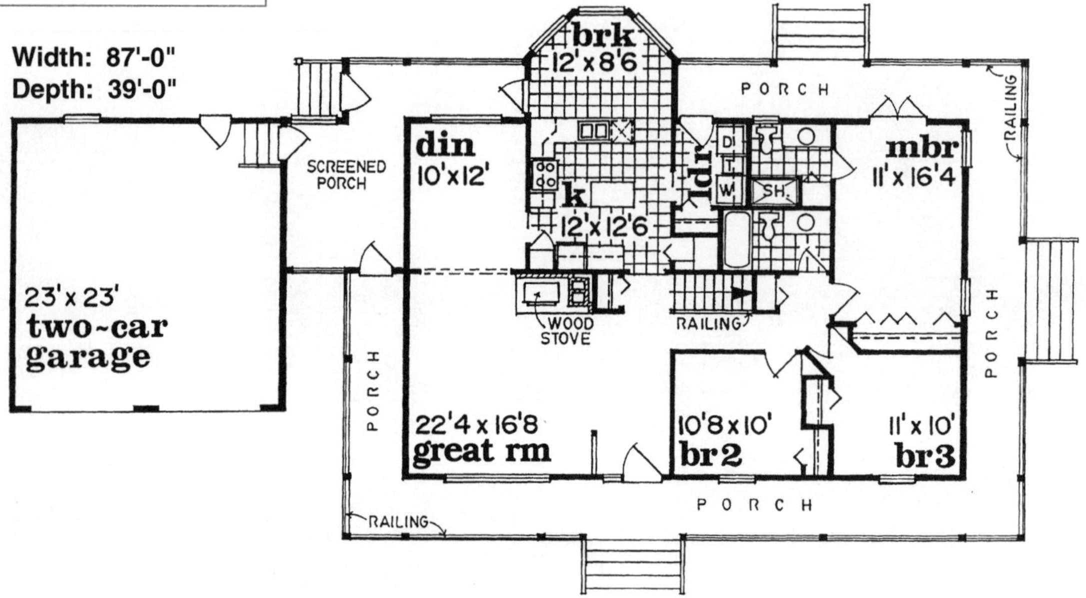
brk
12'x8'6
PORCH
RAILING
din
10'x12'
SCREENED PORCH
k
12'x12'6
ldr.
D
T
W
SH.
mbr
11'x16'4
23'x23'
two-car garage
WOOD STOVE
RAILING
PORCH
PORCH
22'4x16'8
great rm
10'8x10'
br2
11'x10'
br3
PORCH
RAILING

 TO ORDER BLUEPRINTS USE THE FORM ON PAGE 288 OR CALL TOLL-FREE **1-800-DREAM HOME** (373-2646)

LOWE'S

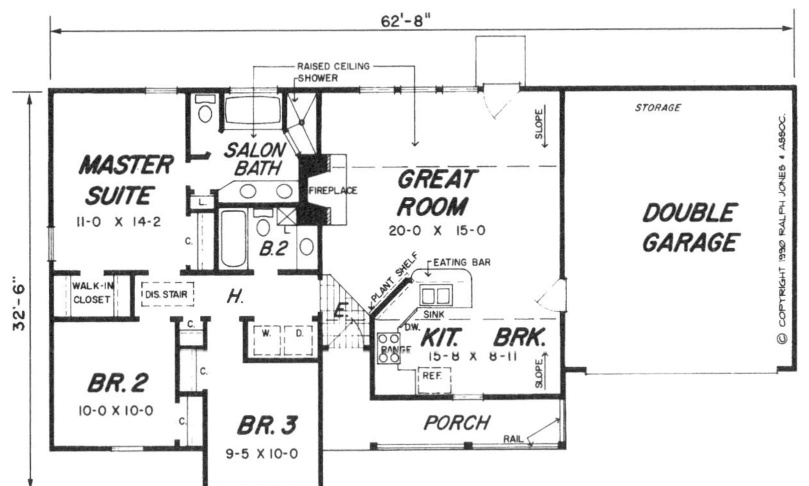
62'-8"
32'-6"
RAISED CEILING
SHOWER
MASTER SUITE
11-0 X 14-2
SALON BATH
B.2
FIREPLACE
GREAT ROOM
20-0 X 15-0
SLOPE
STORAGE
DOUBLE GARAGE
© COPYRIGHT 1990 RALPH JONES & ASSOC.
WALK-IN CLOSET
DIS. STAIR
H.
E.
PLANT SHELF
EATING BAR
SINK
DW.
RANGE
REF.
KIT.
BRK.
15-8 X 8-11
W.
D.
BR. 2
10-0 X 10-0
BR. 3
9-5 X 10-0
PORCH
RAIL

Plan #530-060D-0015

Price Code AA

Total Living Area: 1,192 Sq. Ft.

Home has 3 bedrooms, 2 baths, 2-car garage and slab or crawl space foundation, please specify when ordering.

Special features

- Kitchen eating bar overlooks well-designed great room
- Private bath in master suite
- Extra storage space in garage

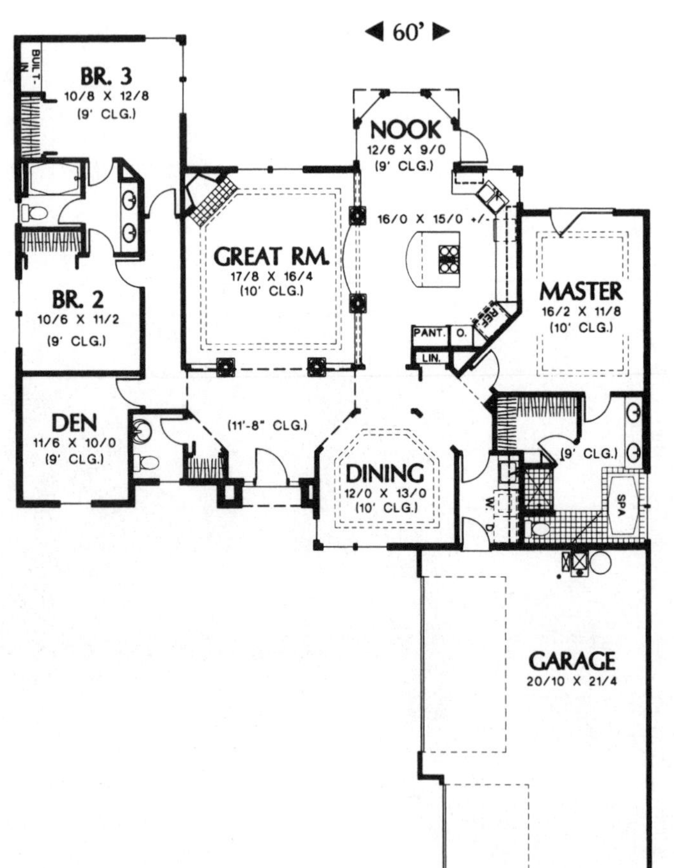
60'
BR. 3
10/8 X 12/8
(9' CLG.)
BUILT-IN
NOOK
12/6 X 9/0
(9' CLG.)
16/0 X 15/0 +/-
GREAT RM.
17/8 X 16/4
(10' CLG.)
MASTER
16/2 X 11/8
(10' CLG.)
BR. 2
10/6 X 11/2
(9' CLG.)
PANT.
LIN.
REF.
DEN
11/6 X 10/0
(9' CLG.)
(11'-8" CLG.)
DINING
12/0 X 13/0
(10' CLG.)
(9' CLG.)
SPA
W
D
79'
GARAGE
20/10 X 21/4

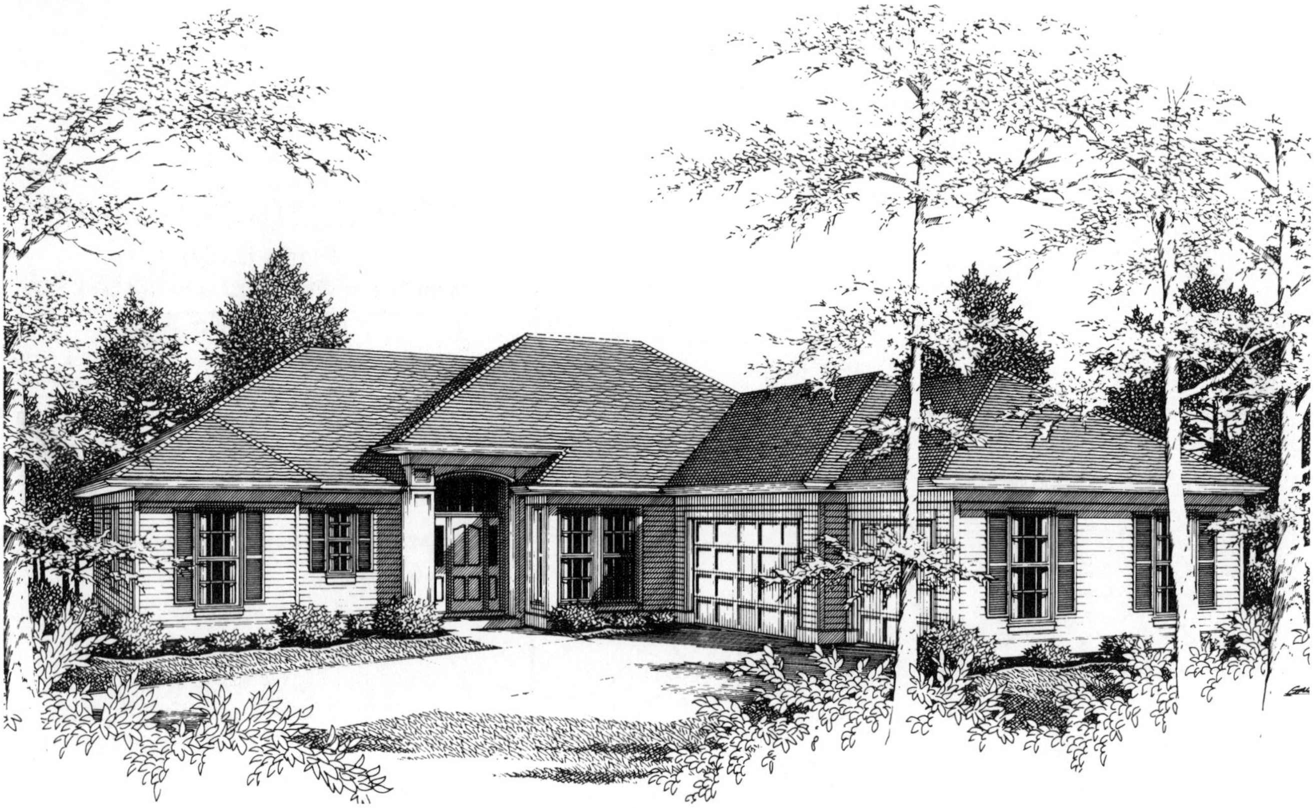

Plan #530-011D-0011

Price Code C

Total Living Area: 2,155 Sq. Ft.

Home has 3 bedrooms, 2 1/2 baths, 3-car side entry garage and crawl space foundation.

Special features

- Great room has a 10' tray ceiling, corner fireplace and columns
- Well-appointed master suite features a 10' tray ceiling
- Two secondary bedrooms share a bath
- Secluded den makes an ideal home office

LOWE'S

Plan #530-039D-0004

Price Code A

Total Living Area: 1,406 Sq. Ft.

Home has 3 bedrooms, 2 baths, 2-car detached garage and slab or crawl space foundation, please specify when ordering.

Special features

- Master bedroom has a sloped ceiling
- Kitchen and dining area merge becoming a gathering place
- Enter the family room from the charming covered front porch to find a fireplace and lots of windows

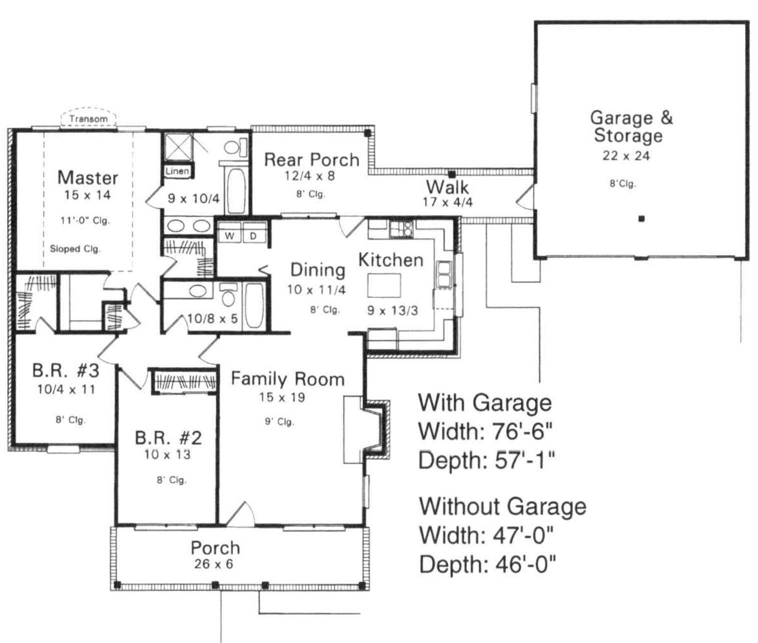
Transom
Master
15 x 14
11'-0" Clg.
Sloped Clg.
Linen
9 x 10/4
Rear Porch
12/4 x 8
8' Clg.
Walk
17 x 4/4
Garage &
Storage
22 x 24
8' Clg.
W D
Dining
10 x 11/4
8' Clg.
Kitchen
9 x 13/3
10/8 x 5
B.R. #3
10/4 x 11
8' Clg.
B.R. #2
10 x 13
8' Clg.
Family Room
15 x 19
9' Clg.
Porch
26 x 6
With Garage
Width: 76'-6"
Depth: 57'-1"
Without Garage
Width: 47'-0"
Depth: 46'-0"

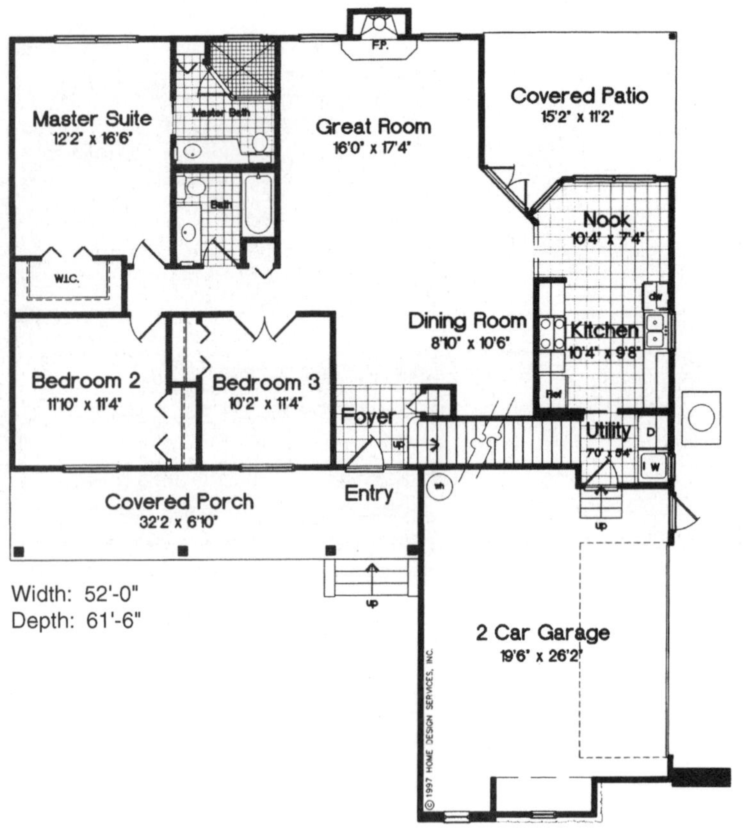
Master Suite
12'2" x 16'6"
Master Bath
Bath
W.I.C.
Great Room
16'0" x 17'4"
F.P.
Covered Patio
15'2" x 11'2"
Nook
10'4" x 7'4"
Dining Room
8'10" x 10'6"
Kitchen
10'4" x 9'8"
Ref
Bedroom 2
11'10" x 11'4"
Bedroom 3
10'2" x 11'4"
Foyer
Utility
7'0" x 5'4"
Covered Porch
32'2 x 6'10"
Entry
2 Car Garage
19'6" x 26'2"
© 1997 HOME DESIGN SERVICES, INC.

Width: 52'-0"
Depth: 61'-6"

Plan #530-047D-0005

Price Code C

Total Living Area: 1,885 Sq. Ft.

Home has 3 bedrooms, 2 baths, 2-car side entry garage and basement foundation.

Special features

- Enormous covered patio
- Dining and great rooms combine to create one large and versatile living area
- Utility room is directly off the kitchen for convenience

LOWE'S

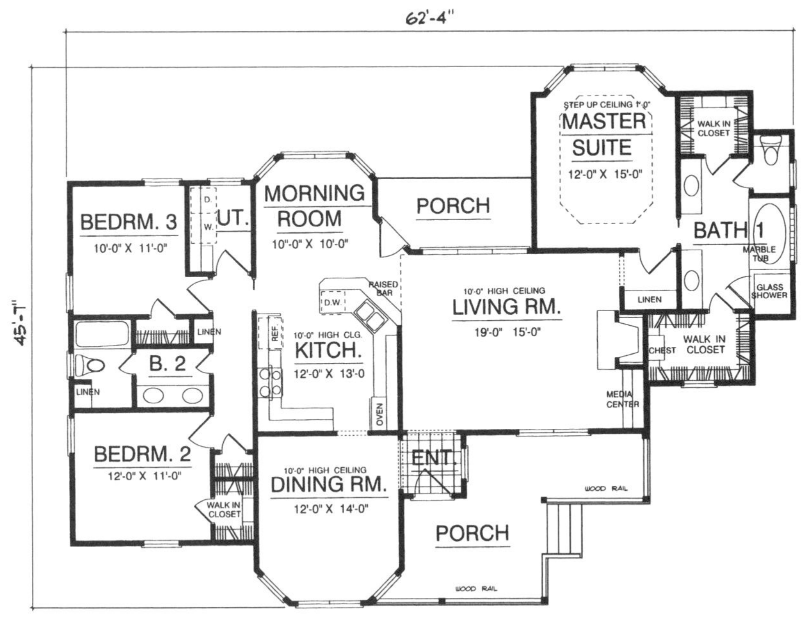
62'-4"
45'-7"
STEP UP CEILING
MASTER
SUITE
12'-0" X 15'-0"
WALK IN
CLOSET
MORNING
ROOM
10'-0" X 10'-0"
PORCH
BEDRM. 3
10'-0" X 11'-0"
UT.
BATH 1
MARBLE
TUB
GLASS
SHOWER
LINEN
RAISED
BAR
D.W.
10'-0" HIGH CEILING
LIVING RM.
19'-0" 15'-0"
REF.
10'-0" HIGH CLG.
KITCH.
12'-0" X 13'-0
LINEN
B. 2
LINEN
CHEST
WALK IN
CLOSET
MEDIA
CENTER
OVEN
BEDRM. 2
12'-0" X 11'-0"
ENT.
10'-0" HIGH CEILING
DINING RM.
12'-0" X 14'-0"
WALK IN
CLOSET
WOOD RAIL
PORCH
WOOD RAIL

Plan #530-030D-0003

Price Code B

Total Living Area: 1,753 Sq. Ft.

Home has 3 bedrooms, 2 baths and slab or crawl space foundation, please specify when ordering.

Special features

- Large front porch has charming appeal
- Kitchen with breakfast bar overlooks morning room and accesses covered porch
- Master suite has amenities such as a private bath, spacious closets and sunny bay window

Formal Country Charm

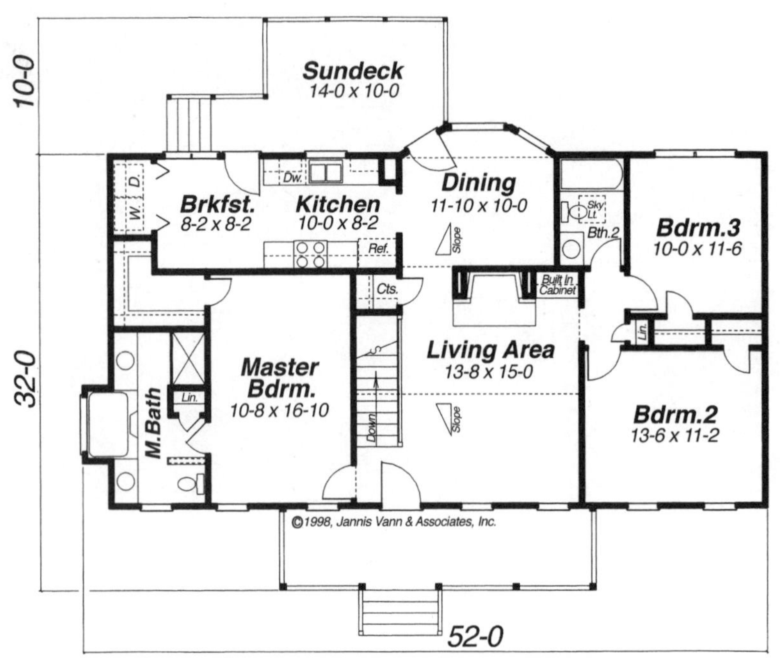
Sundeck
14-0 x 10-0
Brkfst.
8-2 x 8-2
Kitchen
10-0 x 8-2
Dining
11-10 x 10-0
Bdrm.3
10-0 x 11-6
Bth.2
Sky Lt.
W.
D.
Dw.
Ref.
Cts.
Built In Cabinet
Slope
Living Area
13-8 x 15-0
Master Bdrm.
10-8 x 16-10
M.Bath
Lin.
Down
Bdrm.2
13-6 x 11-2
10-0
32-0
52-0
©1998, Jannis Vann & Associates, Inc.

Plan #530-052D-0011

Price Code A

Total Living Area: 1,325 Sq. Ft.

Home has 3 bedrooms, 2 baths, 2-car drive under garage and basement or crawl space foundation, please specify when ordering.

Special features

- Sloped ceiling and a fireplace in the living area create a cozy feeling
- Formal dining and breakfast areas have an efficiently designed kitchen between them
- Master bedroom has a walk-in closet and luxurious private bath

LOWE'S

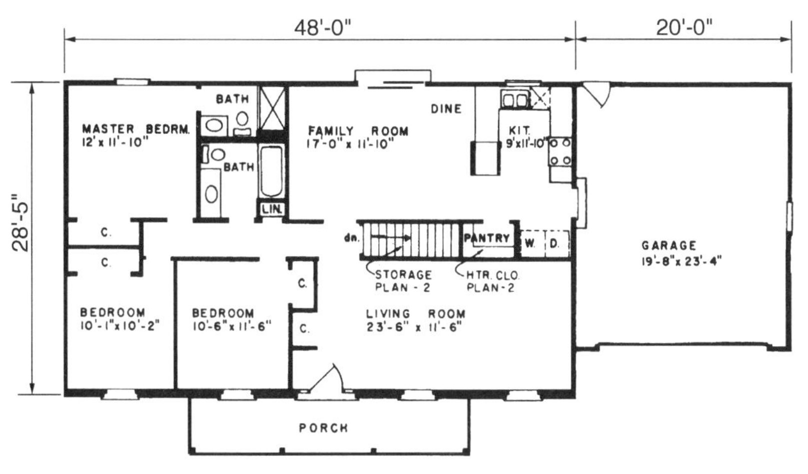
48'-0"
20'-0"
28'-5"
MASTER BEDRM.
12' x 11'-10"
BATH
BATH
LIN.
FAMILY ROOM
17'-0" x 11'-10"
DINE
KIT.
9'x11'-10"
PANTRY
W D
dn.
STORAGE
PLAN - 2
HTR. CLO.
PLAN-2
C.
C.
C.
C.
BEDROOM
10'-1"x10'-2"
BEDROOM
10'-6"x 11'-6"
LIVING ROOM
23'-6" x 11'-6"
GARAGE
19'-8"x 23'-4"
PORCH

Plan #530-008D-0122

Price Code A

Total Living Area: 1,364 Sq. Ft.

Home has 3 bedrooms, 2 baths, 2-car garage and basement foundation, drawings also include crawl space and slab foundations.

Special features

- A large porch and entry door with sidelights lead into a generous living room
- Well-planned U-shaped kitchen features a laundry closet, built-in pantry and open peninsula
- Master bedroom has its own bath with 4' shower
- Convenient to the kitchen is an oversized two-car garage with service door to rear

Plan #530-026D-0070

Price Code B

Total Living Area: 1,666 Sq. Ft.

Home has 3 bedrooms, 2 baths, 2-car garage and basement foundation.

Special features

- Efficient snack island is located in the roomy kitchen
- Stately front entrance welcomes guests
- Bay window adds elegance to the dining room

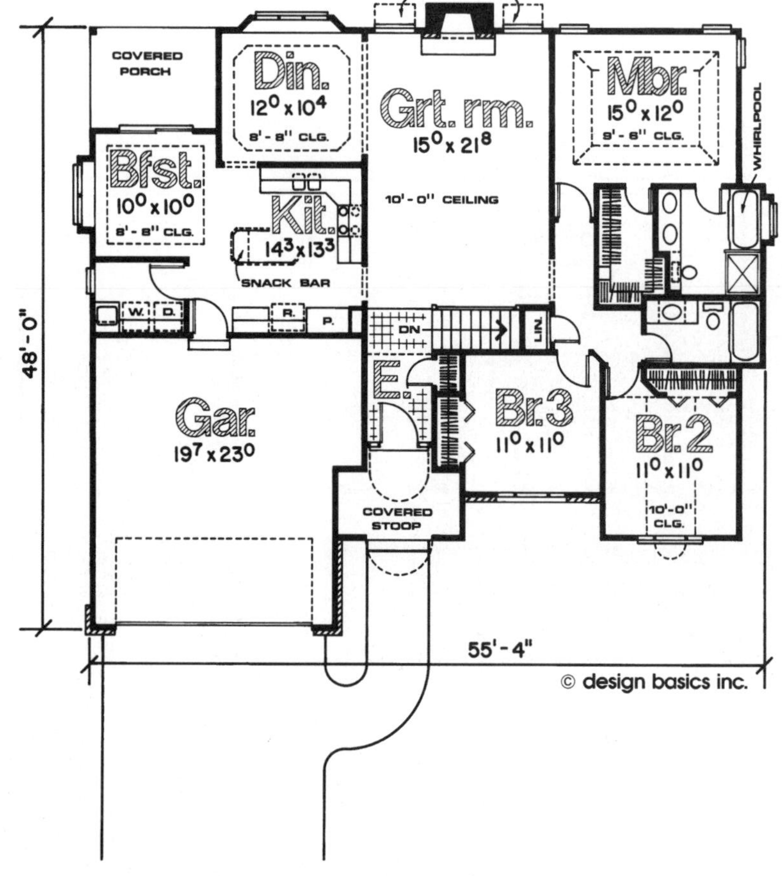
TRANSOMS
COVERED PORCH
Din.
$12^0 \times 10^4$
8'-8" CLG.
Grt. rm.
$15^0 \times 21^8$
10'-0" CEILING
Mbr.
$15^0 \times 12^0$
9'-6" CLG.
WHIRLPOOL
Bfst.
$10^0 \times 10^0$
8'-8" CLG.
Kit.
$14^3 \times 13^3$
SNACK BAR
W.
D.
R.
P.
DN
LIN.
E.
Br.3
$11^0 \times 11^0$
Br.2
$11^0 \times 11^0$
10'-0" CLG.
Gar.
$19^7 \times 23^0$
COVERED STOOP
48'-0"
55'-4"
© design basics inc.

LOWE'S

Plan #530-039D-0005

Price Code A

Total Living Area: 1,474 Sq. Ft.

Home has 3 bedrooms, 2 baths, 2-car detached garage and slab or crawl space foundation, please specify when ordering.

Special features

- Kitchen and dining area include center eat-in island and large pantry
- Laundry facilities and hall bath are roomy
- Both secondary bedrooms have walk-in closets

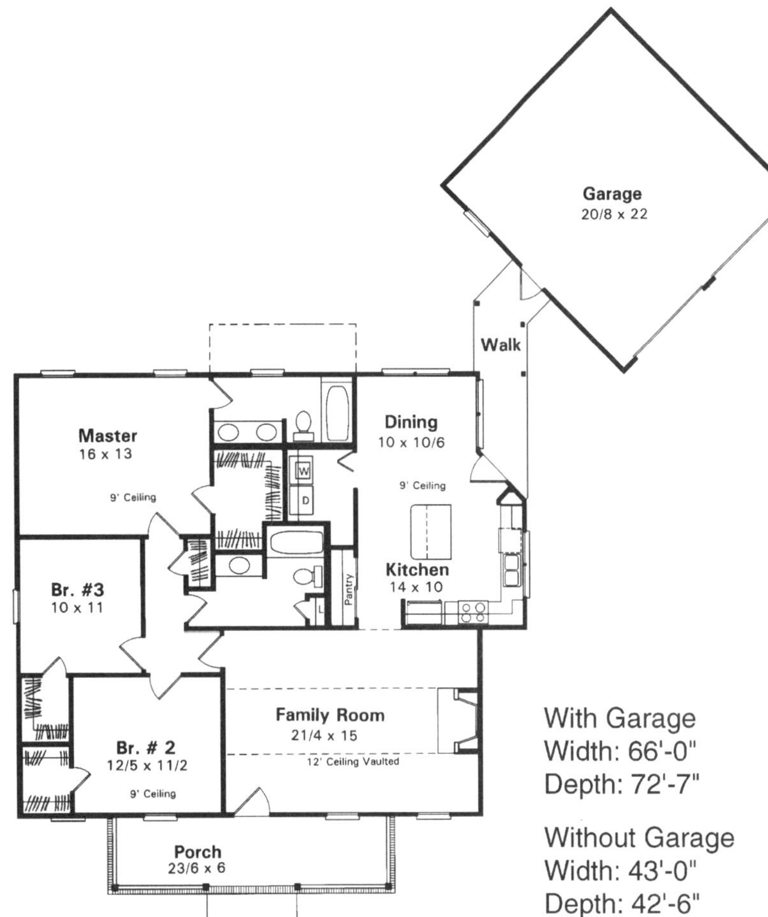
Garage
20/8 x 22
Walk
Master
16 x 13
9' Ceiling
Dining
10 x 10/6
9' Ceiling
W
D
Br. #3
10 x 11
Pantry
Kitchen
14 x 10
Family Room
21/4 x 15
12' Ceiling Vaulted
Br. # 2
12/5 x 11/2
9' Ceiling
Porch
23/6 x 6

With Garage
Width: 66'-0"
Depth: 72'-7"

Without Garage
Width: 43'-0"
Depth: 42'-6"

LOWE'S

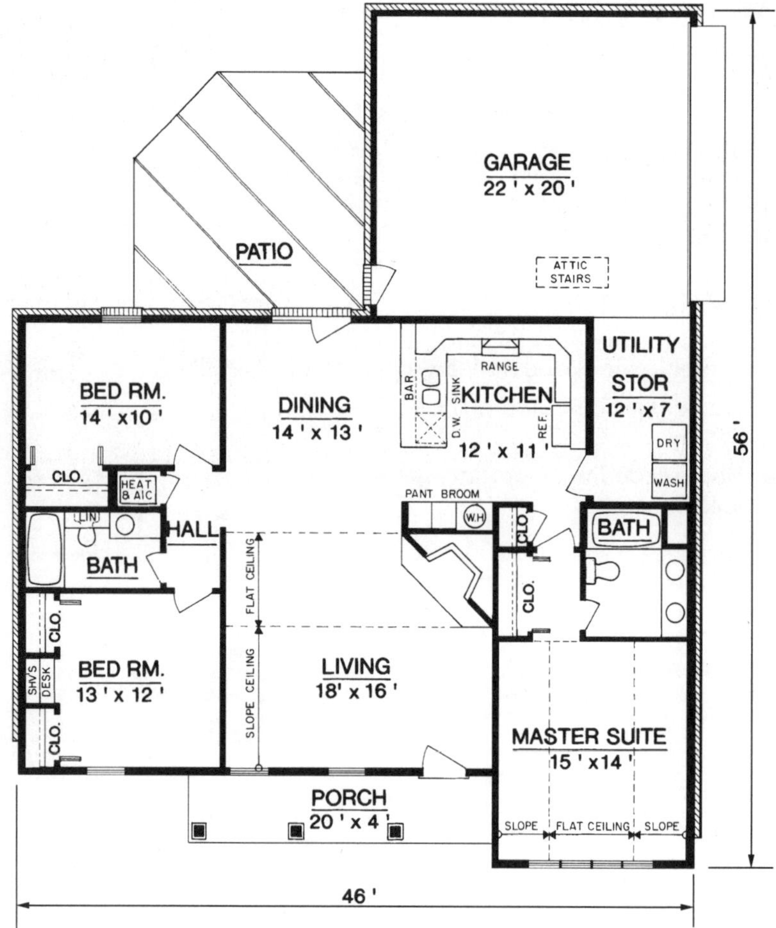
GARAGE
22' x 20'
ATTIC STAIRS
PATIO
BED RM.
14' x10'
CLO.
HEAT & A/C
DINING
14' x 13'
BAR
SINK
RANGE
KITCHEN
D.W.
REF.
12' x 11'
UTILITY
STOR
12' x 7'
DRY
WASH
PANT
BROOM
W.H.
LIN
BATH
HALL
CLO.
BATH
CLO.
FLAT CEILING
SLOPE CEILING
CLO.
SHVS
DESK
BED RM.
13' x 12'
CLO.
LIVING
18' x 16'
MASTER SUITE
15' x14'
PORCH
20' x 4'
SLOPE
FLAT CEILING
SLOPE
46'
56'

Plan #530-020D-0016

Price Code C

Total Living Area: 1,380 Sq. Ft.

Home has 3 bedrooms, 2 baths, 2-car side entry garage and slab foundation, drawings also include crawl space foundation.

Special features

- Living room has a sloped ceiling and corner fireplace
- Kitchen features a breakfast bar overlooking the dining room
- Master suite is separate from other bedrooms for privacy
- Large utility/storage area

TO ORDER BLUEPRINTS USE THE FORM ON PAGE 288 OR CALL TOLL-FREE **1-800-DREAM HOME** (373-2646)

Cozy Home For Family Living

LOWE'S

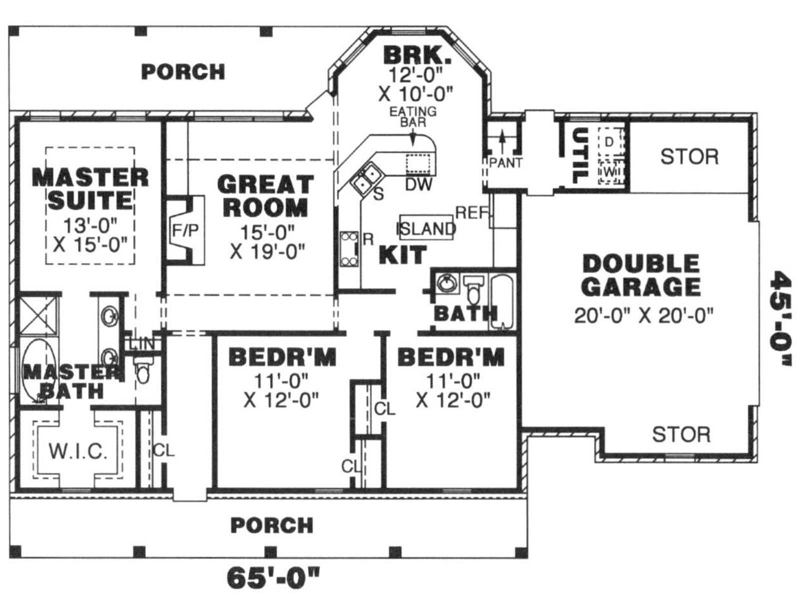
PORCH
BRK.
12'-0"
X 10'-0"
EATING BAR
MASTER SUITE
13'-0"
X 15'-0"
GREAT ROOM
15'-0"
X 19'-0"
F/P
S
DW
PANT
UTIL
D
W
STOR
REF
ISLAND
R
KIT
DOUBLE GARAGE
20'-0" X 20'-0"
BATH
LIN
MASTER BATH
BEDR'M
11'-0"
X 12'-0"
BEDR'M
11'-0"
X 12'-0"
CL
W.I.C.
CL
CL
STOR
PORCH
65'-0"
45'-0"

Plan #530-025D-0006

Price Code B

Total Living Area: 1,612 Sq. Ft.

Home has 3 bedrooms, 2 baths, 2-car side entry garage and slab foundation.

Special features

- Covered porch in rear of home creates an outdoor living area
- Master suite is separated from other bedrooms for privacy
- Eating bar in kitchen extends into breakfast area for additional seating

Country Flair In A Flexible Ranch

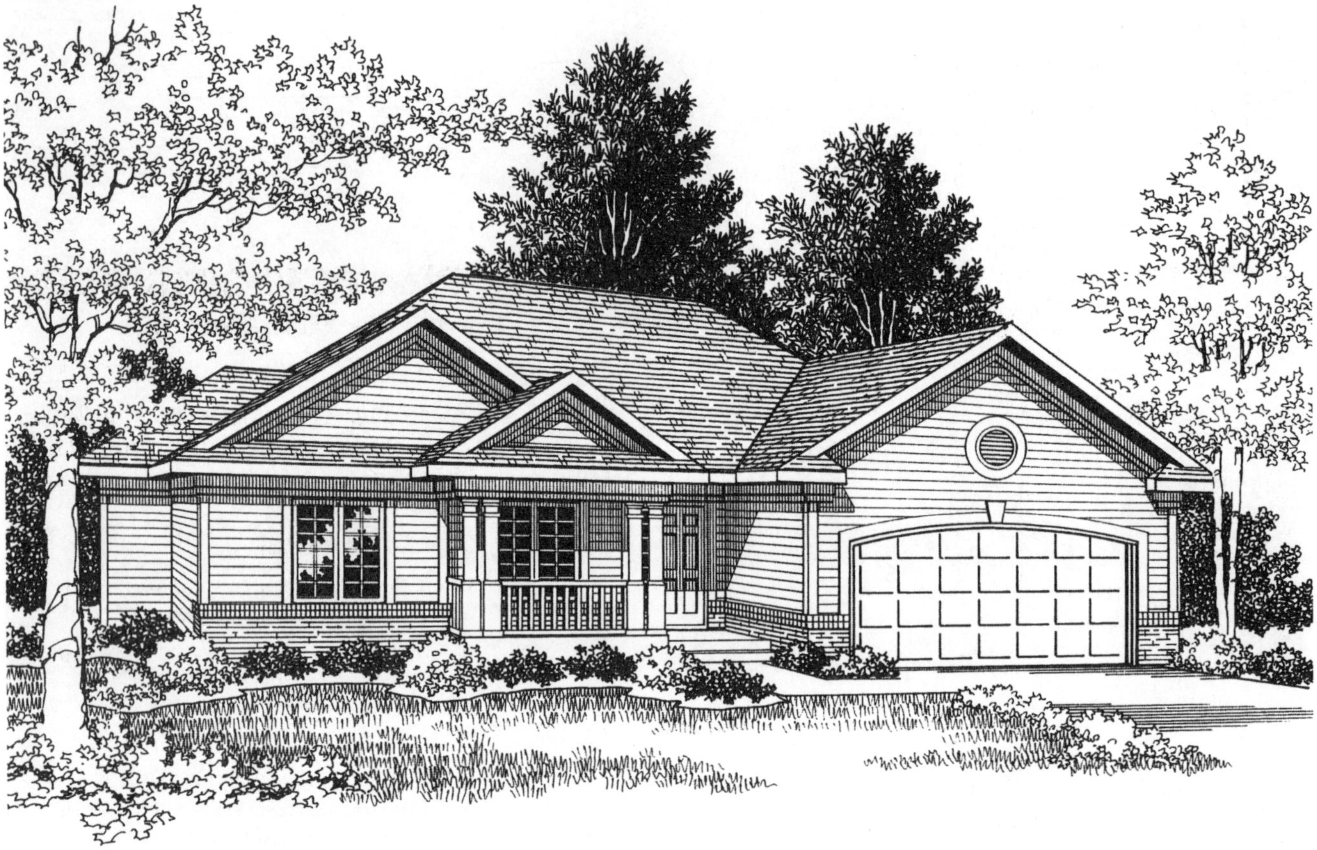

Plan #530-051D-0053

Price Code A

Total Living Area: 1,461 Sq. Ft.

Home has 3 bedrooms, 2 baths, 2-car garage and basement foundation.

Special features

- Casual dining room
- Cathedral ceilings in the great room and dining area give the home a spacious feel
- Relaxing master bedroom boasts an expansive bath and large walk-in closet

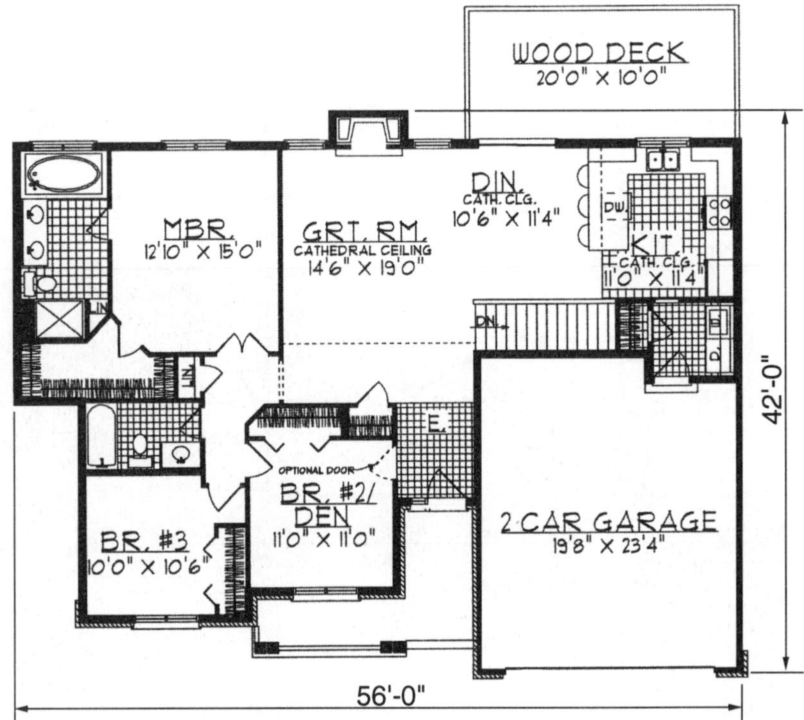
WOOD DECK
20'0" X 10'0"
DIN.
CATH. CLG.
10'6" X 11'4"
MBR.
12'10" X 15'0"
GRT. RM.
CATHEDRAL CEILING
14'6" X 19'0"
DW
KIT.
CATH. CLG.
11'0" X 11'4"
LIN
DN.
LIN
E.
OPTIONAL DOOR
BR. #2/
DEN
11'0" X 11'0"
BR. #3
10'0" X 10'6"
2 CAR GARAGE
19'8" X 23'4"
42'-0"
56'-0"

LOWE'S

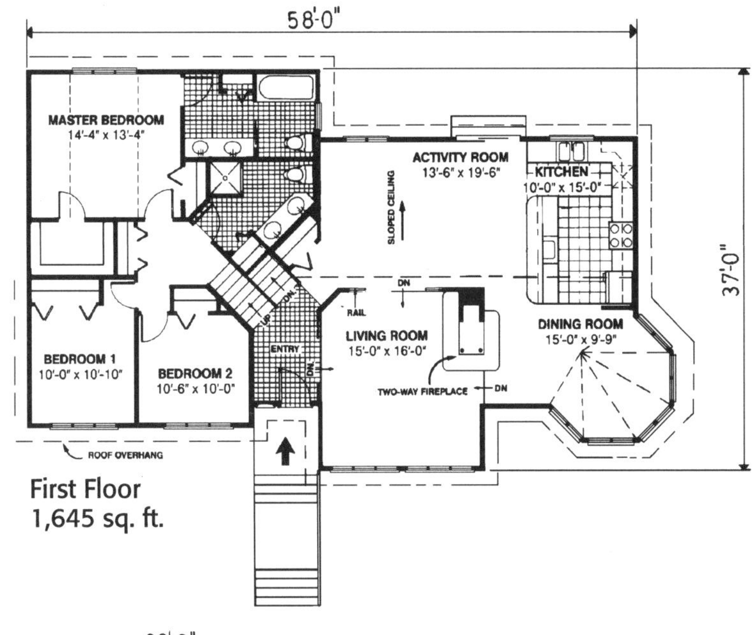
58'-0"
37'-0"
MASTER BEDROOM
14'-4" x 13'-4"
ACTIVITY ROOM
13'-6" x 19'-6"
SLOPED CEILING
KITCHEN
10'-0" x 15'-0"
DN
RAIL
LIVING ROOM
15'-0" x 16'-0"
DINING ROOM
15'-0" x 9'-9"
TWO-WAY FIREPLACE
DN
ENTRY
UP
DN
BEDROOM 1
10'-0" x 10'-10"
BEDROOM 2
10'-6" x 10'-0"
ROOF OVERHANG

First Floor
1,645 sq. ft.

28'-3"
44'-0"
LANDRY
9'-3" x 11'-10"
D.
W.
FAMILY ROOM
17'-6" x 19'-6"
UP
GARAGE
20'-9" x 23'-0"

Lower Level
520 sq. ft.

Plan #530-008D-0070

Price Code C

Total Living Area: 2,165 Sq. Ft.

Home has 3 bedrooms, 2 1/2 baths, 2-car garage and partial basement/slab foundation.

Special features

- Perfect contemporary three-level home for a side to side sloping site
- Breathtaking living room features a fireplace open on three sides, sloped ceiling and gabled-end windows for greeting the sun
- Octagon-shaped dining room adjoins the kitchen with a 10' center island and breakfast bar
- Steps take you to a large family room, combination laundry/bath and two-car garage

LOWE'S

Plan #530-055D-0032

Price Code D

Total Living Area: 2,439 Sq. Ft.

Home has 4 bedrooms, 3 baths, 2-car garage and walk-out basement, basement, crawl space or slab foundation, please specify when ordering.

Special features

- Enter columned gallery area just before reaching the family room with a see-through fireplace
- Master bath has a corner whirlpool tub
- Double-door entrance into the study

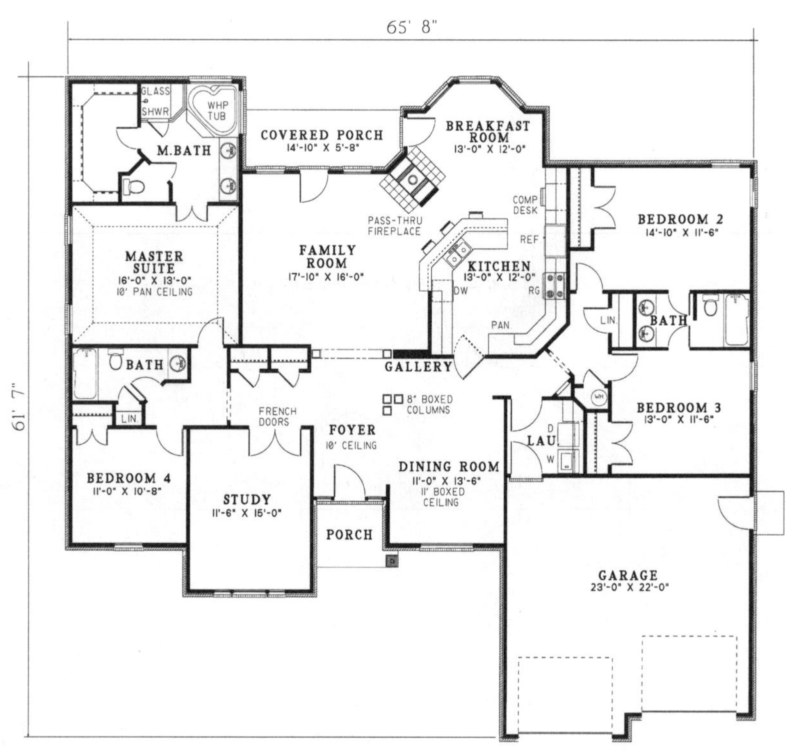
65' 8"
61' 7"
GLASS SHWR
WHP TUB
M.BATH
COVERED PORCH
14'-10" X 5'-8"
BREAKFAST ROOM
13'-0" X 12'-0"
COMP DESK
PASS-THRU FIREPLACE
REF
BEDROOM 2
14'-10" X 11'-6"
MASTER SUITE
16'-0" X 13'-0"
10' PAN CEILING
FAMILY ROOM
17'-10" X 16'-0"
KITCHEN
13'-0" X 12'-0"
DW
RG
PAN
LIN
BATH
BATH
GALLERY
8" BOXED COLUMNS
LIN
FRENCH DOORS
FOYER
10' CEILING
BEDROOM 3
13'-0" X 11'-6"
D
LAU
W
DINING ROOM
11'-0" X 13'-6"
11' BOXED CEILING
BEDROOM 4
11'-0" X 10'-8"
STUDY
11'-6" X 15'-0"
PORCH
GARAGE
23'-0" X 22'-0"

TO ORDER BLUEPRINTS USE THE FORM ON PAGE 288 OR CALL TOLL-FREE **1-800-DREAM HOME** (373-2646)

LOWE'S

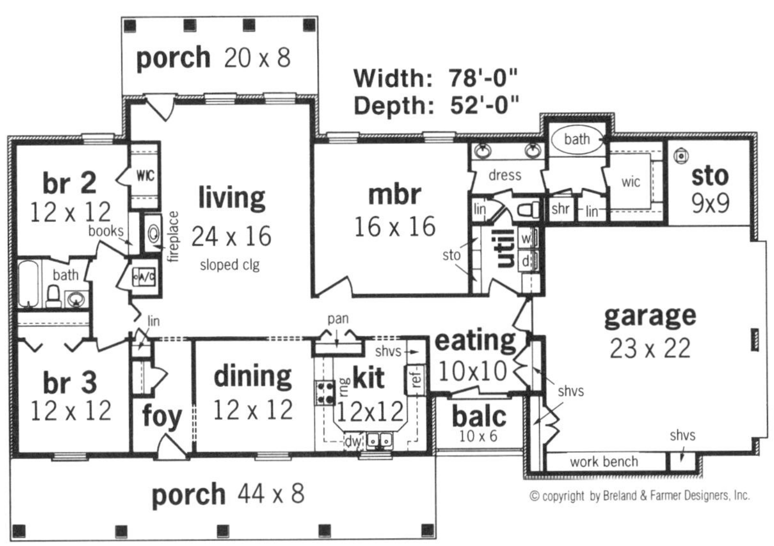
porch 20 x 8
Width: 78'-0"
Depth: 52'-0"
br 2
12 x 12
living
24 x 16
sloped clg
mbr
16 x 16
sto
9x9
util
garage
23 x 22
eating
10x10
br 3
12 x 12
foy
dining
12 x 12
kit
12x12
balc
10 x 6
work bench
porch 44 x 8
© copyright by Breland & Farmer Designers, Inc.

Plan #530-020D-0008

Price Code C

Total Living Area: 1,925 Sq. Ft.

Home has 3 bedrooms, 2 baths, 2-car side entry garage and crawl space foundation, drawings also include slab foundation.

Special features

- Energy efficient home with 2" x 6" exterior walls
- Balcony off eating area adds character
- Master bedroom has a dressing room, bath, walk-in closet and access to the utility room

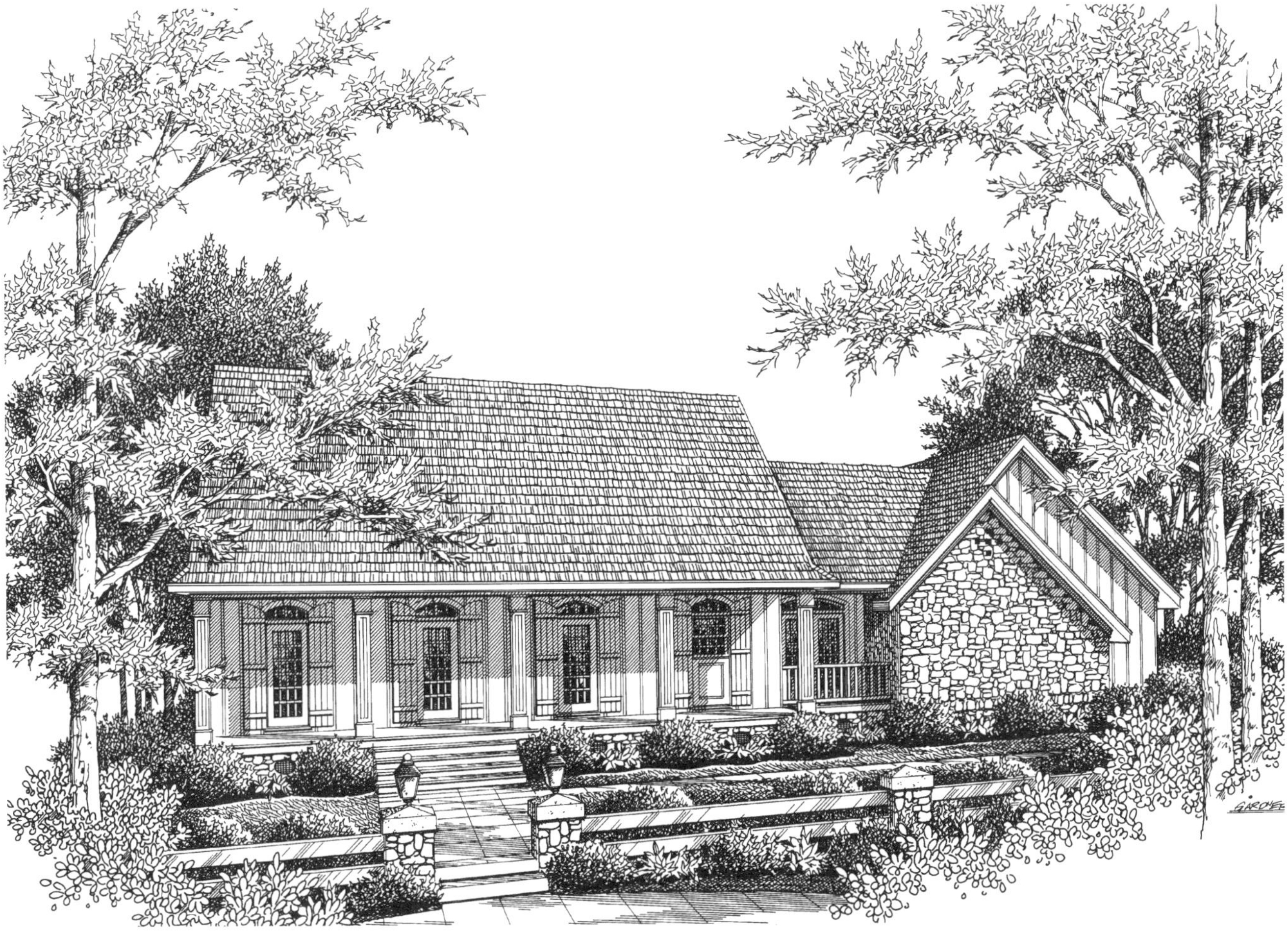

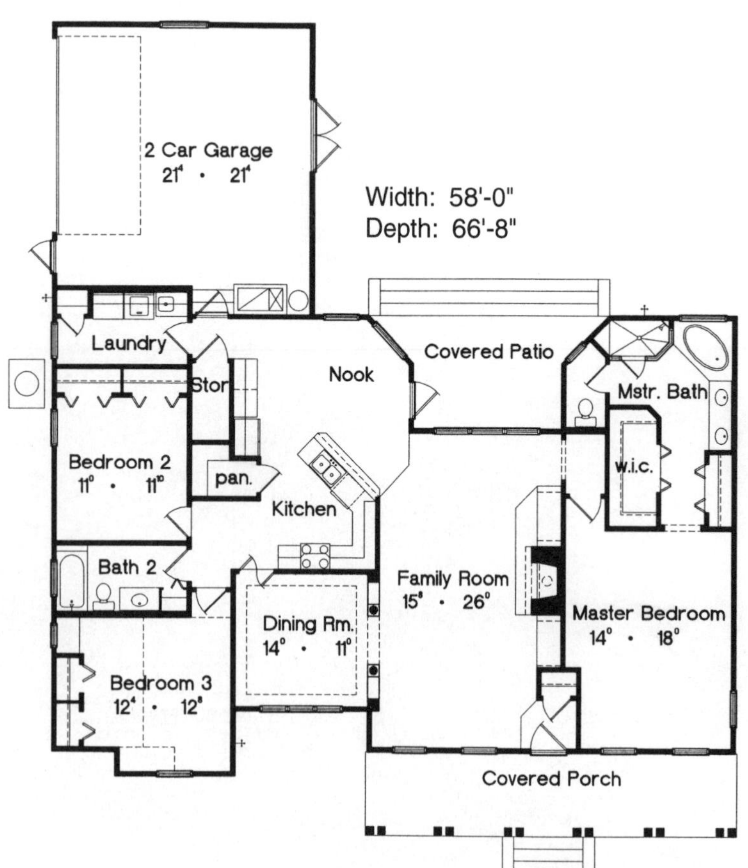
2 Car Garage
$21^4 \cdot 21^4$
Width: 58'-0"
Depth: 66'-8"
Laundry
Stor
Nook
Covered Patio
Mstr. Bath
Bedroom 2
$11^0 \cdot 11^{10}$
pan.
Kitchen
w.i.c.
Bath 2
Family Room
$15^8 \cdot 26^0$
Dining Rm.
$14^0 \cdot 11^0$
Master Bedroom
$14^0 \cdot 18^0$
Bedroom 3
$12^4 \cdot 12^8$
Covered Porch

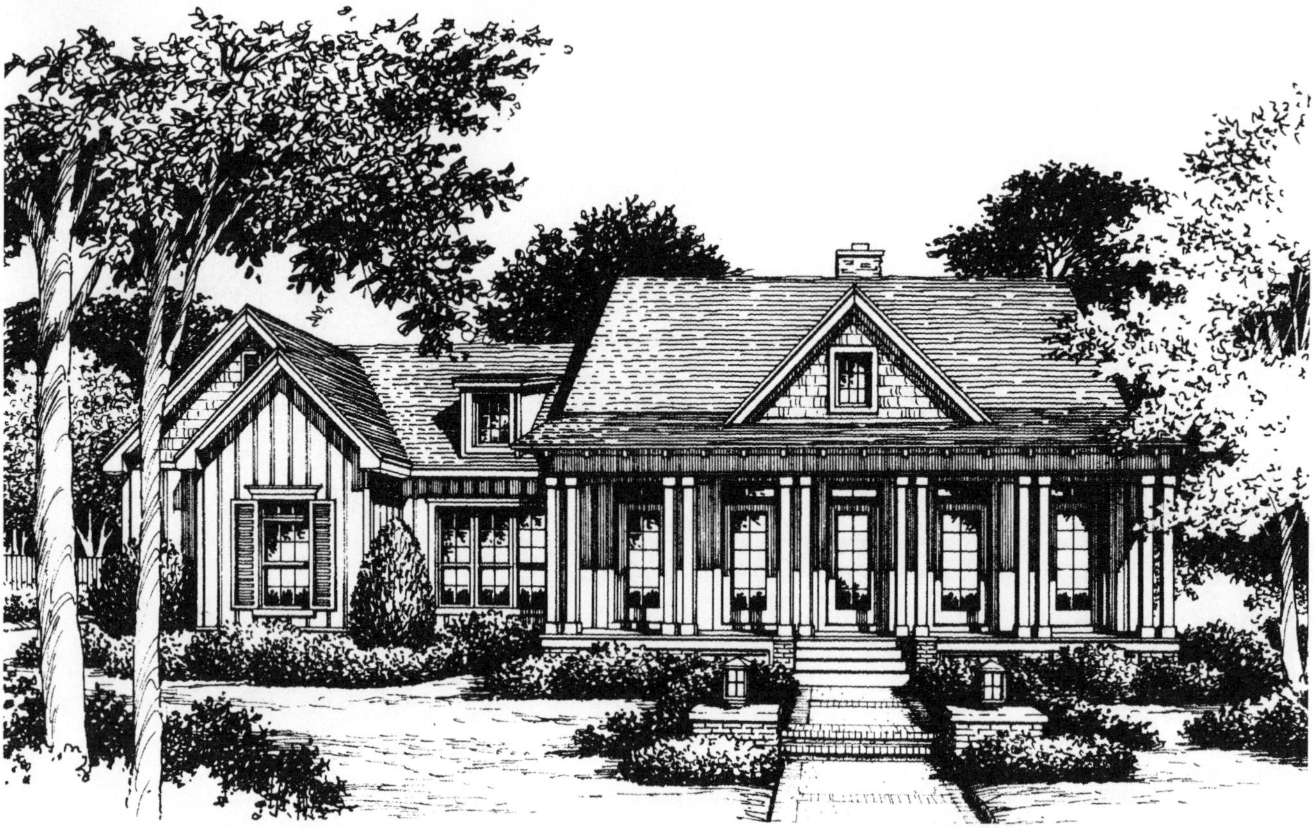

Plan #530-047D-0032

Price Code C

Total Living Area: 1,963 Sq. Ft.

Home has 3 bedrooms, 2 baths, 2-car side entry garage and slab or crawl space foundation, please specify when ordering.

Special features

- Spacious breakfast nook is a great gathering place
- Master bedroom has its own wing with a private bath and lots of closet space
- Large laundry room with closet and sink

LOWE'S

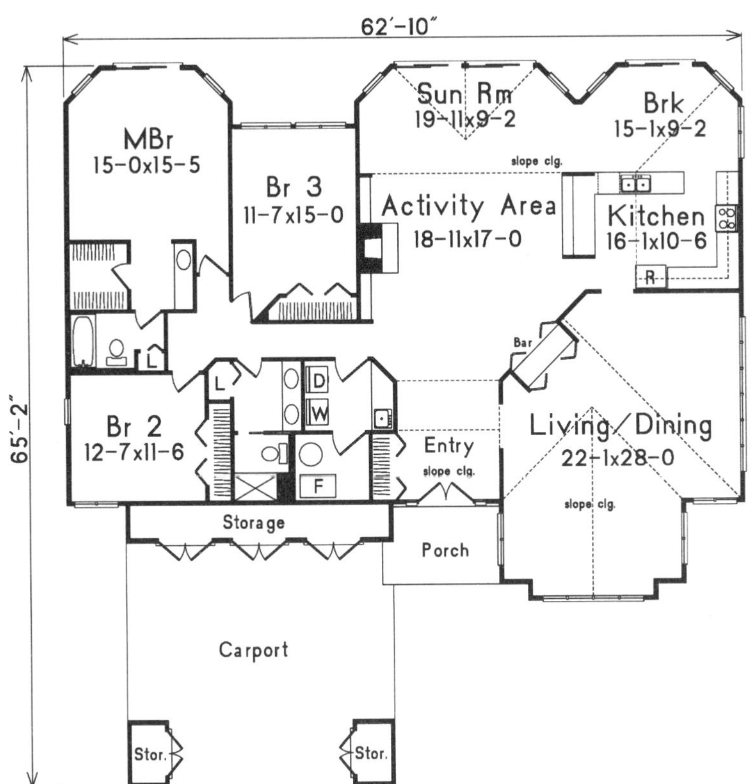
62'-10"
65'-2"
Sun Rm
19-11x9-2
Brk
15-1x9-2
slope clg.
MBr
15-0x15-5
Br 3
11-7x15-0
Activity Area
18-11x17-0
Kitchen
16-1x10-6
R
L
Bar
D
W
L
Br 2
12-7x11-6
Entry
slope clg.
Living/Dining
22-1x28-0
slope clg.
F
Storage
Porch
Carport
Stor.
Stor.

Plan #530-008D-0062

Price Code D

Total Living Area: 2,530 Sq. Ft.

Home has 3 bedrooms, 2 baths, 2-car carport and slab foundation.

Special features

- Spacious activity area with fireplace connects with cheery bayed sun room and breakfast area
- Master bedroom includes sliding glass doors in bay, walk-in closet and private bath
- Convenient kitchen has a see-through counter into activity area
- Storage space lines one whole wall of carport

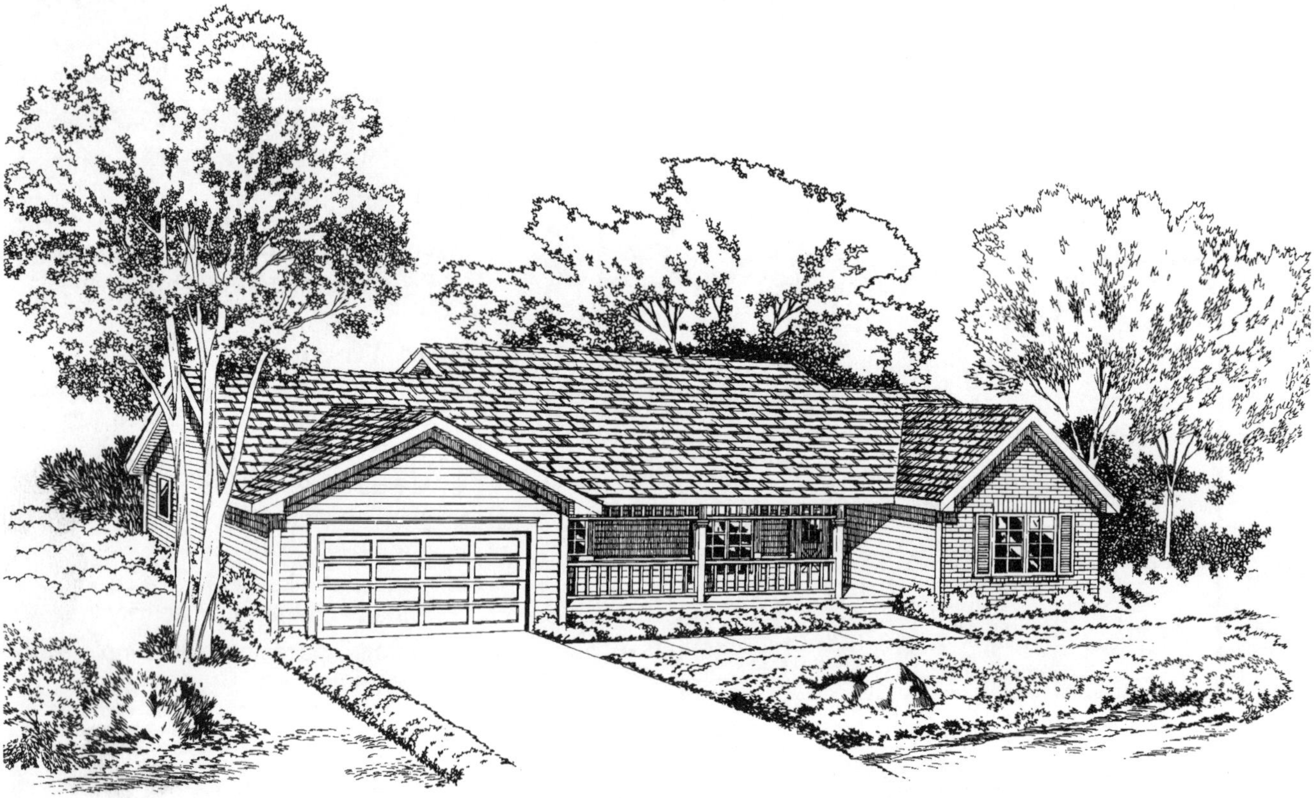

Plan #530-038D-0012

Price Code B

Total Living Area: 1,575 Sq. Ft.

Home has 3 bedrooms, 2 baths, 2-car garage and basement foundation.

Special features

- Two secondary bedrooms share a full bath
- Formal dining room features column accents
- Breakfast room has sliding glass doors leading to an outdoor deck

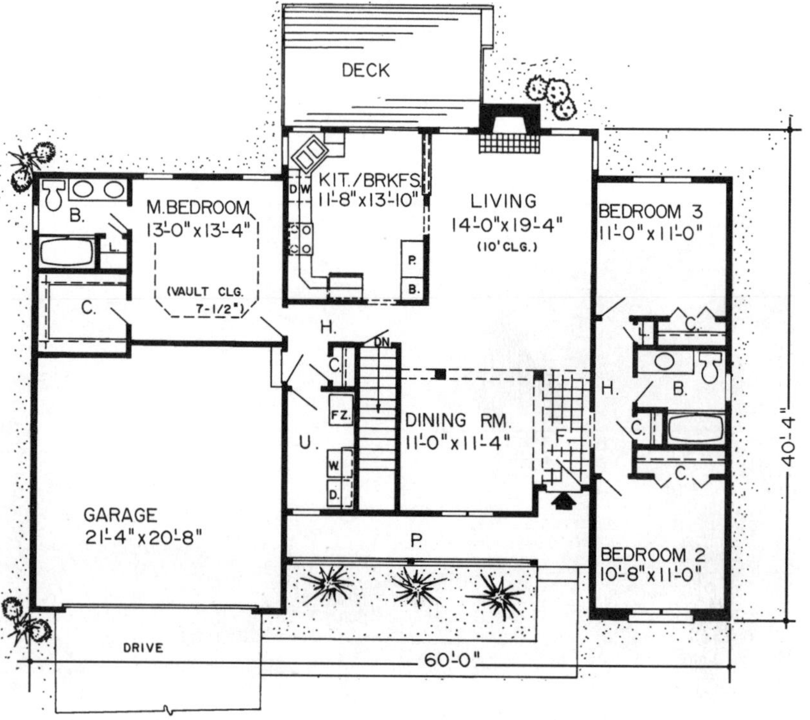
DECK
KIT./BRKFS.
11'-8"x13'-10"
LIVING
14'-0"x19'-4"
(10' CLG.)
M.BEDROOM
13'-0"x13'-4"
(VAULT CLG. 7-1/2")
BEDROOM 3
11'-0"x11'-0"
DINING RM.
11'-0"x11'-4"
GARAGE
21'-4"x20'-8"
BEDROOM 2
10'-8"x11'-0"
DRIVE
60'-0"
40'-4"

LOWE'S

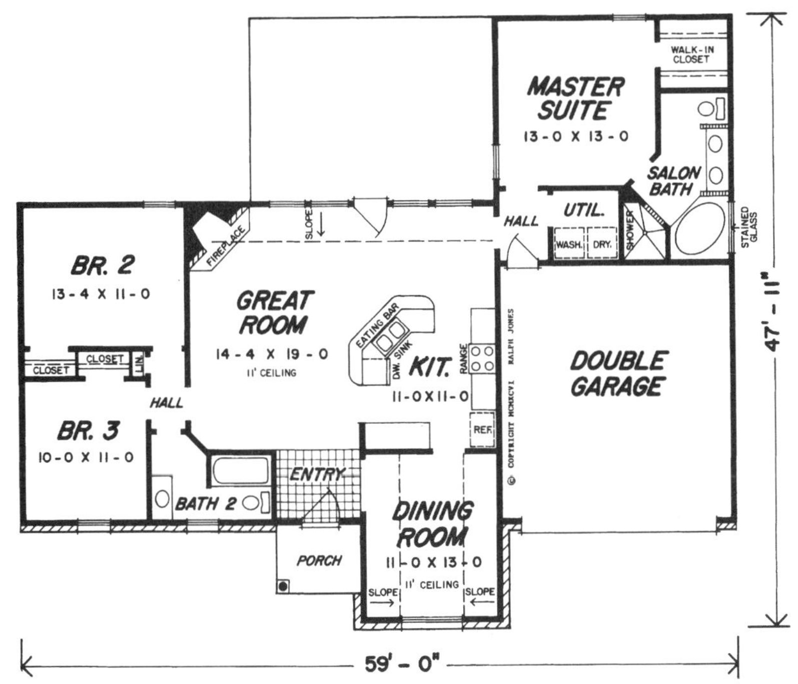
WALK-IN CLOSET
MASTER SUITE
13-0 X 13-0
SALON BATH
STAINED GLASS
UTIL.
WASH.
DRY.
SHOWER
HALL
FIREPLACE
SLOPE
BR. 2
13-4 X 11-0
GREAT ROOM
14-4 X 19-0
11' CEILING
EATING BAR
DW. SINK
KIT.
11-0X11-0
RANGE
REF.
DOUBLE GARAGE
CLOSET
CLOSET
LIN.
HALL
BR. 3
10-0 X 11-0
BATH 2
ENTRY
DINING ROOM
11-0 X 13-0
11' CEILING
SLOPE
SLOPE
PORCH
© COPYRIGHT MCMXCVI RALPH JONES
47'-11"
59'-0"

Plan #530-060D-0026

Price Code A

Total Living Area: 1,497 Sq. Ft.

Home has 3 bedrooms, 2 baths, 2-car garage and slab foundation.

Special features

- Open living area has a kitchen counter overlooking a cozy great room with fireplace
- Sloped ceiling accents dining room
- Master suite has privacy from other bedrooms

© COPYRIGHT MCMXCVI RALPH JONES

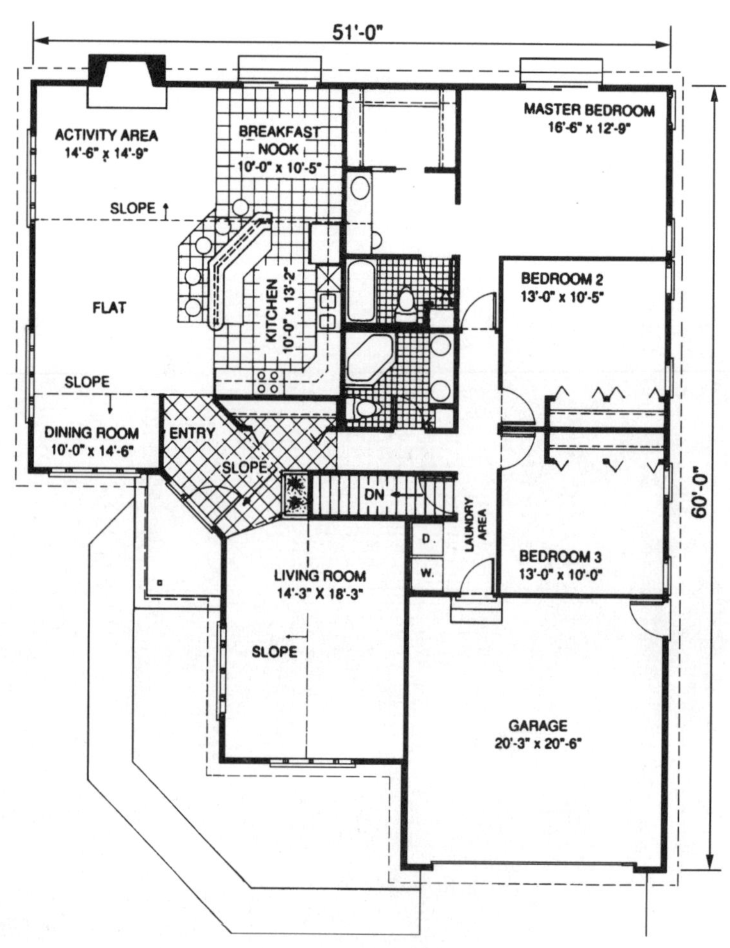
51'-0"
60'-0"
MASTER BEDROOM
16'-6" x 12'-9"
ACTIVITY AREA
14'-6" x 14'-9"
BREAKFAST NOOK
10'-0" x 10'-5"
SLOPE
FLAT
KITCHEN
10'-0" x 13'-2"
BEDROOM 2
13'-0" x 10'-5"
SLOPE
DINING ROOM
10'-0" x 14'-6"
ENTRY
SLOPE
DN
LAUNDRY AREA
D.
W.
BEDROOM 3
13'-0" x 10'-0"
LIVING ROOM
14'-3" X 18'-3"
SLOPE
GARAGE
20'-3" x 20'-6"

Plan #530-008D-0063

Price Code C

Total Living Area: 2,086 Sq. Ft.

Home has 3 bedrooms, 2 baths, 2-car garage and partial basement/crawl space foundation.

Special features

- An angled foyer leads to a vaulted living room with sunken floor
- Kitchen, breakfast nook, dining and activity rooms all have vaulted ceilings
- Skillfully designed kitchen features an angled island with breakfast bar
- Master bedroom is state-of-the-art with a luxury bath and giant walk-in closet

 TO ORDER BLUEPRINTS USE THE FORM ON PAGE 288 OR CALL TOLL-FREE **1-800-DREAM HOME** (373-2646)

LOWE'S

65-0
46-2
MASTER BATH
BRKFST RM
11-4 X 11-6
UTIL
STORAGE
GREAT ROOM
16-10 X 15-6
MASTER BEDROOM
14-6 X 15-6
KITCHEN
11-4 X 13-6
PAN
GARAGE
BATH 2
ENTRY
DINING ROOM
11-6 X 12-0
BEDROOM 2
12-4 X 13-2
PORCH
BEDROOM 3
11-4 X 12-0
NOTE: ALL CEILINGS 10 FT

Plan #530-019D-0009

Price Code C

Total Living Area: 1,862 Sq. Ft.

Home has 3 bedrooms, 2 baths, 2-car garage and crawl space foundation, drawings also include slab foundation.

Special features

- Comfortable traditional has all the amenities of a larger plan in a compact layout
- Angled eating bar separates kitchen and great room while leaving these areas open to one another for entertaining

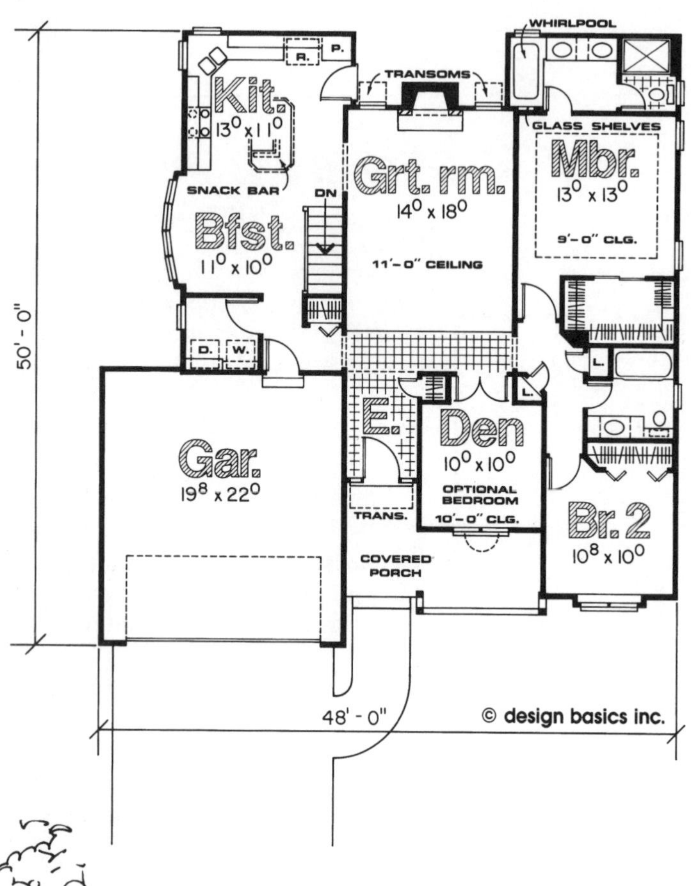
WHIRLPOOL
TRANSOMS
R.
P.
Kit.
$13^{0} \times 11^{0}$
SNACK BAR
DN
Bfst.
$11^{0} \times 10^{0}$
Grt. rm.
$14^{0} \times 18^{0}$
11'-0" CEILING
GLASS SHELVES
Mbr.
$13^{0} \times 13^{0}$
9'-0" CLG.
D.
W.
L.
E.
Den
$10^{0} \times 10^{0}$
OPTIONAL BEDROOM
10'-0" CLG.
TRANS.
Gar.
$19^{8} \times 22^{0}$
COVERED PORCH
Br. 2
$10^{8} \times 10^{0}$
50' - 0"
48' - 0"
© design basics inc.

Plan #530-026D-0130

Price Code A

Total Living Area: 1,479 Sq. Ft.

Home has 2 bedrooms, 2 baths, 2-car garage and basement foundation.

Special features

- Centrally located great room enhanced with fireplace
- Den can easily convert to a third bedroom
- Master bedroom has private bath with large walk-in closet
- Sunny kitchen/breakfast room enjoys view into great room

TO ORDER BLUEPRINTS USE THE FORM ON PAGE 288 OR CALL TOLL-FREE **1-800-DREAM HOME** (373-2646)

LOWE'S

Rear View

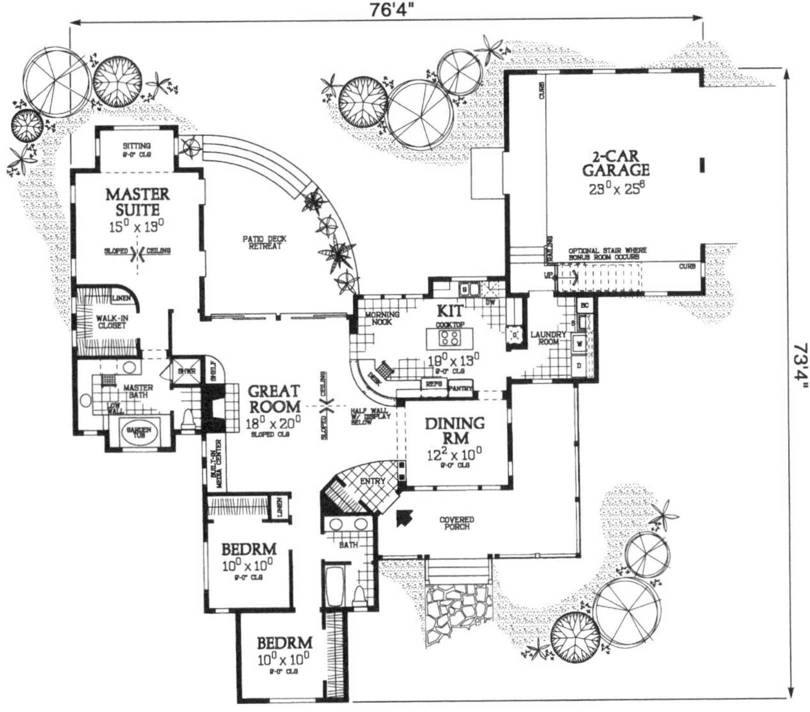
76'4"
73'4"
MASTER SUITE
PATIO DECK RETREAT
2-CAR GARAGE
KIT
GREAT ROOM
DINING RM
BEDRM
BEDRM
COVERED PORCH
ENTRY
LAUNDRY ROOM
MORNING NOOK
WALK-IN CLOSET
MASTER BATH
BATH
SITTING

Plan #530-049D-0008

Price Code C

Total Living Area: 1,937 Sq. Ft.

Home has 3 bedrooms, 2 baths, 2-car side entry garage and crawl space foundation.

Special features

- Upscale great room offers a sloped ceiling, fireplace with extended hearth and built-in shelves for an entertainment center
- Gourmet kitchen includes a cooktop island counter and a quaint morning room
- Master suite features a sloped ceiling, cozy sitting room, walk-in closet and a private bath with whirlpool tub

LOWE'S

Plan #530-008D-0090

Price Code A

Total Living Area: 1,364 Sq. Ft.

Home has 3 bedrooms, 2 baths, optional 2-car garage and basement foundation.

Special features

- Bedrooms are separated from the living area for privacy
- Master bedroom has a private bath and large walk-in closet
- Laundry area is conveniently located near the kitchen
- Bright and spacious great room
- Built-in pantry in the kitchen

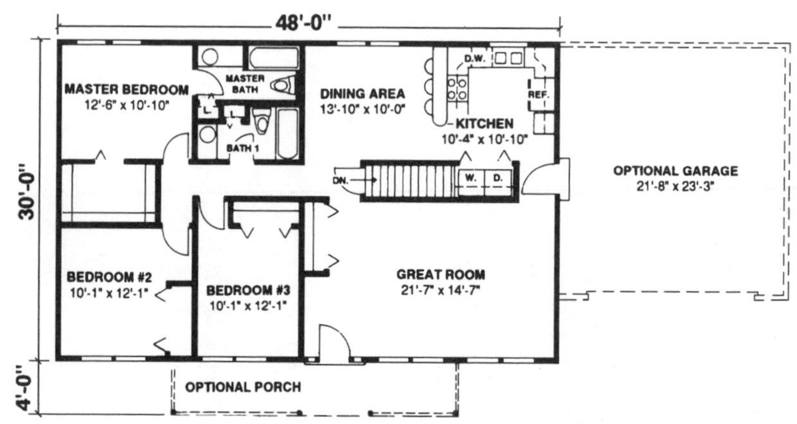
48'-0"
30'-0"
4'-0"
MASTER BEDROOM
12'-6" x 10'-10"
MASTER BATH
BATH 1
DINING AREA
13'-10" x 10'-0"
D.W.
REF.
KITCHEN
10'-4" x 10'-10"
DN.
W.
D.
OPTIONAL GARAGE
21'-8" x 23'-3"
BEDROOM #2
10'-1" x 12'-1"
BEDROOM #3
10'-1" x 12'-1"
GREAT ROOM
21'-7" x 14'-7"
OPTIONAL PORCH

LOWE'S

Width: 56'-4"
Depth: 68'-6"

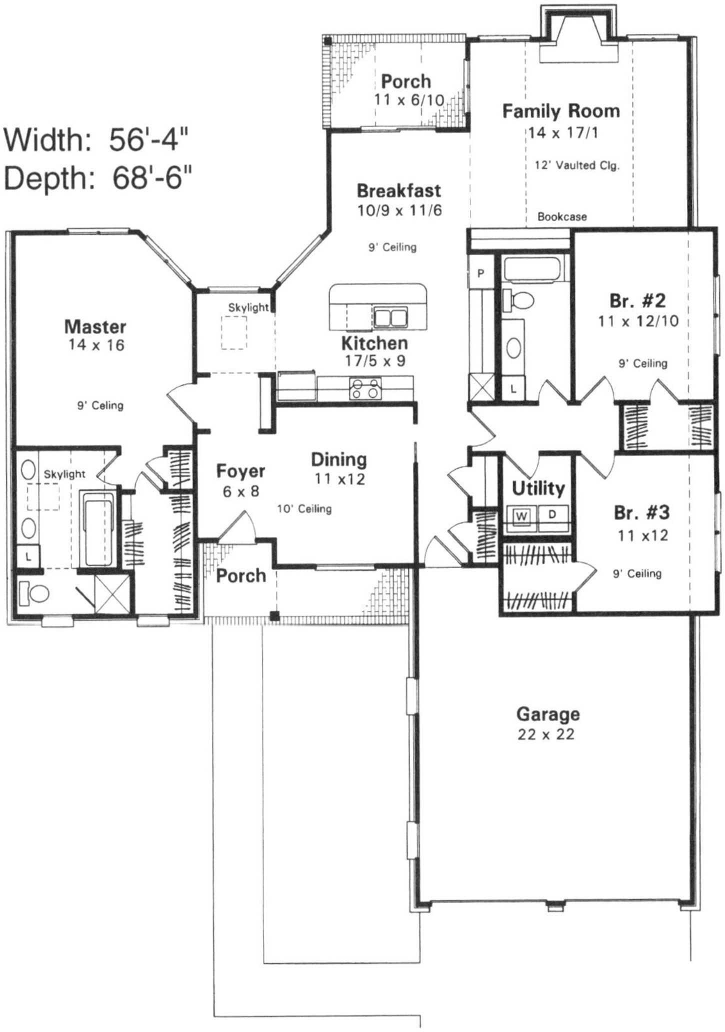

Porch 11 x 6/10
Family Room 14 x 17/1, 12' Vaulted Clg.
Bookcase
Breakfast 10/9 x 11/6, 9' Ceiling
Master 14 x 16, 9' Ceiling
Skylight
Kitchen 17/5 x 9
Br. #2 11 x 12/10, 9' Ceiling
Foyer 6 x 8
Dining 11 x12, 10' Ceiling
Utility
Br. #3 11 x12, 9' Ceiling
Porch
Garage 22 x 22

Plan #530-039D-0013

Price Code C

Total Living Area: 1,842 Sq. Ft.

Home has 3 bedrooms, 2 baths, 2-car garage and slab or crawl space foundation, please specify when ordering.

Special features

- Vaulted family room features a fireplace and an elegant bookcase
- Island countertop in kitchen makes cooking convenient
- Rear facade has an intimate porch area ideal for relaxing

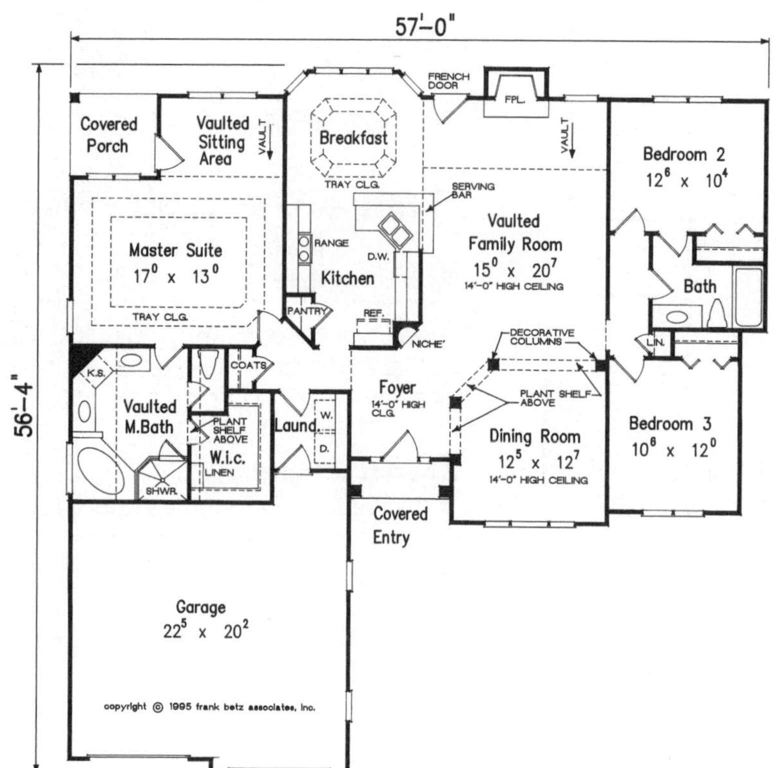
57'-0"
56'-4"
Covered Porch
Vaulted Sitting Area
VAULT
Breakfast
TRAY CLG.
FRENCH DOOR
FPL.
VAULT
Bedroom 2
12^6 x 10^4
SERVING BAR
Vaulted Family Room
15^0 x 20^7
14'-0" HIGH CEILING
Master Suite
17^0 x 13^0
TRAY CLG.
RANGE
D.W.
Kitchen
PANTRY
REF.
NICHE
Bath
LIN.
DECORATIVE COLUMNS
K.S.
COATS
Foyer
14'-0" HIGH CLG.
PLANT SHELF ABOVE
Vaulted M.Bath
PLANT SHELF ABOVE
Laund.
W.
D.
W.i.c.
LINEN
SHWR.
Dining Room
12^5 x 12^7
14'-0" HIGH CEILING
Bedroom 3
10^6 x 12^0
Covered Entry
Garage
22^5 x 20^2
copyright © 1995 frank betz associates, inc.

Plan #530-035D-0028

Price Code B

Total Living Area: 1,779 Sq. Ft.

Home has 3 bedrooms, 2 baths, 2-car garage and walk-out basement, slab or crawl space foundation, please specify when ordering.

Special features

- Well-designed floor plan has a vaulted family room with fireplace and access to the outdoors
- Decorative columns separate the dining area from the foyer
- A vaulted ceiling adds spaciousness in the master bath that also features a walk-in closet

TO ORDER BLUEPRINTS USE THE FORM ON PAGE 288 OR CALL TOLL-FREE **1-800-DREAM HOME** (373-2646)

Sensational Breakfast Area

LOWE'S

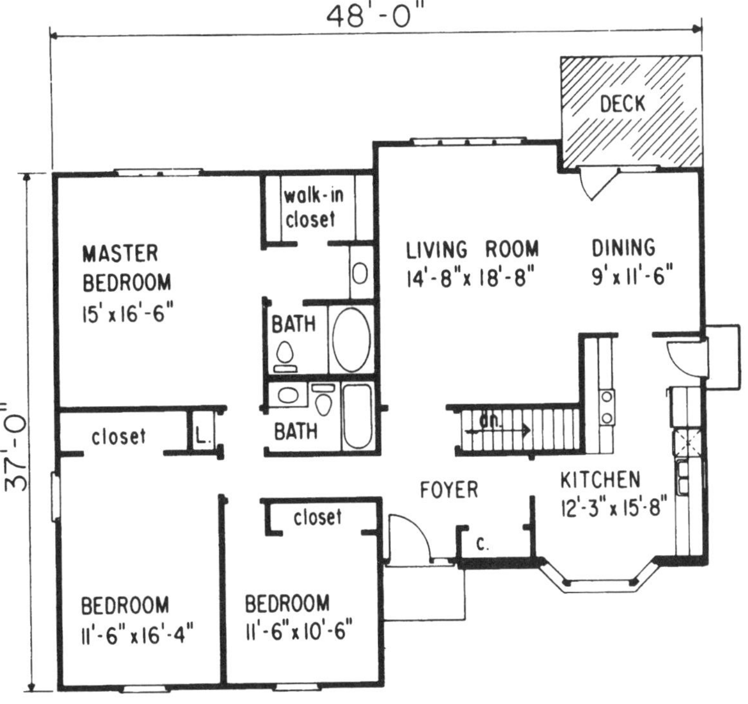
48'-0"
37'-0"
DECK
walk-in closet
MASTER BEDROOM 15' x 16'-6"
LIVING ROOM 14'-8" x 18'-8"
DINING 9' x 11'-6"
BATH
BATH
closet
L.
dn.
FOYER
KITCHEN 12'-3" x 15'-8"
closet
c.
BEDROOM 11'-6" x 16'-4"
BEDROOM 11'-6" x 10'-6"

Plan #530-008D-0047

Price Code B

Total Living Area: 1,610 Sq. Ft.

Home has 3 bedrooms, 2 baths and basement foundation, drawings also include crawl space and slab foundations.

Special features

- Attractive stone facade wraps around cozy breakfast room bay
- Roomy foyer leads to a splendid kitchen with an abundance of storage and counterspace
- The spacious living and dining room combination features access to the rear deck
- Master bedroom features a walk-in closet and compartmented bath with a luxurious garden tub

Bedrooms Share A Wing

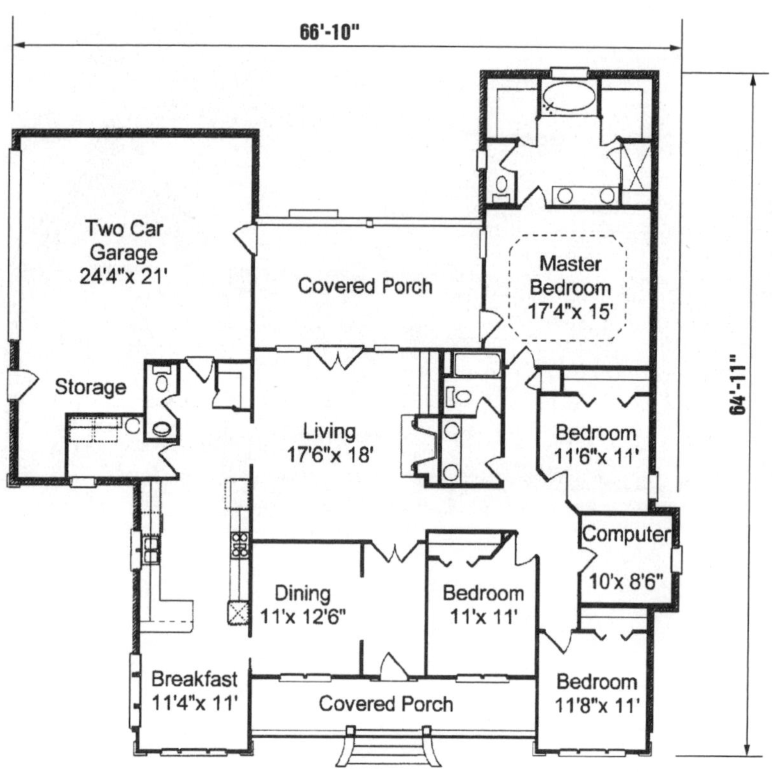
66'-10"
64'-11"
Two Car Garage 24'4"x 21'
Covered Porch
Master Bedroom 17'4"x 15'
Storage
Living 17'6"x 18'
Bedroom 11'6"x 11'
Computer 10'x 8'6"
Dining 11'x 12'6"
Bedroom 11'x 11'
Breakfast 11'4"x 11'
Covered Porch
Bedroom 11'8"x 11'

Plan #530-024D-0025

Price Code D

Total Living Area: 2,450 Sq. Ft.

Home has 4 bedrooms, 2 1/2 baths, 2-car side entry garage and slab foundation.

Special features

- Computer room is situated between bedrooms for easy access
- Two covered porches; one in front and one in rear of home
- Master bedroom includes bath with double walk-in closets and a luxurious step-up tub

 TO ORDER BLUEPRINTS USE THE FORM ON PAGE 288 OR CALL TOLL-FREE **1-800-DREAM HOME** (373-2646)

Quaint Home Made For Country Living

LOWE'S

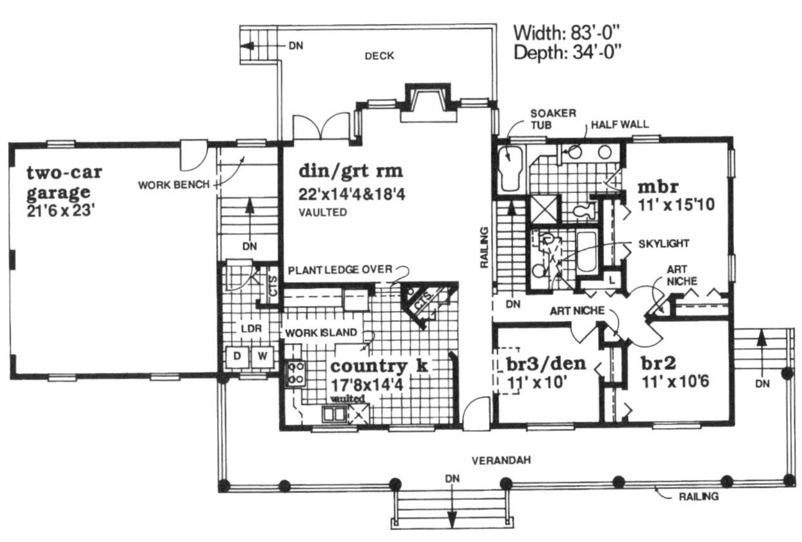
Width: 83'-0"
Depth: 34'-0"
DN
DECK
SOAKER TUB
HALF WALL
two-car garage
21'6 x 23'
WORK BENCH
din/grt rm
22'x14'4&18'4
VAULTED
mbr
11' x 15'10
SKYLIGHT
DN
RAILING
PLANT LEDGE OVER
ART NICHE
DN
ART NICHE
LDR
WORK ISLAND
D W
country k
17'8x14'4
vaulted
br3/den
11' x 10'
br2
11' x 10'6
DN
VERANDAH
DN
RAILING

Plan #530-062D-0051

Price Code B

Total Living Area: 1,578 Sq. Ft.

Home has 3 bedrooms, 2 baths, 2-car side entry garage and basement or crawl space foundation, please specify when ordering.

Special features

- A fireplace warms the great room and is flanked by windows overlooking the rear deck
- Bedrooms are clustered on one side of the home for privacy from living areas
- Master bedroom has a unique art niche at its entry and a private bath with separate tub and shower

Plan #530-035D-0041

Price Code D

Total Living Area: 2,403 Sq. Ft.

Home has 3 bedrooms, 2 1/2 baths, 2-car side entry garage and crawl space, slab or walk-out basement foundation, please specify when ordering.

Special features

- Cozy family room has a high coffered ceiling and a fireplace flanked by bookcases
- Vaulted breakfast room features a wall of windows
- Master suite has a private bath with double walk-in closets and access to a vaulted living room with wet bar

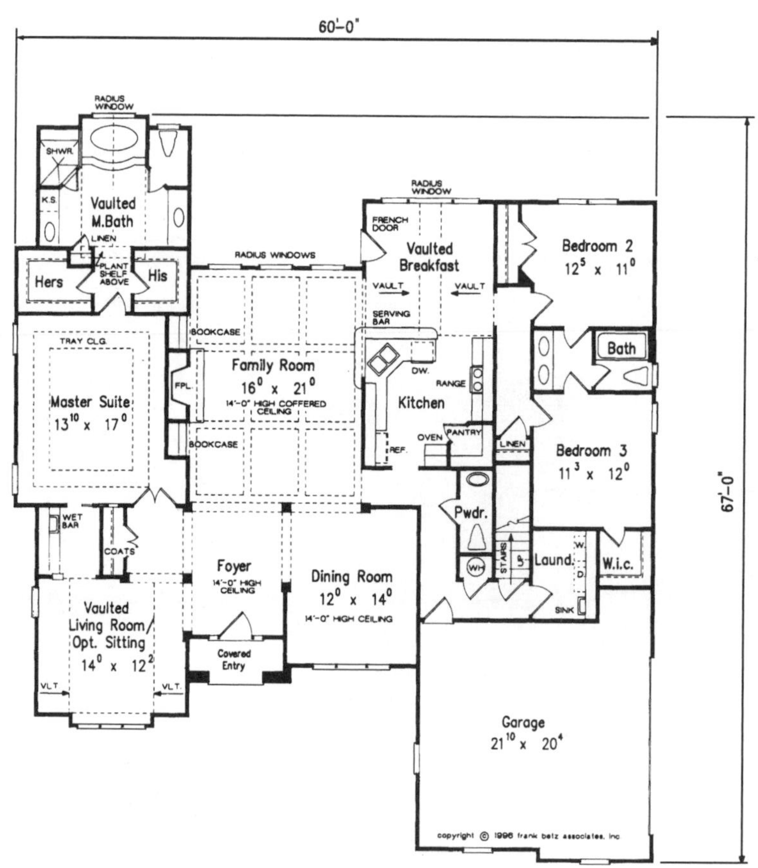
60'-0"
67'-0"
RADIUS WINDOW
SHWR.
K.S.
Vaulted M.Bath
LINEN
Hers
PLANT SHELF ABOVE
His
RADIUS WINDOWS
RADIUS WINDOW
FRENCH DOOR
Vaulted Breakfast
VAULT
VAULT
SERVING BAR
Bedroom 2 12⁵ x 11⁰
Bath
BOOKCASE
Family Room 16⁰ x 21⁰
14'-0" HIGH COFFERED CEILING
FPL
DW.
RANGE
Kitchen
OVEN
PANTRY
REF.
LINEN
Bedroom 3 11³ x 12⁰
TRAY CLG.
Master Suite 13¹⁰ x 17⁰
BOOKCASE
WET BAR
COATS
Foyer
14'-0" HIGH CEILING
Dining Room 12⁰ x 14⁰
14'-0" HIGH CEILING
Pwdr.
WH
STAIRS
Laund.
W
D
W.i.c.
SINK
Vaulted Living Room/Opt. Sitting 14⁰ x 12²
VLT.
VLT.
Covered Entry
Garage 21¹⁰ x 20⁴
copyright © 1996 frank betz associates, inc

LOWE'S

Plan #530-035D-0027

Price Code B

Total Living Area: 1,544 Sq. Ft.

Home has 3 bedrooms, 2 baths, 2-car garage and walk-out basement or crawl space foundation, please specify when ordering.

Special features

- Well-designed floor plan has vaulted family room with fireplace
- Decorative columns separate dining area from foyer
- A vaulted ceiling adds spaciousness to the master bath with walk-in closet
- Bonus room above garage has an additional 284 square feet of living area

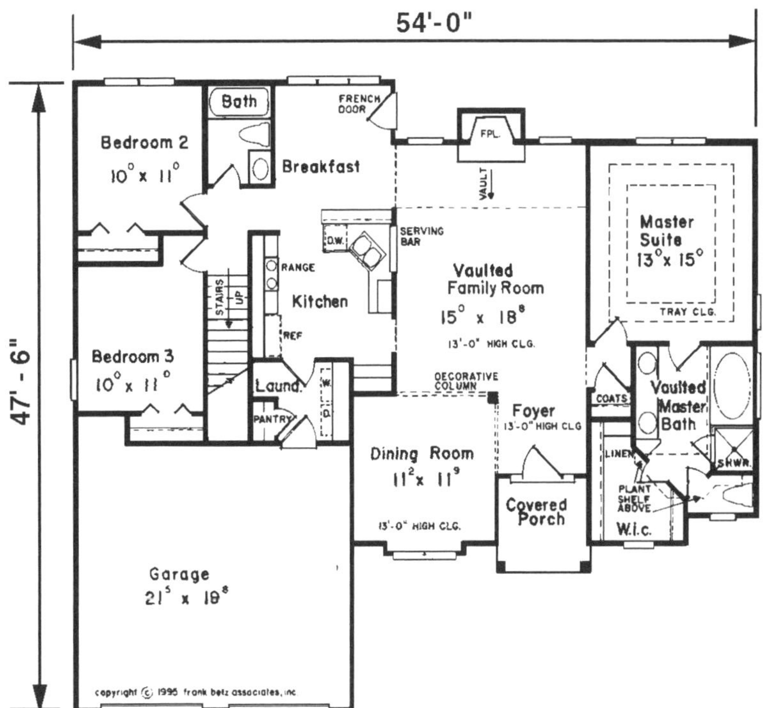
54'-0"
47'-6"
Bath
FRENCH DOOR
Bedroom 2
$10^{0} \times 11^{0}$
Breakfast
FPL.
VAULT
Master Suite
$13^{0} \times 15^{0}$
TRAY CLG.
D.W.
SERVING BAR
RANGE
Kitchen
STAIRS
UP
REF
Vaulted Family Room
$15^{0} \times 18^{8}$
13'-0" HIGH CLG.
Bedroom 3
$10^{0} \times 11^{0}$
Laund.
W
D
PANTRY
DECORATIVE COLUMN
Foyer
13'-0" HIGH CLG
COATS
Vaulted Master Bath
LINEN
SHWR.
PLANT SHELF ABOVE
W.i.c.
Dining Room
$11^{2} \times 11^{9}$
13'-0" HIGH CLG.
Covered Porch
Garage
$21^{5} \times 19^{8}$
copyright © 1995 frank betz associates, inc

LOWE'S

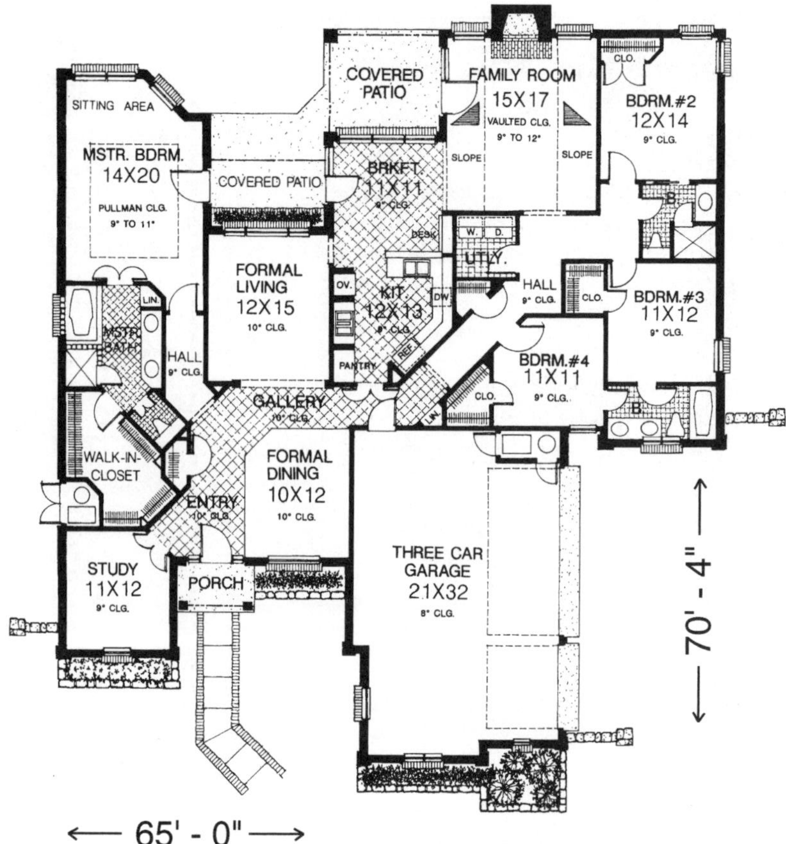
COVERED PATIO
FAMILY ROOM
15X17
VAULTED CLG.
9' TO 12'
SLOPE
SLOPE
CLO.
BDRM.#2
12X14
9' CLG.
SITTING AREA
MSTR. BDRM.
14X20
PULLMAN CLG.
9' TO 11'
COVERED PATIO
BRKFT.
11X11
9' CLG.
DESK
W. D.
UTLY.
B
FORMAL LIVING
12X15
10' CLG.
OV.
KIT
12X13
9' CLG.
DW
HALL
9' CLG.
CLO.
BDRM.#3
11X12
9' CLG.
LIN
MSTR. BATH
HALL
9' CLG.
PANTRY
REF
BDRM.#4
11X11
9' CLG.
CLO.
GALLERY
10' CLG.
LIN
B
WALK-IN-CLOSET
FORMAL DINING
10X12
10' CLG.
ENTRY
10' CLG.
THREE CAR GARAGE
21X32
8' CLG.
STUDY
11X12
9' CLG.
PORCH
70' - 4"
65' - 0"

Plan #530-036D-0049

Price Code D

Total Living Area: 2,591 Sq. Ft.

Home has 4 bedrooms, 3 baths, 3-car side entry garage and slab foundation.

Special features

- Formal living area has a nice view extending past the covered patio
- Family room is adjacent to breakfast area and has a vaulted ceiling and fireplace creating a cozy atmosphere
- Master bedroom has a private sitting area and large private bath
- Gallery adds interest to entry

TO ORDER BLUEPRINTS USE THE FORM ON PAGE 288 OR CALL TOLL-FREE **1-800-DREAM HOME** (373-2646)

Casual Living With This Family Design

LOWE'S

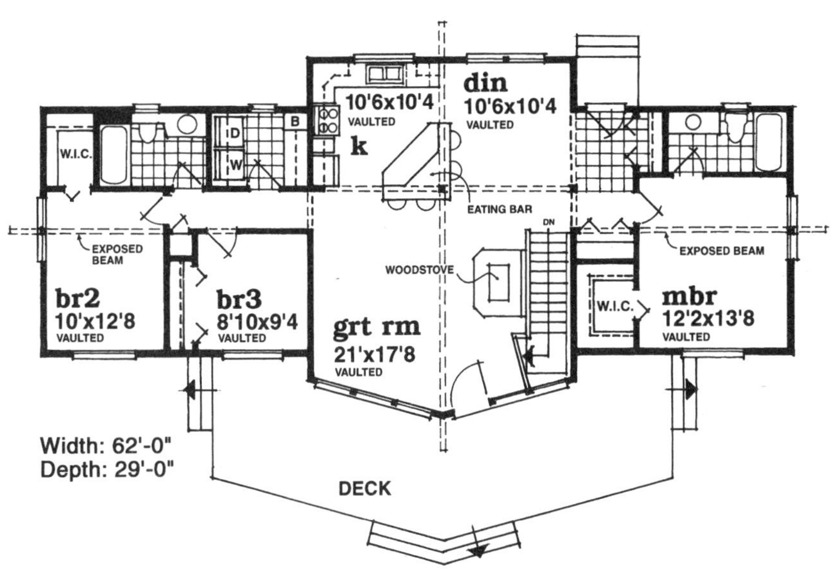
din
10'6x10'4
VAULTED
10'6x10'4
VAULTED
k
W.I.C.
D
W
B
EATING BAR
DN
EXPOSED BEAM
EXPOSED BEAM
WOODSTOVE
br2
10'x12'8
VAULTED
br3
8'10x9'4
VAULTED
grt rm
21'x17'8
VAULTED
W.I.C.
mbr
12'2x13'8
VAULTED
Width: 62'-0"
Depth: 29'-0"
DECK

Plan #530-062D-0053

Price Code A

Total Living Area: 1,405 Sq. Ft.

Home has 3 bedrooms, 2 baths and basement or crawl space foundation, please specify when ordering.

Special features

- An expansive wall of glass gives a spectacular view to the great room and accentuates the high vaulted ceilings throughout the design
- Great room is warmed by a woodstove and is open to the dining room and L-shaped kitchen
- Triangular snack bar graces the kitchen

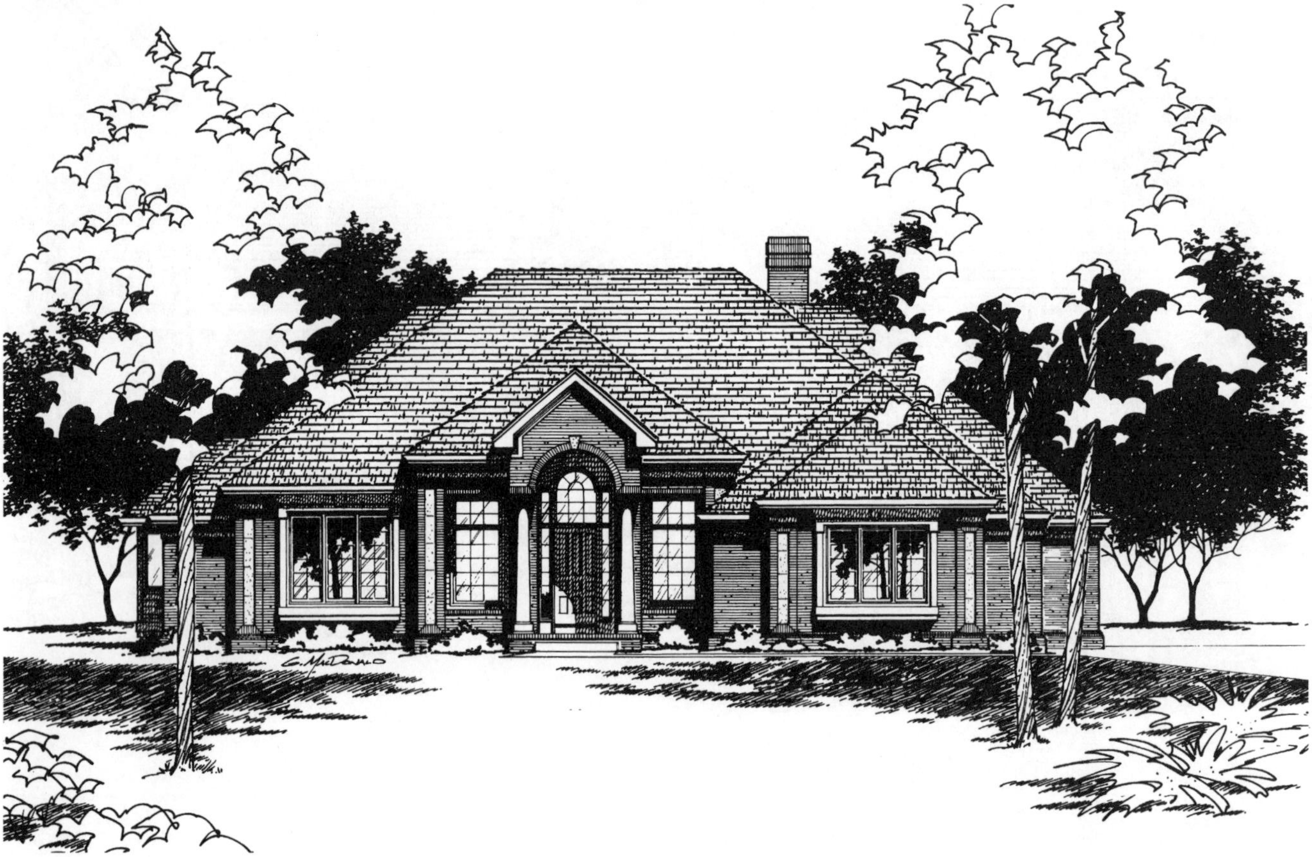

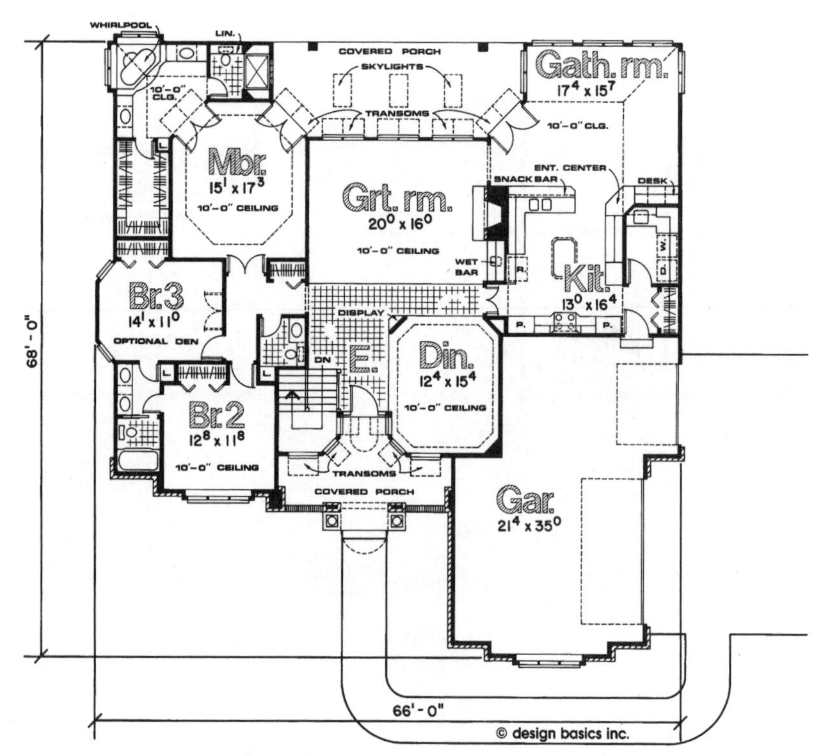
WHIRLPOOL
LIN.
COVERED PORCH
SKYLIGHTS
Gath. rm.
$17^4 \times 15^7$
10'-0" CLG.
TRANSOMS
10'-0" CLG.
Mbr.
$15^1 \times 17^3$
10'-0" CEILING
Grt. rm.
$20^0 \times 16^0$
10'-0" CEILING
ENT. CENTER
SNACK BAR
DESK
WET BAR
Kit.
$13^0 \times 16^4$
Br.3
$14^1 \times 11^0$
OPTIONAL DEN
DISPLAY
DN
E.
Din.
$12^4 \times 15^4$
10'-0" CEILING
Br.2
$12^8 \times 11^8$
10'-0" CEILING
TRANSOMS
COVERED PORCH
Gar.
$21^4 \times 35^0$
68'-0"
66'-0"
© design basics inc.

Plan #530-026D-0097

Price Code D

Total Living Area: 2,456 Sq. Ft.

Home has 3 bedrooms, 2 1/2 baths, 3-car side entry garage and basement foundation.

Special features

- Colossal front entrance intrigues guests
- Luxurious master bedroom features French doors leading outdoors to the covered porch and a one-of-a-kind master bath with numerous amenities
- Massive gathering room walks out to a sunlit covered porch

LOWE'S

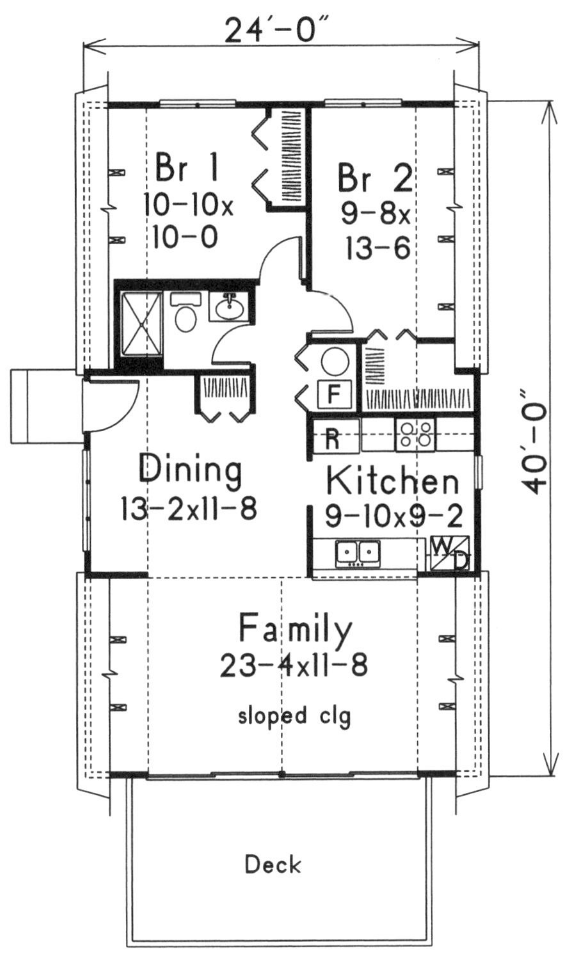
24'-0"
40'-0"
Br 1
10-10x
10-0
Br 2
9-8x
13-6
F
R
Dining
13-2x11-8
Kitchen
9-10x9-2
W
D
Family
23-4x11-8
sloped clg
Deck

Plan #530-008D-0131

Price Code AA

Total Living Area: 960 Sq. Ft.

Home has 2 bedrooms, 1 bath and crawl space foundation.

Special features

- Interesting roof and wood beams overhang a generous-sized deck
- Family room is vaulted and opens to dining area and kitchen
- Pullman-style kitchen has been skillfully designed
- Two bedrooms and hall bath are located at the rear of home

Plan #530-035D-0033

Price Code D

Total Living Area: 2,491 Sq. Ft.

Home has 3 bedrooms, 2 1/2 baths, 2-car side entry garage and crawl space, slab or walk-out basement foundation, please specify when ordering.

Special features

- Impressive master suite has an enormous sitting room with fireplace and access outdoors
- Vaulted family room is cozy with fireplace and conveniently located near breakfast room
- Handy bath between secondary bedrooms is easily accessible
- Optional bonus room above the garage and kitchen has an additional 588 square feet of living area

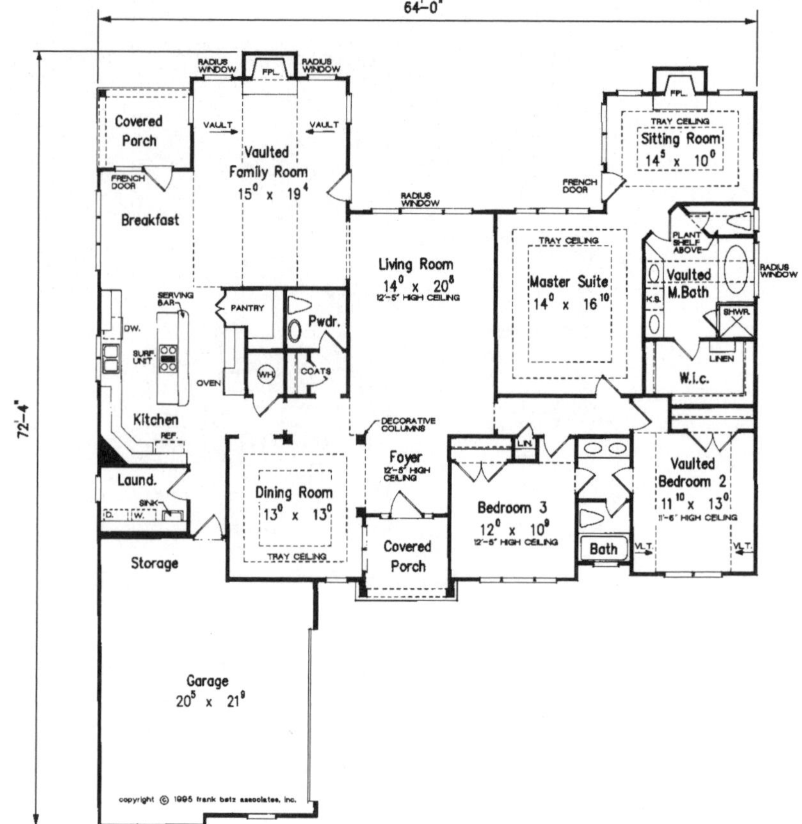
64'-0"
72'-4"
Covered Porch
Vaulted Family Room
15^0 x 19^4
Breakfast
Living Room
14^0 x 20^6
12'-5" HIGH CEILING
Sitting Room
14^5 x 10^0
Master Suite
14^0 x 16^{10}
Vaulted M.Bath
W.i.c.
Pantry
Pwdr.
Coats
Kitchen
Laund.
Dining Room
13^0 x 13^0
Foyer
Covered Porch
Bedroom 3
12^0 x 10^9
Vaulted Bedroom 2
11^{10} x 13^0
Bath
Storage
Garage
20^5 x 21^9
copyright © 1995 frank betz associates, inc.

TO ORDER BLUEPRINTS USE THE FORM ON PAGE 288 OR CALL TOLL-FREE **1-800-DREAM HOME** (373-2646)

LOWE'S

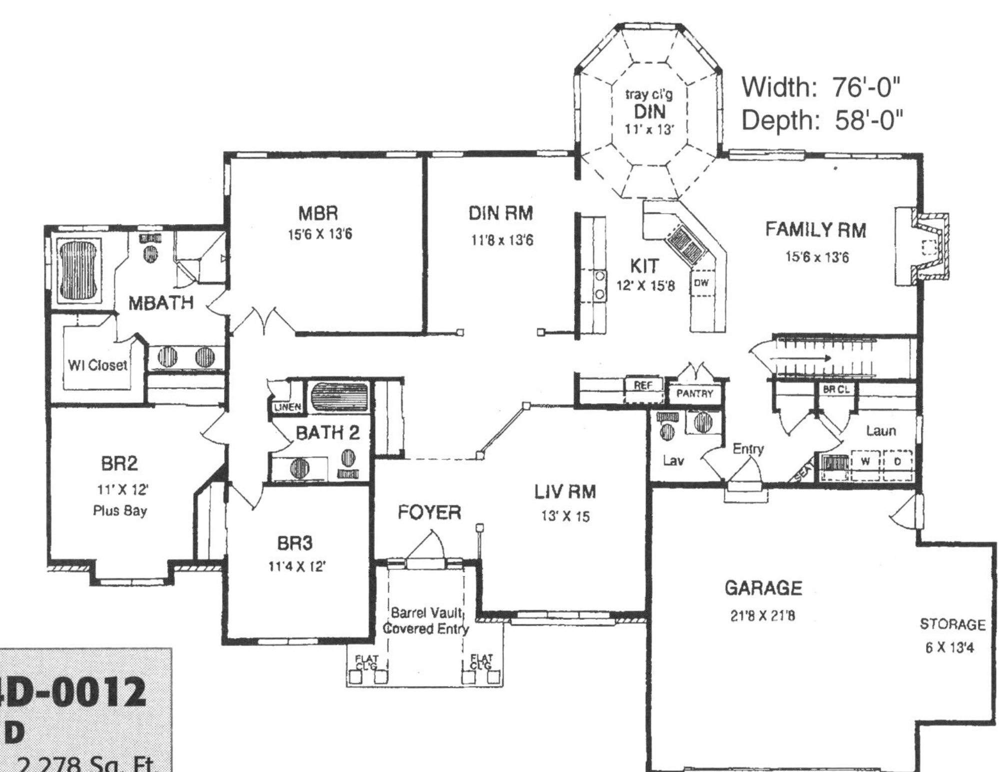
Width: 76'-0"
Depth: 58'-0"
tray cl'g
DIN
11' x 13'
MBR
15'6 X 13'6
DIN RM
11'8 x 13'6
FAMILY RM
15'6 x 13'6
KIT
12' X 15'8
DW
MBATH
WI Closet
REF
PANTRY
BR CL
LINEN
BATH 2
Laun
Lav
Entry
W
D
BR2
11' X 12'
Plus Bay
FOYER
LIV RM
13' X 15
BR3
11'4 X 12'
GARAGE
21'8 X 21'8
Barrel Vault
Covered Entry
STORAGE
6 X 13'4
FLAT CL'G
FLAT CL'G

Plan #530-034D-0012

Price Code D

Total Living Area: 2,278 Sq. Ft.

Home has 3 bedrooms, 2 1/2 baths, 2-car garage and basement foundation.

Special features

- Octagon-shaped dining area is cheerful and bright
- Kitchen with eat-in breakfast bar overlooks family room with fireplace
- Unique box-bay window in bed-room #2

Plan #530-036D-0034

Price Code A

Total Living Area: 1,225 Sq. Ft.

Home has 3 bedrooms, 2 baths, 2-car garage and slab foundation.

Special features

- Utility room accesses the kitchen and garage for convenience
- Extra closets and storage space throughout
- All bedrooms are located on one side of the home for privacy

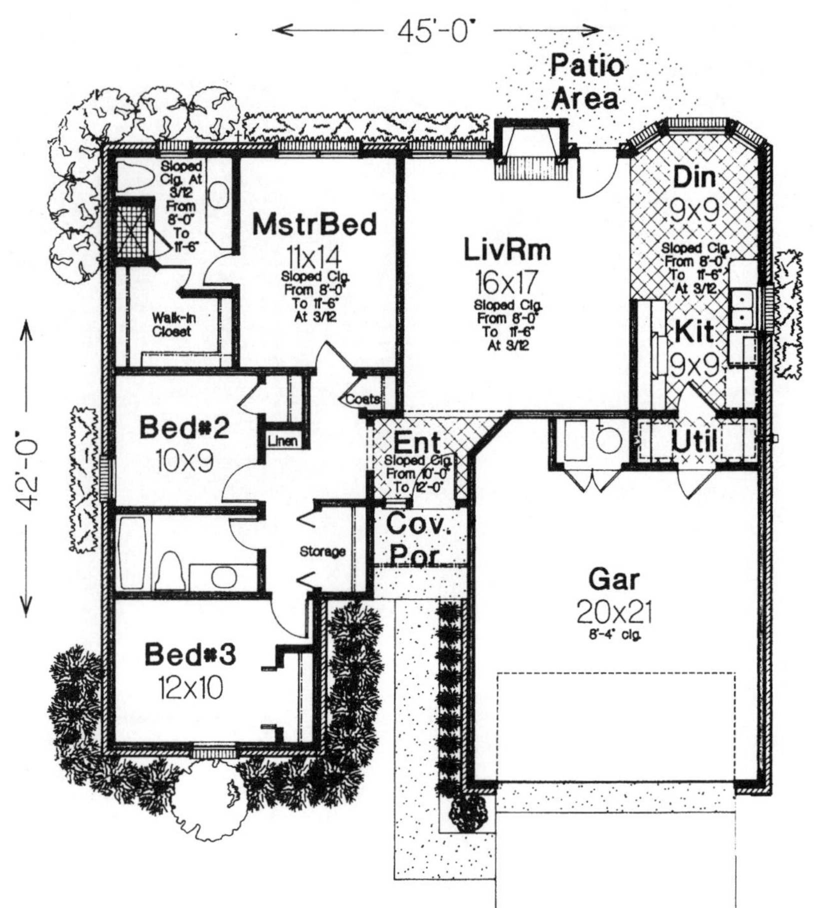
45'-0"
Patio Area
Sloped Clg. At 3/12 From 8'-0" To 11'-6"
MstrBed
11x14
Sloped Clg. From 8'-0" To 11'-6" At 3/12
Walk-in Closet
LivRm
16x17
Sloped Clg. From 8'-0" To 11'-6" At 3/12
Din
9x9
Sloped Clg. From 8'-0" To 11'-6" At 3/12
Kit
9x9
Coats
Linen
Bed#2
10x9
Ent
Sloped Clg. From 10'-0" To 12'-0"
Util
Cov. Por
Storage
Gar
20x21
8'-4" clg.
Bed#3
12x10
42'-0"

TO ORDER BLUEPRINTS USE THE FORM ON PAGE 288 OR CALL TOLL-FREE **1-800-DREAM HOME** (373-2646)

LOWE'S

Plan #530-060D-0016

Price Code A

Total Living Area: 1,214 Sq. Ft.

Home has 3 bedrooms, 2 baths, optional 2-car garage and slab or crawl space foundation, please specify when ordering.

Special features

- Sloped ceiling in great room adds drama
- Utility closet is well located near the bedrooms
- Open kitchen and breakfast area has a cheerful window with seat

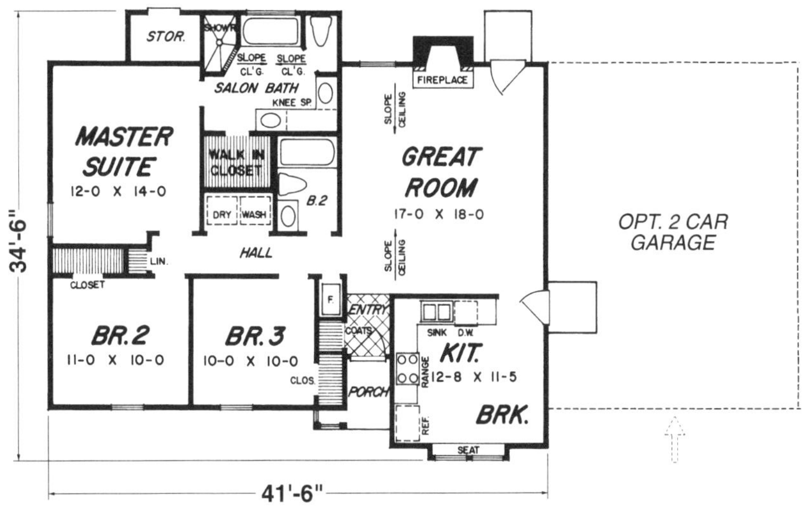
STOR.
SHOWR
SLOPE CL'G.
SLOPE CL'G.
SALON BATH
KNEE SP.
MASTER SUITE
12-0 X 14-0
WALK IN CLOSET
DRY
WASH
B.2
FIREPLACE
SLOPE CEILING
GREAT ROOM
17-0 X 18-0
SLOPE CEILING
OPT. 2 CAR GARAGE
34'-6"
HALL
LIN.
CLOSET
BR.2
11-0 X 10-0
BR.3
10-0 X 10-0
CLOS.
F
ENTRY
COATS
PORCH
SINK
D.W.
KIT.
RANGE
12-8 X 11-5
REF.
BRK.
SEAT
41'-6"

Plan #530-019D-0011

Price Code C

Total Living Area: 1,955 Sq. Ft.

Home has 3 bedrooms, 2 baths, 2-car side entry garage and crawl space foundation, drawings also include slab foundation.

Special features

- Porch adds outdoor area to this design
- Dining and great rooms are visible from foyer through a series of elegant archways
- Kitchen overlooks great room and breakfast room

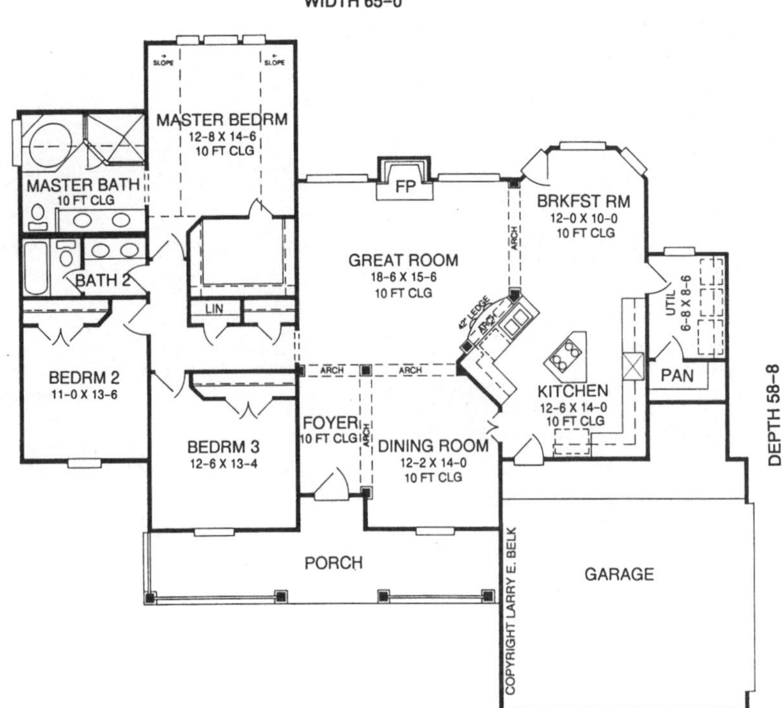
WIDTH 65-0
DEPTH 58-8
MASTER BEDRM
12-8 X 14-6
10 FT CLG
MASTER BATH
10 FT CLG
BATH 2
LIN
BEDRM 2
11-0 X 13-6
BEDRM 3
12-6 X 13-4
FP
GREAT ROOM
18-6 X 15-6
10 FT CLG
BRKFST RM
12-0 X 10-0
10 FT CLG
ARCH
42" LEDGE
UTIL
6-8 X 8-6
PAN
KITCHEN
12-6 X 14-0
10 FT CLG
FOYER
10 FT CLG
DINING ROOM
12-2 X 14-0
10 FT CLG
PORCH
GARAGE
COPYRIGHT LARRY E. BELK

TO ORDER BLUEPRINTS USE THE FORM ON PAGE 288 OR CALL TOLL-FREE **1-800-DREAM HOME** (373-2646)

LOWE'S

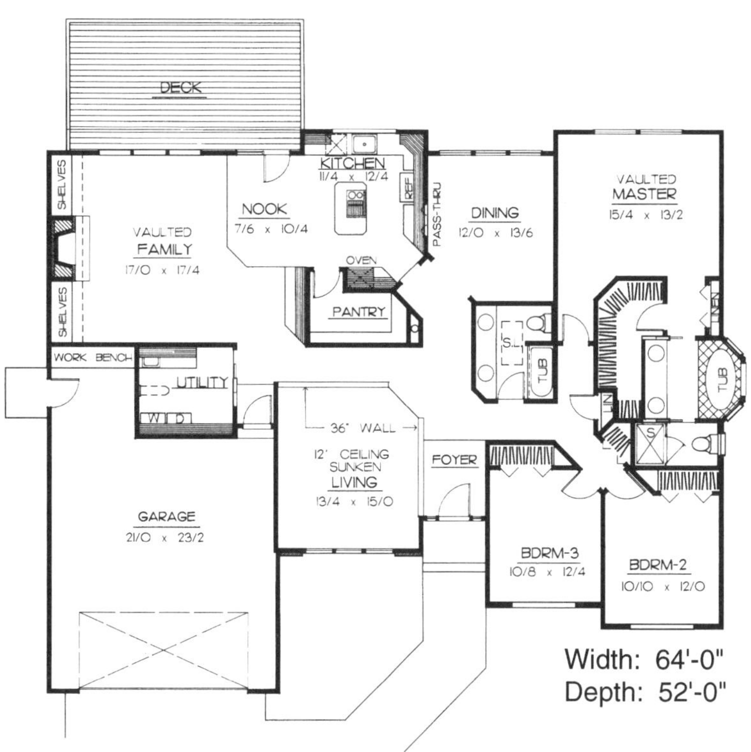
DECK
SHELVES
VAULTED
FAMILY
17/0 x 17/4
NOOK
7/6 x 10/4
KITCHEN
11/4 x 12/4
REF
OVEN
PANTRY
PASS-THRU
DINING
12/0 x 13/6
VAULTED
MASTER
15/4 x 13/2
TUB
S.
WORK BENCH
UTILITY
W D
36" WALL
12' CEILING
SUNKEN
LIVING
13/4 x 15/0
FOYER
GARAGE
21/0 x 23/2
BDRM-3
10/8 x 12/4
BDRM-2
10/10 x 12/0

Width: 64'-0"
Depth: 52'-0"

Plan #530-015D-0003

Price Code D

Total Living Area: 2,255 Sq. Ft.

Home has 3 bedrooms, 2 baths, 2-car garage and crawl space foundation.

Special features

- Well-lit foyer with transom overlooks sunken formal living room with 12' ceiling
- Family room and kitchen are situated separately for a more casual living area
- Breakfast nook offers access to the deck and overlooks the family room with a fireplace surrounded by built-in shelves
- Master suite has a vaulted ceiling and huge walk-in closet

LOWE'S

Plan #530-008D-0045

Price Code B

Total Living Area: 1,540 Sq. Ft.

Home has 3 bedrooms, 2 baths, 2-car garage and basement foundation, drawings also include crawl space and slab foundations.

Special features

- Porch entrance into foyer leads to an impressive dining area with full window and a half-circle window above
- Kitchen/breakfast room features a center island and cathedral ceiling
- Great room with cathedral ceiling and exposed beams is accessible from the foyer
- Master bedroom includes a full bath and walk-in closet
- Two additional bedrooms share a full bath

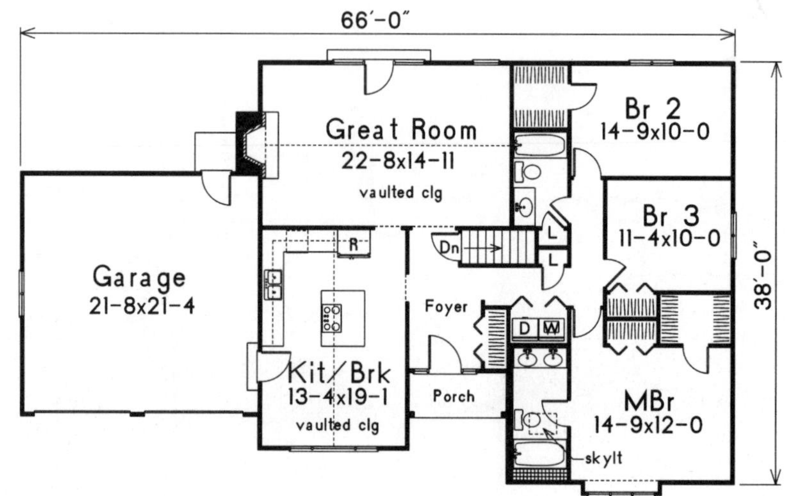
66'-0"
38'-0"
Great Room
22-8x14-11
vaulted clg
Br 2
14-9x10-0
Br 3
11-4x10-0
Garage
21-8x21-4
Dn
Foyer
Kit/Brk
13-4x19-1
vaulted clg
Porch
MBr
14-9x12-0
skylt

LOWE'S

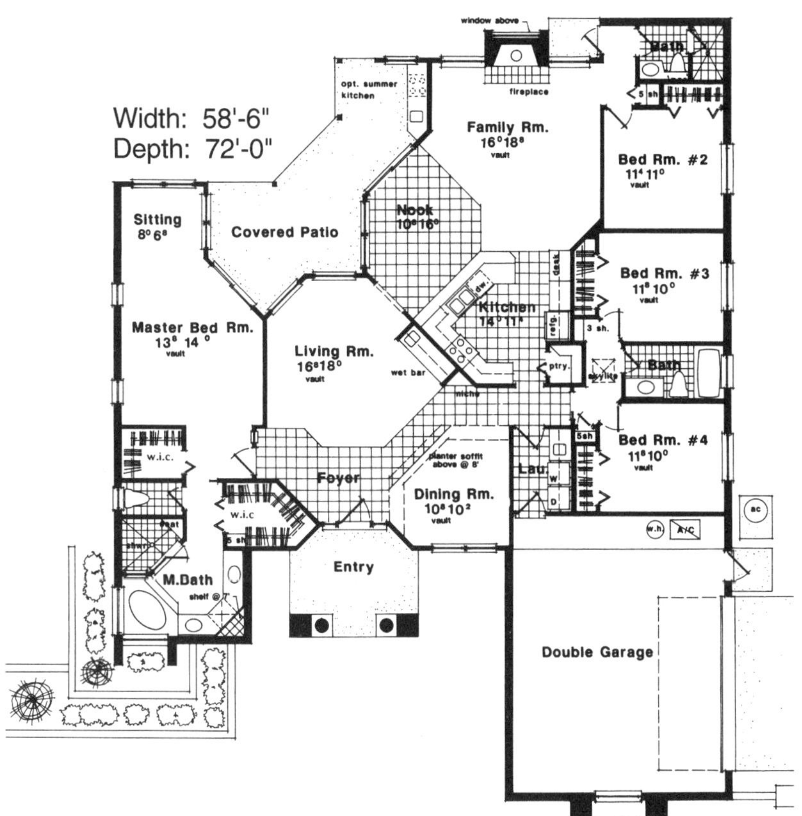
Width: 58'-6"
Depth: 72'-0"
window above
opt. summer kitchen
fireplace
Family Rm.
Bath
Bed Rm. #2
Sitting
Covered Patio
Nook
Bed Rm. #3
Kitchen
Master Bed Rm.
Living Rm.
wet bar
ptry.
Bath
Bed Rm. #4
w.i.c.
Foyer
Lau
Dining Rm.
planter soffit above @ 8'
w.i.c
M.Bath
Entry
Double Garage

Plan #530-047D-0039

Price Code D

Total Living Area: 2,224 Sq. Ft.

Home has 4 bedrooms, 3 baths, 2-car side entry garage and slab foundation.

Special features

- Vaulted living room features a wet bar
- Pass-through kitchen with V-shaped counter and walk-in pantry overlooks family room
- Master bedroom includes a sitting area, two walk-in closets and a full bath with tub surrounded by windows

LOWE'S

Plan #530-015D-0019

Price Code AA

Total Living Area: 1,018 Sq. Ft.

Home has 3 bedrooms, 2 baths, 2-car garage and crawl space foundation.

Special features

- Bayed living room provides charm while dining room offers access to patio area
- Well-defined use of space is a plus in this home
- Two-car garage offers space for washer and dryer

Width: 43'-6"
Depth: 49'-0"

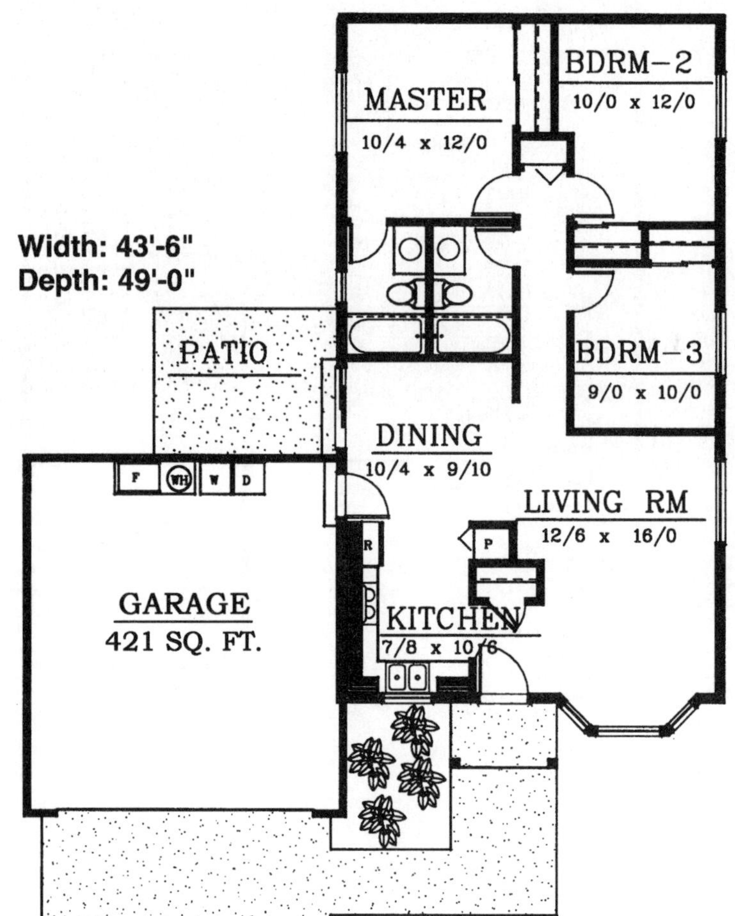
MASTER
10/4 x 12/0
BDRM-2
10/0 x 12/0
BDRM-3
9/0 x 10/0
PATIO
DINING
10/4 x 9/10
LIVING RM
12/6 x 16/0
GARAGE
421 SQ. FT.
KITCHEN
7/8 x 10/6
F
WH
W
D
R
P

LOWE'S

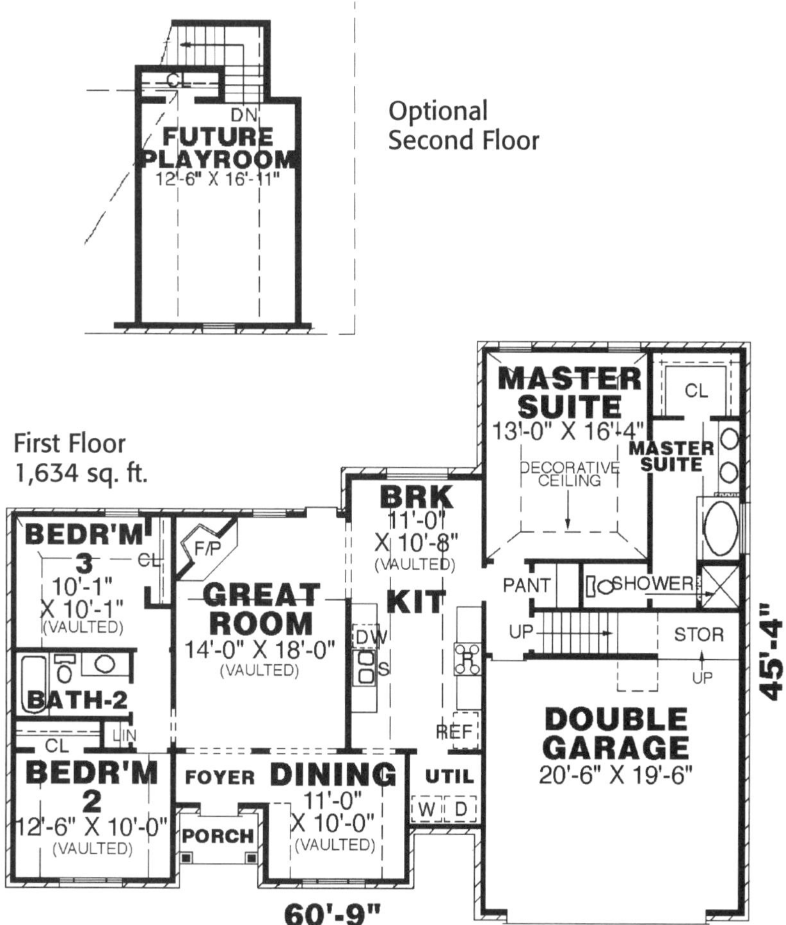
Optional
Second Floor
FUTURE PLAYROOM
12'-6" X 16'-11"
DN
CL
First Floor
1,634 sq. ft.
MASTER SUITE
13'-0" X 16'-4"
DECORATIVE CEILING
MASTER SUITE
CL
SHOWER
PANT
BRK
11'-0" X 10'-8"
(VAULTED)
KIT
BEDR'M 3
10'-1" X 10'-1"
(VAULTED)
F/P
GREAT ROOM
14'-0" X 18'-0"
(VAULTED)
DW
BATH-2
LIN
UP
STOR
REF
DOUBLE GARAGE
20'-6" X 19'-6"
BEDR'M 2
12'-6" X 10'-0"
(VAULTED)
FOYER
DINING
11'-0" X 10'-0"
(VAULTED)
UTIL
W D
PORCH
60'-9"
45'-4"

Plan #530-025D-0012

Price Code B

Total Living Area: 1,634 Sq. Ft.

Home has 3 bedrooms, 2 baths, 2-car garage and slab foundation.

Special features

- Enter the foyer to find a nice-sized dining room to the right and a cozy great room with fireplace straight ahead
- Secluded master suite offers privacy from other bedrooms and living areas
- Plenty of storage throughout this home
- Future playroom on the second floor has an additional 256 square feet of living area

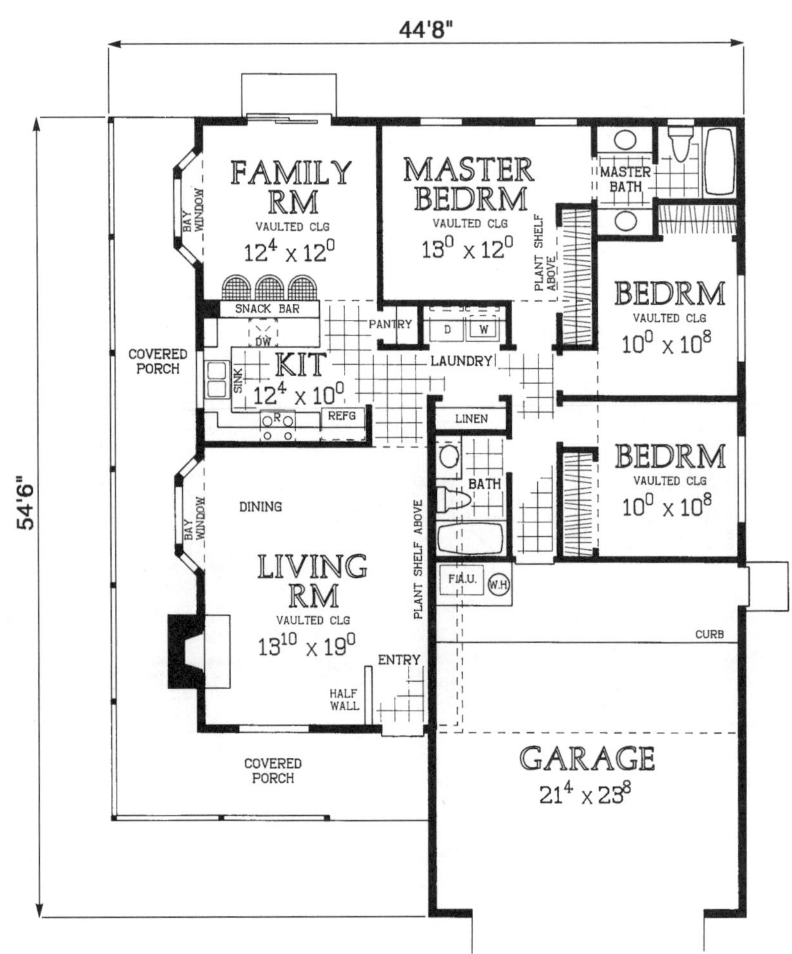
44'8"
54'6"
FAMILY RM
VAULTED CLG
12⁴ x 12⁰
BAY WINDOW
MASTER BEDRM
VAULTED CLG
13⁰ x 12⁰
MASTER BATH
PLANT SHELF ABOVE
BEDRM
VAULTED CLG
10⁰ x 10⁸
SNACK BAR
PANTRY
D
W
DW
COVERED PORCH
KIT
12⁴ x 10⁰
SINK
LAUNDRY
R
REFG
LINEN
BEDRM
VAULTED CLG
10⁰ x 10⁸
BATH
DINING
BAY WINDOW
LIVING RM
VAULTED CLG
13¹⁰ x 19⁰
PLANT SHELF ABOVE
F.A.U.
W.H.
CURB
ENTRY
HALF WALL
COVERED PORCH
GARAGE
21⁴ x 23⁸

Plan #530-049D-0005

Price Code A

Total Living Area: 1,389 Sq. Ft.

Home has 3 bedrooms, 2 baths, 2-car garage and slab foundation.

Special features

- Formal living room has a warming fireplace and delightful bay window
- U-shaped kitchen shares a snack bar with the bayed family room
- Lovely master bedroom has its own private bath

TO ORDER BLUEPRINTS USE THE FORM ON PAGE 288 OR CALL TOLL-FREE **1-800-DREAM HOME** (373-2646)

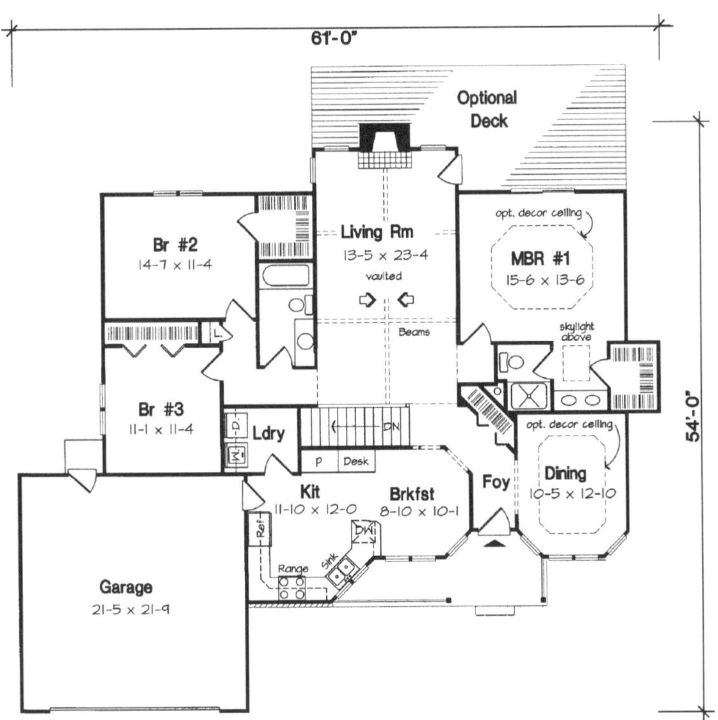
61'-0"
54'-0"
Optional Deck
Living Rm
13-5 x 23-4
vaulted
Beams
opt. decor ceiling
MBR #1
15-6 x 13-6
skylight above
Br #2
14-7 x 11-4
Br #3
11-1 x 11-4
Ldry
DN
P
Desk
Kit
11-10 x 12-0
Brkfst
8-10 x 10-1
Foy
opt. decor ceiling
Dining
10-5 x 12-10
Ref
Range
Sink
DW
Garage
21-5 x 21-9

Plan #530-038D-0049

Price Code B

Total Living Area: 1,686 Sq. Ft.

Home has 3 bedrooms, 2 baths, 2-car garage and basement, crawl space or slab foundation, please specify when ordering.

Special features

- Breakfast room surrounded with windows connects to the kitchen for convenience
- Master bedroom is separate from secondary bedrooms for privacy
- Vaulted living room features spectacular exposed beams creating a dramatic atmosphere

Rear View

LOWE'S

Plan #530-028D-0006

Price Code B

Total Living Area: 1,700 Sq. Ft.

Home has 3 bedrooms, 2 baths and crawl space or slab foundation, please specify when ordering.

Special features

- Oversized laundry room has large pantry and storage area as well as access to the outdoors
- Master bedroom is separated from other bedrooms for privacy
- Raised snack bar in kitchen allows extra seating for dining

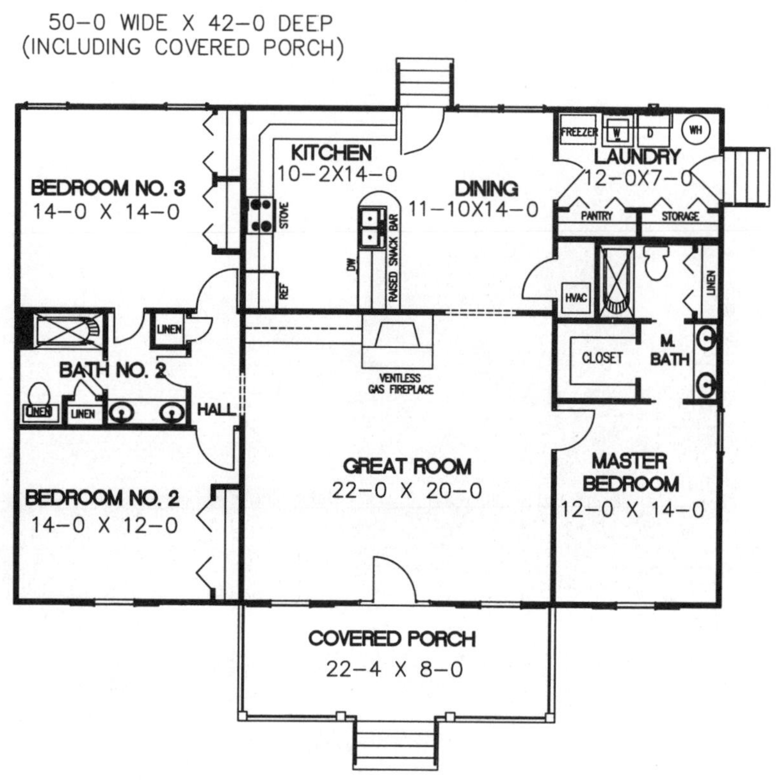
50-0 WIDE X 42-0 DEEP
(INCLUDING COVERED PORCH)
KITCHEN
10-2X14-0
DINING
11-10X14-0
LAUNDRY
12-0X7-0
FREEZER
W
D
WH
PANTRY
STORAGE
BEDROOM NO. 3
14-0 X 14-0
STOVE
DW
REF
RAISED SNACK BAR
HVAC
LINEN
CLOSET
M. BATH
BATH NO. 2
LINEN
LINEN
LINEN
HALL
VENTLESS GAS FIREPLACE
GREAT ROOM
22-0 X 20-0
MASTER BEDROOM
12-0 X 14-0
BEDROOM NO. 2
14-0 X 12-0
COVERED PORCH
22-4 X 8-0

TO ORDER BLUEPRINTS USE THE FORM ON PAGE 288 OR CALL TOLL-FREE **1-800-DREAM HOME** (373-2646)

LOWE'S

Plan #530-039D-0002

Price Code A

Total Living Area: 1,333 Sq. Ft.

Home has 3 bedrooms, 2 baths, 2-car attached carport and slab or crawl space foundation, please specify when ordering.

Special features

- Country charm with a covered front porch
- Dining area looks into the family room with fireplace
- Master suite has a walk-in closet and private bath

Width: 55'-6"
Depth: 64'-3"

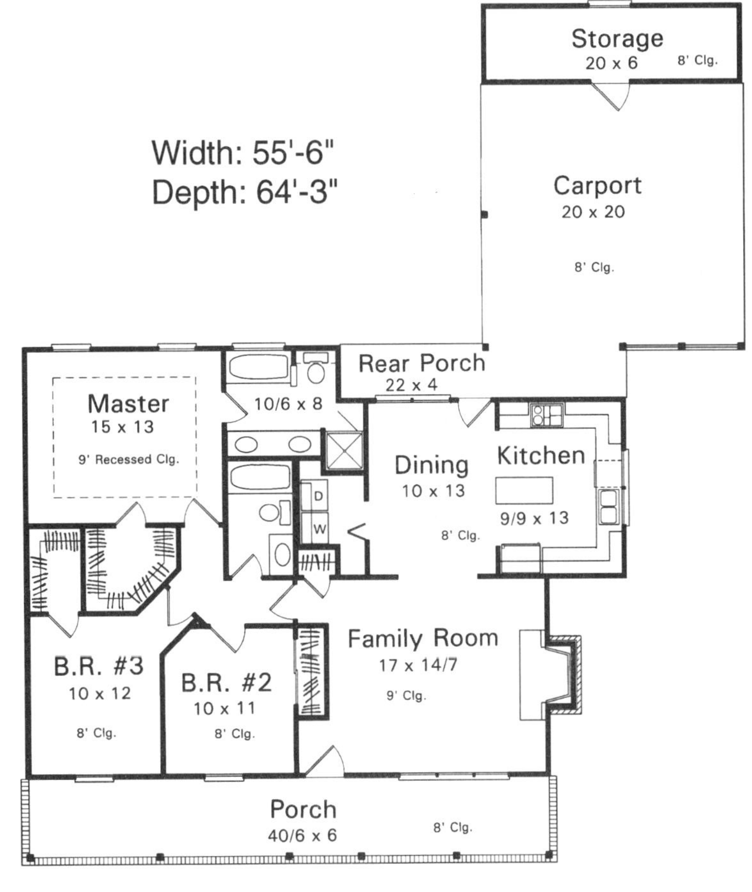
Storage
20 x 6
8' Clg.
Carport
20 x 20
8' Clg.
Rear Porch
22 x 4
Master
15 x 13
9' Recessed Clg.
10/6 x 8
Dining
10 x 13
8' Clg.
Kitchen
9/9 x 13
D
W
B.R. #3
10 x 12
8' Clg.
B.R. #2
10 x 11
8' Clg.
Family Room
17 x 14/7
9' Clg.
Porch
40/6 x 6
8' Clg.

Plan #530-026D-0137

Price Code B

Total Living Area: 1,758 Sq. Ft.

Home has 3 bedrooms, 2 baths, 2-car garage and basement foundation.

Special features

- Secluded covered porch off the breakfast area is a charming touch
- Great room and dining area combine for terrific entertaining possibilities
- Master bedroom has all the amenities
- Spacious foyer opens into a large great room with 11' ceiling

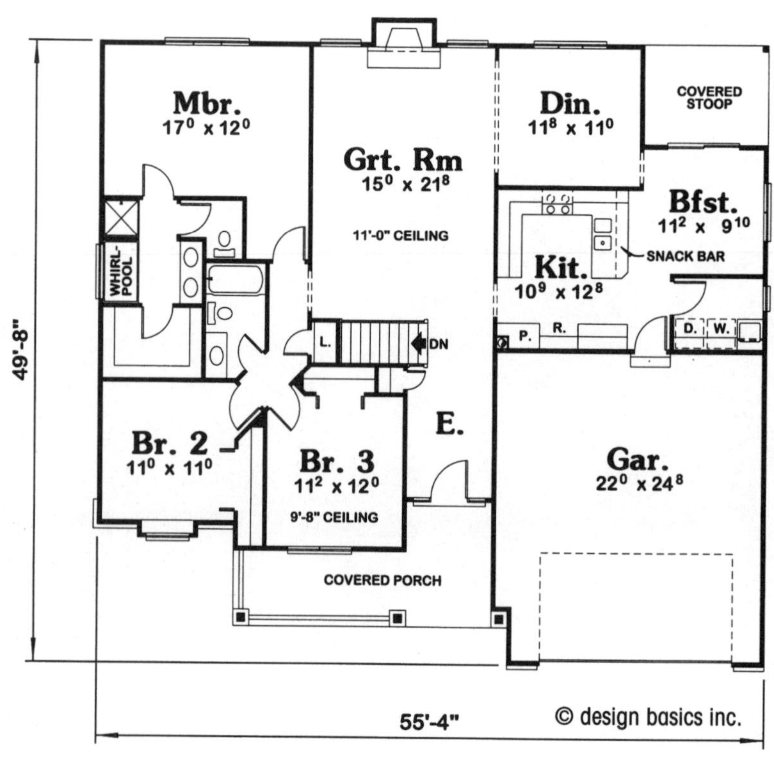
Mbr.
17^0 x 12^0
Grt. Rm
15^0 x 21^8
11'-0" CEILING
Din.
11^8 x 11^0
COVERED STOOP
Bfst.
11^2 x 9^{10}
SNACK BAR
Kit.
10^9 x 12^8
WHIRL-POOL
L.
DN
P.
R.
D.
W.
E.
Br. 2
11^0 x 11^0
Br. 3
11^2 x 12^0
9'-8" CEILING
Gar.
22^0 x 24^8
COVERED PORCH
49'-8"
55'-4"
© design basics inc.

TO ORDER BLUEPRINTS USE THE FORM ON PAGE 288 OR CALL TOLL-FREE **1-800-DREAM HOME** (373-2646)

LOWE'S

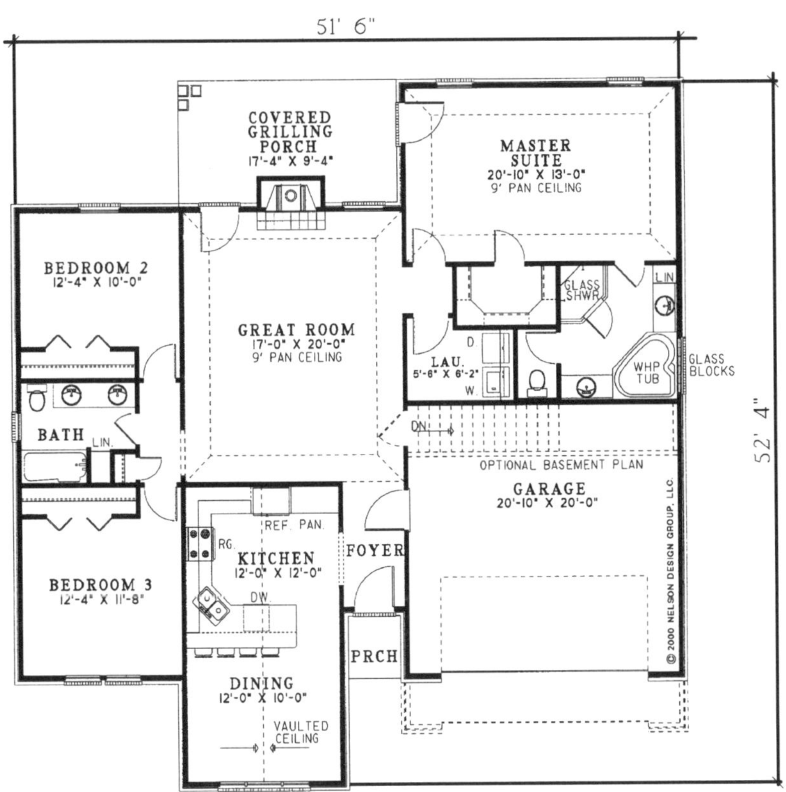
51' 6"
COVERED GRILLING PORCH 17'-4" X 9'-4"
MASTER SUITE 20'-10" X 13'-0" 9' PAN CEILING
BEDROOM 2 12'-4" X 10'-0"
GREAT ROOM 17'-0" X 20'-0" 9' PAN CEILING
GLASS SHWR
LIN
D
LAU. 5'-6" X 6'-2"
W
WHP TUB
GLASS BLOCKS
BATH
LIN.
DN
OPTIONAL BASEMENT PLAN
GARAGE 20'-10" X 20'-0"
52' 4"
REF. PAN.
RG.
KITCHEN 12'-0" X 12'-0"
DW
FOYER
BEDROOM 3 12'-4" X 11'-8"
PRCH
DINING 12'-0" X 10'-0"
VAULTED CEILING
© 2000 NELSON DESIGN GROUP, LLC

Plan #530-055D-0024

Price Code B

Total Living Area: 1,680 Sq. Ft.

Home has 3 bedrooms, 2 baths, 2-car garage and walk-out basement, basement, crawl space or slab foundation, please specify when ordering.

Special features

- Enormous and luxurious master suite
- Kitchen and dining room have vaulted ceilings creating an open feeling
- Double sinks grace secondary bath

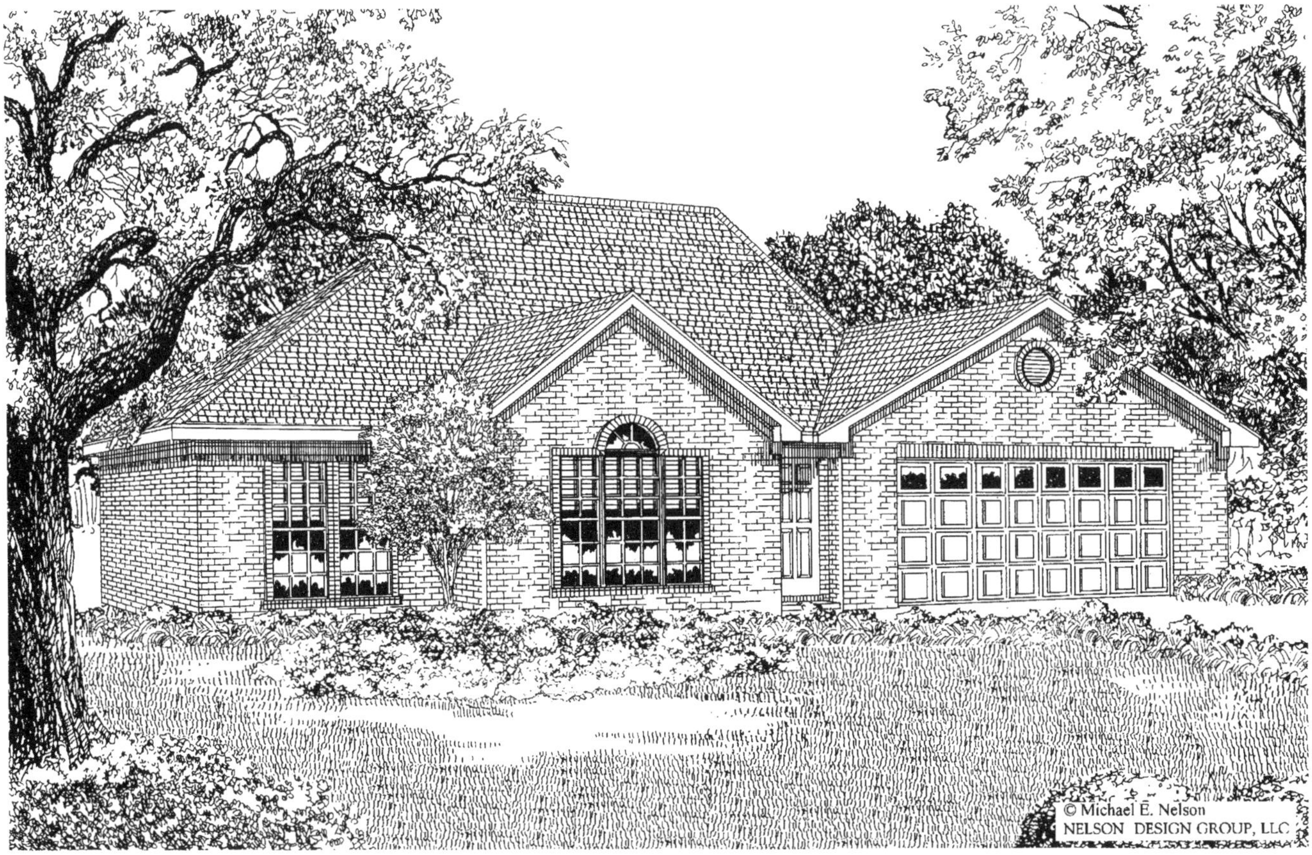

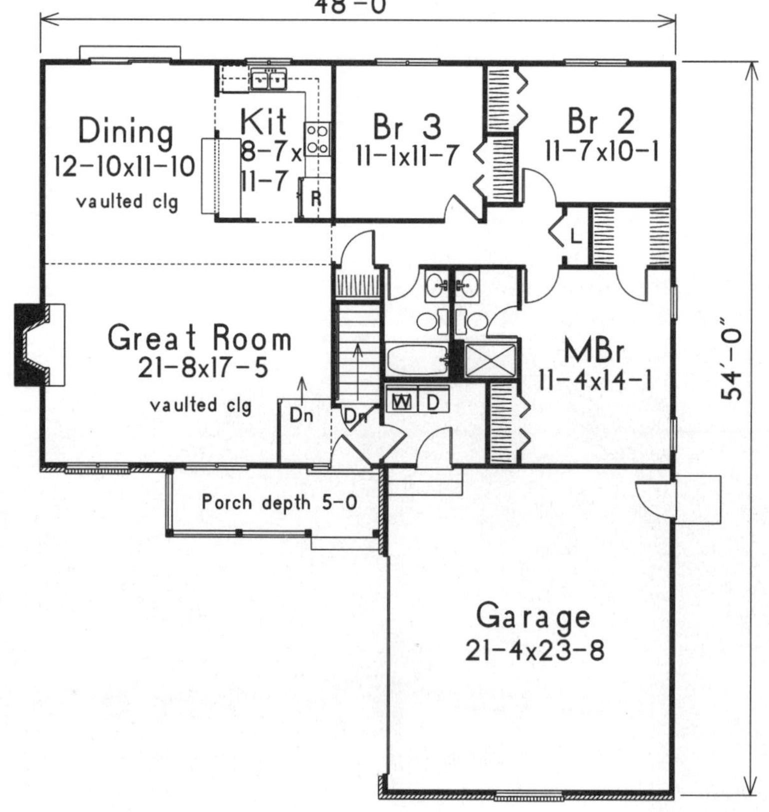
48'-0"
54'-0"
Dining
12-10x11-10
vaulted clg
Kit
8-7x
11-7
R
Br 3
11-1x11-7
Br 2
11-7x10-1
L
Great Room
21-8x17-5
vaulted clg
Dn
Dn
W
D
MBr
11-4x14-1
Porch depth 5-0
Garage
21-4x23-8

Plan #530-008D-0010

Price Code A

Total Living Area: 1,440 Sq. Ft.

Home has 3 bedrooms, 2 baths, 2-car side entry garage and basement foundation, drawings also include crawl space and slab foundations.

Special features

- Foyer adjoins massive-sized great room with sloping ceiling and tall masonry fireplace
- The kitchen connects to the spacious dining room and features a pass-through to the breakfast bar
- Master bedroom enjoys a private bath and two closets
- An oversized two-car side entry garage offers plenty of storage for bicycles, lawn equipment, etc.

 TO ORDER BLUEPRINTS USE THE FORM ON PAGE 288 OR CALL TOLL-FREE **1-800-DREAM HOME** (373-2646)

LOWE'S

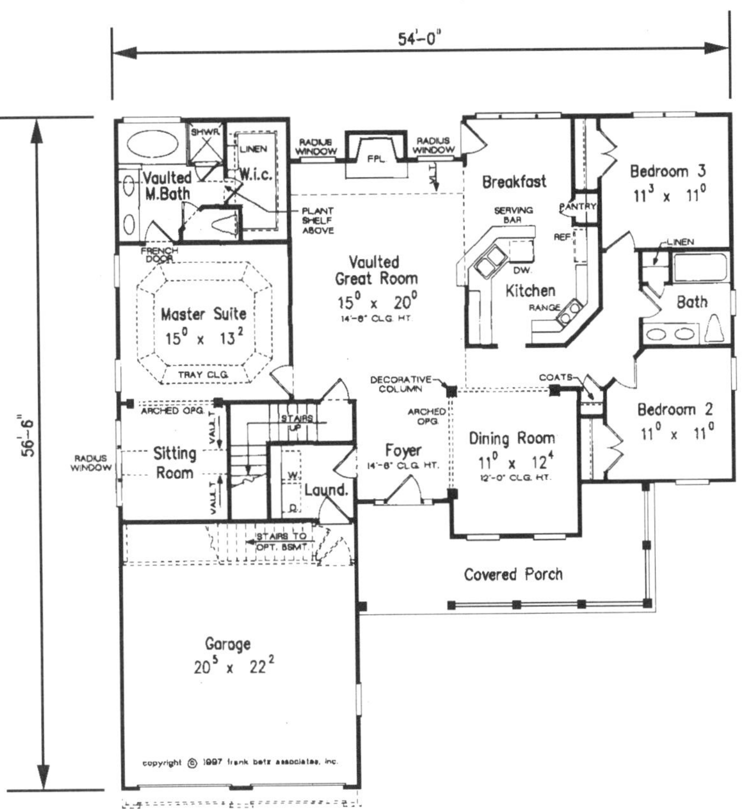

54'-0"
56'-6"
Vaulted M.Bath
SHWR.
LINEN
W.i.c.
RADIUS WINDOW
FPL.
RADIUS WINDOW
PLANT SHELF ABOVE
Breakfast
SERVING BAR
PANTRY
Bedroom 3
11³ x 11⁰
REF.
DW.
Kitchen
RANGE
LINEN
Bath
FRENCH DOOR
Vaulted Great Room
15⁰ x 20⁰
14'-8" CLG. HT.
Master Suite
15⁰ x 13²
TRAY CLG.
DECORATIVE COLUMN
COATS
Bedroom 2
11⁰ x 11⁰
ARCHED OPG.
STAIRS UP
ARCHED OPG.
Dining Room
11⁰ x 12⁴
12'-0" CLG. HT.
RADIUS WINDOW
Sitting Room
Foyer
14'-8" CLG. HT.
Laund.
STAIRS TO OPT. BSMT.
Covered Porch
Garage
20⁵ x 22²
copyright © 1997 frank betz associates, inc.
GARAGE LOCATION W/ BASEMENT

Plan #530-035D-0045

Price Code B

Total Living Area: 1,749 Sq. Ft.

Home has 3 bedrooms, 2 baths, 2-car garage and walk-out basement, slab or crawl space foundation, please specify when ordering.

Special features

- Tray ceiling in master suite
- A breakfast bar overlooks the vaulted great room
- Additional bedrooms are located away from master suite for privacy
- Optional bonus room above the garage has an additional 308 square feet of living area

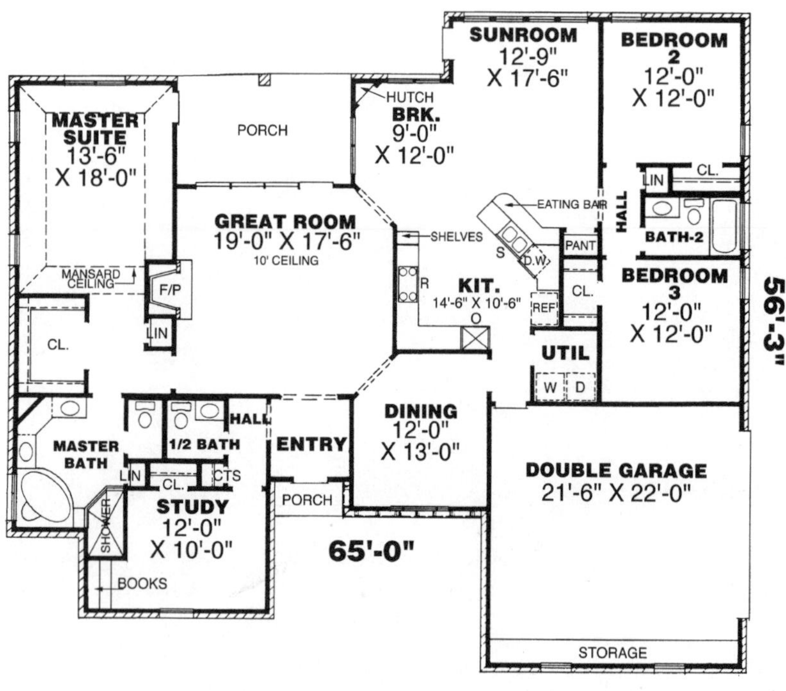
SUNROOM
12'-9"
X 17'-6"
BEDROOM
2
12'-0"
X 12'-0"
MASTER
SUITE
13'-6"
X 18'-0"
PORCH
HUTCH
BRK.
9'-0"
X 12'-0"
CL.
LIN
EATING BAR
HALL
BATH-2
GREAT ROOM
19'-0" X 17'-6"
10' CEILING
SHELVES
S
D.W.
PANT
MANSARD
CEILING
F/P
R
KIT.
14'-6" X 10'-6"
O
REF
CL.
BEDROOM
3
12'-0"
X 12'-0"
56'-3"
LIN
CL.
UTIL
W
D
HALL
DINING
12'-0"
X 13'-0"
MASTER
BATH
1/2 BATH
ENTRY
DOUBLE GARAGE
21'-6" X 22'-0"
LIN
CL.
CTS
PORCH
SHOWER
STUDY
12'-0"
X 10'-0"
65'-0"
BOOKS
STORAGE

Plan #530-025D-0028

Price Code D

Total Living Area: 2,350 Sq. Ft.

Home has 3 bedrooms, 2 1/2 baths, 2-car side entry garage and walk-out basement, crawl space or slab foundation, please specify when ordering.

Special features

- Luxurious master suite enjoys a large bath and an enormous walk-in closet
- Built-in hutch in breakfast room is eye-catching
- The terrific study is located in its own private hall and includes a half bath, two closets and a bookcase

TO ORDER BLUEPRINTS USE THE FORM ON PAGE 288 OR CALL TOLL-FREE **1-800-DREAM HOME** (373-2646)

LOWE'S

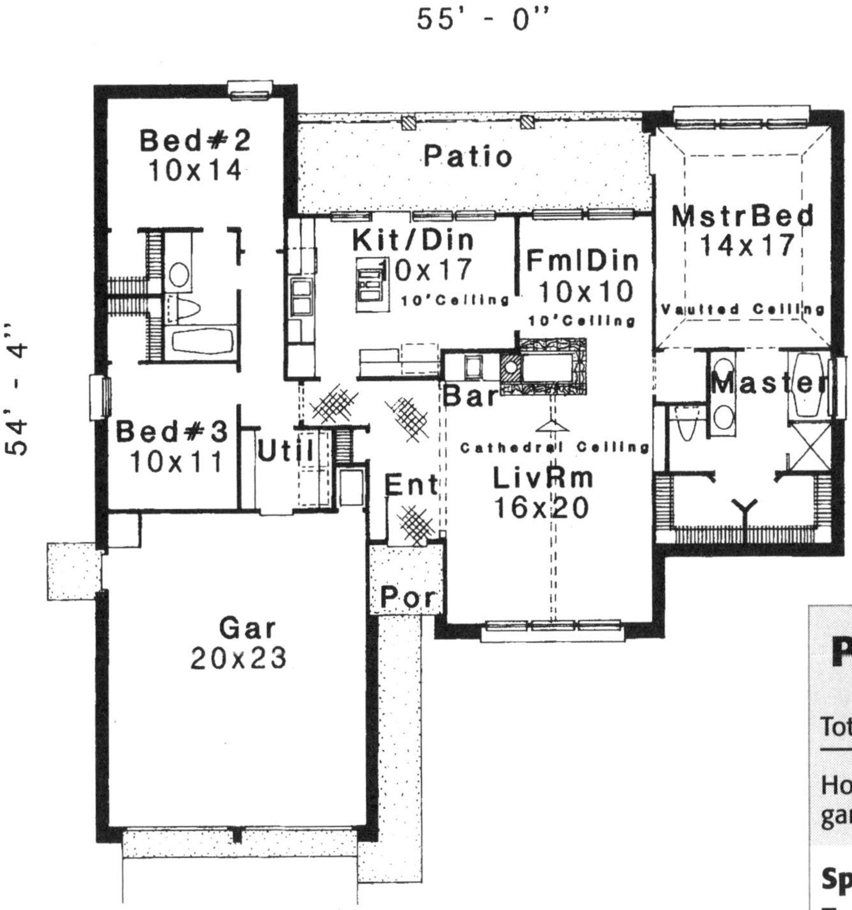

55' - 0"

54' - 4"

Bed#2
10x14

Patio

MstrBed
14x17
Vaulted Ceiling

Kit/Din
10x17
10'Ceiling

FmlDin
10x10
10'Ceiling

Bed#3
10x11

Util

Bar

Master

Cathedral Ceiling

Ent

LivRm
16x20

Por

Gar
20x23

Plan #530-036D-0006

Price Code B

Total Living Area: 1,624 Sq. Ft.

Home has 3 bedrooms, 2 baths, 2-car garage and slab foundation.

Special features

- Massive living room with cathedral ceiling has wet bar for entertaining
- Large double walk-in closets connect to master bath
- Kitchen includes island for easy food preparation

LOWE'S

Plan #530-008D-0054

Price Code B

Total Living Area: 1,574 Sq. Ft.

Home has 3 bedrooms, 2 baths, 2-car garage and basement foundation, drawings also include crawl space foundation.

Special features

- Foyer enters into an open great room with corner fireplace and rear dining room with adjoining kitchen
- Two secondary bedrooms share a full bath
- Master bedroom has a spacious private bath
- Garage accesses home through the spacious utility room

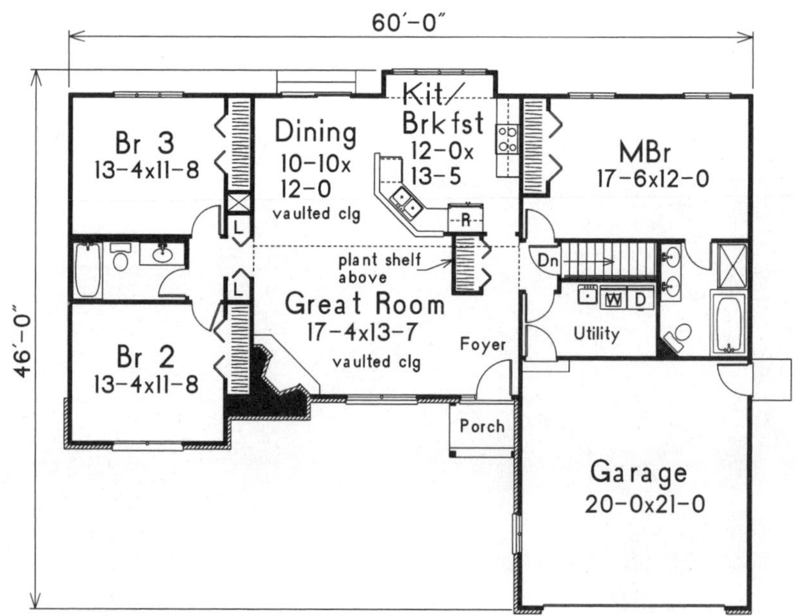
60'-0"
46'-0"
Br 3
13-4x11-8
Dining
10-10x
12-0
vaulted clg
Kit/
Brkfst
12-0x
13-5
R
MBr
17-6x12-0
plant shelf
above
Great Room
17-4x13-7
vaulted clg
Dn
W D
Utility
Br 2
13-4x11-8
Foyer
Porch
Garage
20-0x21-0

 TO ORDER BLUEPRINTS USE THE FORM ON PAGE 288 OR CALL TOLL-FREE **1-800-DREAM HOME** (373-2646)

Unique Window Seat In Bedrooms

LOWE'S

Plan #530-052D-0017

Price Code A

Total Living Area: 1,418 Sq. Ft.

Home has 3 bedrooms, 2 baths, 2-car garage and basement, crawl space or slab foundation, please specify when ordering.

Special features

- A corner fireplace warms the living room
- Luxurious master bedroom features a tray ceiling and secluded location for privacy
- Dining area accesses outdoor patio/ deck

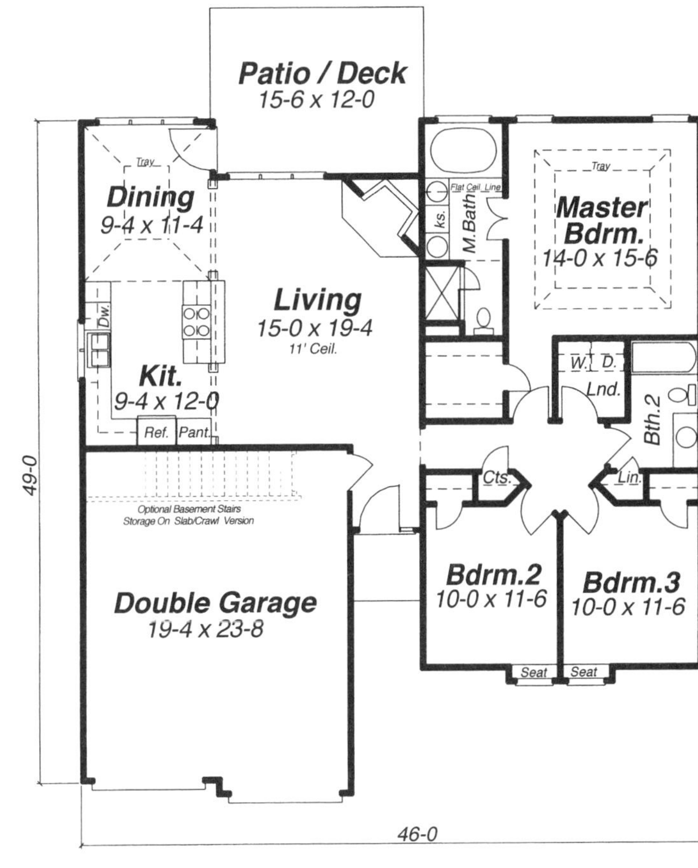
Patio / Deck
15-6 x 12-0
Tray
Dining
9-4 x 11-4
Living
15-0 x 19-4
11' Ceil.
Flat Ceil. Line
ks.
M.Bath
Tray
Master Bdrm.
14-0 x 15-6
Dw.
Kit.
9-4 x 12-0
Ref.
Pant.
W. D.
Lnd.
Bth.2
Cts.
Lin.
Optional Basement Stairs
Storage On Slab/Crawl Version
49-0
Double Garage
19-4 x 23-8
Bdrm.2
10-0 x 11-6
Bdrm.3
10-0 x 11-6
Seat
Seat
46-0

LOWE'S

Whirlpool With Skylight Above

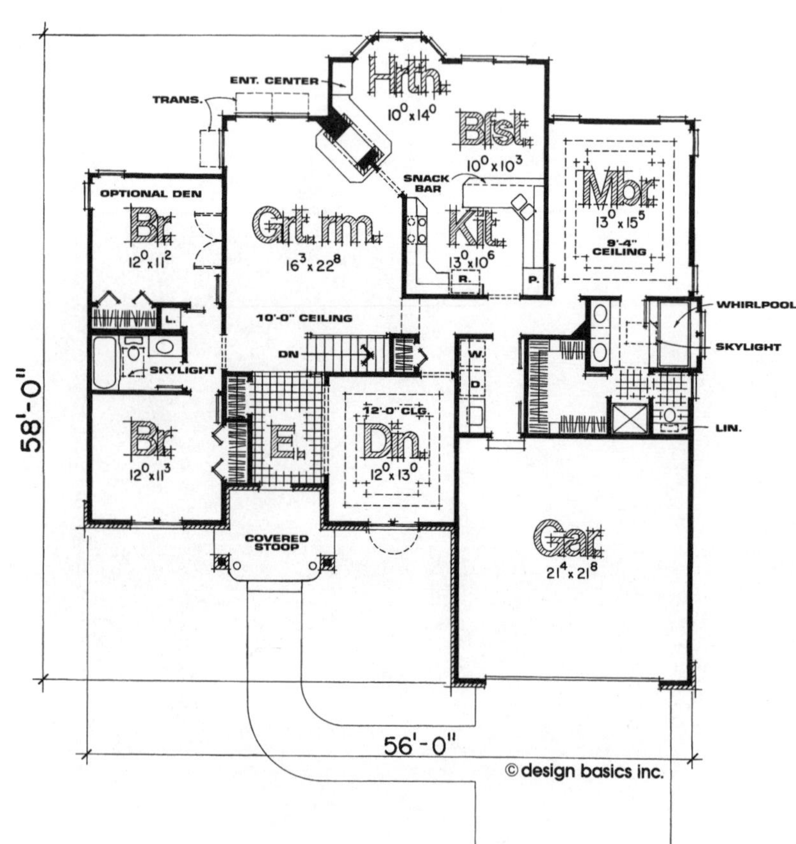
ENT. CENTER
TRANS.
Hrth.
$10^0 \times 14^0$
Bfst.
$10^0 \times 10^3$
SNACK BAR
OPTIONAL DEN
Br.
$12^0 \times 11^2$
Grt. rm.
$16^3 \times 22^8$
Kit.
$13^0 \times 10^6$
Mbr.
$13^0 \times 15^5$
9'-4" CEILING
R.
P.
L.
WHIRLPOOL
10'-0" CEILING
SKYLIGHT
DN
W.
D.
SKYLIGHT
12'-0" CLG.
Br.
$12^0 \times 11^3$
E.
Dn.
$12^0 \times 13^0$
LIN.
58'-0"
COVERED STOOP
Gar.
$21^4 \times 21^8$
56'-0"
© design basics inc.

Plan #530-026D-0112

Price Code C

Total Living Area: 1,911 Sq. Ft.

Home has 3 bedrooms, 2 baths, 2-car garage and basement foundation.

Special features

- Large entry opens into a beautiful great room with an angled see-through fireplace
- Terrific design includes kitchen and breakfast area with adjacent sunny bayed hearth room
- Private master bedroom with bath features skylight and walk-in closet

TO ORDER BLUEPRINTS USE THE FORM ON PAGE 288 OR CALL TOLL-FREE **1-800-DREAM HOME** (373-2646)

LOWE'S

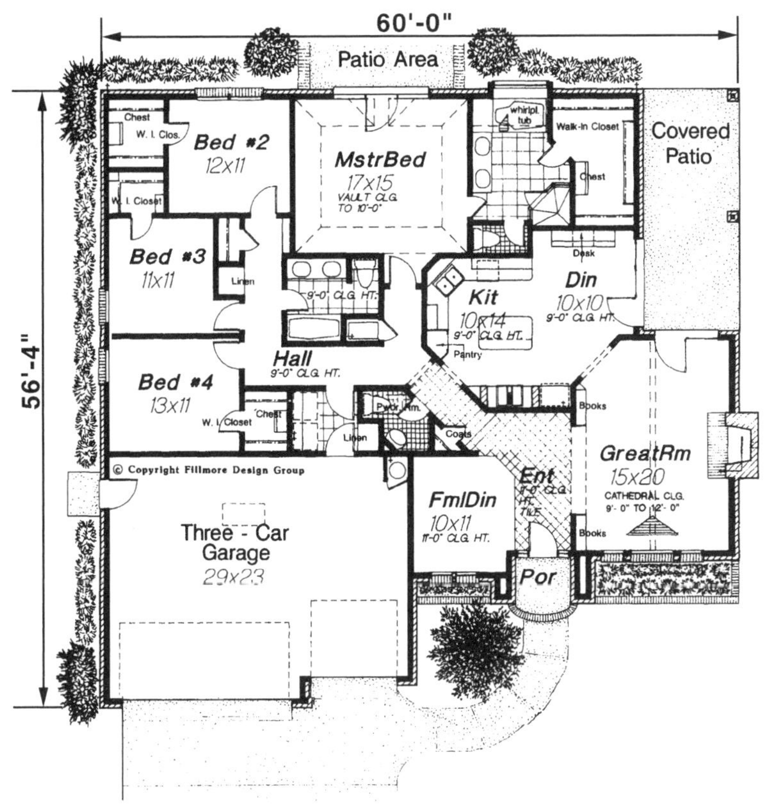
60'-0"
Patio Area
56'-4"
Covered Patio
Bed #2
12x11
MstrBed
17x15
VAULT CLG. TO 10'-0"
Bed #3
11x11
Bed #4
13x11
Hall
9'-0" CLG. HT.
Kit
10x14
9'-0" CLG. HT.
Din
10x10
9'-0" CLG. HT.
GreatRm
15x20
CATHEDRAL CLG. 9'-0" TO 12'-0"
FmlDin
10x11
11'-0" CLG. HT.
Ent
Por
Three - Car Garage
29x23
© Copyright Fillmore Design Group

Plan #530-036D-0024

Price Code C

Total Living Area: 2,118 Sq. Ft.

Home has 4 bedrooms, 2 1/2 baths, 3-car garage and slab foundation.

Special features

- 9' ceilings throughout this home
- Massive great room located off entry for formal gatherings
- Large master bath has whirlpool tub and an oversized walk-in closet for extra storage

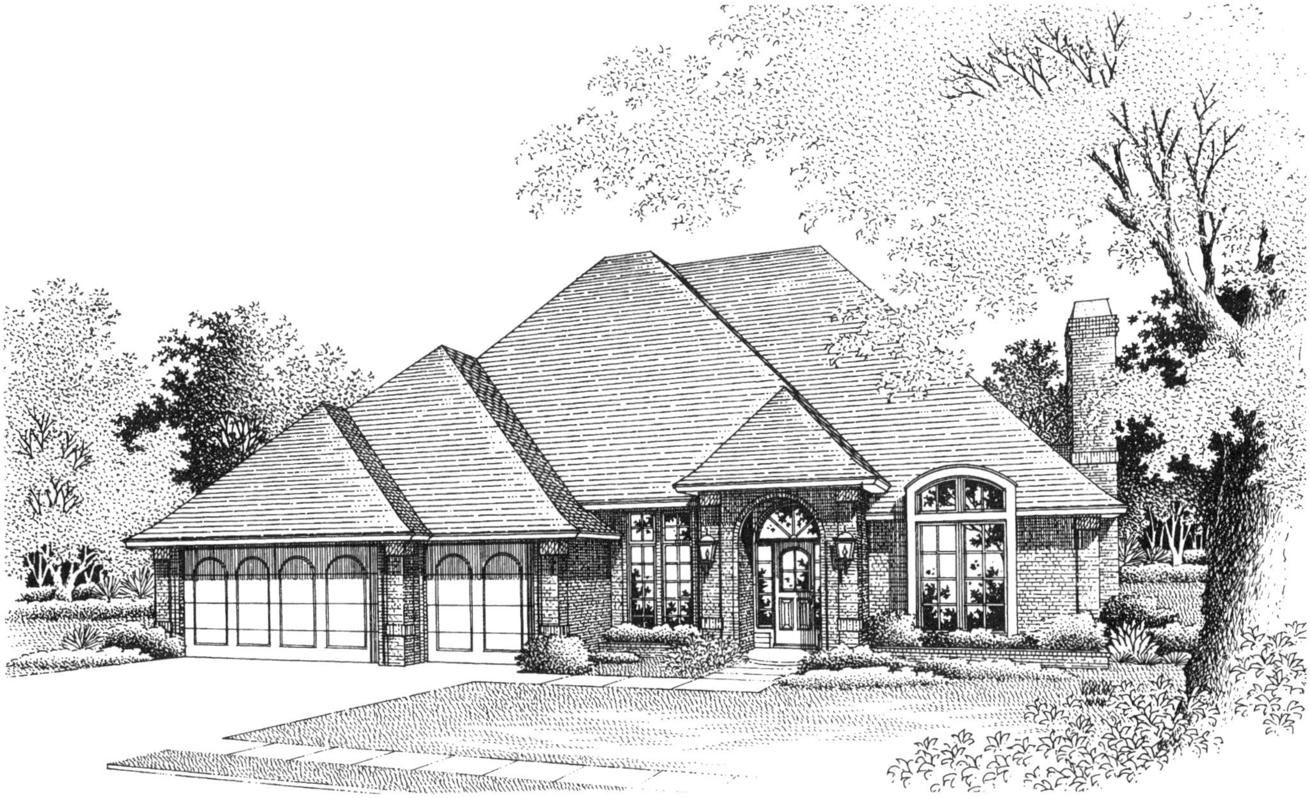

Plan #530-020D-0017

Price Code D

Total Living Area: 2,424 Sq. Ft.

Home has 3 bedrooms, 2 baths, 2-car side entry carport and slab foundation, drawings also include crawl space foundation.

Special features

- Utility room is next to the kitchen for convenience
- Large closets in all bedrooms
- Open living area for added spaciousness

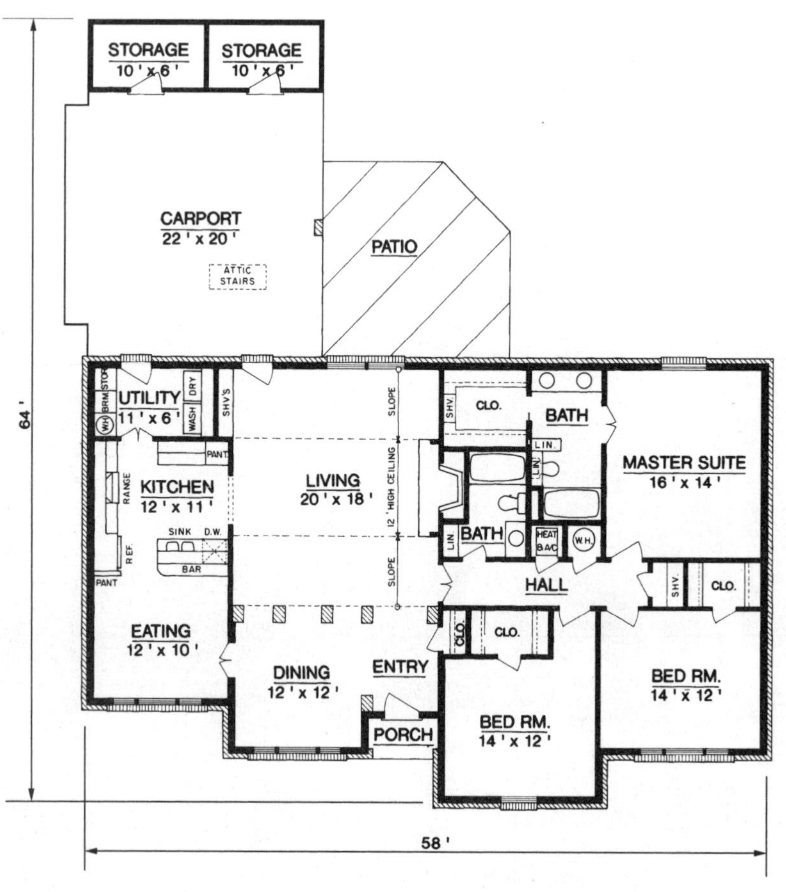
STORAGE 10' x 6'
STORAGE 10' x 6'
CARPORT 22' x 20'
ATTIC STAIRS
PATIO
64'
UTILITY 11' x 6'
KITCHEN 12' x 11'
LIVING 20' x 18'
12' HIGH CEILING
SLOPE
BATH
MASTER SUITE 16' x 14'
BATH
HALL
EATING 12' x 10'
DINING 12' x 12'
ENTRY
PORCH
BED RM. 14' x 12'
BED RM. 14' x 12'
58'

LOWE'S

Plan #530-052D-0005

Price Code A

Total Living Area: 1,268 Sq. Ft.

Home has 3 bedrooms, 2 baths, 2-car drive under garage and basement foundation.

Special features

- Raised gable porch is a focal point creating a dramatic look
- 10' ceilings throughout living and dining areas
- Open kitchen is well designed
- Master bedroom offers a tray ceiling and private bath with both a garden tub and a 4' shower

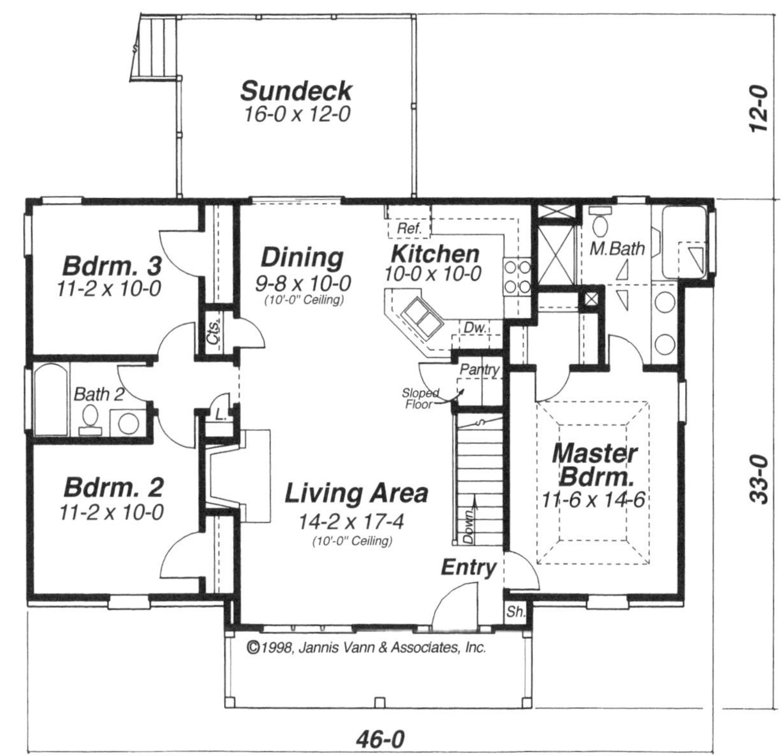
Sundeck
16-0 x 12-0
12-0
Bdrm. 3
11-2 x 10-0
Dining
9-8 x 10-0
(10'-0" Ceiling)
Ref.
Kitchen
10-0 x 10-0
M.Bath
Cts.
Dw.
Pantry
Bath 2
Sloped Floor
L.
Master Bdrm.
11-6 x 14-6
33-0
Bdrm. 2
11-2 x 10-0
Living Area
14-2 x 17-4
(10'-0" Ceiling)
Down
Entry
Sh.
©1998, Jannis Vann & Associates, Inc.
46-0

Vaulted Ceilings Add A Sense Of Spaciousness

Plan #530-062D-0050

Price Code A

Total Living Area: 1,408 Sq. Ft.

Home has 3 bedrooms, 2 baths, 2-car side entry garage and basement or crawl space foundation, please specify when ordering.

Special features

- A bright country kitchen boasts an abundance of counterspace and cupboards
- The front entry is sheltered by a broad veranda
- A spa tub is brightened by a box-bay window in the master bath

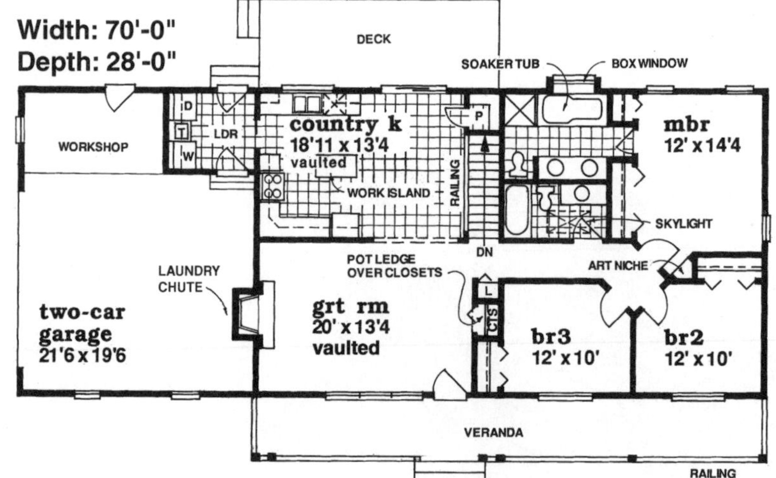
Width: 70'-0"
Depth: 28'-0"
DECK
SOAKER TUB
BOX WINDOW
WORKSHOP
D
T
W
LDR
country k
18'11 x 13'4
vaulted
WORK ISLAND
P
RAILING
mbr
12' x 14'4
SKYLIGHT
DN
POT LEDGE
OVER CLOSETS
ART NICHE
LAUNDRY
CHUTE
two-car
garage
21'6 x 19'6
grt rm
20' x 13'4
vaulted
L
C/S
br3
12' x 10'
br2
12' x 10'
VERANDA
RAILING

TO ORDER BLUEPRINTS USE THE FORM ON PAGE 288 OR CALL TOLL-FREE **1-800-DREAM HOME** (373-2646)

LOWE'S

Plan #530-055D-0029

Price Code D

Total Living Area: 2,525 Sq. Ft.

Home has 3 bedrooms, 2 1/2 baths, 2-car side entry garage and basement or walk-out basement foundation, please specify when ordering.

Special features

- Glorious sun room off great room has French doors leading to the optional grilling porch
- Enormous laundry room includes a sink and loads of counterspace to make chores much easier
- Formal living/study as well as the dining room are accented with decorative columns

63' 4"
59' 10"
OPTIONAL GRILLING PORCH
18'-10" X 13'-0"
GARAGE
20'-0" X 26'-10"
GLASS SHWR
LIN
FRENCH DOORS
SUN ROOM
18'-6" X 7'-8"
MASTER SUITE
10' BOX CEILING
14'-8" X 14'-8"
M.BATH
8'-6" X 22'-10"
WHP TUB
KNEE SPACE
MEDIA CENTER
GREAT RM.
10' BOX CEILING
18'-6" X 17'-6"
TO ATTIC STORAGE
UP
STORAGE
LAU.
11'-8" X 7'-8"
SEWING
W
D
BEDROOM 2
10'-10" X 11'-8"
BUILT-INS
LIN
GALLERY
8" COLUMNS
REF
RG
KITCHEN
14'-8" X 14'-0"
ISLAND
PANTRY
DW
FORMAL LIVING / STUDY
12' CEILING
12'-0" X 12'-4"
FOYER
12' CEILING
6'-8" X 11'-4"
DINING RM.
12' CEILING
12'-0" X 12'-4"
BRKFST RM. / HEARTH RM.
14'-8" X 10'-0"
BEDROOM 3
14'-8" X 11'-8"
BUILT-INS
4' PORCH

Plan #530-008D-0011

Price Code B

Total Living Area: 1,550 Sq. Ft.

Home has 3 bedrooms, 2 baths, 2-car side entry garage and basement foundation, drawings also include crawl space and slab foundations.

Special features

- Convenient mud room between the garage and kitchen
- Oversized dining area allows plenty of space for entertaining
- Master bedroom has a private bath and ample closet space
- Large patio off the family room brings the outdoors in

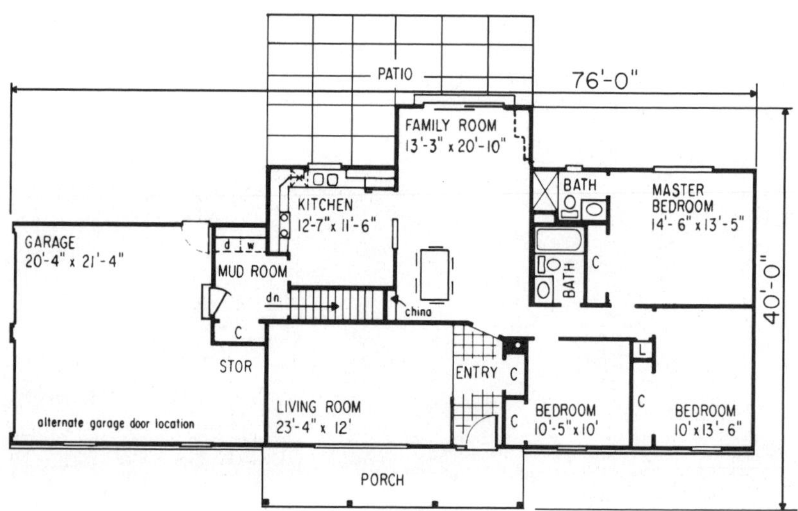
PATIO
76'-0"
40'-0"
FAMILY ROOM
13'-3" x 20'-10"
KITCHEN
12'-7" x 11'-6"
BATH
MASTER BEDROOM
14'-6" x 13'-5"
GARAGE
20'-4" x 21'-4"
MUD ROOM
d w
dn.
china
BATH
C
STOR
ENTRY
LIVING ROOM
23'-4" x 12'
BEDROOM
10'-5" x 10'
BEDROOM
10' x 13'-6"
alternate garage door location
PORCH

LOWE'S

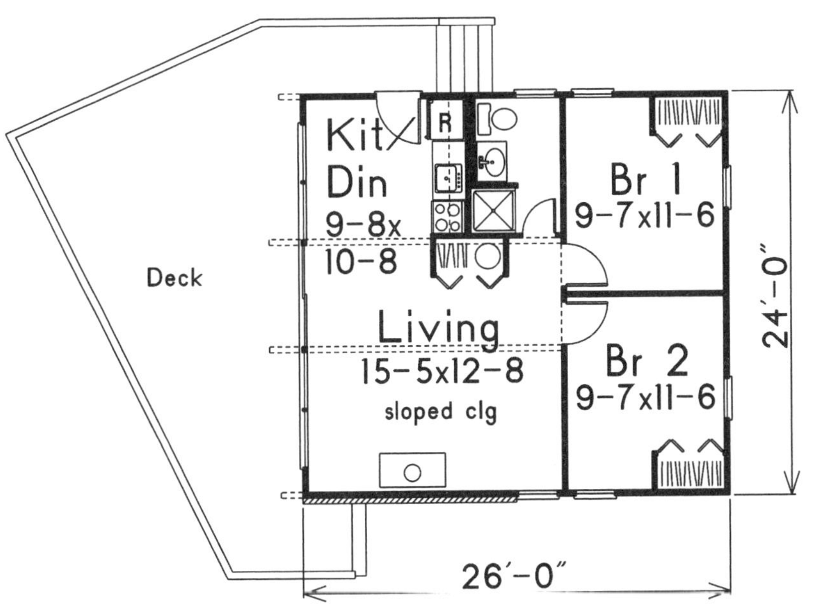
Deck
Kit/
Din
9-8x
10-8
R
Br 1
9-7x11-6
Living
15-5x12-8
sloped clg
Br 2
9-7x11-6
24'-0"
26'-0"

Plan #530-008D-0133

Price Code AAA

Total Living Area: 624 Sq. Ft.

Home has 2 bedrooms, 1 bath and a pier foundation.

Special features

- The combination of stone, vertical siding, lots of glass and a low roof line creates a cozy retreat
- Vaulted living area features a free-standing fireplace that heats the adjacent stone wall
- Efficient kitchen includes a dining area and view onto an angular deck
- Two bedrooms share a hall bath with shower

Plan #530-035D-0011

Price Code C

Total Living Area: 1,945 Sq. Ft.

Home has 4 bedrooms, 2 baths, 2-car side entry garage and walk-out basement, crawl space or slab foundation, please specify when ordering.

Special features

- Master suite is separate from other bedrooms for privacy
- Vaulted breakfast room is directly off great room
- Kitchen includes a built-in desk area
- Elegant dining room has an arched window

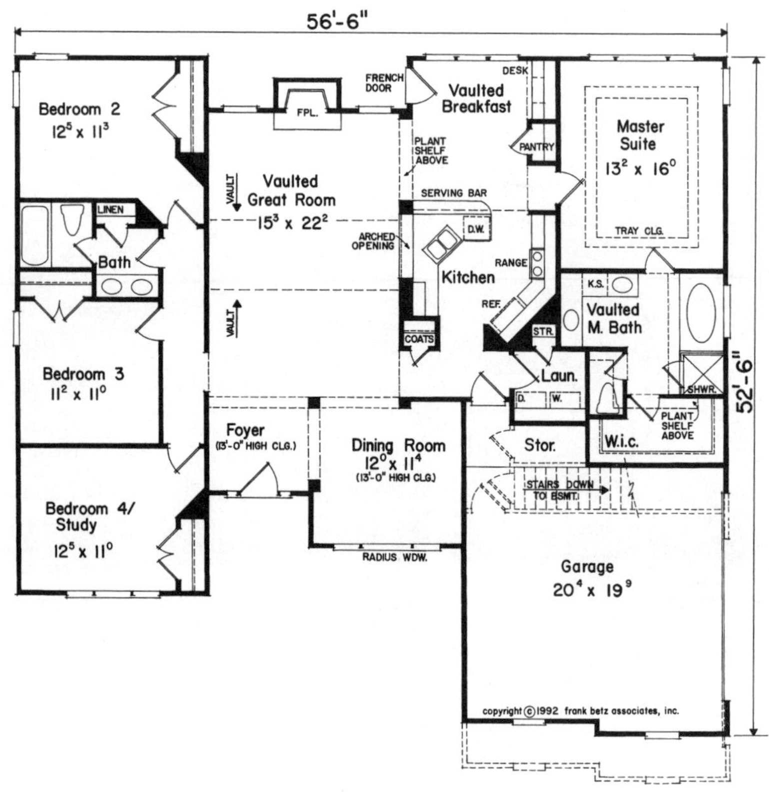
56'-6"
52'-6"
Bedroom 2
12^5 x 11^3
FPL.
FRENCH DOOR
Vaulted Breakfast
DESK
PANTRY
Master Suite
13^2 x 16^0
TRAY CLG.
PLANT SHELF ABOVE
VAULT
Vaulted Great Room
15^3 x 22^2
SERVING BAR
D.W.
ARCHED OPENING
LINEN
Bath
Kitchen
RANGE
REF.
K.S.
Vaulted M. Bath
STR.
COATS
Bedroom 3
11^2 x 11^0
Laun.
D.
W.
SHWR.
Foyer
(13'-0" HIGH CLG.)
Dining Room
12^0 x 11^4
(13'-0" HIGH CLG.)
Stor.
PLANT SHELF ABOVE
W.i.c.
STAIRS DOWN TO BSMT.
Bedroom 4/ Study
12^5 x 11^0
RADIUS WDW.
Garage
20^4 x 19^9
copyright ©1992 frank betz associates, inc.

TO ORDER BLUEPRINTS USE THE FORM ON PAGE 288 OR CALL TOLL-FREE **1-800-DREAM HOME** (373-2646)

LOWE'S

Plan #530-055D-0027

Price Code A

Total Living Area: 1,353 Sq. Ft.

Home has 3 bedrooms, 2 baths, 2-car garage and basement, walk-out basement, slab or crawl space foundation, please specify when ordering.

Special features

- All bedrooms are located together and away from living areas
- Dining room overlooks great room with fireplace
- Kitchen has counterspace for eating as well as plenty of storage

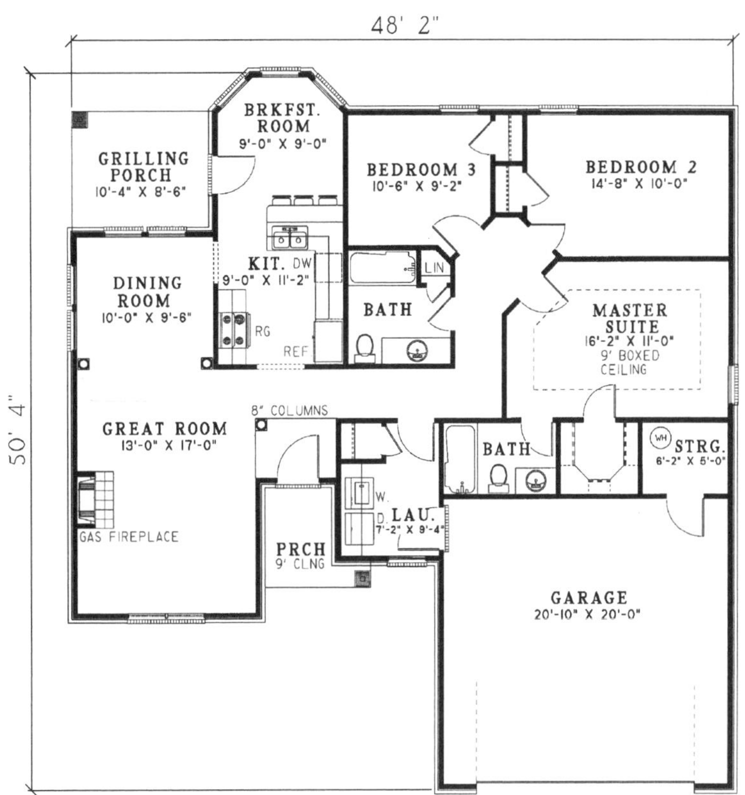
48' 2"
50' 4"
BRKFST. ROOM
9'-0" X 9'-0"
GRILLING PORCH
10'-4" X 8'-6"
BEDROOM 3
10'-6" X 9'-2"
BEDROOM 2
14'-8" X 10'-0"
KIT.
9'-0" X 11'-2"
DW
LIN
DINING ROOM
10'-0" X 9'-6"
BATH
RG
REF
MASTER SUITE
16'-2" X 11'-0"
9' BOXED CEILING
8" COLUMNS
GREAT ROOM
13'-0" X 17'-0"
BATH
WH
STRG.
6'-2" X 5'-0"
W.
D.
LAU.
7'-2" X 9'-4"
GAS FIREPLACE
PRCH
9' CLNG
GARAGE
20'-10" X 20'-0"

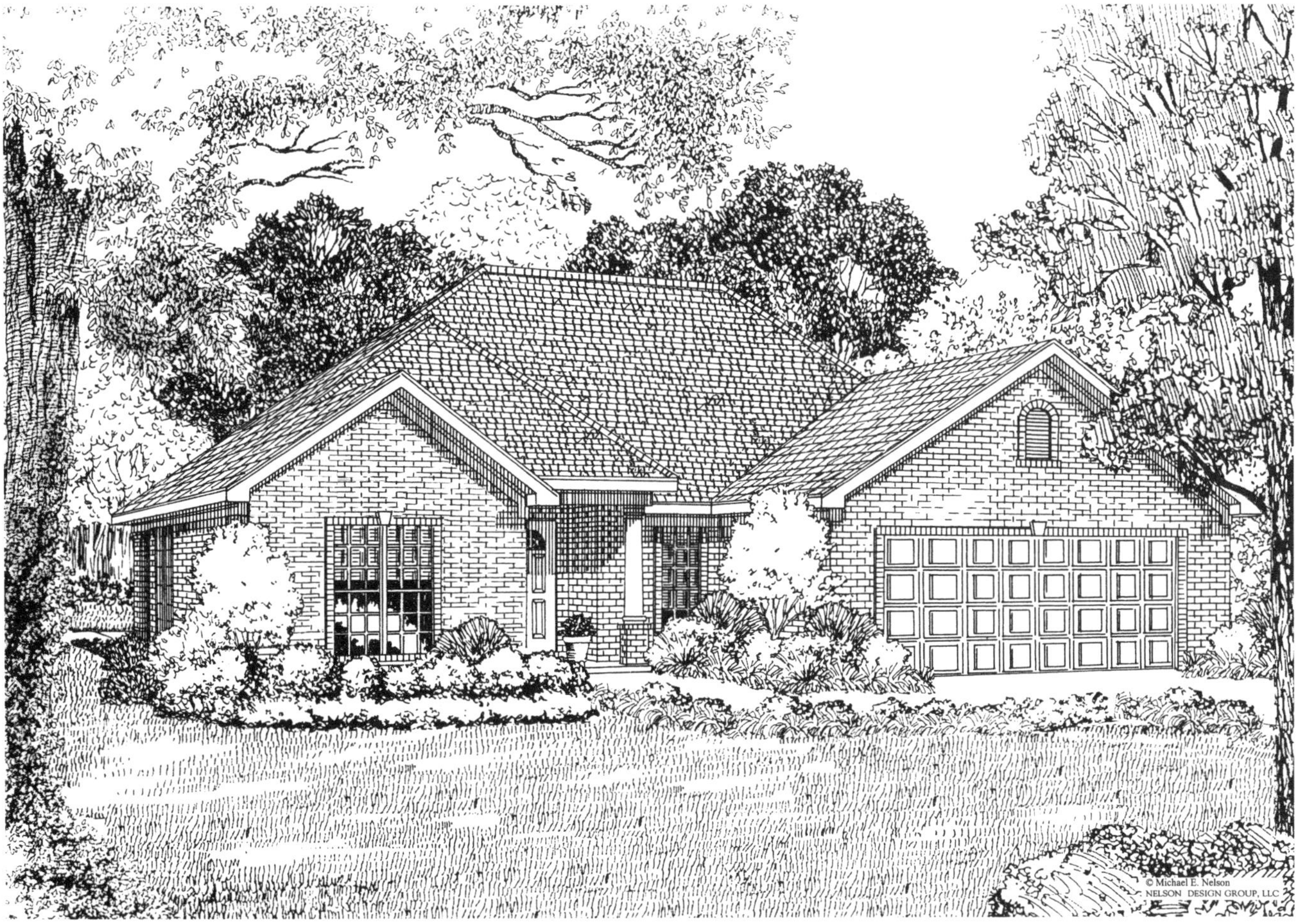

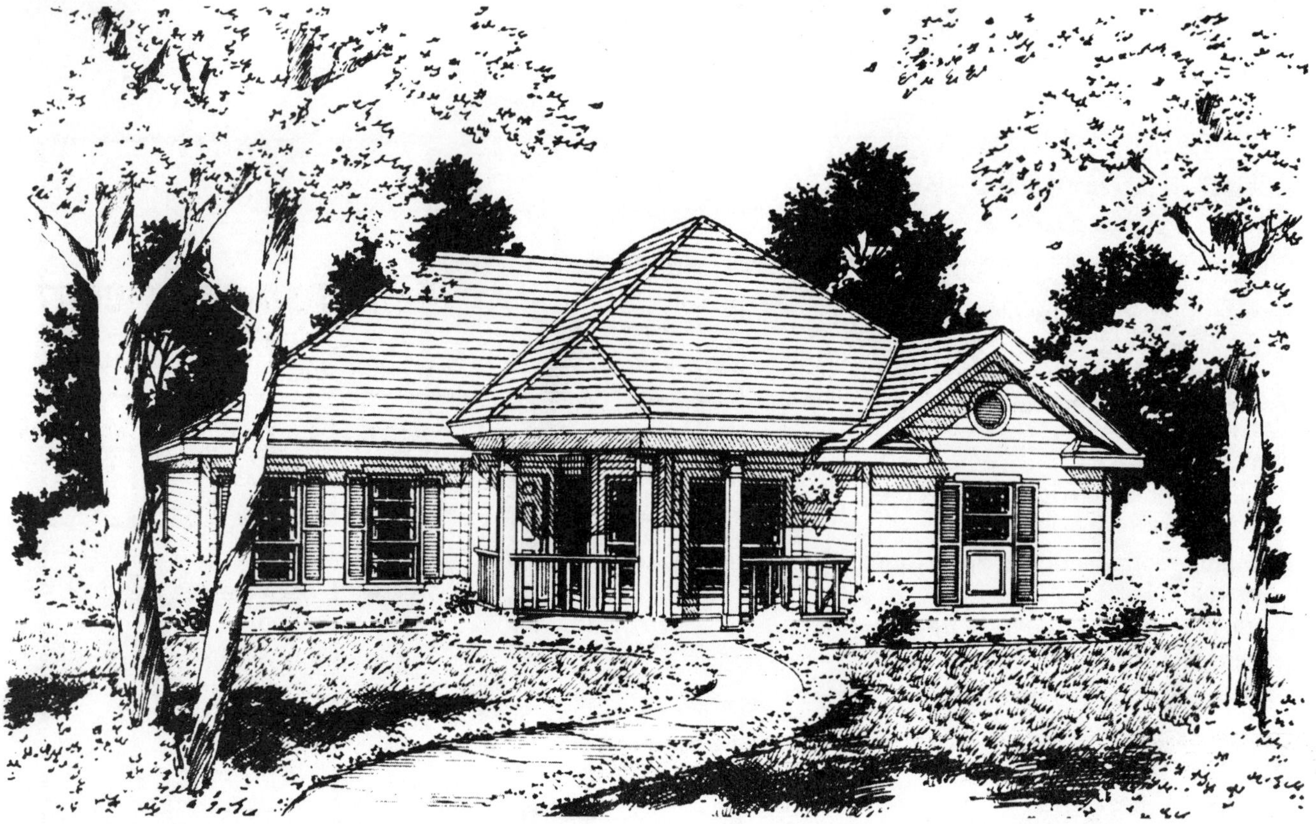

Plan #530-024D-0002

Price Code A

Total Living Area: 1,405 Sq. Ft.

Home has 3 bedrooms, 2 baths and slab foundation.

Special features

- Compact design has all the luxuries of a larger home
- Master bedroom has its privacy away from other bedrooms
- Living room has corner fireplace, access to the outdoors and easily reaches the dining area and kitchen
- Large utility room has access to the outdoors

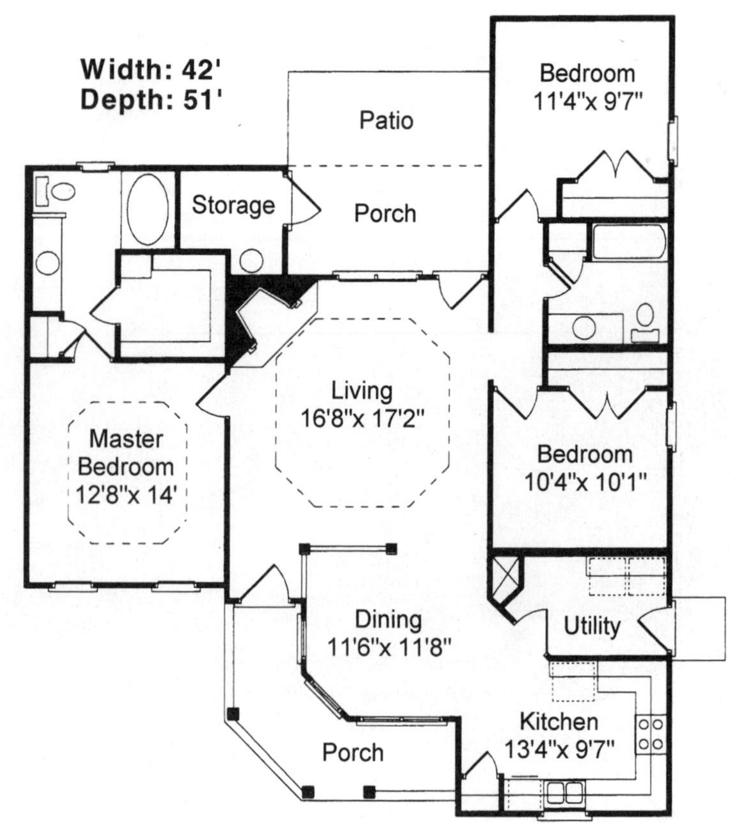
Width: 42'
Depth: 51'
Bedroom
11'4"x 9'7"
Patio
Storage
Porch
Living
16'8"x 17'2"
Master
Bedroom
12'8"x 14'
Bedroom
10'4"x 10'1"
Dining
11'6"x 11'8"
Utility
Kitchen
13'4"x 9'7"
Porch

LOWE'S

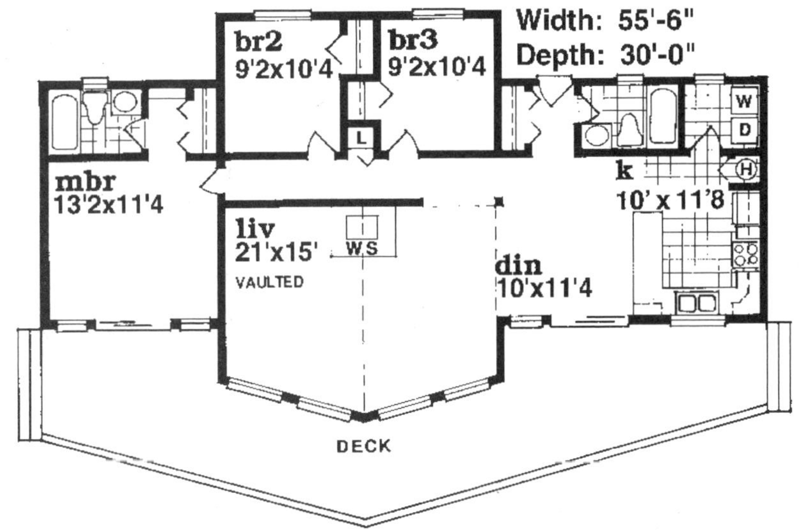
Width: 55'-6"
Depth: 30'-0"
br2
9'2x10'4
br3
9'2x10'4
W
D
L
H
mbr
13'2x11'4
k
10' x 11'8
liv
21'x15'
WS
VAULTED
din
10'x11'4
DECK

Plan #530-062D-0047

Price Code A

Total Living Area: 1,230 Sq. Ft.

Home has 3 bedrooms, 2 baths and crawl space or basement foundation, please specify when ordering.

Special features

- Full-width deck creates plenty of outdoor living area
- The master bedroom accesses the deck through sliding glass doors and features a private bath
- Vaulted living room has a wood-stove

Plan #530-055D-0030

Price Code C

Total Living Area: 2,107 Sq. Ft.

Home has 4 bedrooms, 2 1/2 baths, 2-car garage and crawl space, basement, walk-out basement or slab foundation, please specify when ordering.

Special features

- Master bedroom is separate from other bedrooms for privacy
- Spacious breakfast room and kitchen include center island with eating space
- Centralized great room has fireplace and easy access to any area in the home

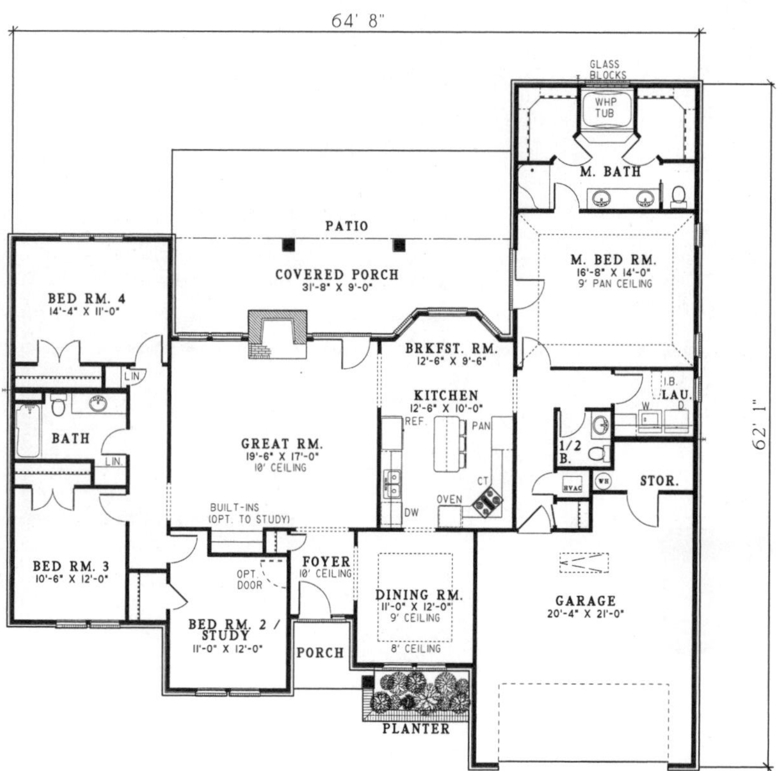
64' 8"
GLASS BLOCKS
WHP TUB
M. BATH
PATIO
COVERED PORCH
31'-8" X 9'-0"
M. BED RM.
16'-8" X 14'-0"
9' PAN CEILING
BED RM. 4
14'-4" X 11'-0"
BRKFST. RM.
12'-6" X 9'-6"
KITCHEN
12'-6" X 10'-0"
REF.
PAN
LIN
BATH
GREAT RM.
19'-6" X 17'-0"
10' CEILING
I.B.
LAU.
W
D
1/2 B.
62' 1"
HVAC
WH
STOR.
CT
OVEN
DW
BUILT-INS (OPT. TO STUDY)
BED RM. 3
10'-6" X 12'-0"
OPT. DOOR
FOYER
10' CEILING
DINING RM.
11'-0" X 12'-0"
9' CEILING
GARAGE
20'-4" X 21'-0"
BED RM. 2 / STUDY
11'-0" X 12'-0"
PORCH
8' CEILING
PLANTER

 TO ORDER BLUEPRINTS USE THE FORM ON PAGE 288 OR CALL TOLL-FREE **1-800-DREAM HOME** (373-2646)

LOWE'S

M MAXON

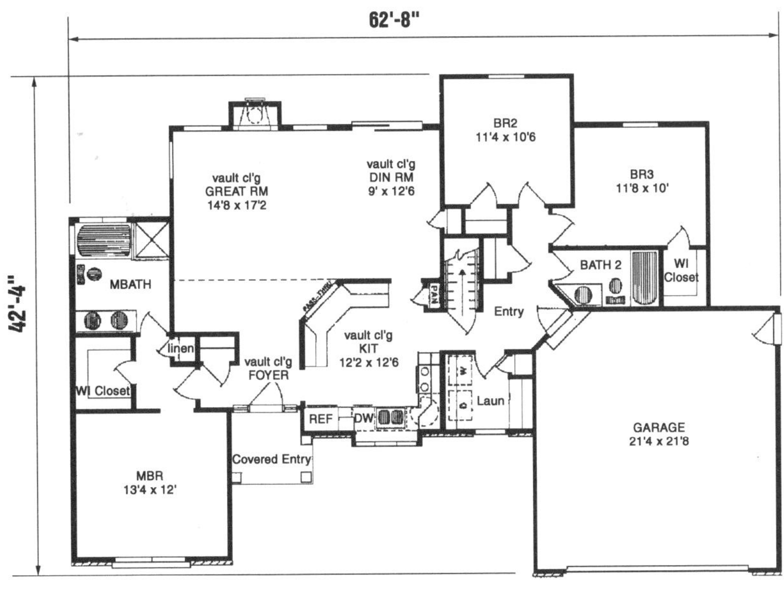
62'-8"
42'-4"
BR2
11'4 x 10'6
BR3
11'8 x 10'
vault cl'g
GREAT RM
14'8 x 17'2
vault cl'g
DIN RM
9' x 12'6
MBATH
BATH 2
WI
Closet
PAN
Entry
vault cl'g
KIT
12'2 x 12'6
linen
vault cl'g
FOYER
WI Closet
REF
DW
Laun
GARAGE
21'4 x 21'8
MBR
13'4 x 12'
Covered Entry

Plan #530-034D-0001

Price Code A

Total Living Area: 1,436 Sq. Ft.

Home has 3 bedrooms, 2 baths, 2-car garage and basement foundation.

Special features

- Covered entry is inviting
- Kitchen has handy breakfast bar which overlooks great room and dining room
- Private master bedroom with bath and walk-in closet is separate from other bedrooms

LOWE'S

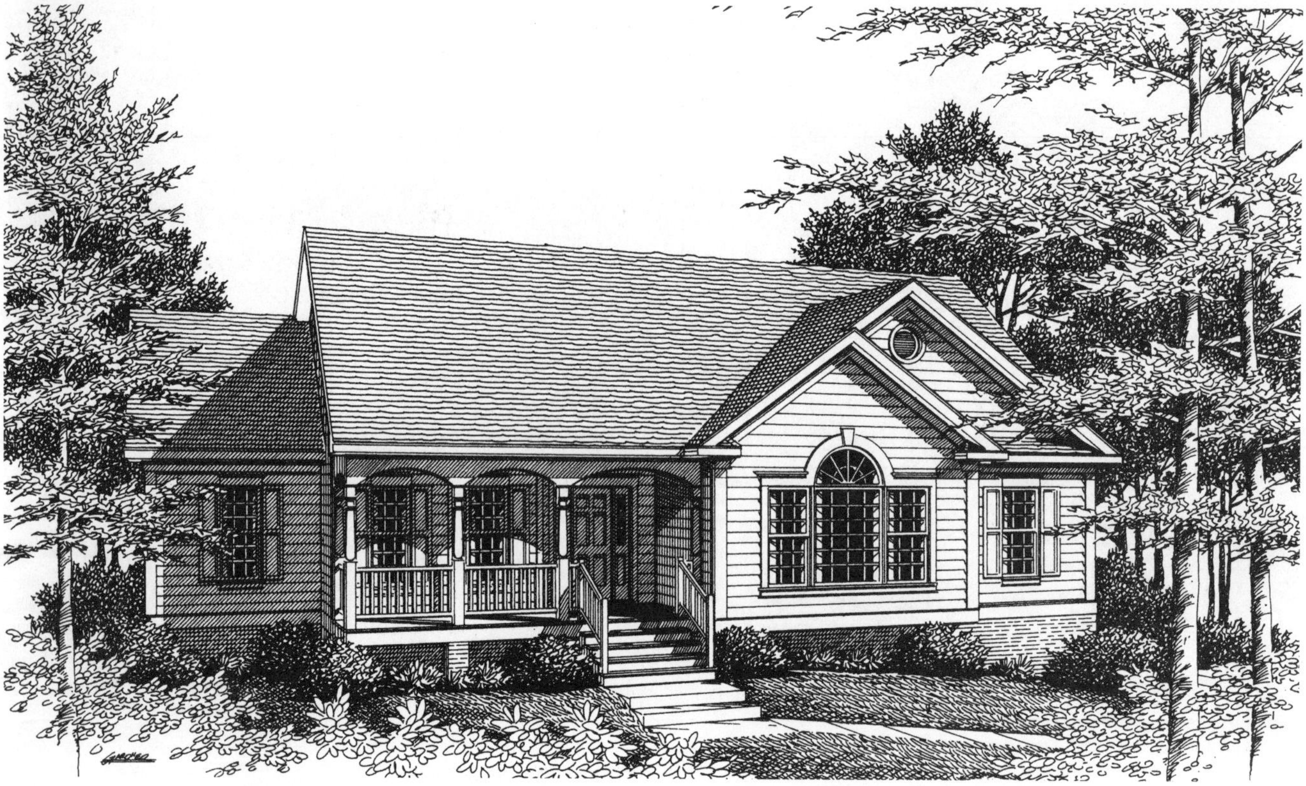

Scalloped Porch Cornice

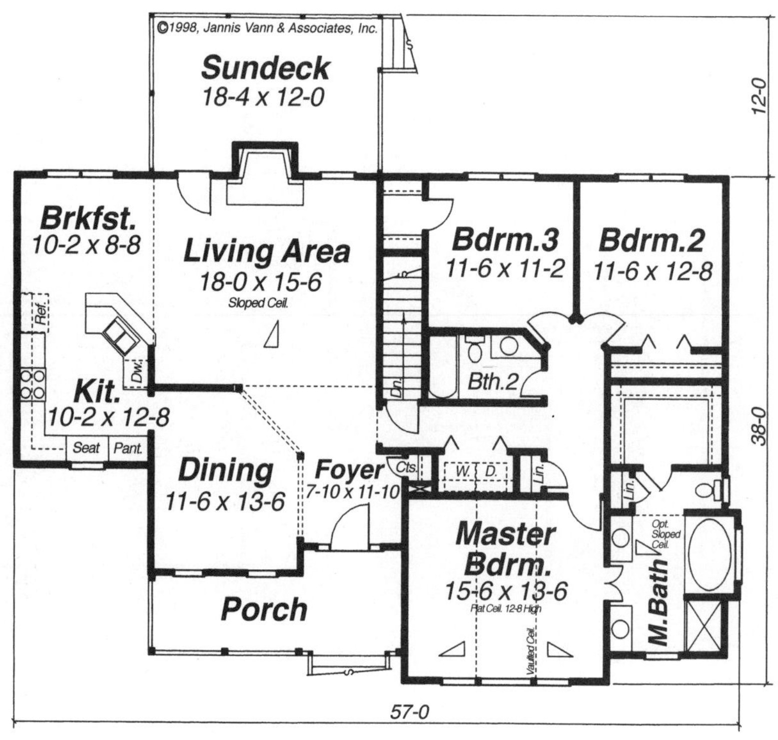
©1998, Jannis Vann & Associates, Inc.
Sundeck
18-4 x 12-0
Brkfst.
10-2 x 8-8
Living Area
18-0 x 15-6
Sloped Ceil.
Bdrm.3
11-6 x 11-2
Bdrm.2
11-6 x 12-8
Ref.
Dw.
Kit.
10-2 x 12-8
Seat
Pant.
Dn.
Bth.2
Dining
11-6 x 13-6
Foyer
7-10 x 11-10
Cts.
W. D.
Lin.
Master
Bdrm.
15-6 x 13-6
Flat Ceil. 12-8 High
Vaulted Ceil.
Opt. Sloped Ceil.
M.Bath
Porch
57-0
38-0
12-0

Plan #530-052D-0036

Price Code B

Total Living Area: 1,772 Sq. Ft.

Home has 3 bedrooms, 2 baths, 3-car drive under garage and basement foundation.

Special features

- Dramatic palladian window and scalloped porch are attention grabbers
- Island kitchen sink allows for easy access and views into the living and breakfast areas
- Washer and dryer closet is easily accessible from all bedrooms

LOWE'S

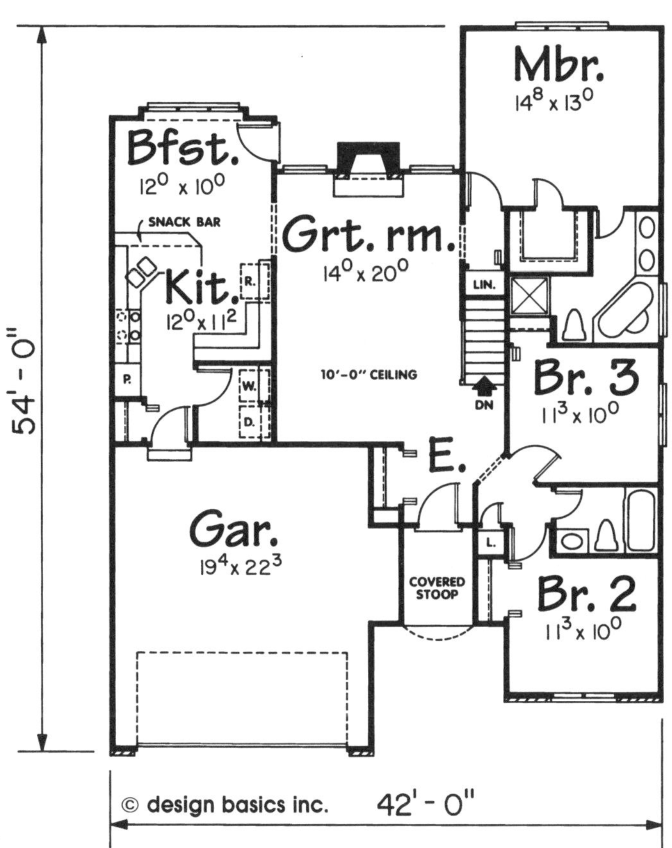
Mbr.
14^8 x 13^0
Bfst.
12^0 x 10^0
SNACK BAR
Grt. rm.
14^0 x 20^0
Kit.
12^0 x 11^2
R.
LIN.
10'-0" CEILING
P.
W.
D.
DN
Br. 3
11^3 x 10^0
E.
Gar.
19^4 x 22^3
L.
COVERED STOOP
Br. 2
11^3 x 10^0
54' - 0"
42' - 0"
© design basics inc.

Plan #530-026D-0154

Price Code A

Total Living Area: 1,392 Sq. Ft.

Home has 3 bedrooms, 2 baths, 2-car garage and basement foundation.

Special features

- Centralized great room welcomes guests with a warm fireplace
- Master bedroom has a separate entrance for added privacy
- Kitchen includes breakfast room, snack counter and laundry area

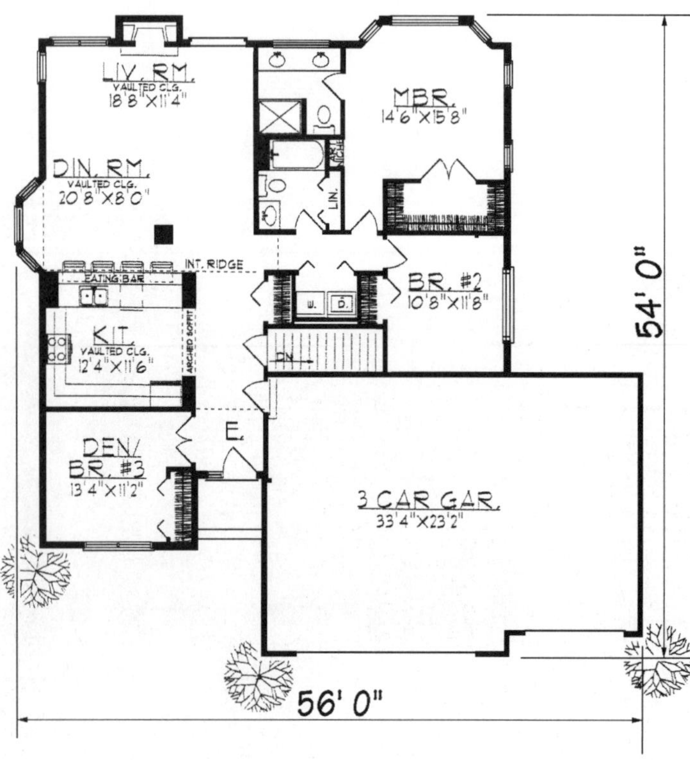

LIV. RM.
VAULTED CLG.
18'8"X11'4"
MBR.
14'6"X15'8"
DIN. RM.
VAULTED CLG.
20'8"X8'0"
LIN.
INT. RIDGE
EATING BAR
BR. #2
10'8"X11'8"
KIT.
VAULTED CLG.
12'4"X11'6"
ARCHED SOFFIT
DN.
E.
DEN/
BR. #3
13'4"X11'2"
3 CAR GAR.
33'4"X23'2"
54' 0"
56' 0"

Plan #530-051D-0064

Price Code A

Total Living Area: 1,462 Sq. Ft.

Home has 2 bedrooms, 2 baths, 3-car garage and basement foundation.

Special features

- Arch soffit frames the entrance of the kitchen
- Living room has fireplace with surrounding windows
- Bay window in master bedroom adds light and beauty
- Den can easily be converted to a third bedroom

LOWE'S

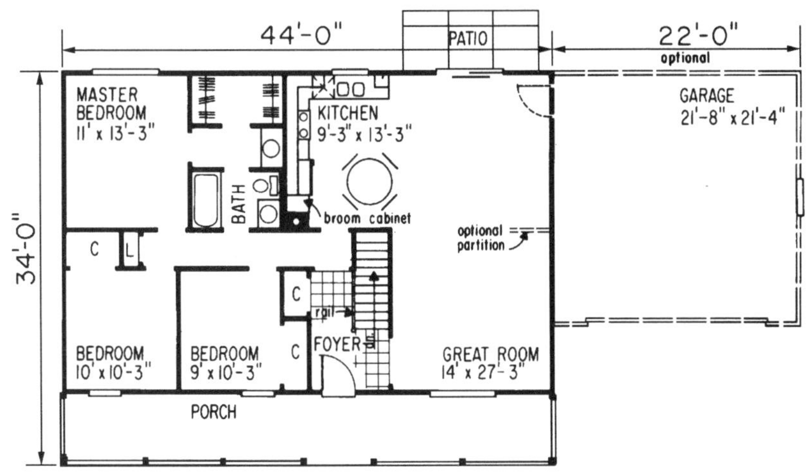
44'-0"
PATIO
22'-0"
optional
34'-0"
MASTER BEDROOM
11' x 13'-3"
KITCHEN
9'-3" x 13'-3"
GARAGE
21'-8" x 21'-4"
BATH
broom cabinet
optional partition
C
L
C
rail
BEDROOM
10' x 10'-3"
BEDROOM
9' x 10'-3"
C
FOYER
GREAT ROOM
14' x 27'-3"
PORCH

Plan #530-008D-0012

Price Code A

Total Living Area: 1,232 Sq. Ft.

Home has 3 bedrooms, 1 bath, optional 2-car garage and basement foundation, drawings also include crawl space and slab foundations.

Special features

- Ideal porch for quiet quality evenings
- Great room opens to dining room for those large dinner gatherings
- Functional L-shaped kitchen includes broom cabinet
- Master bedroom contains a large walk-in closet and compartmented bath

LOWE'S

Appealing Gabled Facade

Plan #530-025D-0009

Price Code B

Total Living Area: 1,680 Sq. Ft.

Home has 4 bedrooms, 2 baths, 2-car garage and slab foundation.

Special features

- Vaulted great room has a wet bar making it an ideal space for entertaining
- Spacious dining area features an eating bar for additional seating
- Fourth bedroom could easily be converted to a study

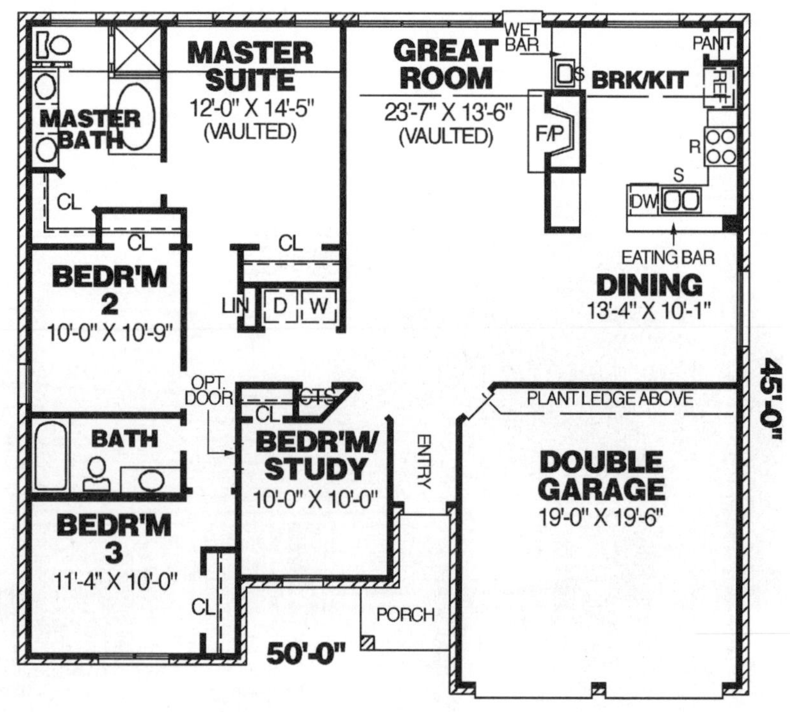
MASTER SUITE
12'-0" X 14'-5"
(VAULTED)
GREAT ROOM
23'-7" X 13'-6"
(VAULTED)
WET BAR
PANT
BRK/KIT
REF
F/P
R
S
DW
MASTER BATH
CL
CL
CL
EATING BAR
DINING
13'-4" X 10'-1"
BEDR'M 2
10'-0" X 10'-9"
LIN
D
W
OPT. DOOR
CTS
CL
PLANT LEDGE ABOVE
45'-0"
BATH
BEDR'M/ STUDY
10'-0" X 10'-0"
ENTRY
DOUBLE GARAGE
19'-0" X 19'-6"
BEDR'M 3
11'-4" X 10'-0"
CL
PORCH
50'-0"

TO ORDER BLUEPRINTS USE THE FORM ON PAGE 288 OR CALL TOLL-FREE **1-800-DREAM HOME** (373-2646)

LOWE'S

Plan #530-052D-0045

Price Code C

Total Living Area: 1,865 Sq. Ft.

Home has 3 bedrooms, 2 baths, 2-car garage and walk-out basement foundation.

Special features

- French doors next to stately fireplace in living room lead to sundeck
- Open living and dining rooms create a spacious feel
- Angled wall in master bedroom adds interest

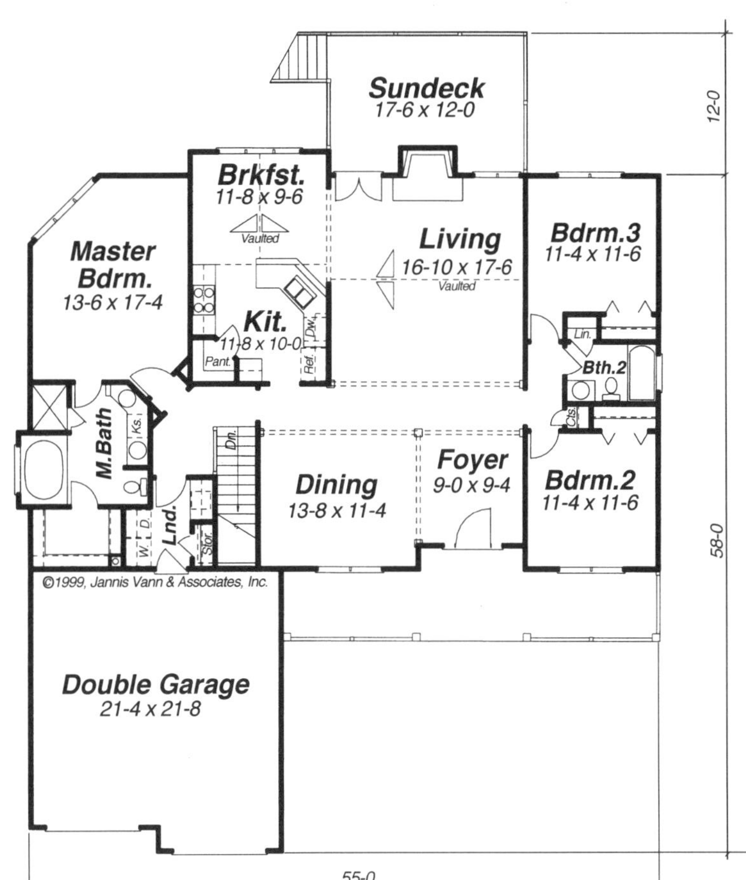
Sundeck
17-6 x 12-0
12-0
Brkfst.
11-8 x 9-6
Vaulted
Living
16-10 x 17-6
Vaulted
Bdrm.3
11-4 x 11-6
Master
Bdrm.
13-6 x 17-4
Kit.
11-8 x 10-0
Pant.
Ref.
Dw.
Lin.
Bth.2
Cts.
M.Bath
Ks.
Dn.
Dining
13-8 x 11-4
Foyer
9-0 x 9-4
Bdrm.2
11-4 x 11-6
58-0
W.
D.
Lnd.
Stor.
©1999, Jannis Vann & Associates, Inc.
Double Garage
21-4 x 21-8
55-0

LOWE'S

FREILING

Plan #530-051D-0039

Price Code C

Total Living Area: 1,976 Sq. Ft.

Home has 3 bedrooms, 2 1/2 baths, 3-car garage and basement foundation.

Special features

- Formal dining room has a butler's pantry for entertaining
- Open living room offers a fireplace, built-in cabinetry and an exceptional view to the outdoors
- Kitchen has work island and planning desk

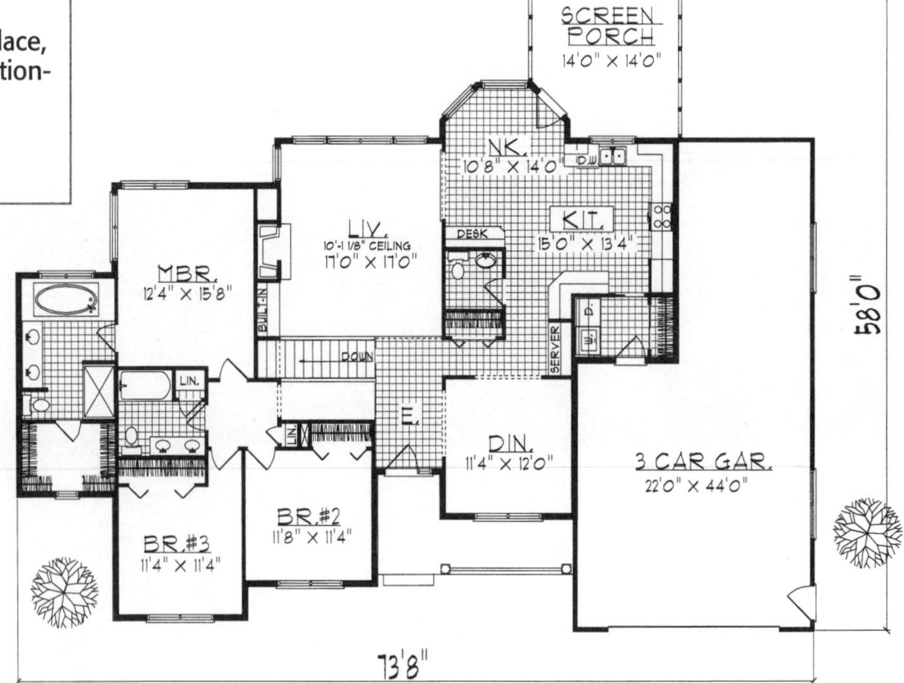
SCREEN PORCH
14'0" x 14'0"
NK.
10'8" x 14'0"
DW
LIV.
10'-1 1/8" CEILING
17'0" x 17'0"
KIT.
15'0" x 13'4"
DESK
MBR.
12'4" x 15'8"
BUILT-IN
DOWN
SERVER
LIN.
E.
DIN.
11'4" x 12'0"
3 CAR GAR.
22'0" x 44'0"
LIN
BR.#2
11'8" x 11'4"
BR.#3
11'4" x 11'4"
58'0"
73'8"

 TO ORDER BLUEPRINTS USE THE FORM ON PAGE 288 OR CALL TOLL-FREE **1-800-DREAM HOME** (373-2646)

Plan #530-008D-0013

Price Code A

Total Living Area: 1,345 Sq. Ft.

Home has 3 bedrooms, 2 baths, 2-car side entry garage and basement foundation, drawings also include crawl space and slab foundations.

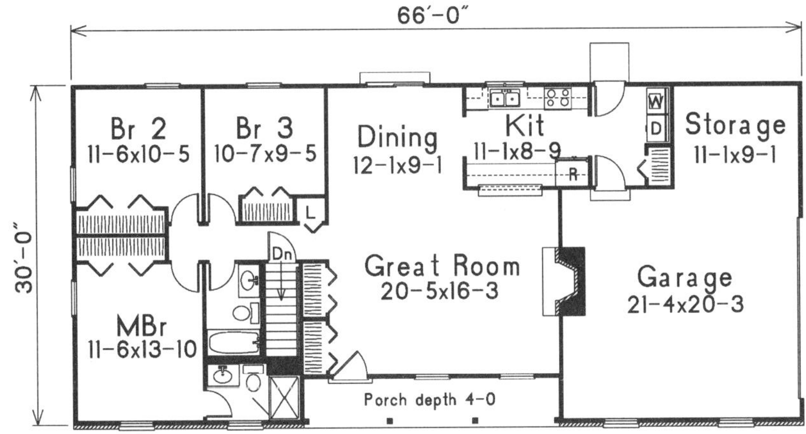
66'-0"
30'-0"
Br 2
11-6x10-5
Br 3
10-7x9-5
Dining
12-1x9-1
Kit
11-1x8-9
W
D
R
Storage
11-1x9-1
L
Dn
Great Room
20-5x16-3
Garage
21-4x20-3
MBr
11-6x13-10
Porch depth 4-0

Special features

- Brick front details add a touch of elegance
- Master bedroom has a private full bath
- Great room combines with the dining area creating a sense of spaciousness
- Garage includes a handy storage area which could easily convert to a workshop space

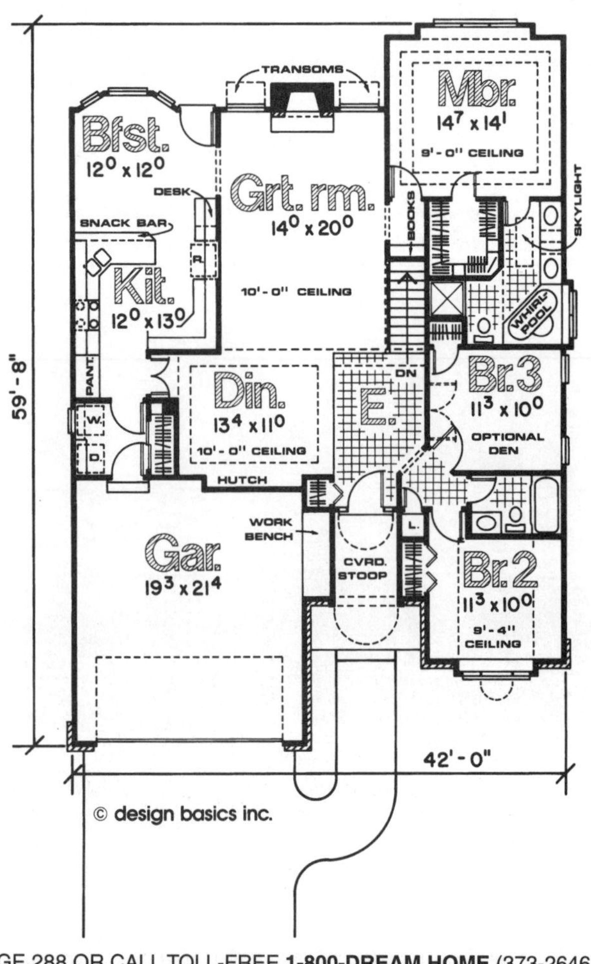
TRANSOMS
Mbr.
$14^7 \times 14^1$
9'-0" CEILING
SKYLIGHT
Bfst.
$12^0 \times 12^0$
DESK
SNACK BAR
Grt. rm.
$14^0 \times 20^0$
10'-0" CEILING
BOOKS
R
Kit.
$12^0 \times 13^0$
WHIRL POOL
PANT.
W.
D.
Din.
$13^4 \times 11^0$
10'-0" CEILING
HUTCH
DN
E.
Br. 3
$11^3 \times 10^0$
OPTIONAL DEN
L.
WORK BENCH
Gar.
$19^3 \times 21^4$
CVRD. STOOP
Br. 2
$11^3 \times 10^0$
9'-4" CEILING
59'-8"
42'-0"
© design basics inc.

Plan #530-026D-0082

Price Code B

Total Living Area: 1,636 Sq. Ft.

Home has 3 bedrooms, 2 baths, 2-car garage and basement foundation.

Special features

- Narrow front facade fits most unique lots
- Soaring front entrance invites guests
- Formal master bedroom and bath feature tray ceilings and a whirlpool tub

Impressive Ranch Features Attractive Courtyard

LOWE'S

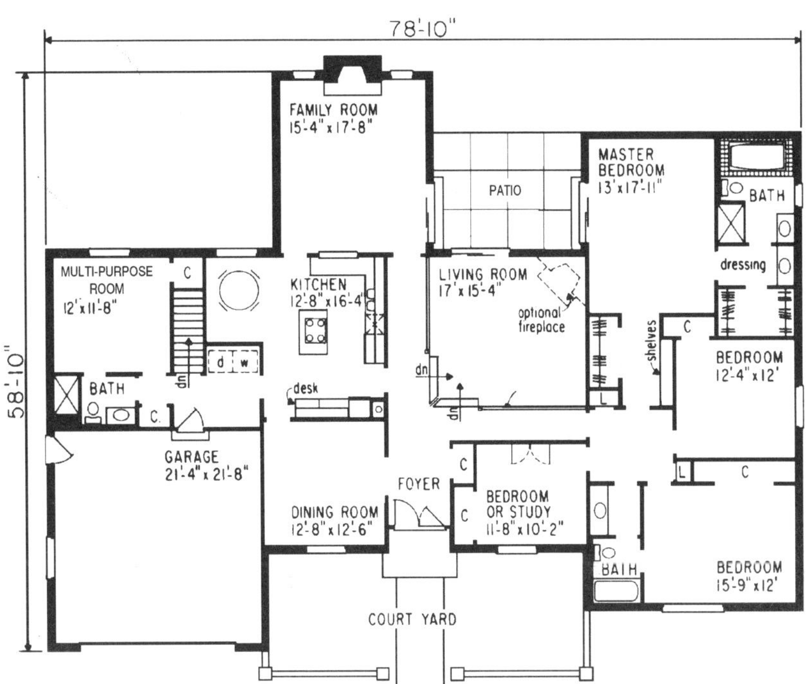
78'-10"
58'-10"
FAMILY ROOM
15'-4" x 17'-8"
PATIO
MASTER BEDROOM
13' x 17'-11"
BATH
dressing
MULTI-PURPOSE ROOM
12' x 11'-8"
KITCHEN
12'-8" x 16'-4"
LIVING ROOM
17' x 15'-4"
optional fireplace
shelves
BEDROOM
12'-4" x 12'
BATH
desk
GARAGE
21'-4" x 21'-8"
FOYER
BEDROOM OR STUDY
11'-8" x 10'-2"
DINING ROOM
12'-8" x 12'-6"
BATH
BEDROOM
15'-9" x 12'
COURT YARD

Plan #530-008D-0009

Price Code E

Total Living Area: 2,851 Sq. Ft.

Home has 4 bedrooms, 3 baths, 2-car garage and basement foundation, drawings also include crawl space and slab foundations.

Special features

- Foyer with double-door entrance leads to unique sunken living room with patio view
- Multi-purpose room is perfect for a home office, hobby room or fifth bedroom
- Master bedroom boasts abundant closet space and access to patio
- Family room has access to kitchen and features a fireplace flanked by windows

LOWE'S

Plan #530-015D-0008

Price Code B

Total Living Area: 1,785 Sq. Ft.

Home has 3 bedrooms, 2 baths, 2-car garage and basement, crawl space or slab foundation, please specify when ordering.

Special features

- Vaulted foyer opens to the living room which features a graceful archway framed by decorative columns and overhead plant shelves
- Bayed dining room also features an 11' ceiling and a French door that opens to a covered patio
- Open floor plan allows this home to be wheelchair accessible

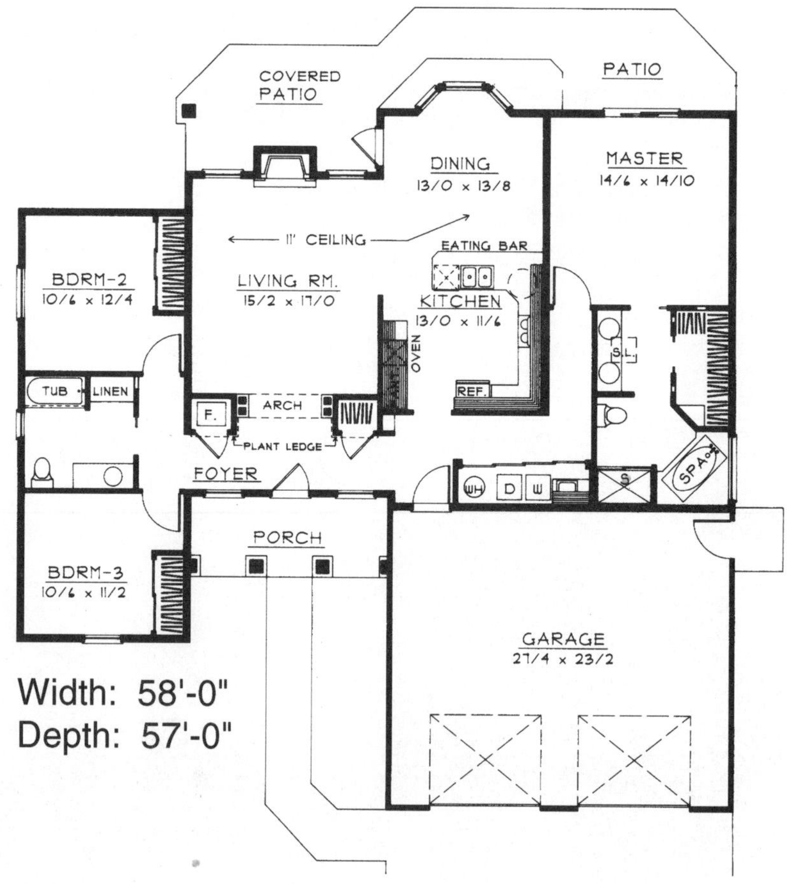
COVERED PATIO
PATIO
DINING 13/0 x 13/8
MASTER 14/6 x 14/10
11' CEILING
EATING BAR
BDRM-2 10/6 x 12/4
LIVING RM. 15/2 x 17/0
KITCHEN 13/0 x 11/6
OVEN
REF.
TUB
LINEN
F.
ARCH
PLANT LEDGE
FOYER
WH
D
W
SPA
PORCH
BDRM-3 10/6 x 11/2
GARAGE 27/4 x 23/2
Width: 58'-0"
Depth: 57'-0"

 TO ORDER BLUEPRINTS USE THE FORM ON PAGE 288 OR CALL TOLL-FREE **1-800-DREAM HOME** (373-2646)

LOWE'S

Plan #530-019D-0016

Price Code E

Total Living Area: 2,678 Sq. Ft.

Home has 4 bedrooms, 2 1/2 baths, 2-car side entry garage and crawl space foundation, drawings also include slab foundation.

Special features

- An elegant arched opening graces the entrance
- Kitchen has double ovens, walk-in pantry and an eating bar
- Master bedroom has a beautiful bath spotlighting a step-up tub

HERS
HIS
STEP
MASTER BATH
11 FT TRAY CLG
SEAT
FP
PORCH
9 FT CLG
FAMILY ROOM
13-6 X 16-6
9 FT CLG
BRKFST RM
10-8 X 11-6
9 FT CLG
MASTER BEDRM
15-0 X 17-4
11 FT TRAY CLG
COVERED PORCH
9 FT CLG
BEDRM 4
14-8 X 12-8
9 FT CLG
DEPTH 67-9
42" LEDGE
KITCHEN
13-6 X 11-4
9 FT CLG
PWDR
UTIL
12-8 X 5-8
9 FT CLG
LIVING ROOM
18-4 X 18-6
11 FT CLG
BATH 2
PAN
ARCH
DINING ROOM
14-0 X 13-6
11 FT CLG
GARAGE
BEDRM 3
11-0 X 13-4
9 FT CLG
BEDRM 2/
STUDY
11-6 X 13-0
11 FT TRAY CLG
FOYER
11 FT CLG
COPYRIGHT LARRY E. BELK
PORCH
9 FT CLG
WIDTH 70-2

Plan #530-043D-0005

Price Code B

Total Living Area: 1,734 Sq. Ft.

Home has 3 bedrooms, 2 baths, 2-car garage and crawl space foundation.

Special features

- Large entry boasts a coffered ceiling and display niches
- Sunken great room has 10' ceiling
- Kitchen island includes an eating counter
- 9' ceiling in the master bedroom
- Master bath features a corner tub and double sinks

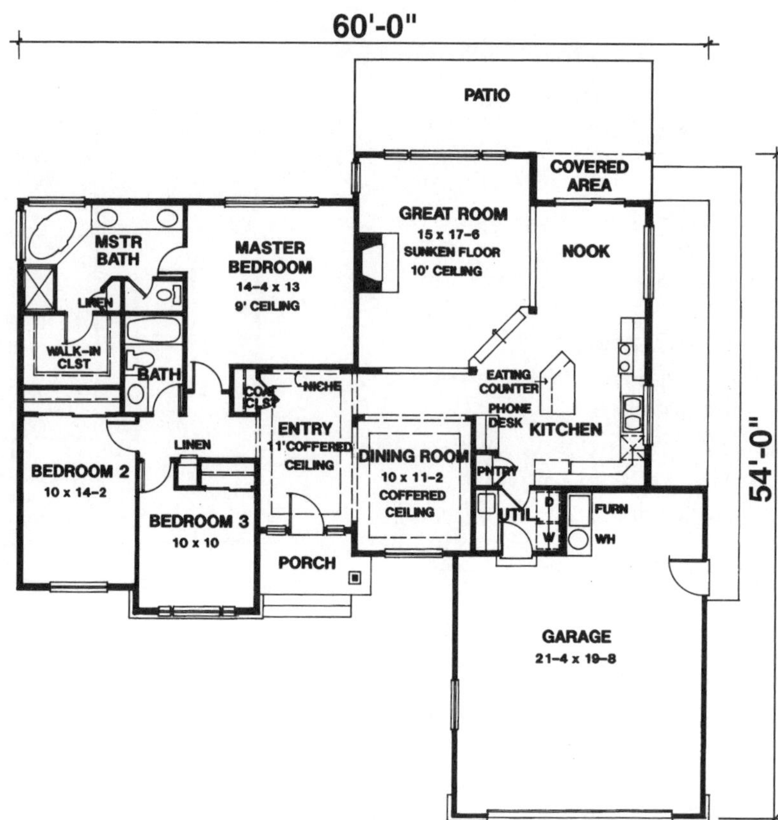
60'-0"
PATIO
COVERED AREA
GREAT ROOM
15 x 17-6
SUNKEN FLOOR
10' CEILING
NOOK
MSTR BATH
MASTER BEDROOM
14-4 x 13
9' CEILING
LINEN
WALK-IN CLST
BATH
COAT CLST
NICHE
EATING COUNTER
PHONE DESK
KITCHEN
ENTRY
11' COFFERED CEILING
DINING ROOM
10 x 11-2
COFFERED CEILING
PNTRY
UTIL
D
W
FURN
WH
BEDROOM 2
10 x 14-2
LINEN
BEDROOM 3
10 x 10
PORCH
GARAGE
21-4 x 19-8
54'-0"

Charming One-Story Traditional

LOWE'S

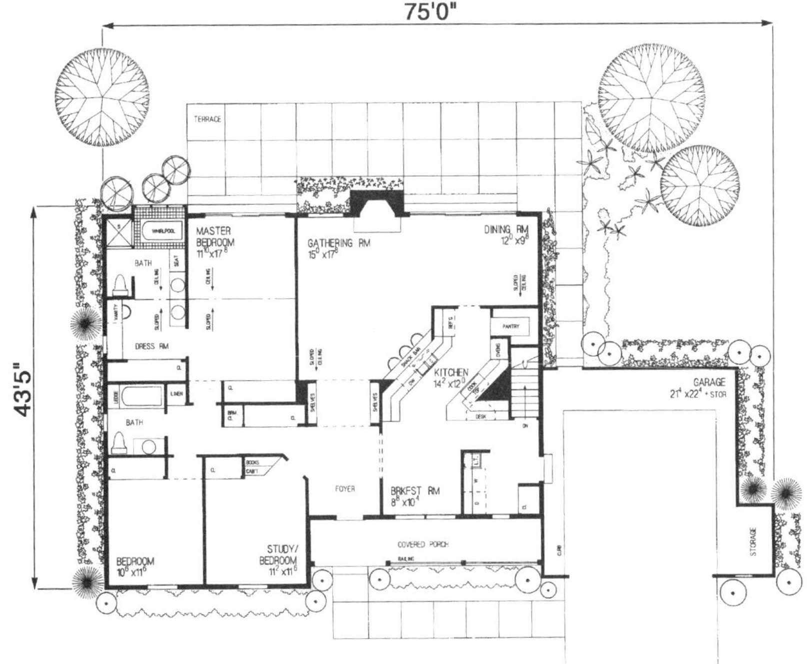
75'0"
43'5"
TERRACE
MASTER BEDROOM
GATHERING RM
DINING RM
BATH
WHIRLPOOL
DRESS RM
LINEN
KITCHEN
PANTRY
GARAGE
FOYER
BRKFST RM
COVERED PORCH
BEDROOM
STUDY/ BEDROOM
STORAGE

Plan #530-049D-0003

Price Code C

Total Living Area: 1,830 Sq. Ft.

Home has 3 bedrooms, 2 baths, 2-car garage and basement foundation.

Special features

- A uniquely shaped galley-style kitchen shares a snack bar with the spacious gathering room that features a fireplace
- Dining room has sliding glass doors to the rear terrace as well as the master bedroom
- Master bedroom includes a luxury bath with a whirlpool tub and separate dressing room

LOWE'S

Plan #530-031D-0005

Price Code B

Total Living Area: 1,735 Sq. Ft.

Home has 3 bedrooms, 2 baths, 2-car garage and slab foundation.

Special features

- Luxurious master bath has a spa tub, shower, double vanity and large walk-in closet
- Peninsula in the kitchen has a sink and dishwasher
- Massive master bedroom has a step-up ceiling and private location

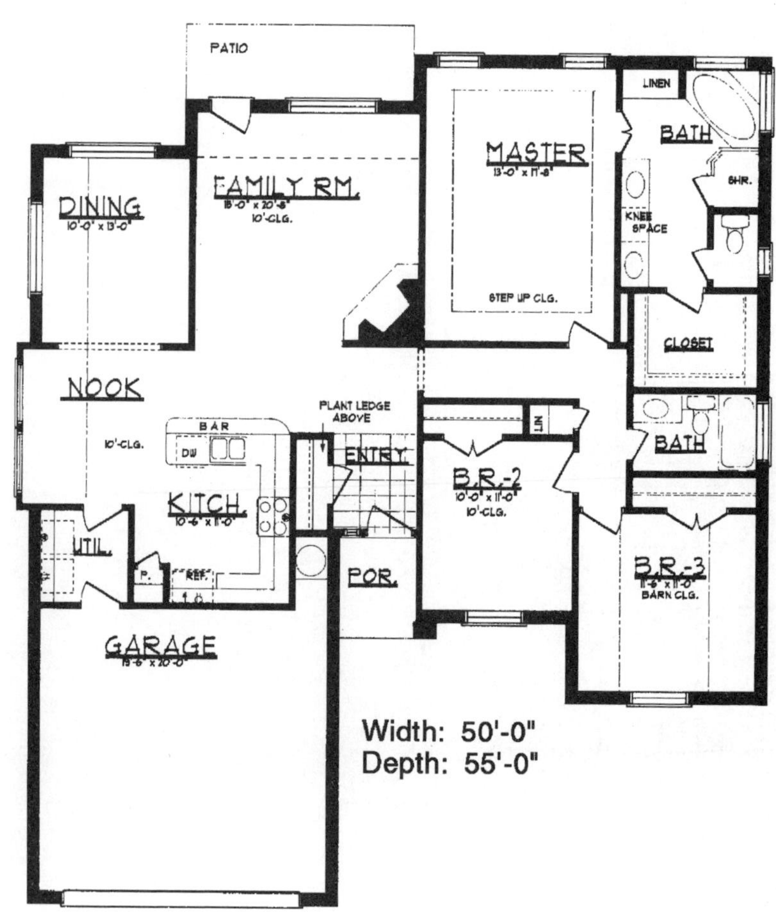
PATIO
LINEN
BATH
MASTER
STEP UP CLG.
SHR.
KNEE SPACE
FAMILY RM.
10'-CLG.
DINING
10'-0" x 13'-0"
CLOSET
NOOK
PLANT LEDGE ABOVE
BAR
10'-CLG.
DW
ENTRY
LIN
BATH
B.R.-2
10'-CLG.
KITCH.
UTIL.
P.
REF.
POR.
B.R.-3
BARN CLG.
GARAGE
Width: 50'-0"
Depth: 55'-0"

 TO ORDER BLUEPRINTS USE THE FORM ON PAGE 288 OR CALL TOLL-FREE **1-800-DREAM HOME** (373-2646)

LOWE'S

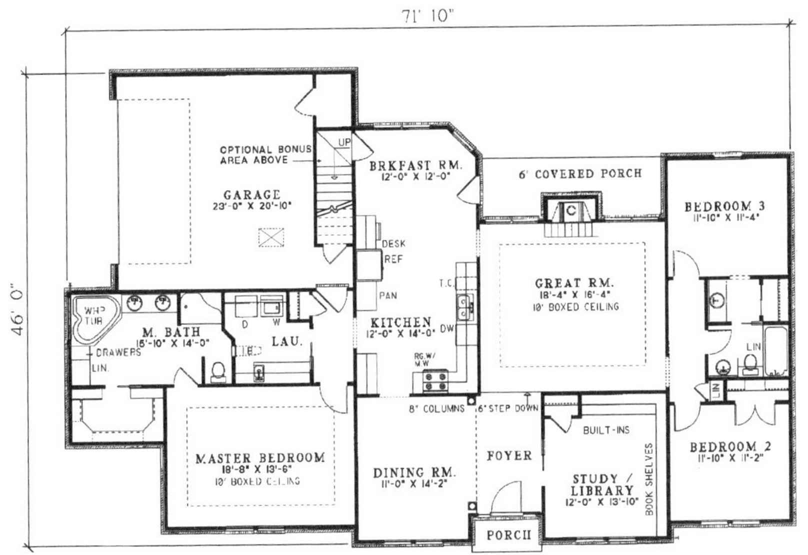
71' 10"
46' 0"
OPTIONAL BONUS AREA ABOVE
GARAGE
23'-0" X 20'-10"
UP
BRKFAST RM.
12'-0" X 12'-0"
6' COVERED PORCH
BEDROOM 3
11'-10" X 11'-4"
DESK
REF
PAN
T.C.
GREAT RM.
18'-4" X 16'-4"
10' BOXED CEILING
KITCHEN
12'-0" X 14'-0"
DW
RG.W/ M.W.
WHP TUB
M. BATH
15'-10" X 14'-0"
DRAWERS
LIN.
D
W
LAU.
LIN
8' COLUMNS
6" STEP DOWN
BUILT-INS
MASTER BEDROOM
18'-8" X 13'-6"
10' BOXED CEILING
DINING RM.
11'-0" X 14'-2"
FOYER
STUDY / LIBRARY
12'-0" X 13'-10"
BOOK SHELVES
BEDROOM 2
11'-10" X 11'-2"
PORCH

Plan #530-055D-0015

Price Code C

Total Living Area: 2,092 Sq. Ft.

Home has 3 bedrooms, 2 baths, 2-car side entry garage and slab or crawl space foundation, please specify when ordering.

Special features

- Master bedroom has a private luxury bath
- Kitchen and breakfast room are centrally located
- Study/library is secluded from living areas

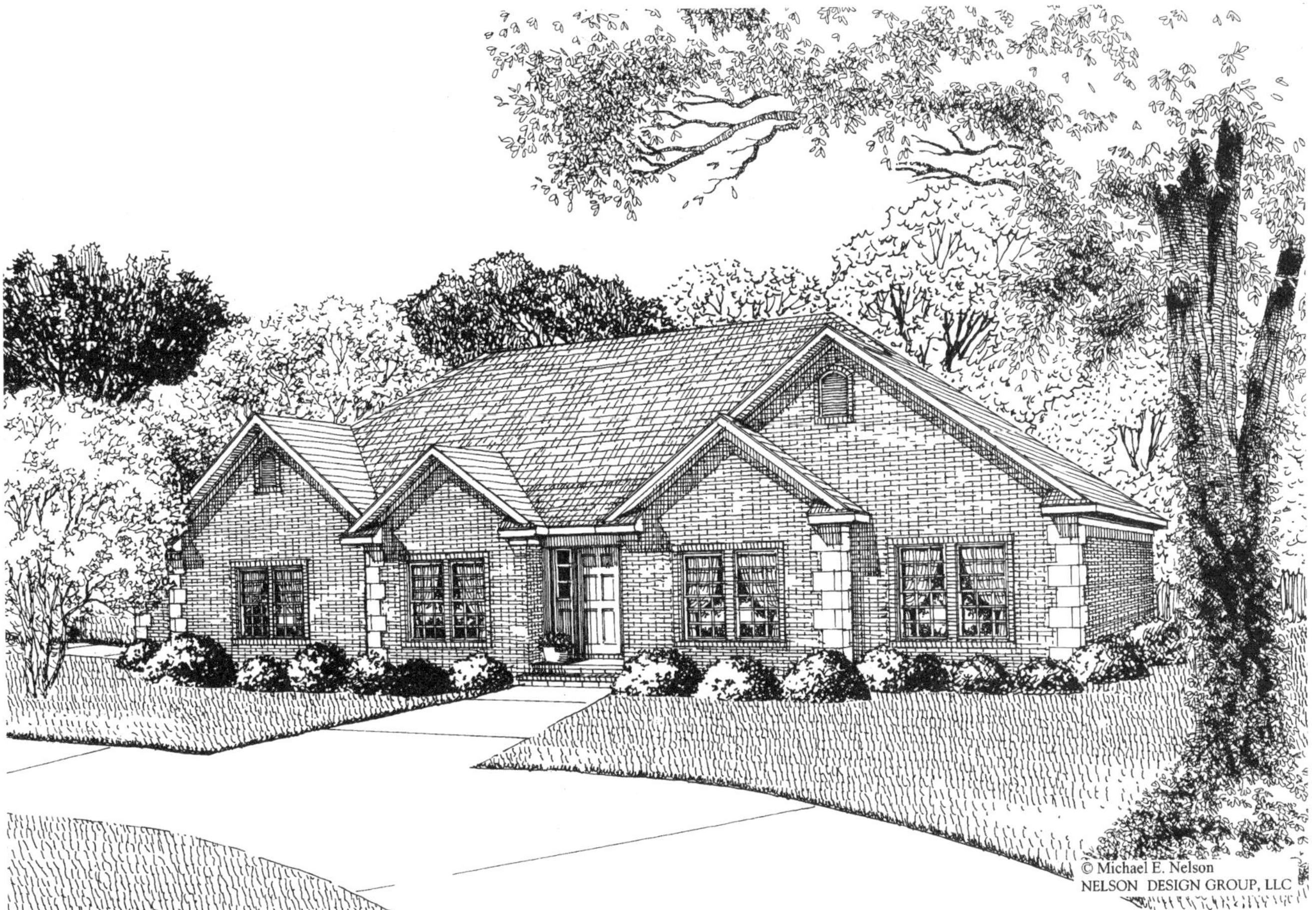

Plan #530-051D-0027

Price Code B

Total Living Area: 1,540 Sq. Ft.

Home has 3 bedrooms, 2 baths, 2-car garage and basement foundation.

Special features

- Spacious master bedroom has a large walk-in closet and sweeping windows overlooking yard
- First floor laundry is conveniently located between the garage and kitchen
- Living room features a cathedral ceiling and corner fireplace

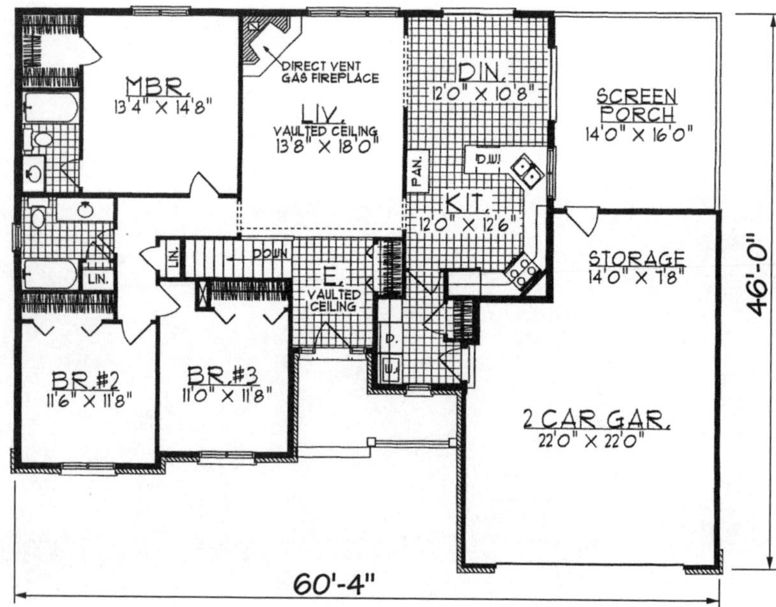

MBR.
13'4" X 14'8"
DIRECT VENT GAS FIREPLACE
LIV.
VAULTED CEILING
13'8" X 18'0"
DIN.
12'0" X 10'8"
SCREEN PORCH
14'0" X 16'0"
PAN.
D.W.
KIT.
12'0" X 12'6"
STORAGE
14'0" X 7'8"
LIN.
DOWN
E.
VAULTED CEILING
LIN.
D.
W.
BR.#2
11'6" X 11'8"
BR.#3
11'0" X 11'8"
2 CAR GAR.
22'0" X 22'0"
46'-0"
60'-4"

Stone And Brick Facade

LOWE'S

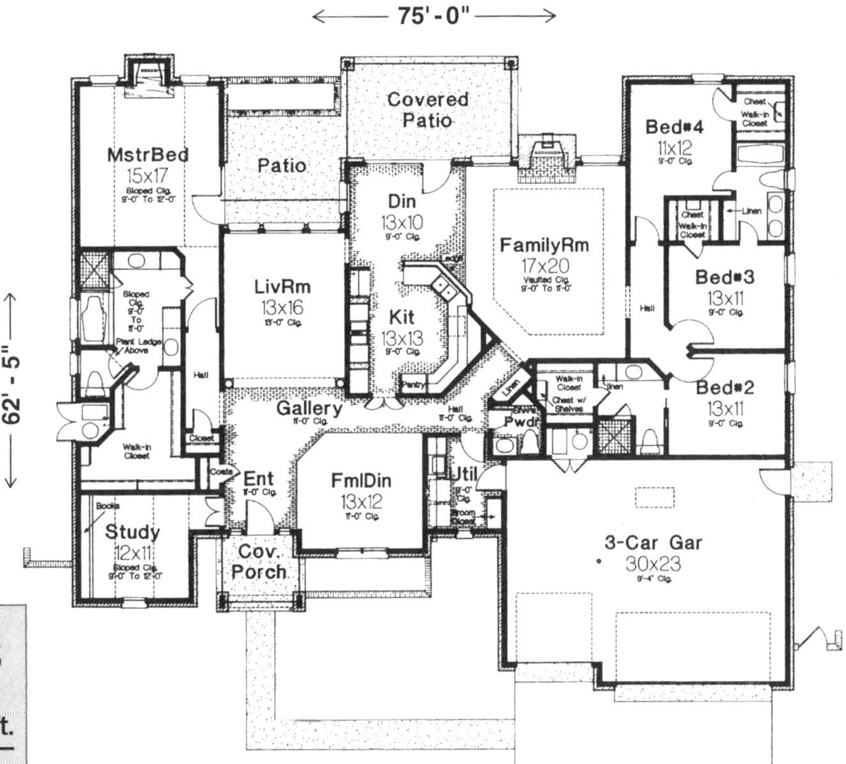
75'-0"
62'-5"
Covered Patio
MstrBed
15x17
Sloped Clg.
9'-0" To 12'-0"
Patio
Din
13x10
9'-0" Clg.
FamilyRm
17x20
Vaulted Clg.
9'-0" To 11'-0"
Bed#4
11x12
9'-0" Clg.
Bed#3
13x11
9'-0" Clg.
LivRm
13x16
13'-0" Clg.
Kit
13x13
9'-0" Clg.
Gallery
11'-0" Clg.
Bed#2
13x11
9'-0" Clg.
Walk-in Closet
Hall
Pwdr
Ent
11'-0" Clg.
FmlDin
13x12
11'-0" Clg.
Util
Study
12x11
Sloped Clg.
9'-0" To 12'-0"
Cov.
Porch
3-Car Gar
30x23
9'-4" Clg.

Plan #530-036D-0042

Price Code E

Total Living Area: 2,945 Sq. Ft.

Home has 4 bedrooms, 3 1/2 baths, 3-car garage and slab foundation.

Special features

- Private study has a double-door entry, sloped ceiling and bookshelves
- Super master bedroom boasts a gas log fireplace for coziness
- Large family room features a fireplace and is adjacent to secondary bedrooms

LOWE'S

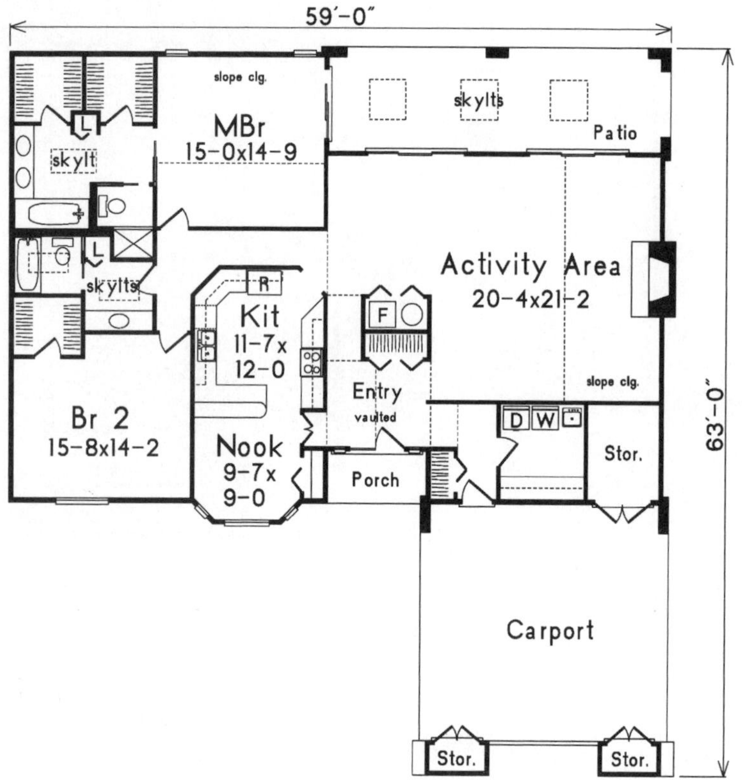
59'-0"
63'-0"
slope clg.
MBr
15-0x14-9
skylts
Patio
skylt
skylts
Activity Area
20-4x21-2
Kit
11-7x
12-0
Entry
vaulted
slope clg.
Br 2
15-8x14-2
Nook
9-7x
9-0
Porch
Stor.
Carport
Stor.
Stor.

Plan #530-008D-0055

Price Code C

Total Living Area: 1,996 Sq. Ft.

Home has 2 bedrooms, 2 baths, 2-car side entry carport and slab foundation.

Special features

- Centrally located activity area has a fireplace and double sliding glass doors accessing the covered patio with skylights
- Spacious master bedroom includes a private bath with skylight and double walk-in closets
- Private nook with a double-door entry makes an ideal office area
- Plenty of closet space throughout with walk-in closets in the bedrooms and several hall closets

LOWE'S

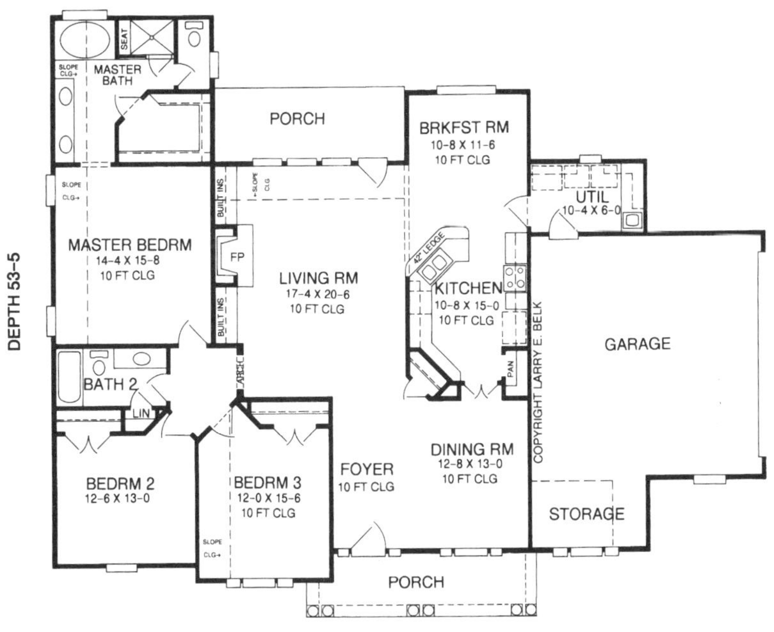
MASTER BATH
SEAT
PORCH
BRKFST RM
10-8 X 11-6
10 FT CLG
UTIL
10-4 X 6-0
MASTER BEDRM
14-4 X 15-8
10 FT CLG
FP
BUILT INS
LIVING RM
17-4 X 20-6
10 FT CLG
KITCHEN
10-8 X 15-0
10 FT CLG
PAN
GARAGE
DEPTH 53-5
BATH 2
LIN
BEDRM 2
12-6 X 13-0
BEDRM 3
12-0 X 15-6
10 FT CLG
FOYER
10 FT CLG
DINING RM
12-8 X 13-0
10 FT CLG
COPYRIGHT LARRY E. BELK
STORAGE
PORCH
WIDTH 65-10

Plan #530-019D-0013

Price Code C

Total Living Area: 1,932 Sq. Ft.

Home has 3 bedrooms, 2 baths, 2-car side entry garage and crawl space foundation, drawings also include slab foundation.

Special features

- Double arches form entrance to this elegantly styled home
- Two palladian windows add distinction to facade
- Kitchen has an angled eating bar opening to the breakfast and living rooms

Spacious Ranch For A Growing Family

Plan #530-035D-0001

Price Code B

Total Living Area: 1,715 Sq. Ft.

Home has 3 bedrooms, 2 baths, 2-car garage and walk-out basement, crawl space or slab foundation, please specify when ordering.

Special features

- Vaulted great room is spacious and bright
- Master suite enjoys a sitting room and private bath
- Kitchen has plenty of counterspace and cabinetry

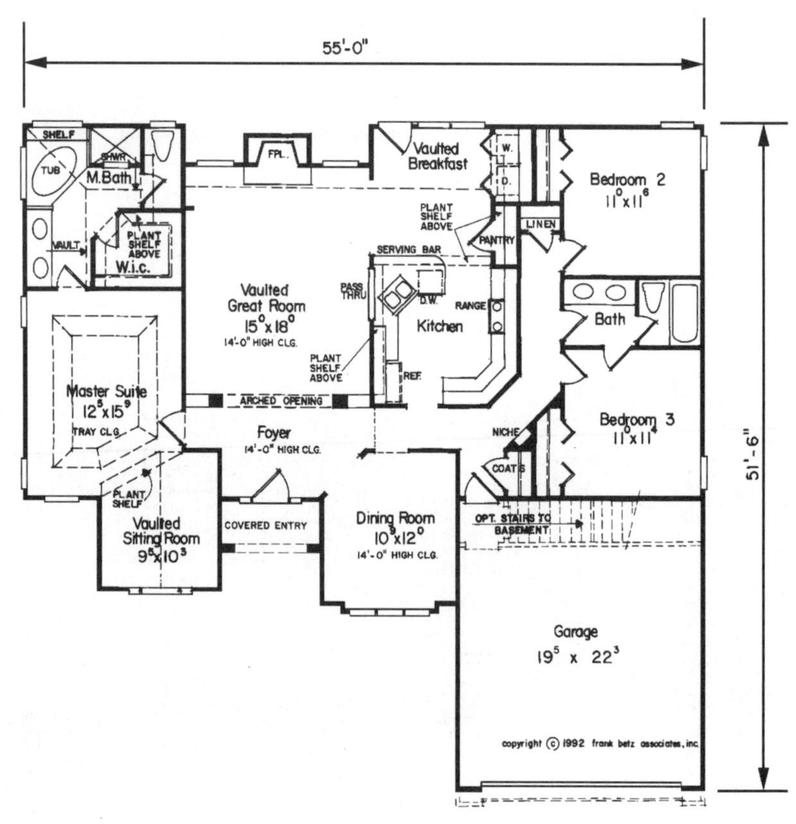
55'-0"
SHELF
TUB
SHWR
M.Bath
FPL.
Vaulted Breakfast
W.
D.
Bedroom 2
$11^0 x 11^6$
PLANT SHELF ABOVE
LINEN
PANTRY
VAULT
PLANT SHELF ABOVE
W.i.c.
SERVING BAR
Vaulted Great Room
$15^0 x 18^0$
14'-0" HIGH CLG.
PASS THRU
D.W.
RANGE
Kitchen
Bath
PLANT SHELF ABOVE
REF.
Master Suite
$12^5 x 15^9$
TRAY CLG.
ARCHED OPENING
Foyer
14'-0" HIGH CLG.
NICHE
Bedroom 3
$11^0 x 11^4$
COATS
51'-6"
PLANT SHELF
Vaulted Sitting Room
$9^5 x 10^3$
COVERED ENTRY
Dining Room
$10^9 x 12^0$
14'-0" HIGH CLG.
OPT. STAIRS TO BASEMENT
Garage
$19^5 x 22^3$
copyright (c) 1992 frank betz associates, inc.

LOWE'S

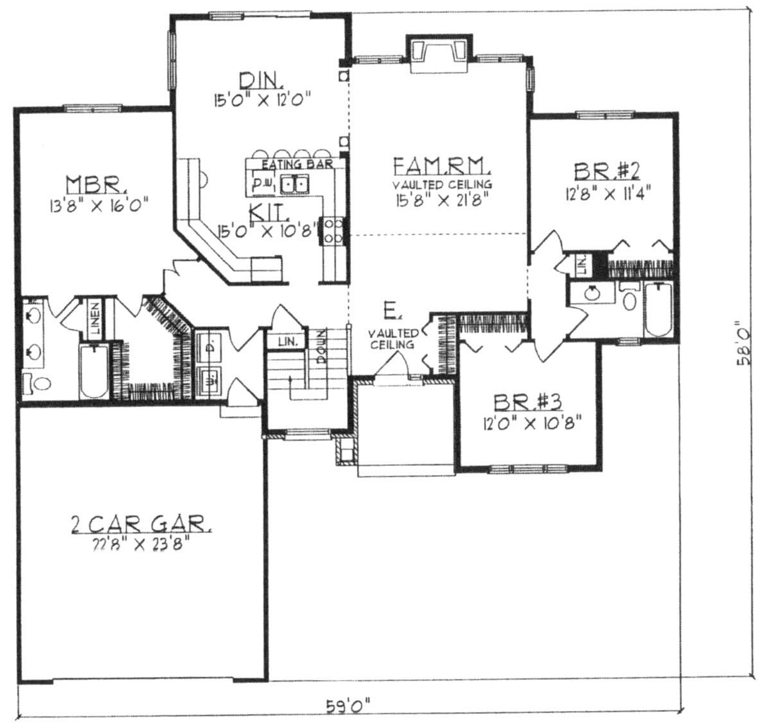
DIN.
15'0" X 12'0"
EATING BAR
KIT.
15'0" X 10'8"
FAM.RM.
VAULTED CEILING
15'8" X 21'8"
BR.#2
12'8" X 11'4"
MBR.
13'8" X 16'0"
LINEN
LIN.
DOWN
E.
VAULTED CEILING
BR.#3
12'0" X 10'8"
2 CAR GAR.
22'8" X 23'8"
58'0"
59'0"

Plan #530-051D-0034

Price Code B

Total Living Area: 1,756 Sq. Ft.

Home has 3 bedrooms, 2 baths, 2-car garage and basement foundation.

Special features

- Room for expansion on lower level
- Master bedroom enjoys a private bath and large walk-in closet
- Kitchen features a built-in desk and breakfast counter

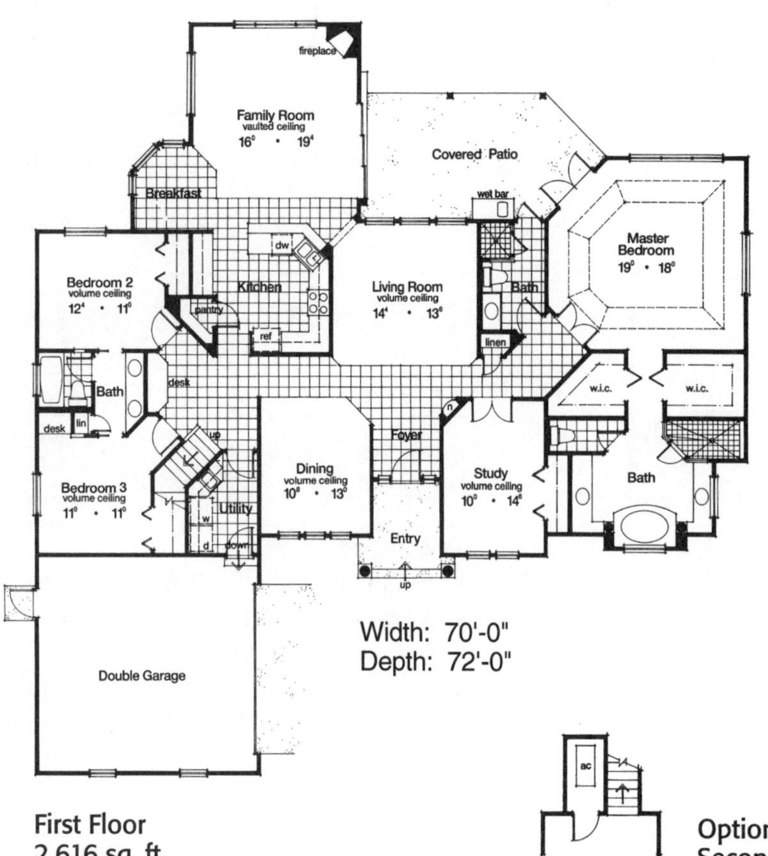
fireplace
Family Room
vaulted ceiling
16^{0} • 19^{4}
Covered Patio
Breakfast
wet bar
Master Bedroom
19^{0} • 18^{0}
dw
Bedroom 2
volume ceiling
12^{4} • 11^{0}
Kitchen
Living Room
volume ceiling
14^{4} • 13^{6}
Bath
pantry
ref
linen
w.i.c.
w.i.c.
Bath
desk
desk
lin
Foyer
up
Dining
volume ceiling
10^{8} • 13^{0}
Study
volume ceiling
10^{0} • 14^{8}
Bath
Bedroom 3
volume ceiling
11^{0} • 11^{0}
Utility
w
d
down
Entry
up
Double Garage
Width: 70'-0"
Depth: 72'-0"

First Floor
2,616 sq. ft.

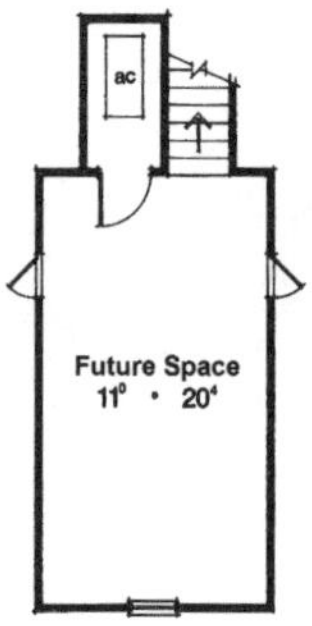

Plan #530-047D-0045

Price Code E

Total Living Area: 2,616 Sq. Ft.

Home has 3 bedrooms, 3 baths, 2-car side entry garage and slab foundation.

Special features

- Archway joins formal living and family rooms
- Master bedroom has a private bath and access to a covered patio
- Breakfast nook overlooks family room with cozy corner fireplace
- Future space on the second floor has an additional 287 square feet of living area

ac

Future Space
11^{0} • 20^{4}

Optional
Second Floor

LOWE'S

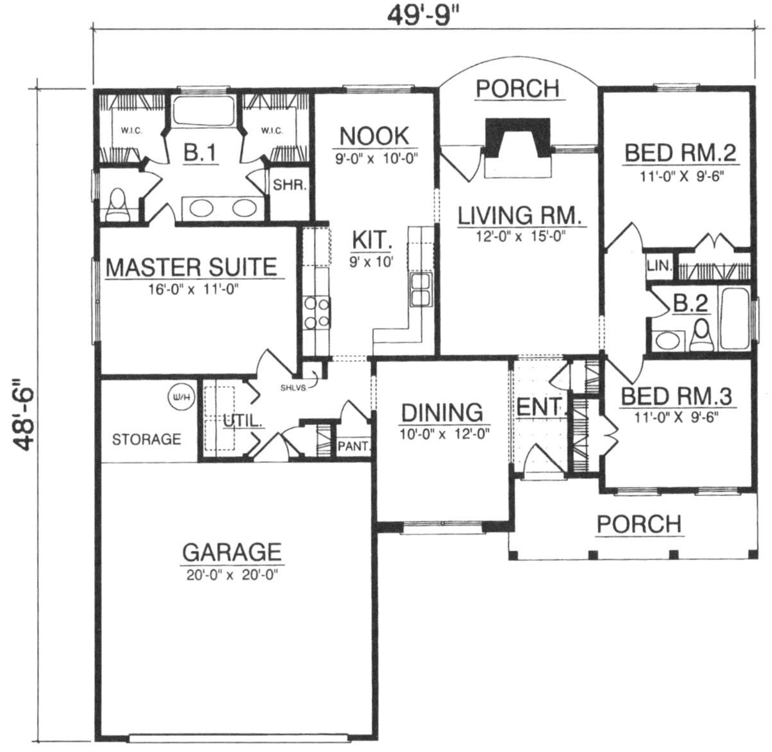
49'-9"
48'-6"
PORCH
W.I.C.
B.1
W.I.C.
SHR.
NOOK
9'-0" x 10'-0"
BED RM.2
11'-0" X 9'-6"
LIVING RM.
12'-0" x 15'-0"
KIT.
9' x 10'
MASTER SUITE
16'-0" x 11'-0"
LIN.
B.2
SHLVS
W/H
UTIL.
STORAGE
PANT.
DINING
10'-0" x 12'-0"
ENT.
BED RM.3
11'-0" X 9'-6"
PORCH
GARAGE
20'-0" x 20'-0"

Plan #530-030D-0001

Price Code A

Total Living Area: 1,374 Sq. Ft.

Home has 3 bedrooms, 2 baths, 2-car garage and slab or crawl space foundation, please specify when ordering.

Special features

- Garage has extra storage space
- Spacious living room has a fireplace
- Well-designed kitchen enjoys an adjacent breakfast nook
- Secluded master suite maintains privacy

LOWE'S

Architectural Accents Throughout

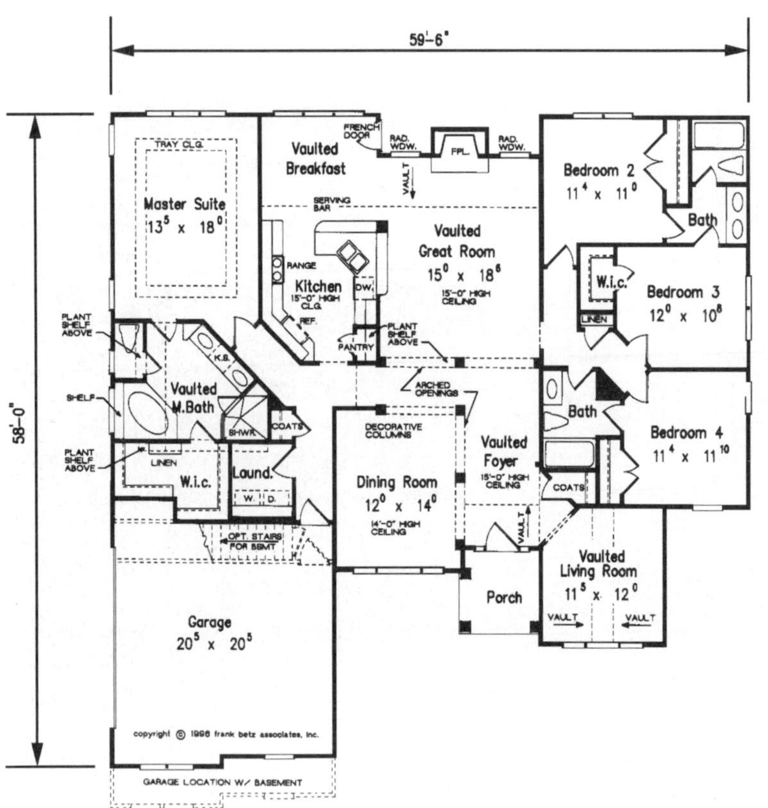
59'-6"
58'-0"
TRAY CLG.
Master Suite
13^{5} x 18^{0}
FRENCH DOOR
Vaulted Breakfast
RAD. WDW.
FPL.
RAD. WDW.
VAULT
SERVING BAR
Vaulted Great Room
15^{0} x 18^{8}
15'-0" HIGH CEILING
RANGE
Kitchen
15'-0" HIGH CLG.
DW.
REF.
PANTRY
PLANT SHELF ABOVE
PLANT SHELF ABOVE
K.S.
SHELF
Vaulted M.Bath
SHWR.
COATS
PLANT SHELF ABOVE
LINEN
W.i.c.
Laund.
W. D.
OPT. STAIRS FOR BSMT
ARCHED OPENINGS
DECORATIVE COLUMNS
Dining Room
12^{0} x 14^{0}
14'-0" HIGH CEILING
Vaulted Foyer
15'-0" HIGH CEILING
VAULT
Porch
COATS
Bedroom 2
11^{4} x 11^{0}
Bath
W.i.c.
Bedroom 3
12^{0} x 10^{8}
LINEN
Bath
Bedroom 4
11^{4} x 11^{10}
Vaulted Living Room
11^{5} x 12^{0}
VAULT
VAULT
Garage
20^{5} x 20^{5}
copyright © 1996 frank betz associates, inc.
GARAGE LOCATION W/ BASEMENT

Plan #530-035D-0037

Price Code D

Total Living Area: 2,279 Sq. Ft.

Home has 4 bedrooms, 3 baths, 2-car side entry garage and slab, crawl space or walk-out basement foundation, please specify when ordering.

Special features

- Formal vaulted living room is secluded and quiet
- Breakfast room connects to the great room
- Master suite is separate from the other bedrooms for privacy

TO ORDER BLUEPRINTS USE THE FORM ON PAGE 288 OR CALL TOLL-FREE **1-800-DREAM HOME** (373-2646)

Corner Fireplace In Grand Room

LOWE'S

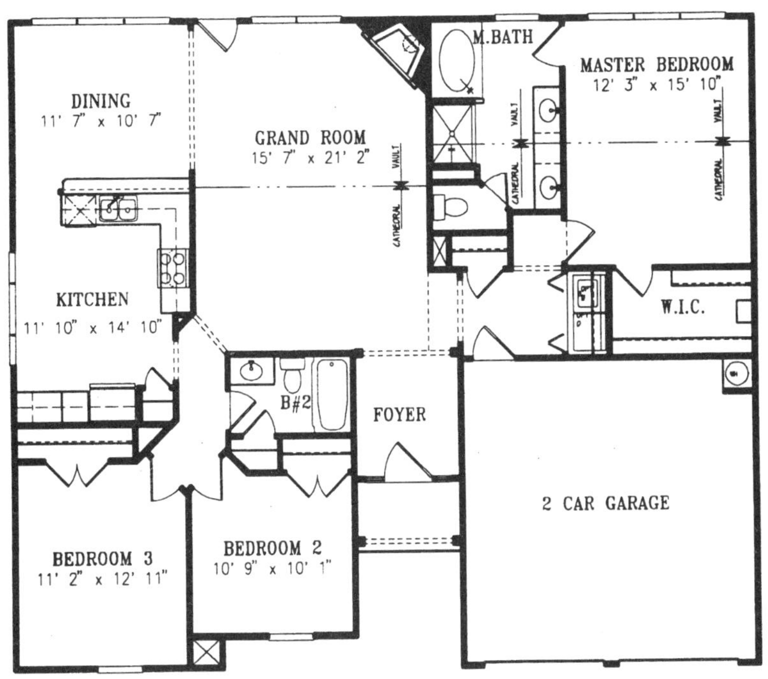
DINING
11' 7" x 10' 7"
GRAND ROOM
15' 7" x 21' 2"
M.BATH
MASTER BEDROOM
12' 3" x 15' 10"
CATHEDRAL VAULT
KITCHEN
11' 10" x 14' 10"
W.I.C.
B#2
FOYER
2 CAR GARAGE
BEDROOM 3
11' 2" x 12' 11"
BEDROOM 2
10' 9" x 10' 1"

Width: 50'-0"
Depth: 42'-0"

Plan #530-056D-0009

Price Code B

Total Living Area: 1,606 Sq. Ft.

Home has 3 bedrooms, 2 baths, 2-car garage and slab foundation.

Special features

- Kitchen has a snack bar which overlooks the dining area for convenience
- Master bedroom has lots of windows with a private bath and large walk-in closet
- Cathedral vault in the great room adds spaciousness

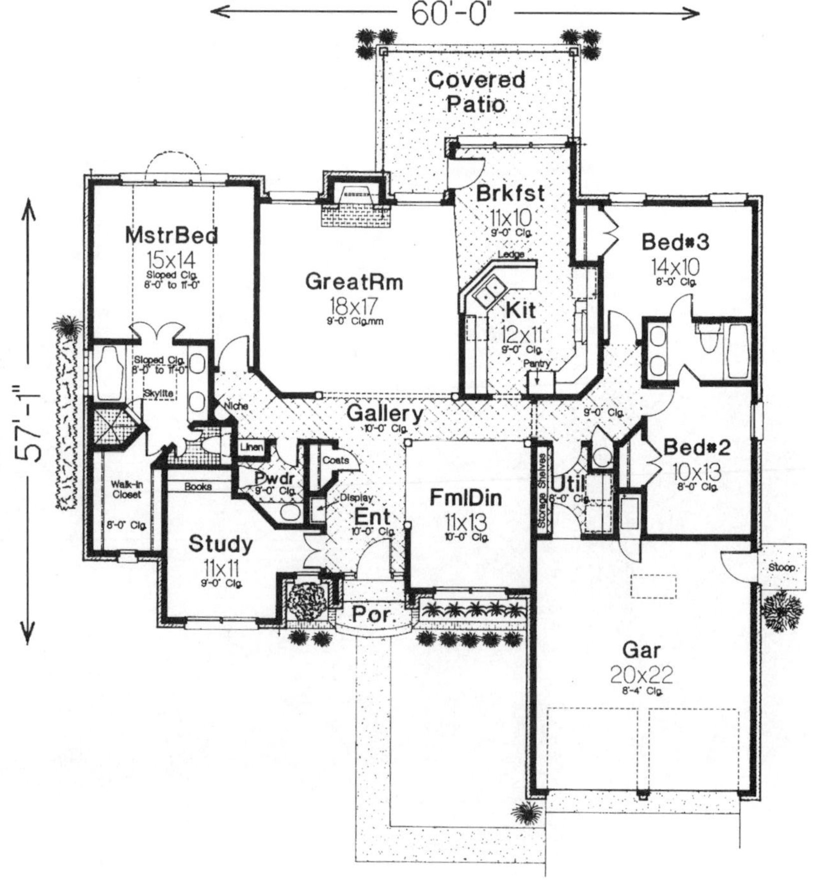
60'-0"
57'-1"
Covered Patio
Brkfst
11x10
9'-0" Clg.
MstrBed
15x14
Sloped Clg.
8'-0" to 11'-0"
GreatRm
18x17
9'-0" Clg.mm
Kit
12x11
9'-0" Clg.
Ledge
Pantry
Bed#3
14x10
8'-0" Clg.
Sloped Clg.
8'-0" to 11'-0"
Skylite
Niche
Gallery
10'-0" Clg.
9'-0" Clg.
Bed#2
10x13
8'-0" Clg.
Linen
Coats
Pwdr
9'-0" Clg.
Walk-in Closet
8'-0" Clg.
Books
Display
Ent
10'-0" Clg.
FmlDin
11x13
10'-0" Clg.
Storage Shelves
Util
8'-0" Clg.
Study
11x11
9'-0" Clg.
Stoop
Por.
Gar
20x22
8'-4" Clg.

Plan #530-036D-0040

Price Code C

Total Living Area: 2,061 Sq. Ft.

Home has 3 bedrooms, 2 1/2 baths, 2-car garage and crawl space or slab foundation, please specify when ordering.

Special features

- Charming stone facade entry
- Centrally located great room
- Private study in the front of the home is ideal as a home office
- Varied ceiling heights throughout this home

 TO ORDER BLUEPRINTS USE THE FORM ON PAGE 288 OR CALL TOLL-FREE **1-800-DREAM HOME** (373-2646)

LOWE'S

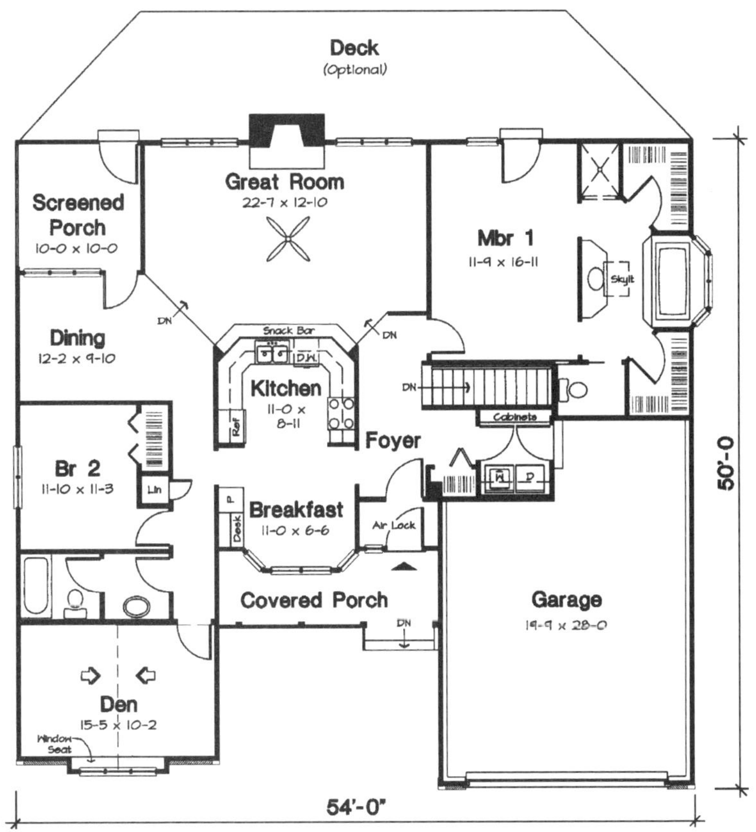
Deck
(Optional)
Screened Porch
10-0 x 10-0
Great Room
22-7 x 12-10
Mbr 1
11-9 x 16-11
Sklyt
Dining
12-2 x 9-10
Snack Bar
DW
Kitchen
11-0 x 8-11
Ref
DN
Foyer
Cabinets
Br 2
11-10 x 11-3
Lin
Breakfast
11-0 x 6-6
Desk
Air Lock
Covered Porch
Garage
19-9 x 28-0
Den
15-5 x 10-2
Window Seat
54'-0"
50'-0

Plan #530-038D-0039

Price Code B

Total Living Area: 1,771 Sq. Ft.

Home has 2 bedrooms, 2 baths, 2-car garage and basement, crawl space or slab foundation, please specify when ordering.

Special features

- Den has a sloped ceiling and charming window seat
- Private master bedroom has access to the outdoors
- Central kitchen allows for convenient access when entertaining

LOWE'S

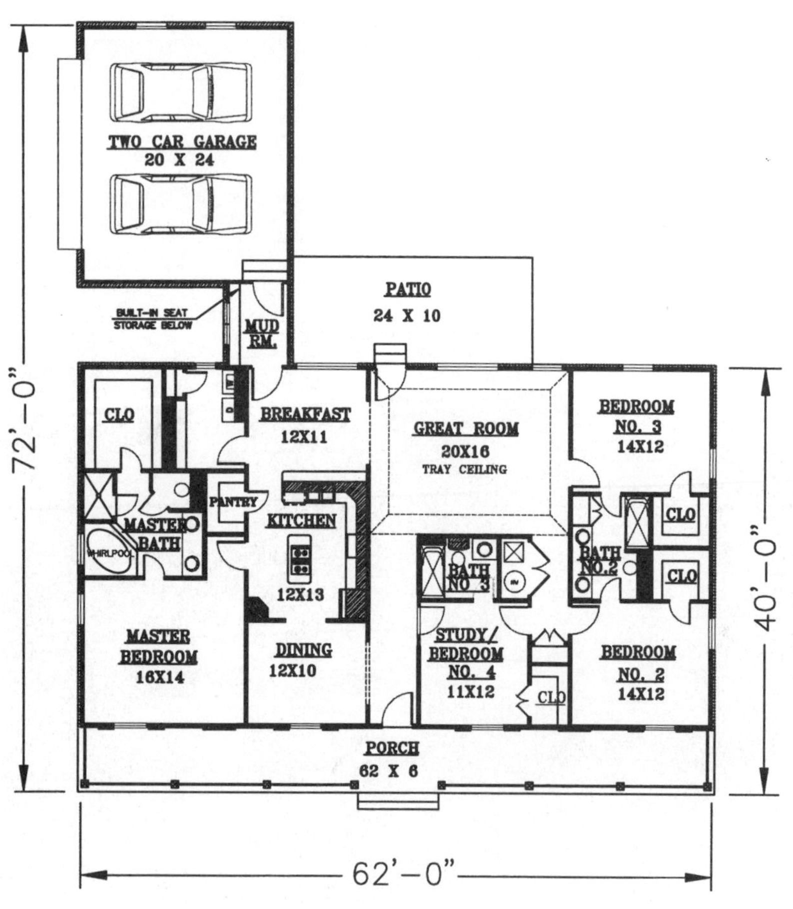
TWO CAR GARAGE
20 X 24
PATIO
24 X 10
BUILT-IN SEAT
STORAGE BELOW
MUD RM.
CLO
BREAKFAST
12X11
GREAT ROOM
20X16
TRAY CEILING
BEDROOM NO. 3
14X12
PANTRY
KITCHEN
12X13
MASTER BATH
WHIRLPOOL
BATH NO 3
BATH NO.2
CLO
CLO
MASTER BEDROOM
16X14
DINING
12X10
STUDY/ BEDROOM NO. 4
11X12
CLO
BEDROOM NO. 2
14X12
PORCH
62 X 6
72'-0"
40'-0"
62'-0"

Plan #530-028D-0008

Price Code C

Total Living Area: 2,156 Sq. Ft.

Home has 4 bedrooms, 3 baths, 2-car side entry garage and basement, crawl space or slab foundation, please specify when ordering.

Special features

- Secluded master bedroom has spa-style bath with corner whirlpool tub, large shower, double sinks and a walk-in closet
- Kitchen overlooks rear patio
- Plenty of windows add an open, airy feel to the great room

 TO ORDER BLUEPRINTS USE THE FORM ON PAGE 288 OR CALL TOLL-FREE **1-800-DREAM HOME** (373-2646)

LOWE'S

50'-0"
MASTER SUITE
16'-10" X 11'-6"
9' PAN CEILING
GREAT RM.
20'-0" X 15'-6"
9' BOXED CEILING
BEDROOM 3
11'-10" X 11'-0"
LIN
LIN
M.BATH
10'-6" X 16'-0"
SKL
K.S
KITCHEN
10'-0" X 10'-0"
DW
RG
REF
DINING
10'-6" X 11'-10"
FOYER
BATH
LIN
HVAC
PAN
LAU.
D
W
WH
STORAGE
COVERED PORCH
BEDROOM 2
11'-10" X 11'-0"
VAULTED CEILING
GARAGE
21'-0" X 21'-0"
53'-8"

Plan #530-055D-0026

Price Code B

Total Living Area: 1,538 Sq. Ft.

Home has 3 bedrooms, 2 baths, 2-car garage and walk-out basement, basement, crawl space or slab foundation, please specify when ordering.

Special features

- Dining and great rooms highlighted in this design
- Master suite has many amenities
- Kitchen and laundry room are accessible from any room in the house

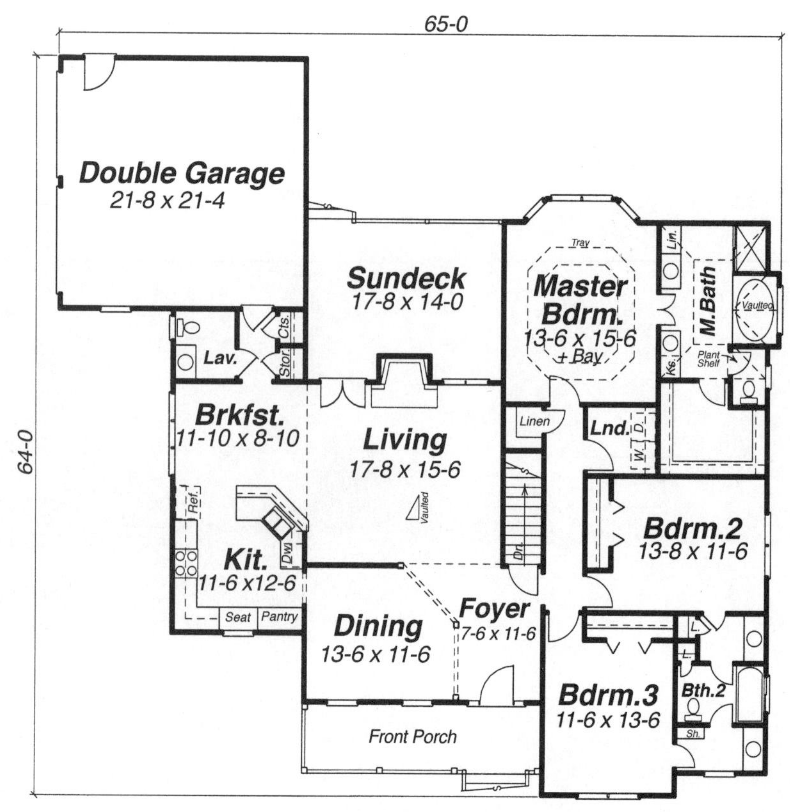
65-0
64-0
Double Garage
21-8 x 21-4
Sundeck
17-8 x 14-0
Tray
Master
Bdrm.
13-6 x 15-6
+ Bay
Lin.
M.Bath
Vaulted
Plant Shelf
Ks.
Cls.
Lav.
Stor.
Brkfst.
11-10 x 8-10
Living
17-8 x 15-6
Vaulted
Linen
Lnd.
W
D
Ref.
Bdrm.2
13-8 x 11-6
Kit.
11-6 x12-6
Dw
Dn
Seat
Pantry
Foyer
7-6 x 11-6
Dining
13-6 x 11-6
Bdrm.3
11-6 x 13-6
Bth.2
Sh
Front Porch

Plan #530-052D-0058

Price Code C

Total Living Area: 2,012 Sq. Ft.

Home has 3 bedrooms, 2 1/2 baths, 2-car side entry garage and walk-out basement foundation.

Special features

- Kitchen with eat-in breakfast bar overlooks breakfast room
- Sunny living room is open and airy with vaulted ceiling
- Secondary bedrooms with convenient vanities skillfully share bath

LOWE'S

Plan #530-008D-0084

Price Code B

Total Living Area: 1,704 Sq. Ft.

Home has 3 bedrooms, 2 baths, 2-car garage and basement foundation.

Special features

- Open living and dining areas combine for added spaciousness
- Master bedroom features a private bath and walk-in closet
- Sunny kitchen/nook has space for dining
- Cabinet bar in hallway leading to the living area is designed for entertaining

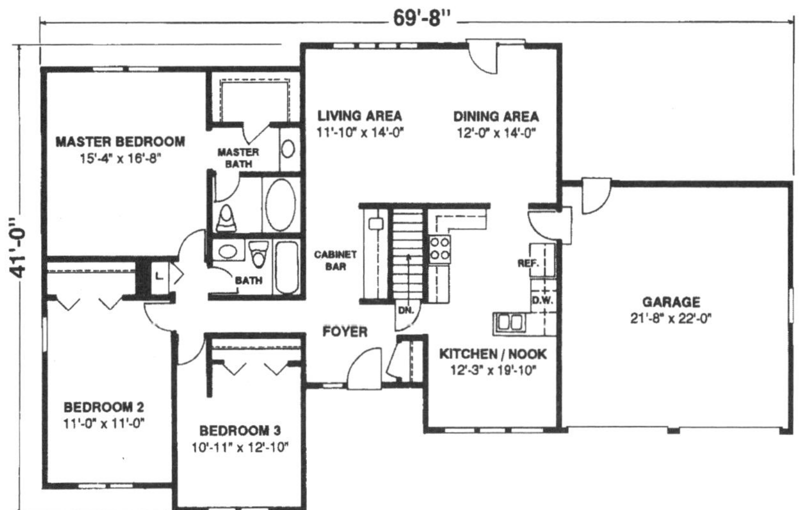
69'-8"
41'-0"
MASTER BEDROOM
15'-4" x 16'-8"
MASTER BATH
LIVING AREA
11'-10" x 14'-0"
DINING AREA
12'-0" x 14'-0"
CABINET BAR
BATH
L
DN.
REF.
D.W.
GARAGE
21'-8" x 22'-0"
FOYER
KITCHEN / NOOK
12'-3" x 19'-10"
BEDROOM 2
11'-0" x 11'-0"
BEDROOM 3
10'-11" x 12'-10"

LOWE'S

Plan #530-024D-0009

Price Code B

Total Living Area: 1,704 Sq. Ft.

Home has 3 bedrooms, 2 baths and slab foundation.

Special features

- Open floor plan combines foyer, dining and living rooms together for an open airy feeling
- Kitchen has island that adds work-space and storage
- Bedrooms are situated together and secluded from the rest of the home

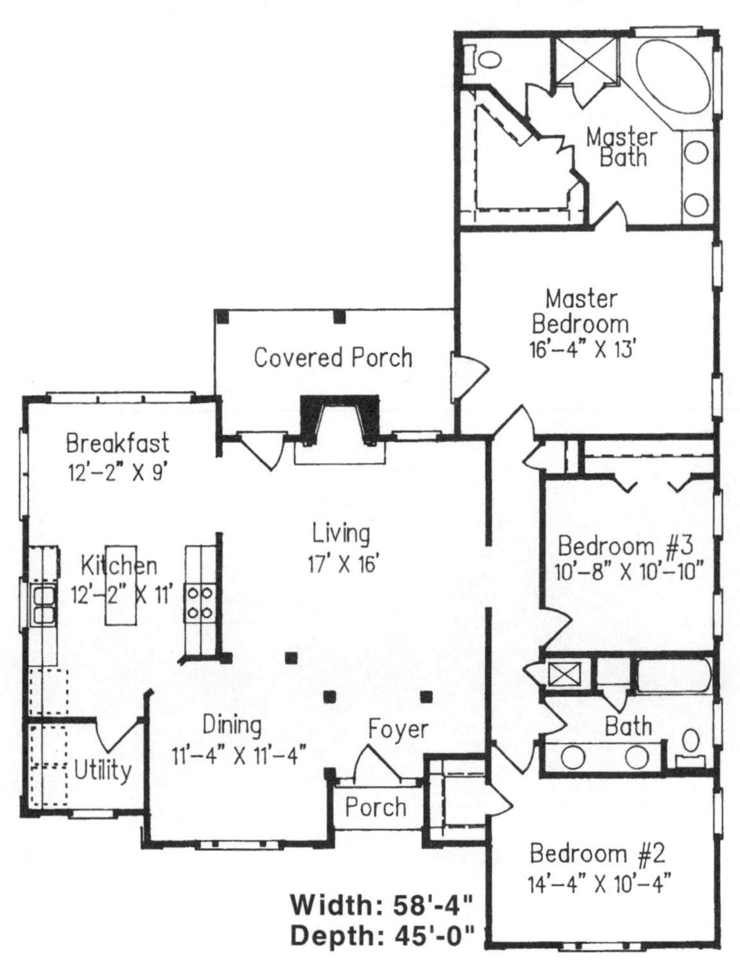
Master Bath
Master Bedroom
16'-4" X 13'
Covered Porch
Breakfast
12'-2" X 9'
Living
17' X 16'
Bedroom #3
10'-8" X 10'-10"
Kitchen
12'-2" X 11'
Dining
11'-4" X 11'-4"
Foyer
Bath
Utility
Porch
Bedroom #2
14'-4" X 10'-4"
Width: 58'-4"
Depth: 45'-0"

 TO ORDER BLUEPRINTS USE THE FORM ON PAGE 288 OR CALL TOLL-FREE **1-800-DREAM HOME** (373-2646)

LOWE'S

Plan #530-008D-0102

Price Code AA

Total Living Area: 1,102 Sq. Ft.

Home has 2 bedrooms, 1 bath, 2-car garage and basement foundation, drawings also include crawl space foundation.

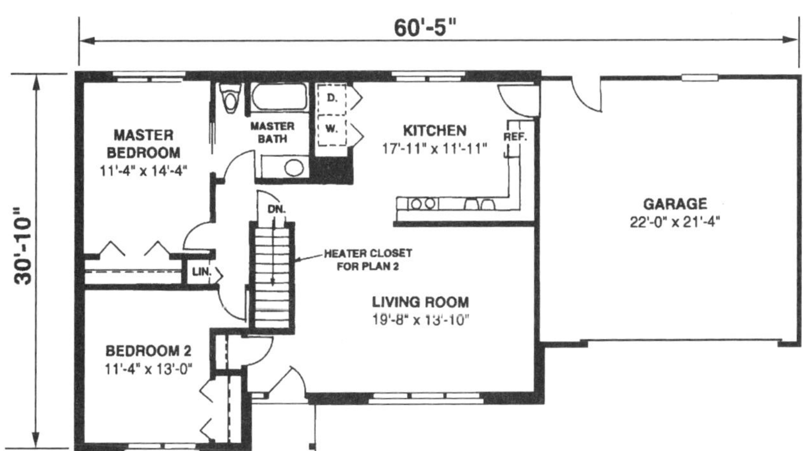
60'-5"
30'-10"
MASTER BEDROOM
11'-4" x 14'-4"
MASTER BATH
D.
W.
KITCHEN
17'-11" x 11'-11"
REF.
GARAGE
22'-0" x 21'-4"
DN.
HEATER CLOSET FOR PLAN 2
LIN.
LIVING ROOM
19'-8" x 13'-10"
BEDROOM 2
11'-4" x 13'-0"

Special features

- Compact design with a dressy exterior
- Spacious living room with separate entry and coat closet
- Eat-in kitchen with first floor laundry
- Master bedroom and second bedroom share a roomy full bath

Plan #530-056D-0024

Price Code AA

Total Living Area: 1,093 Sq. Ft.

Home has 2 bedrooms, 2 baths, 2-car garage and slab foundation.

Special features

- Family room with fireplace overlooks large covered porch
- Vaulted family and dining rooms are adjacent to kitchen
- Bedroom #2 has its own entrance into bath
- Plant shelf accents vaulted foyer
- Centrally located laundry area

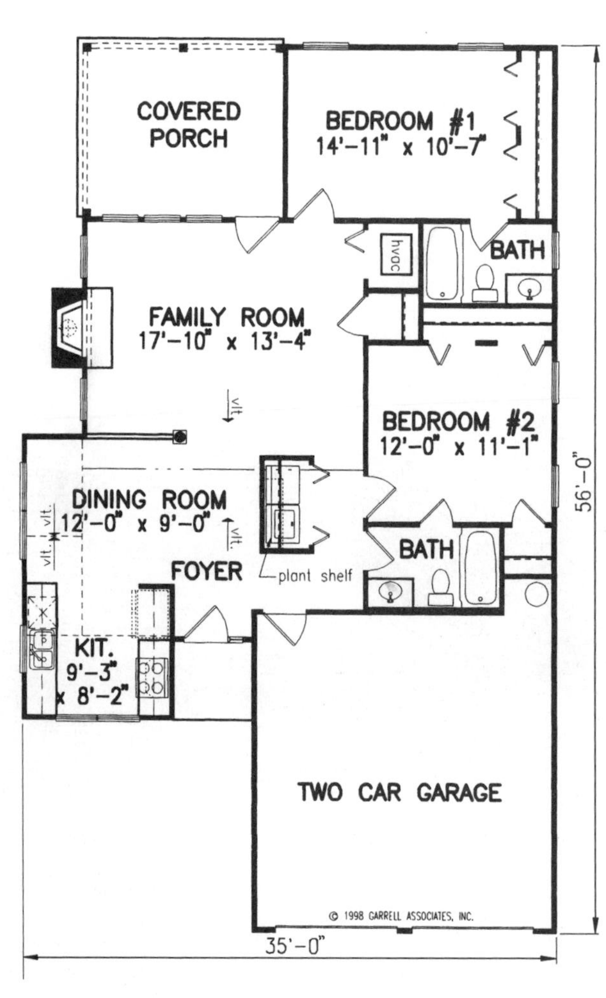

COVERED PORCH
BEDROOM #1
14'–11" x 10'–7"
BATH
hvac
FAMILY ROOM
17'–10" x 13'–4"
vlt.
BEDROOM #2
12'–0" x 11'–1"
DINING ROOM
12'–0" x 9'–0"
vlt.
vlt.
vlt.
vlt.
FOYER
plant shelf
BATH
KIT.
9'–3"
x 8'–2"
TWO CAR GARAGE
© 1998 GARRELL ASSOCIATES, INC.
56'–0"
35'–0"

LOWE'S

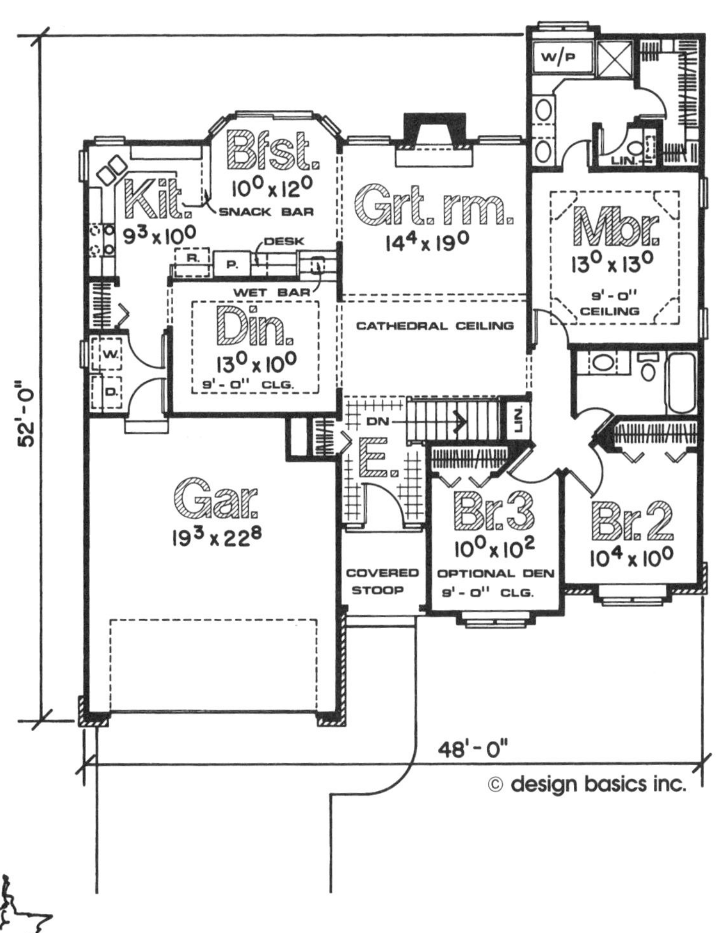
W/P
LIN.
Bfst.
10^{0} x 12^{0}
SNACK BAR
Kit.
9^{3} x 10^{0}
Grt. rm.
14^{4} x 19^{0}
Mbr.
13^{0} x 13^{0}
9'-0" CEILING
R.
P.
DESK
WET BAR
Din.
13^{0} x 10^{0}
9'-0" CLG.
CATHEDRAL CEILING
W.
D.
DN
LIN.
E.
Gar.
19^{3} x 22^{8}
Br. 3
10^{0} x 10^{2}
OPTIONAL DEN
9'-0" CLG.
Br. 2
10^{4} x 10^{0}
COVERED STOOP
52'-0"
48'-0"
© design basics inc.

Plan #530-026D-0072

Price Code A

Total Living Area: 1,496 Sq. Ft.

Home has 3 bedrooms, 2 baths, 2-car garage and basement foundation.

Special features

- Wet bar is open to dining and breakfast rooms for entertaining
- Expansive great room with cathedral ceiling has plenty of room
- Great room has fireplace flanked by bright windows

Plan #530-055D-0017

Price Code B

Total Living Area: 1,525 Sq. Ft.

Home has 3 bedrooms, 2 baths, 2-car garage and basement, walk-out basement, crawl space or slab foundation, please specify when ordering.

Special features

- Corner fireplace is highlighted in the great room
- Unique glass block window over the whirlpool tub in the master bath brightens the interior
- Open bar overlooks both the kitchen and great room
- Breakfast room leads to an outdoor grilling and covered porch

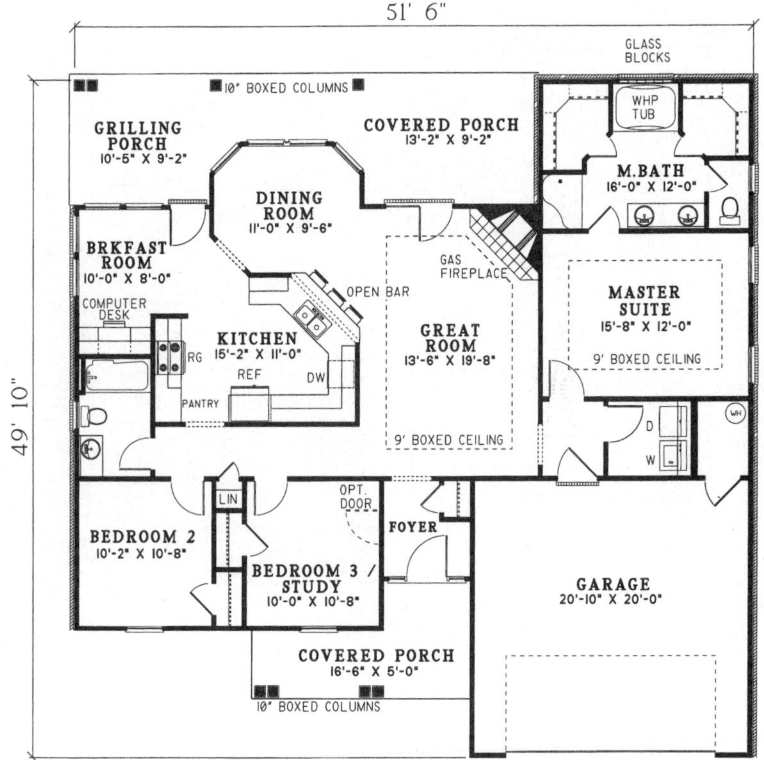
51' 6"
GLASS BLOCKS
10" BOXED COLUMNS
GRILLING PORCH 10'-5" X 9'-2"
COVERED PORCH 13'-2" X 9'-2"
WHP TUB
M.BATH 16'-0" X 12'-0"
DINING ROOM 11'-0" X 9'-6"
BRKFAST ROOM 10'-0" X 8'-0"
GAS FIREPLACE
OPEN BAR
COMPUTER DESK
KITCHEN 15'-2" X 11'-0"
RG
REF
DW
PANTRY
GREAT ROOM 13'-6" X 19'-8"
9' BOXED CEILING
MASTER SUITE 15'-8" X 12'-0"
9' BOXED CEILING
49' 10"
WH
D
W
LIN
OPT. DOOR
FOYER
BEDROOM 2 10'-2" X 10'-8"
BEDROOM 3 / STUDY 10'-0" X 10'-8"
GARAGE 20'-10" X 20'-0"
COVERED PORCH 16'-6" X 5'-0"
10" BOXED COLUMNS

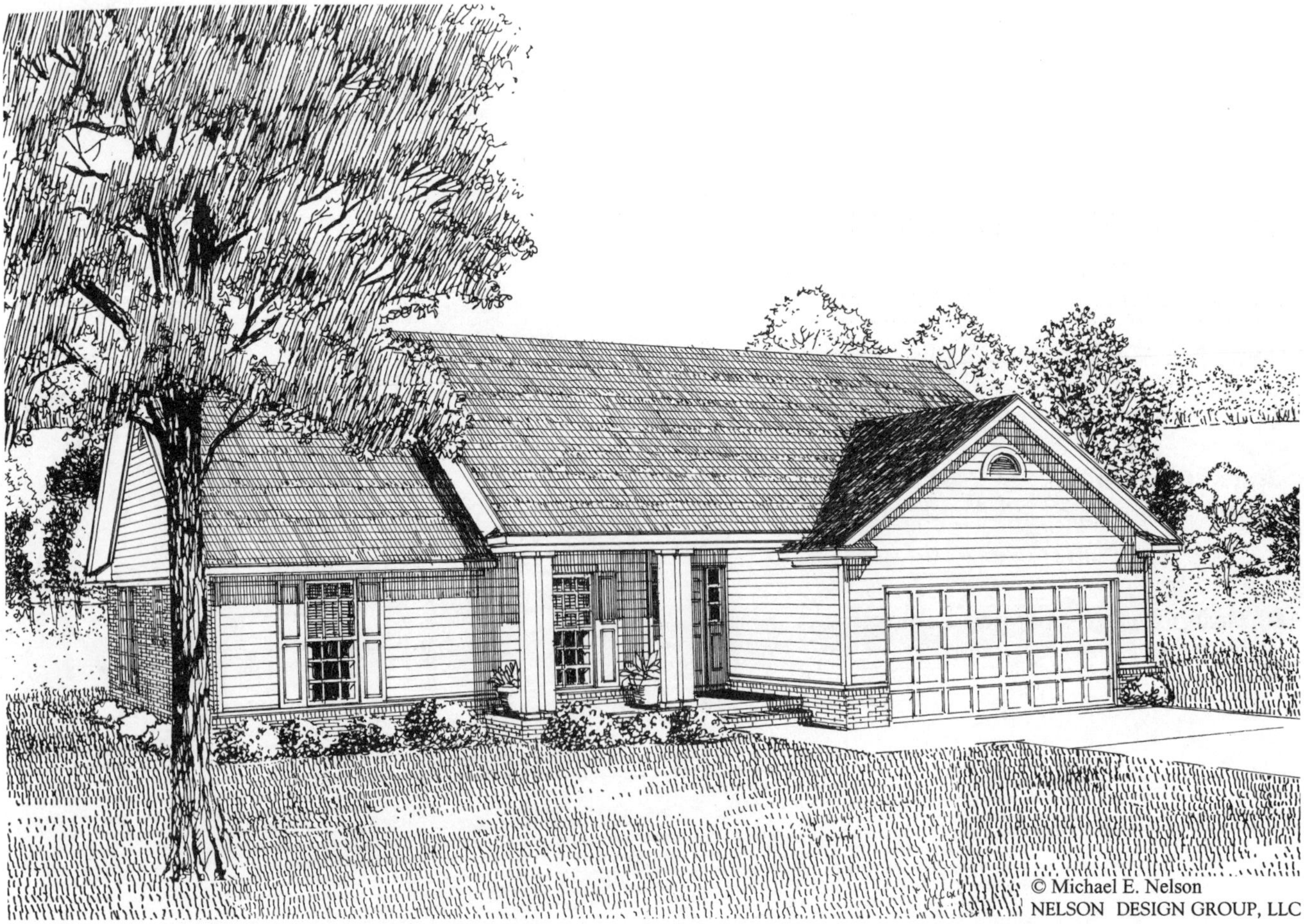

Stylish Ranch

LOWE'S

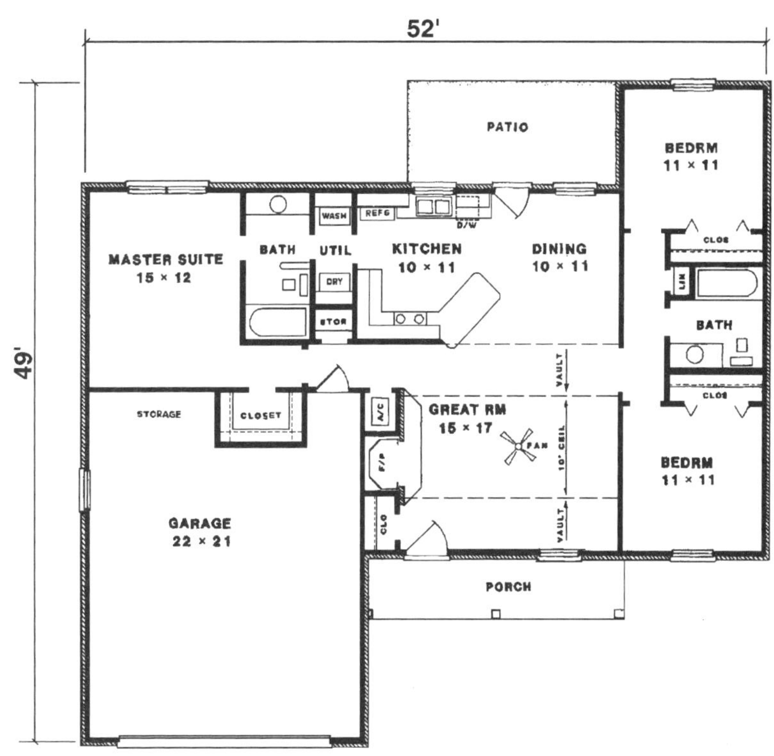
52'
49'
PATIO
BEDRM
11 × 11
MASTER SUITE
15 × 12
BATH
UTIL
WASH
REF'G
D/W
DRY
STOR
KITCHEN
10 × 11
DINING
10 × 11
CLOS
LIN
BATH
CLOS
STORAGE
CLOSET
A/C
GREAT RM
15 × 17
FAN
VAULT
10' CEIL
VAULT
F/P
CLO
BEDRM
11 × 11
GARAGE
22 × 21
PORCH

Plan #530-069D-0005

Price Code A

Total Living Area: 1,267 Sq. Ft.

Home has 3 bedrooms, 2 baths, 2-car garage and slab or crawl space foundation, please specify when ordering.

Special features

- 10' vaulted ceiling in the great room
- Open floor plan creates a spacious feeling
- Master suite is separated from the other bedrooms for privacy

Striking Plant Shelf

Plan #530-011D-0005

Price Code C

Total Living Area: 1,467 Sq. Ft.

Home has 3 bedrooms, 2 baths, 2-car garage and crawl space foundation.

Special features

- Vaulted ceilings, an open floor plan and a wealth of windows create an inviting atmosphere
- Efficiently arranged kitchen has an island with built-in cooktop and a snack counter
- Plentiful storage and closet space throughout this home

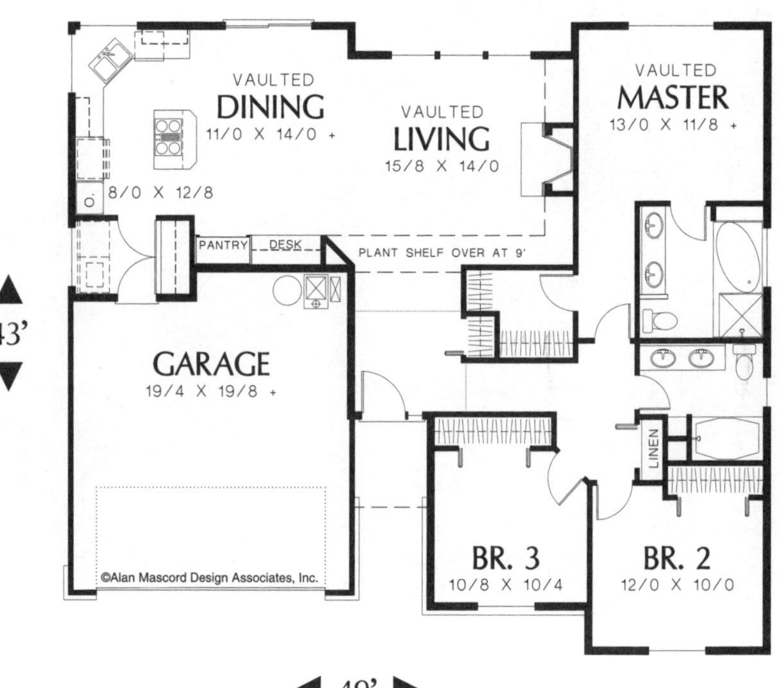
VAULTED
DINING
11/0 X 14/0 +
VAULTED
LIVING
15/8 X 14/0
VAULTED
MASTER
13/0 X 11/8 +
8/0 X 12/8
PANTRY
DESK
PLANT SHELF OVER AT 9'
GARAGE
19/4 X 19/8 +
LINEN
BR. 3
10/8 X 10/4
BR. 2
12/0 X 10/0
©Alan Mascord Design Associates, Inc.

43'

49'

LOWE'S

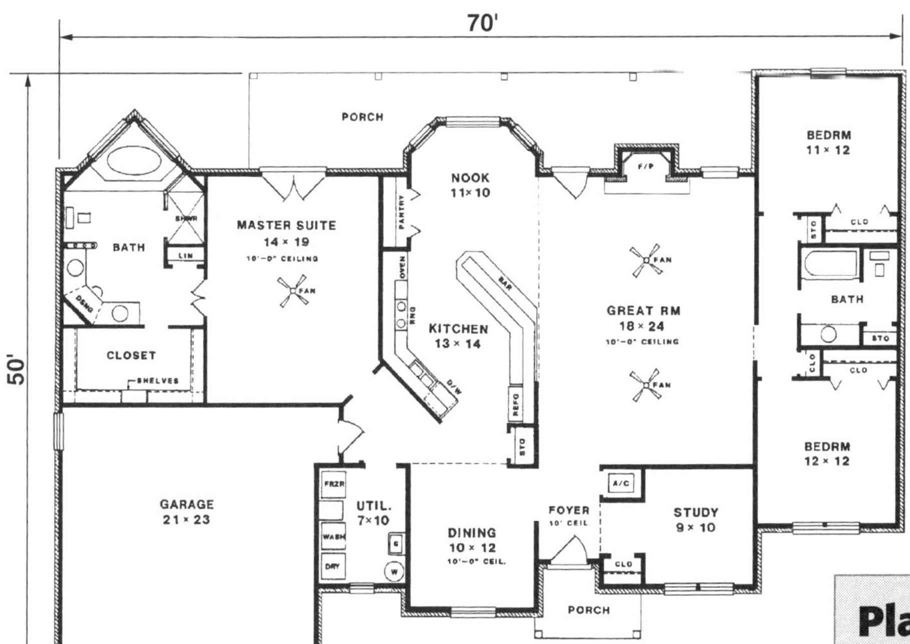
70'
50'
PORCH
NOOK
11×10
F/P
BEDRM
11 × 12
PANTRY
MASTER SUITE
14 × 19
10'-0" CEILING
BATH
SHWR
LIN
FAN
OVEN
RNG
BAR
KITCHEN
13 × 14
GREAT RM
18 × 24
10'-0" CEILING
CLO
STO
BATH
CLOSET
SHELVES
D/W
REFG
STO
BEDRM
12 × 12
GARAGE
21 × 23
FRZR
UTIL.
7×10
WASH
DRY
A/C
DINING
10 × 12
10'-0" CEIL.
FOYER
10' CEIL
STUDY
9 × 10
CLO
PORCH

Plan #530-069D-0019

Price Code C

Total Living Area: 2,162 Sq. Ft.

Home has 3 bedrooms, 2 baths, 2-car garage and crawl space or slab foundation, please specify when ordering.

Special features

- 10' ceilings in great room, dining room, master suite and foyer
- Enormous great room overlooks kitchen with oversized snack bar
- Luxurious master bath boasts a triangular whirlpool tub drenched in light from large windows

Unique Fireplace In Great Room

Plan #530-026D-0089

Price Code B

Total Living Area: 1,580 Sq. Ft.

Home has 3 bedrooms, 2 baths, 2-car garage and basement foundation.

Special features

- Snack bar skillfully separates efficient kitchen and breakfast room
- Spacious great room with high ceiling and fireplace creates an inviting atmosphere
- Garage includes storage shelves for organization

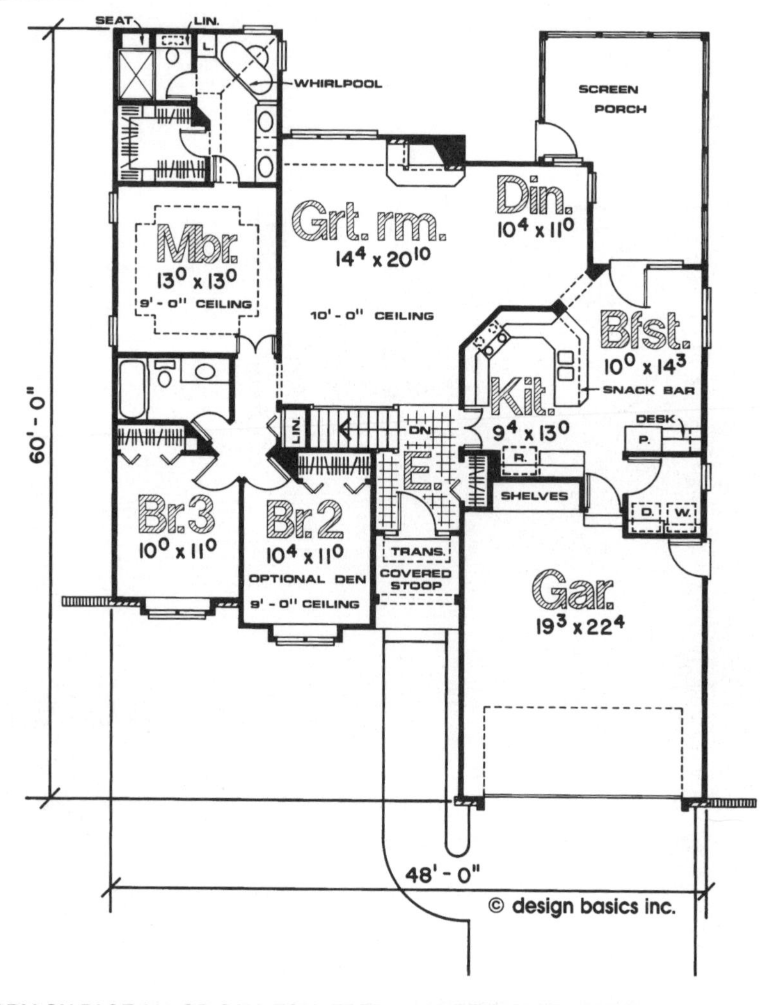
SEAT
LIN.
WHIRLPOOL
SCREEN PORCH
Grt. rm.
14^4 x 20^{10}
10'-0" CEILING
Din.
10^4 x 11^0
Mbr.
13^0 x 13^0
9'-0" CEILING
Bfst.
10^0 x 14^3
SNACK BAR
Kit.
9^4 x 13^0
DESK
P.
R.
LIN.
DN
E.
SHELVES
D.
W.
Br.3
10^0 x 11^0
Br.2
10^4 x 11^0
OPTIONAL DEN
9'-0" CEILING
TRANS.
COVERED STOOP
Gar.
19^3 x 22^4
60'-0"
48'-0"
© design basics inc.

LOWE'S

Plan #530-030D-0004

Price Code B

Total Living Area: 1,791 Sq. Ft.

Home has 3 bedrooms, 2 baths, 2-car garage and slab or crawl space foundation, please specify when ordering.

Special features

- Dining area has a 10' high sloped ceiling
- Kitchen opens to the large living room with fireplace and has access to a covered porch
- Master suite features a private bath, double walk-in closets and whirlpool tub

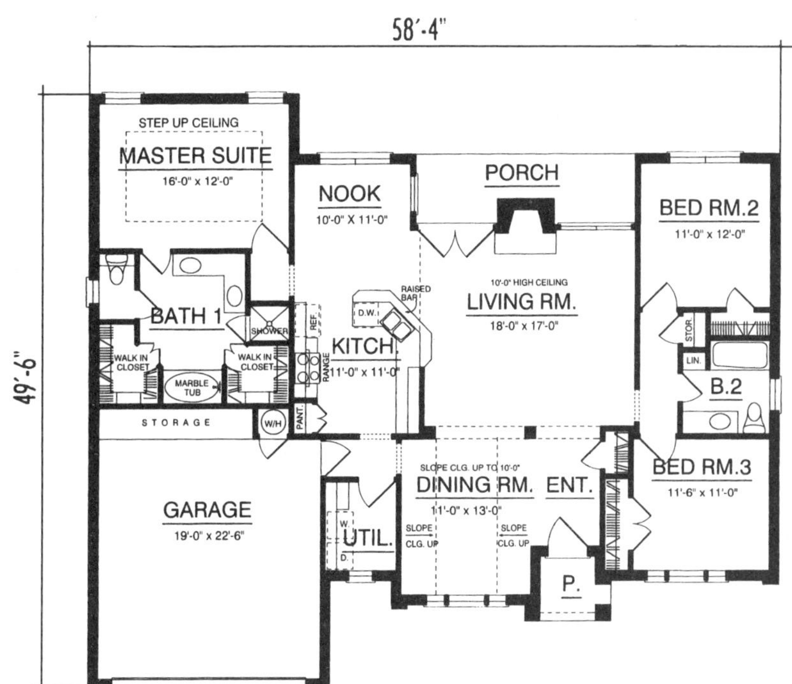
58'-4"
49'-6"
STEP UP CEILING
MASTER SUITE
16'-0" x 12'-0"
NOOK
10'-0" X 11'-0"
PORCH
BED RM.2
11'-0" x 12'-0"
RAISED BAR
D.W.
10'-0" HIGH CEILING
LIVING RM.
18'-0" x 17'-0"
BATH 1
SHOWER
REF.
KITCH.
11'-0" x 11'-0"
RANGE
WALK IN CLOSET
WALK IN CLOSET
MARBLE TUB
STOR
LIN.
B.2
STORAGE
W/H
PANT.
SLOPE CLG. UP TO 10'-0"
DINING RM.
11'-0" x 13'-0"
ENT.
BED RM.3
11'-6" x 11'-0"
GARAGE
19'-0" x 22'-6"
UTIL.
W
D
SLOPE CLG. UP
SLOPE CLG. UP
P.

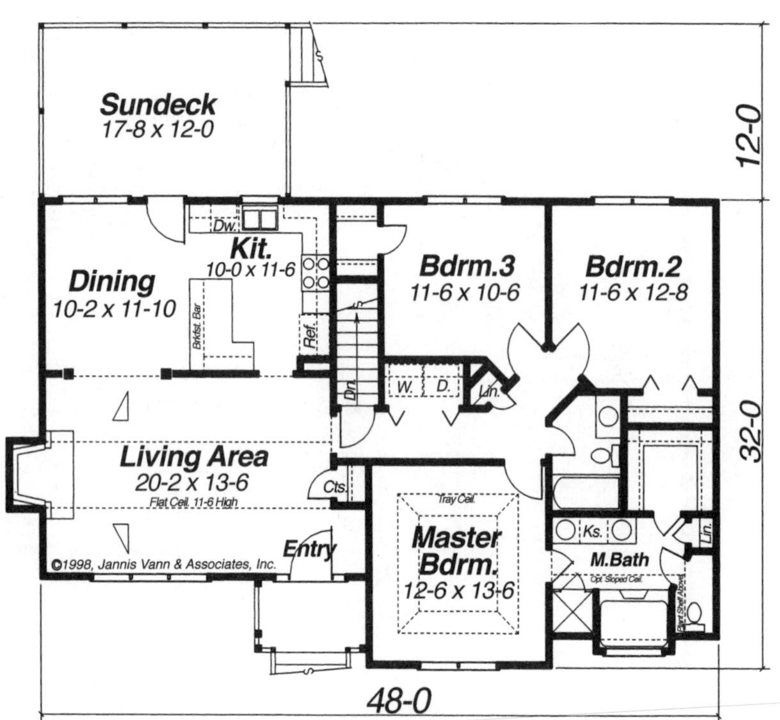
Sundeck
17-8 x 12-0
12-0
Dw.
Kit.
10-0 x 11-6
Dining
10-2 x 11-10
Brkfst. Bar
Ref.
Bdrm.3
11-6 x 10-6
Bdrm.2
11-6 x 12-8
W.
D.
Lin.
Dn.
Living Area
20-2 x 13-6
Flat Ceil. 11-6 High
Cts.
32-0
Tray Ceil.
Master
Bdrm.
12-6 x 13-6
Ks.
Lin.
M.Bath
Entry
©1998, Jannis Vann & Associates, Inc.
48-0

Plan #530-052D-0013

Price Code A

Total Living Area: 1,379 Sq. Ft.

Home has 3 bedrooms, 2 baths, 2-car drive under garage and basement foundation.

Special features

- Living area has a spacious feel with 11'-6" ceiling
- Kitchen has an eat-in breakfast bar open to the dining area
- Laundry area is located near the bedrooms
- Large cased opening with columns opens to the living and dining areas

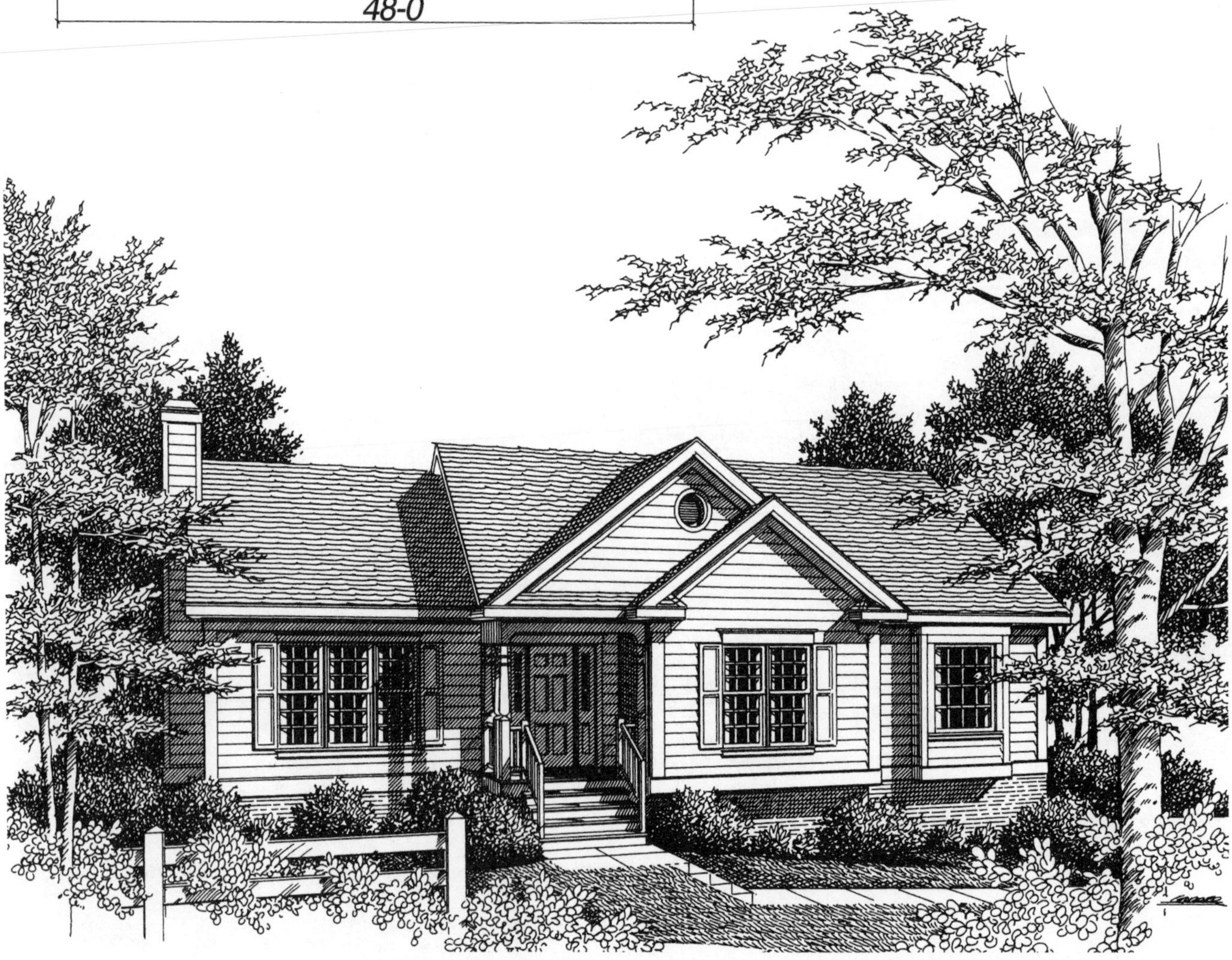

LOWE'S

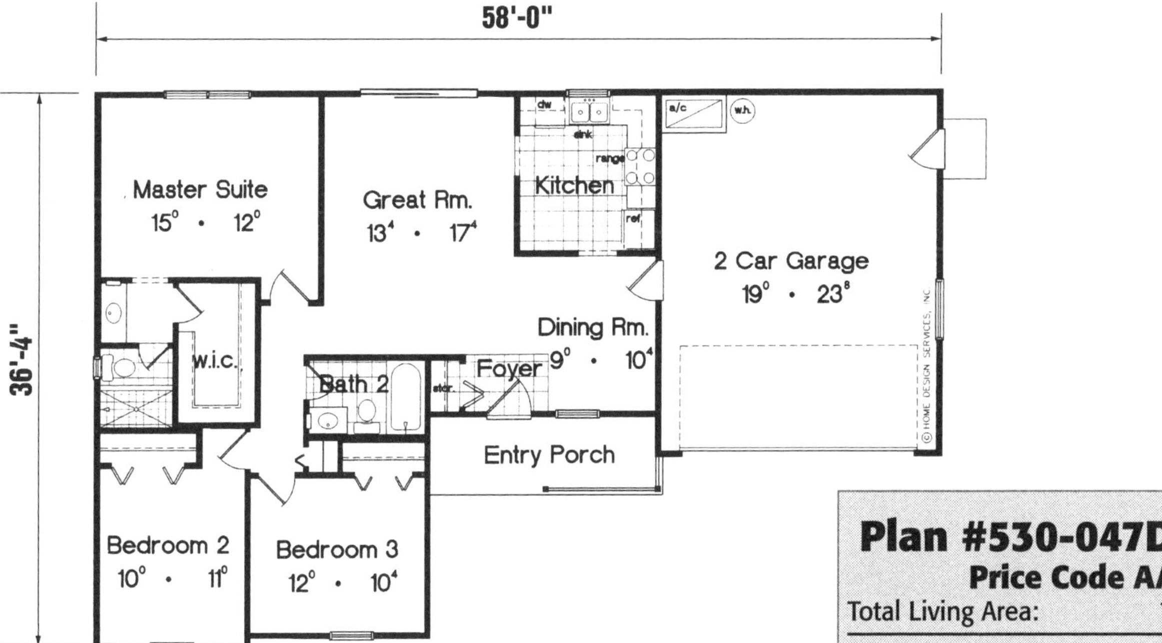
58'-0"
36'-4"
Master Suite
15^{0} · 12^{0}
Great Rm.
13^{4} · 17^{4}
Kitchen
dw
sink
range
ref
a/c
w.h.
2 Car Garage
19^{0} · 23^{8}
Dining Rm.
9^{0} · 10^{4}
w.i.c.
Bath 2
stor.
Foyer
Entry Porch
Bedroom 2
10^{0} · 11^{0}
Bedroom 3
12^{0} · 10^{4}
© HOME DESIGN SERVICES, INC

Plan #530-047D-0002

Price Code AA

Total Living Area: 1,167 Sq. Ft.

Home has 3 bedrooms, 2 baths, 2-car garage and slab foundation.

Special features

- Master suite includes a private bath
- Handy coat closet in foyer
- Lots of storage space throughout

Plan #530-031D-0009

Price Code C

Total Living Area: 1,960 Sq. Ft.

Home has 3 bedrooms, 2 baths, 2-car garage and slab foundation.

Special features

- Open floor plan is suitable for an active family
- Desk space in bedroom #3 is ideal for a young student
- Effective design creates an enclosed courtyard in the rear of the home

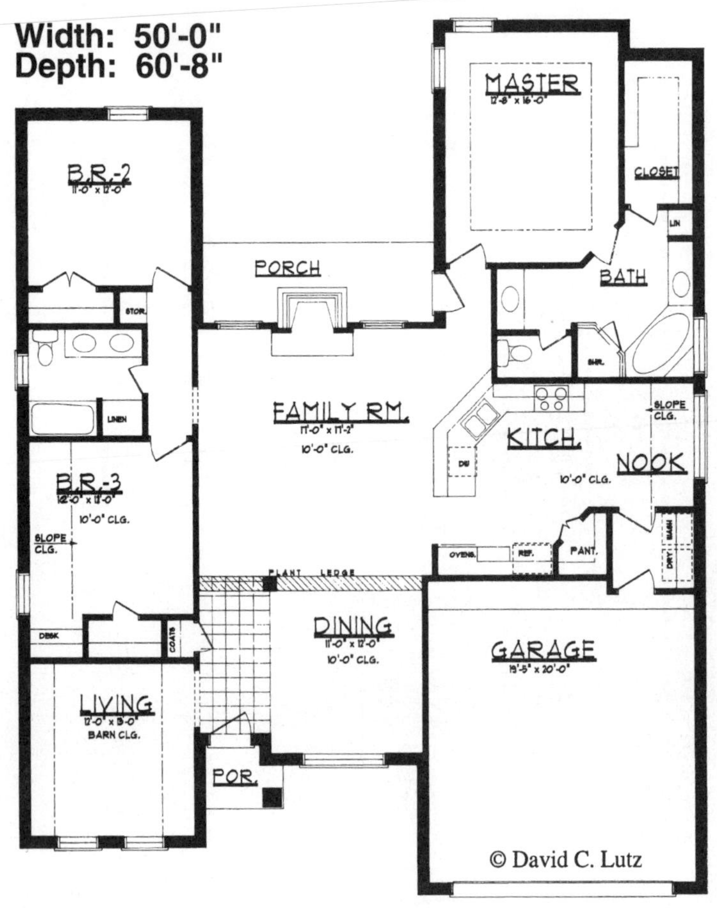
Width: 50'-0"
Depth: 60'-8"
MASTER
CLOSET
B.R.-2
PORCH
BATH
FAMILY RM.
10'-0" CLG.
KITCH.
NOOK
B.R.-3
SLOPE CLG.
DINING
GARAGE
LIVING
BARN CLG.
POR.
© David C. Lutz

LOWE'S

Plan #530-008D-0026

Price Code AA

Total Living Area: 1,120 Sq. Ft.

Home has 3 bedrooms, 2 baths, 1-car carport and basement foundation, drawings also include crawl space and slab foundations.

Special features

- Kitchen/family room creates a useful spacious area
- Rustic, colonial design is perfect for many surroundings
- Oversized living room is ideal for entertaining
- Carport includes a functional storage area

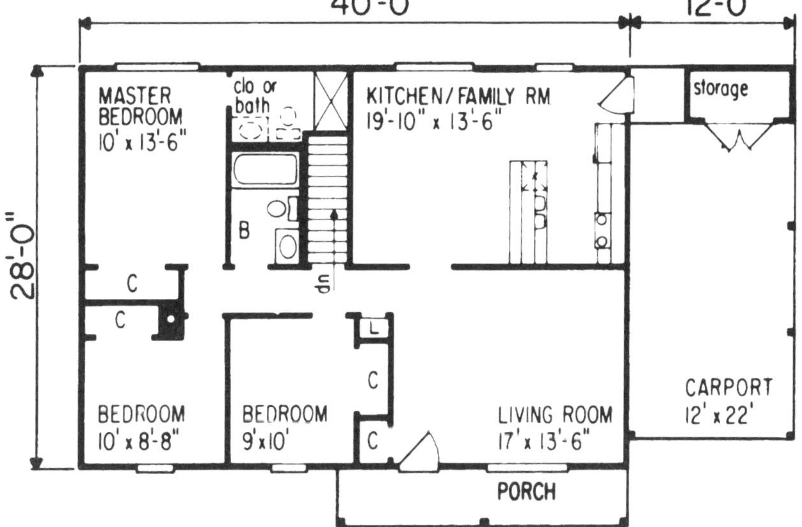
40'-0"
12'-0"
28'-0"
MASTER BEDROOM 10' x 13'-6"
clo or bath
KITCHEN/FAMILY RM 19'-10" x 13'-6"
storage
B
up
C
C
L
C
C
BEDROOM 10' x 8'-8"
BEDROOM 9'x10'
LIVING ROOM 17' x 13'-6"
CARPORT 12' x 22'
PORCH

Plan #530-026D-0142

Price Code C

Total Living Area: 2,188 Sq. Ft.

Home has 3 bedrooms, 2 baths, 3-car side entry garage and basement foundation.

Special features

- Master bedroom includes a private covered porch, sitting area and two large walk-in closets
- Spacious kitchen has center island, snack bar and laundry access
- Great room has a 10' ceiling and a dramatic corner fireplace

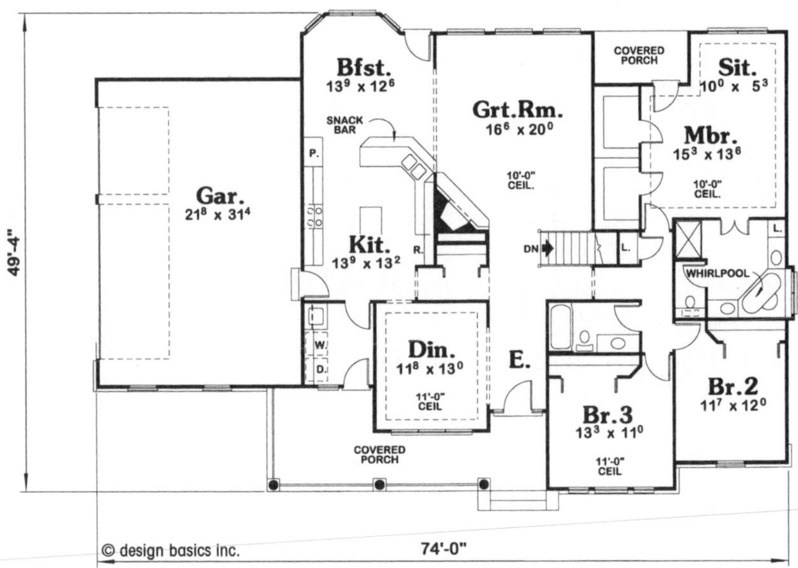
Bfst.
13^{9} x 12^{6}
SNACK BAR
Grt.Rm.
16^{6} x 20^{0}
10'-0" CEIL.
COVERED PORCH
Sit.
10^{0} x 5^{3}
Mbr.
15^{3} x 13^{6}
10'-0" CEIL.
Gar.
21^{8} x 31^{4}
P.
Kit.
13^{9} x 13^{2}
R.
DN
L.
WHIRLPOOL
W.
D.
Din.
11^{8} x 13^{0}
11'-0" CEIL
E.
Br.3
13^{3} x 11^{0}
11'-0" CEIL
Br.2
11^{7} x 12^{0}
COVERED PORCH
49'-4"
© design basics inc.
74'-0"

 TO ORDER BLUEPRINTS USE THE FORM ON PAGE 288 OR CALL TOLL-FREE **1-800-DREAM HOME** (373-2646)

LOWE'S

Plan #530-047D-0036

Price Code C

Total Living Area: 2,140 Sq. Ft.

Home has 4 bedrooms, 3 baths, 2-car side entry garage and slab foundation.

Special features

- Living and dining areas are traditionally separated by foyer
- Media wall and fireplace are located in cozy family room
- Generous master bedroom has sliding glass doors onto the patio, a walk-in closet and a private bath

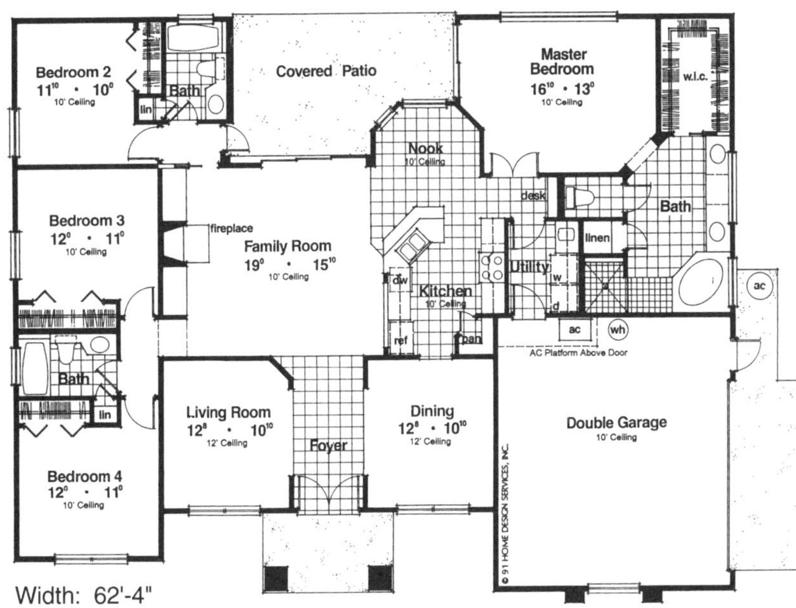
Bedroom 2
11^{10} · 10^{0}
10' Ceiling
Bath
lin
Covered Patio
Master Bedroom
16^{10} · 13^{0}
10' Ceiling
w.i.c.
Nook
10' Ceiling
desk
Bath
Bedroom 3
12^{0} · 11^{0}
10' Ceiling
fireplace
Family Room
19^{0} · 15^{10}
10' Ceiling
linen
Utility
w
d
dw
Kitchen
10' Ceiling
ref
pan
ac
wh
ac
AC Platform Above Door
Bath
lin
Living Room
12^{8} · 10^{10}
12' Ceiling
Foyer
Dining
12^{8} · 10^{10}
12' Ceiling
Double Garage
10' Ceiling
Bedroom 4
12^{0} · 11^{0}
10' Ceiling
© 91 HOME DESIGN SERVICES, INC.

Width: 62'-4"
Depth: 51'-0"

Cottage Style Adds Charm

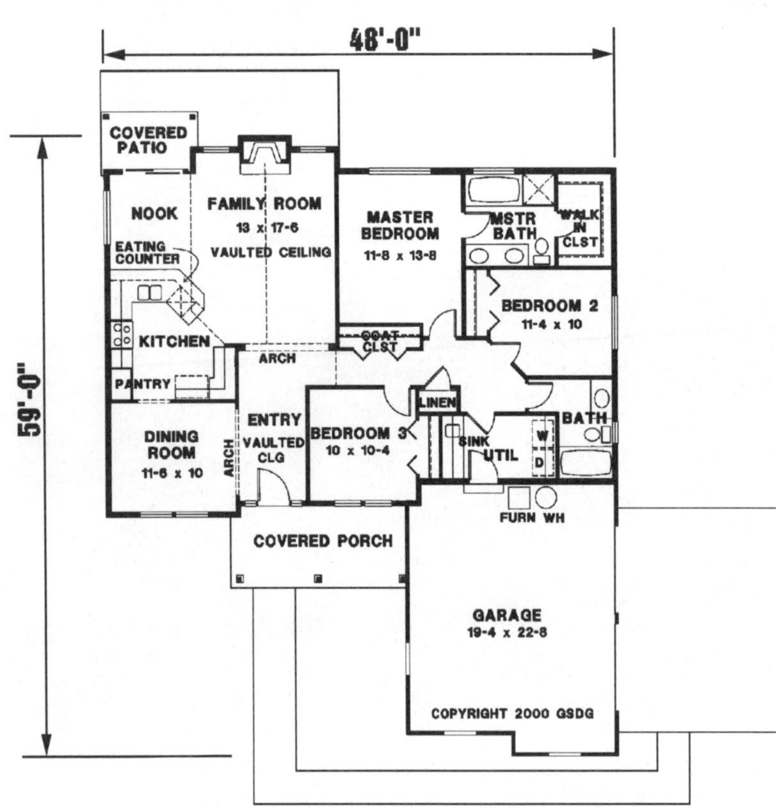

48'-0"
59'-0"
COVERED PATIO
NOOK
EATING COUNTER
FAMILY ROOM
13 x 17-6
VAULTED CEILING
MASTER BEDROOM
11-8 x 13-8
MSTR BATH
WALK IN CLST
BEDROOM 2
11-4 x 10
KITCHEN
COAT CLST
ARCH
PANTRY
LINEN
DINING ROOM
11-6 x 10
ARCH
ENTRY
VAULTED CLG
BEDROOM 3
10 x 10-4
SINK
UTIL
W
D
BATH
FURN
WH
COVERED PORCH
GARAGE
19-4 x 22-8
COPYRIGHT 2000 GSDG

Plan #530-043D-0008

Price Code A

Total Living Area: 1,496 Sq. Ft.

Home has 3 bedrooms, 2 baths, 2-car side entry garage and crawl space foundation.

Special features

- Large utility room with sink and extra counterspace
- Covered patio off breakfast nook extends dining to the outdoors
- Eating counter in kitchen overlooks vaulted family room

TO ORDER BLUEPRINTS USE THE FORM ON PAGE 288 OR CALL TOLL-FREE **1-800-DREAM HOME** (373-2646)

Narrow Lot Charmer

LOWE'S

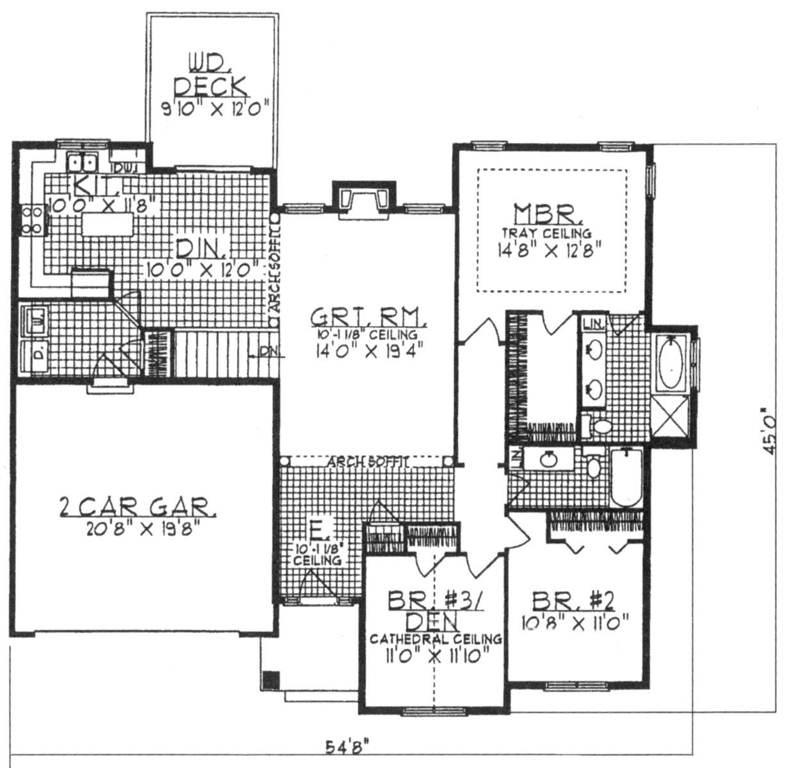
WD. DECK
9'10" X 12'0"
KIT.
10'0" X 11'8"
DIN.
10'0" X 12'0"
ARCH SOFFIT
GRT. RM.
10'-1 1/8" CEILING
14'0" X 19'4"
MBR.
TRAY CEILING
14'8" X 12'8"
LIN.
DN.
ARCH SOFFIT
2 CAR GAR.
20'8" X 19'8"
E.
10'-1 1/8" CEILING
BR. #3/ DEN
CATHEDRAL CEILING
11'0" X 11'10"
BR. #2
10'8" X 11'0"
45'0"
54'8"

Plan #530-051D-0052

Price Code B

Total Living Area: 1,600 Sq. Ft.

Home has 3 bedrooms, 2 baths, 2-car garage and basement foundation.

Special features

- Optional den with cathedral ceiling
- Kitchen has a large island for additional counterspace
- Master bedroom has a large walk-in closet and a full bath with double vanity

Our Blueprint Packages Offer...

Quality plans for building your future, with extras that provide unsurpassed value, ensure good construction and long-term enjoyment.

A quality home - one that looks good, functions well, and provides years of enjoyment - is a product of many things - design, materials, craftsmanship. But it's also the result of outstanding blueprints - the actual plans and specifications that tell the builder exactly how to build your home.

And with our BLUEPRINT PACKAGES you get the absolute best. A complete set of blueprints is available for every design in this book. These "working drawings," are highly detailed, resulting in two key benefits:

- *Better understanding by the contractor of how to build your home, and...*
- *More accurate construction estimates.*

Other helpful building aids are also available to help make your dream home a reality.

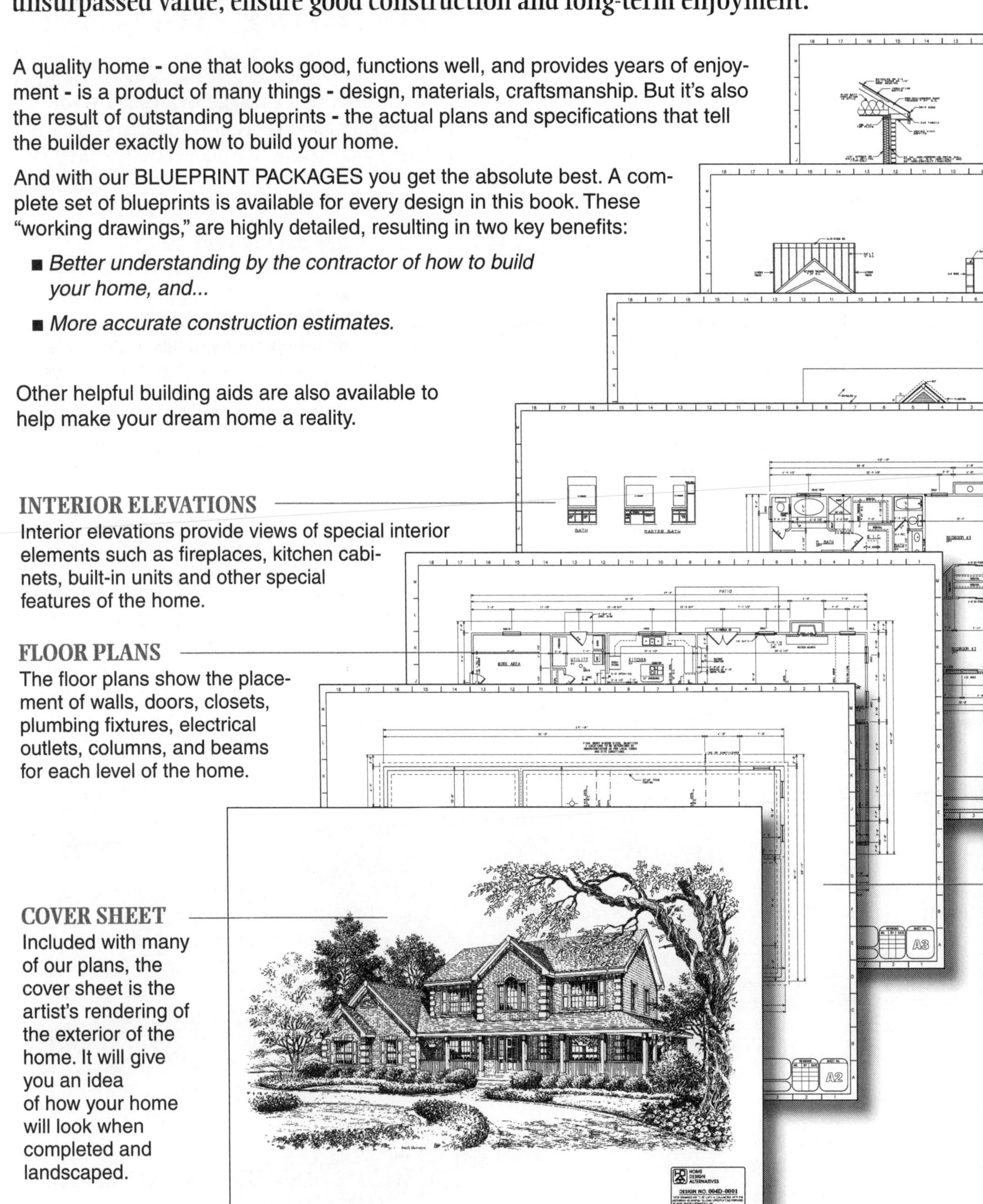

INTERIOR ELEVATIONS

Interior elevations provide views of special interior elements such as fireplaces, kitchen cabinets, built-in units and other special features of the home.

FLOOR PLANS

The floor plans show the placement of walls, doors, closets, plumbing fixtures, electrical outlets, columns, and beams for each level of the home.

COVER SHEET

Included with many of our plans, the cover sheet is the artist's rendering of the exterior of the home. It will give you an idea of how your home will look when completed and landscaped.

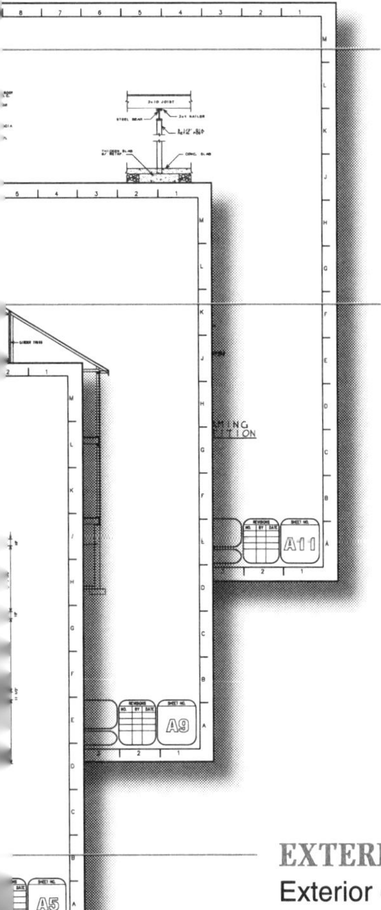

DETAILS

Details show how to construct certain components of your home, such as the roof system, stairs, deck, etc.

SECTIONS

Sections show detail views of the home or portions of the home as if it were sliced from the roof to the foundation. This sheet shows important areas such as load-bearing walls, stairs, joists, trusses and other structural elements, which are critical for proper construction.

EXTERIOR ELEVATIONS

Exterior elevations illustrate the front, rear and both sides of the house, with all details of exterior materials and the required dimensions.

FOUNDATION PLAN

The foundation plan shows the layout of the basement, crawl space, slab, or pier foundation. All necessary notations and dimensions are included. See plan page for the foundation types included. If the home plan you choose does not have your desired foundation type, our Customer Service Representatives can advise you on how to customize your foundation to suit your specific needs or site conditions.

Other Helpful Building Aids...

Your Blueprint Package will contain the necessary construction information to build your home. We also offer the following products and services to save you time and money in the building process.

Express Delivery

Most orders are processed within 24 hours of receipt. Please allow 7-10 business days for delivery. If you need to place a rush order, please call us by 11:00 a.m. Monday-Friday CST and ask for express service (allow 1-2 business days).

Technical Assistance

If you have questions, call our technical support line at 1-314-770-2228 between 8:00 a.m. and 5:00 p.m. Monday-Friday CST. Whether it involves design modifications or field assistance, our designers are extremely familiar with all of our designs and will be happy to help you. We want your home to be everything you expect it to be.

Material List

Material lists are available for many of our plans. Each list gives you the quantity, dimensions and description of the building materials necessary to construct your home. You'll get faster and more accurate bids from your contractor while saving money by paying for only the materials you need. See the Home Plans Index on pages 286-287 for availability. **Cost: $125**

HOME DESIGN ALTERNATIVES, INC.

HOME PLANS INDEX

Shaded Plans Denote Lowe's Signature Series Plans

Plan Number	Sq. Ft.	Price Code	Page	Mat. List	Right Read. Reverse	Can. Ship.
530-001D-0007	2,874	E	15	•		
530-001D-0013	1,882	D	22	•		
530-001D-0018	988	AA	75	•		
530-001D-0021	1,416	A	80	•		
530-001D-0024	1,360	A	5	•		
530-001D-0030	1,416	A	73	•		
530-001D-0031	1,501	B	7	•		
530-001D-0033	1,624	B	128	•		
530-001D-0035	1,396	A	103	•		
530-001D-0041	1,000	AA	41	•		
530-001D-0045	1,197	AA	21	•		
530-001D-0048	1,400	A	55	•		
530-001D-0053	1,344	A	122	•		
530-001D-0058	1,720	B	116	•		
530-001D-0067	1,285	B	127	•		
530-001D-0088	800	AAA	123	•		
530-001D-0091	1,344	A	118	•		
530-003D-0002	1,676	B	16	•		
530-003D-0005	1,708	B	39	•		
530-004D-0002	1,823	C	48	•		
530-005D-0001	1,400	B	8	•		
530-006D-0001	1,643	B	42	•		
530-006D-0003	1,674	B	27	•		
530-007D-0002	3,814	G	12	•		
530-007D-0004	2,531	D	47	•		
530-007D-0007	2,523	D	34	•		
530-007D-0010	1,721	C	11	•		
530-007D-0012	2,563	D	58	•		
530-007D-0017	1,882	C	110	•		
530-007D-0018	1,941	C	64	•		
530-007D-0030	1,140	AA	30	•		
530-007D-0031	1,092	AA	109	•		
530-007D-0037	1,403	A	94	•		
530-007D-0039	1,563	B	104	•		
530-007D-0044	1,516	B	72	•		
530-007D-0045	1,321	A	74	•		
530-007D-0048	2,758	E	113	•		
530-007D-0049	1,791	C	101	•		
530-007D-0050	2,723	E	14	•		
530-007D-0053	2,334	D	120	•		
530-007D-0055	2,029	D	69	•		
530-007D-0056	3,199	E	9	•		
530-007D-0057	2,808	F	53	•		
530-007D-0058	4,826	G	114	•		
530-007D-0060	1,268	B	124	•		
530-007D-0061	1,340	A	81	•		
530-007D-0062	2,483	D	6	•		
530-007D-0065	2,218	D	90	•		
530-007D-0066	2,408	D	13	•		
530-007D-0067	1,761	B	78	•		
530-007D-0068	1,384	B	99	•		
530-007D-0069	2,070	C	84	•		
530-007D-0077	1,977	C	134	•		
530-007D-0078	2,514	D	136	•		
530-007D-0085	1,787	B	115	•		
530-007D-0102	1,452	A	138	•		
530-007D-0105	1,084	AA	144	•		
530-007D-0106	1,200	A	140	•		
530-007D-0107	1,161	AA	142	•		
530-014D-0005	1,314	A	45	•		
530-014D-0007	1,453	A	86	•		
530-014D-0009	1,428	A	38	•		
530-014D-0010	2,563	D	98	•		
530-014D-0015	1,941	C	87	•		
530-017D-0005	1,367	B	63	•		
530-017D-0008	1,466	B	106	•		
530-018D-0003	2,517	D	44	•		
530-018D-0005	2,598	D	117	•		
530-018D-0006	1,742	B	24	•		
530-018D-0008	2,109	C	17	•		

Plan Number	Sq. Ft.	Price Code	Page	Mat. List	Right Read. Reverse	Can. Ship.
530-021D-0001	2,396	D	88	•		
530-021D-0004	1,800	C	25	•		
530-021D-0005	2,177	C	49	•		
530-021D-0006	1,600	C	10	•		
530-021D-0007	1,868	D	68	•		
530-021D-0009	2,252	D	37	•		
530-021D-0011	1,800	D	107	•		
530-021D-0012	1,672	C	119	•		
530-021D-0014	1,856	C	96	•		
530-022D-0005	1,360	A	60	•		
530-022D-0011	1,630	B	54	•		
530-022D-0018	1,368	A	28	•		
530-022D-0020	988	AA	35	•		
530-022D-0025	2,847	E	62	•		
530-023D-0010	2,558	D	29	•		
530-027D-0002	3,796	F	105	•		
530-027D-0003	2,061	D	125	•		
530-027D-0006	2,076	C	93	•		
530-027D-0008	3,411	F	77	•		
530-027D-0009	3,808	F	36	•		
530-033D-0012	1,546	C	89	•		
530-037D-0003	1,996	D	79	•		
530-037D-0006	1,772	C	50	•		
530-037D-0008	1,707	C	71	•		
530-037D-0010	1,770	B	82	•		
530-037D-0020	1,994	D	33	•		
530-037D-0021	2,260	D	59	•		
530-037D-0031	1,923	C	19	•		
530-040D-0003	1,475	B	92	•		
530-040D-0008	1,631	B	85	•		
530-040D-0026	1,393	B	70	•		
530-041D-0001	2,003	D	46	•		
530-041D-0004	1,195	AA	43	•		
530-045D-0003	1,958	C	97	•		
530-045D-0009	1,684	B	40	•		
530-045D-0014	987	AA	66	•		
530-048D-0002	2,467	D	121	•		
530-048D-0004	2,397	E	112	•		
530-048D-0005	2,287	E	20	•		
530-048D-0008	2,089	C	61	•		
530-048D-0011	1,550	B	51	•		
530-053D-0002	1,668	C	23	•		
530-053D-0029	1,220	A	31	•		
530-053D-0032	1,404	A	65	•		
530-053D-0037	1,388	A	56	•		
530-053D-0042	1,458	A	95	•		
530-053D-0044	1,340	A	100	•		
530-053D-0049	1,261	A	18	•		
530-053D-0050	2,718	E	91	•		
530-053D-0051	2,731	E	52	•		
530-053D-0052	2,513	D	76	•		
530-053D-0053	1,609	B	111	•		
530-053D-0055	1,803	C	57	•		
530-058D-0015	2,308	D	102	•		
530-058D-0016	1,558	B	67	•		
530-058D-0017	2,412	D	108	•		
530-058D-0021	1,477	A	126	•		
530-058D-0022	1,578	B	129	•		
530-058D-0023	1,883	C	131	•		
530-058D-0024	1,598	B	135	•		
530-058D-0025	2,164	C	133	•		
530-058D-0026	1,819	C	130	•		
530-058D-0043	1,277	A	132	•		
530-061D-0001	1,747	B	83	•		
530-061D-0002	1,950	C	32	•		
530-061D-0003	2,255	D	26	•		
530-068D-0005	1,433	A	137	•		
530-068D-0007	1,599	B	143	•		
530-068D-0008	2,651	E	139	•		
530-068D-0010	1,849	C	141	•		

Plan Number	Sq. Ft.	Price Code	Page	Mat. List	Right Read. Reverse	Can. Ship.
530-008D-0004	1,643	B	158	•		
530-008D-0009	2,851	E	243	•		
530-008D-0010	1,440	A	214	•		
530-008D-0011	1,550	B	226	•		
530-008D-0012	1,232	A	237	•		
530-008D-0013	1,345	A	241	•		
530-008D-0026	1,120	AA	279	•		
530-008D-0045	1,540	B	204	•		
530-008D-0047	1,610	B	189	•		
530-008D-0054	1,574	B	218	•		
530-008D-0055	1,996	C	252	•		
530-008D-0062	2,530	D	179	•		
530-008D-0063	2,086	C	182	•		
530-008D-0070	2,165	C	175	•		
530-008D-0084	1,704	B	265			
530-008D-0090	1,364	A	186	•		
530-008D-0094	1,364	A	147	•		
530-008D-0102	1,102	AA	267	•		
530-008D-0110	1,500	B	156			
530-008D-0122	1,364	A	169	•		
530-008D-0131	960	AA	197	•		
530-008D-0133	624	AAA	227	•		
530-008D-0148	784	AAA	149	•		
530-008D-0153	792	AAA	155	•		
530-011D-0005	1,467	C	272	•	•	
530-011D-0011	2,155	C	164	•	•	
530-015D-0003	2,255	D	203	•		
530-015D-0008	1,785	B	244	•		
530-015D-0018	2,710	E	160			
530-015D-0019	1,018	AA	206			
530-019D-0009	1,862	C	183			
530-019D-0010	1,890	C	159			
530-019D-0011	1,955	C	202			
530-019D-0013	1,932	C	253			
530-019D-0016	2,678	E	245			
530-020D-0008	1,925	C	177			
530-020D-0015	1,191	AA	152			
530-020D-0016	1,380	C	172			
530-020D-0017	2,424	D	222			
530-024D-0002	1,405	A	230			
530-024D-0009	1,704	B	266			
530-024D-0025	2,450	D	190			
530-025D-0003	1,379	A	154			
530-025D-0006	1,612	B	173			
530-025D-0009	1,680	B	238			
530-025D-0012	1,634	B	207			
530-025D-0028	2,350	D	216			
530-026D-0070	1,666	B	170	•		
530-026D-0072	1,496	A	269	•		
530-026D-0082	1,636	B	242	•		
530-026D-0089	1,580	B	274	•		
530-026D-0097	2,456	D	196	•		
530-026D-0112	1,911	C	220	•	•	
530-026D-0130	1,479	A	184	•		
530-026D-0137	1,758	B	212	•	•	
530-026D-0142	2,188	C	280	•		
530-026D-0154	1,392	A	235	•		
530-026D-0155	1,691	B	151	•		
530-028D-0004	1,785	B	148		•	
530-028D-0006	1,700	B	210			
530-028D-0008	2,156	C	262		•	
530-030D-0001	1,374	A	257			
530-030D-0003	1,753	B	167			
530-030D-0004	1,791	B	275			
530-031D-0005	1,735	B	248			
530-031D-0009	1,960	C	278			
530-031D-0011	2,164	C	146			
530-034D-0001	1,436	A	233			
530-034D-0003	1,629	B	157			
530-034D-0012	2,278	D	199			

HOME PLANS INDEX - *continued*

Plan Number	Sq. Ft.	Price Code	Page	Mat. List	Right Read. Reverse	Can. Ship.
530-035D-0001	1,715	B	254	•		
530-035D-0011	1,945	C	228	•		
530-035D-0027	1,544	B	193	•		
530-035D-0028	1,779	B	188	•		
530-035D-0033	2,491	D	198			
530-035D-0037	2,279	D	258	•		
530-035D-0041	2,403	D	192	•		
530-035D-0045	1,749	B	215	•		
530-036D-0006	1,624	B	217			
530-036D-0024	2,118	C	221			
530-036D-0034	1,225	A	200			
530-036D-0040	2,061	C	260			
530-036D-0042	2,945	E	251			
530-036D-0049	2,591	D	194			
530-038D-0008	1,738	B	161	•	•	
530-038D-0012	1,575	B	180	•		
530-038D-0039	1,771	B	261	•		
530-038D-0049	1,686	B	209	•		
530-039D-0001	1,253	A	150	•		
530-039D-0002	1,333	A	211	•		
530-039D-0004	1,406	A	165	•		
530-039D-0005	1,474	A	171	•		
530-039D-0013	1,842	C	187	•		
530-043D-0001	3,158	E	153			
530-043D-0005	1,734	B	246			
530-043D-0008	1,496	A	282			
530-047D-0002	1,167	AA	277			
530-047D-0005	1,885	C	166			
530-047D-0032	1,963	C	178			
530-047D-0036	2,140	C	281	•		
530-047D-0039	2,224	D	205	•		
530-047D-0045	2,616	E	256			
530-049D-0003	1,830	C	247	•		
530-049D-0005	1,389	A	208	•		
530-049D-0007	1,118	AA	145	•		
530-049D-0008	1,937	C	185	•		
530-051D-0027	1,540	B	250	•		
530-051D-0034	1,756	B	255			
530-051D-0039	1,976	C	240			
530-051D-0052	1,600	B	283			
530-051D-0053	1,461	A	174			
530-051D-0064	1,462	A	236			
530-052D-0005	1,268	A	223			
530-052D-0011	1,325	A	168	•		
530-052D-0013	1,379	A	276			
530-052D-0017	1,418	A	219			
530-052D-0036	1,772	B	234			
530-052D-0045	1,865	C	239			
530-052D-0058	2,012	C	264			
530-055D-0015	2,092	C	249	•	•	
530-055D-0017	1,525	B	270	•	•	
530-055D-0024	1,680	B	213	•	•	
530-055D-0026	1,538	B	263	•	•	
530-055D-0027	1,353	A	229	•	•	
530-055D-0029	2,525	D	225	•	•	
530-055D-0030	2,107	C	232	•	•	
530-055D-0032	2,439	D	176	•	•	
530-056D-0009	1,606	B	259			
530-056D-0024	1,093	AA	268			
530-060D-0015	1,192	AA	163			
530-060D-0016	1,214	A	201			
530-060D-0026	1,497	A	181			
530-062D-0041	1,541	B	162	•	•	•
530-062D-0047	1,230	A	231	•	•	•
530-062D-0050	1,408	A	224	•	•	•
530-062D-0051	1,578	B	191	•		•
530-062D-0053	1,405	A	195	•		•
530-069D-0005	1,267	A	271	•		
530-069D-0019	2,162	C	273	•		

OTHER GREAT PRODUCTS TO HELP YOU BUILD YOUR DREAM HOME

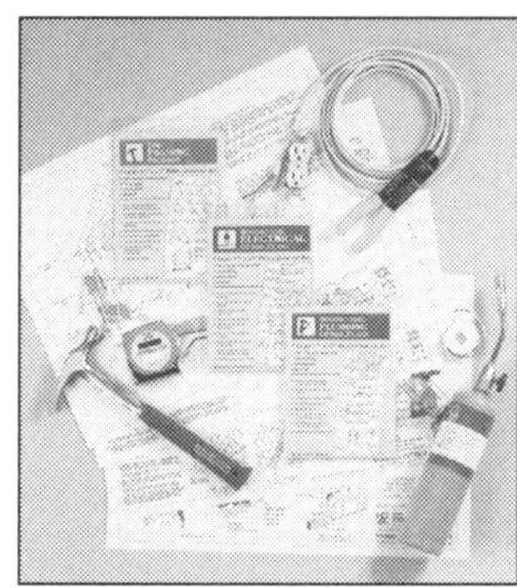

FRAMING, PLUMBING AND ELECTRICAL PLAN PACKAGES

Three separate packages offer homebuilders details for constructing various foundations; numerous floor, wall and roof framing techniques; simple to complex residential wiring; sump and water softener hookups; plumbing connection methods; installation of septic systems, and more. Each package includes three-dimensional illustrations and a glossary of terms. Purchase one or all three. **Cost: $20.00 each or all three for $40.00**

Note: These drawings do not pertain to a specific home plan.

THE LEGAL KIT

Avoid many legal pitfalls and build your home with confidence using the forms and contracts featured in this kit. Included are request for proposal documents, various fixed price and cost plus contracts, instructions on how and when to use each form, warranty statements and more. Save time and money before you break ground on your new home or start a remodeling project. All forms are reproducible. The kit is ideal for homebuilders and contractors. **Cost: $35.00**

WHAT KIND OF PLAN PACKAGE DO YOU NEED?

Now that you've found the home plan you've been looking for, here are some suggestions on how to make your Dream Home a reality. To get started, order the type of plans that fit your particular situation.

Your Choices:

The 1-Set Study package - We offer a 1-set plan package so you can study your home in detail. This one set is considered a study set and is marked "not for construction." It is a copyright violation to reproduce blueprints.

The Minimum 5-Set package - If you're ready to start the construction process, this 5-set package is the minimum number of blueprint sets you will need. It will require keeping close track of each set so they can be used by multiple subcontractors and tradespeople.

The Standard 8-set package - For best results in terms of cost, schedule and quality of construction, we recommend you order eight (or more) sets of blueprints. Besides one set for yourself, additional sets of blueprints will be required by your mortgage lender, local building department, general contractor and all subcontractors working on foundation, electrical, plumbing, heating/air conditioning, carpentry work, etc.

Reproducible Masters - If you wish to make some minor design changes, you'll want to order reproducible masters. These drawings contain the same information as the blueprints but are printed on erasable and reproducible paper which clearly indicates your right to copy or reproduce. This will allow your builder or a local design professional to make the necessary drawing changes without the major expense of redrawing the plans. This package also allows you to print copies of the modified plans as needed. The right of building only one structure from these plans is licensed exclusively to the buyer. You may not use this design to build a second or multiple dwelling(s) without purchasing another blueprint. Each violation of the Copyright Law is punishable in a fine.

Mirror Reverse Sets - Plans can be printed in mirror reverse. These plans are useful when the house would fit your site better if all the rooms were on the opposite side than shown. They are simply a mirror image of the original drawings causing the lettering and dimensions to read backwards. Therefore, when ordering mirror reverse drawings, you must purchase at least one set of right-reading plans. Some of our plans are offered mirror reverse right-reading. This means the plan, lettering and dimensions are flipped but read correctly. See the Home Plans Index for availability.

How To Order

For fastest service, Call Toll-Free
1-800-DREAM HOME
(1-800-373-2646) 24 HOURS A DAY

Three Easy Ways To Order

1. CALL toll-free 1-877-373-2646 for credit card orders. MasterCard, Visa, Discover and American Express are accepted.
2. FAX your order to 1-314-770-2226.
3. MAIL the Order Form to:

HDA, Inc.
944 Anglum Road
St. Louis, MO 63042

Order Form

Please send me -

PLAN NUMBER 530 - ____________________

PRICE CODE ______ *(see pages 286-287)*

Specify Foundation Type *(see plan page for availability)*

☐ Slab ☐ Crawl space ☐ Pier
☐ Basement ☐ Walk-out basement

☐ Reproducible Masters $ ________
☐ Eight-Set Plan Package $ ________
☐ Five-Set Plan Package $ ________
☐ One-Set Study Package *(no mirror reverse)* $ ________
☐ Additional Plan Sets*
______ (Qty.) at $45.00 each $ ________

Mirror Reverse*
☐ Right-reading $150 one-time charge
(see index on pages 286-287 for availability) $ ________
☐ Print in Mirror Reverse *(where right-reading is not available)*
_____ (Qty.) at $15.00 each $ ________
☐ Material List* $125 *(see pages 286-287)* $ ________
☐ Legal Kit *(see page 287)* $ ________

Detail Plan Packages: *(see page 287)*
☐ Framing ☐ Electrical ☐ Plumbing $ ________
SUBTOTAL $ ________

Sales Tax - MO residents add 6% $ ________
☐ Shipping / Handling *(see chart at right)* $ ________
TOTAL ENCLOSED *(US funds only)* $ ________

I hereby authorize HDA, Inc. to charge this purchase to my credit card account (check one):

☐ MasterCard ☐ VISA ☐ DISCOVER NOVUS ☐ AMERICAN EXPRESS Cards

Credit Card number ____________________

Expiration date ____________________

Signature ____________________

Name ____________________
(Please print or type)

Street Address ____________________
(Please **do not** use PO Box)

City ____________________

State __________ Zip ____________________

Daytime phone number (____) - ____________

I'm a ☐ Builder/Contractor ☐ Homeowner ☐ Renter

I ☐ have ☐ have not selected my general contractor

Thank you for your order!

Important Information To Know Before You Order

Exchange Policies - Since blueprints are printed in response to your order, we cannot honor requests for refunds. However, if for some reason you find that the plan you have purchased does not meet your requirements, you may exchange that plan for another plan in our collection within 90 days of purchase. At the time of the exchange, you will be charged a processing fee of 25% of your original plan package price, plus the difference in price between the plan packages (if applicable) and the cost to ship the new plans to you.

Please note: Reproducible drawings can only be exchanged if the package is unopened.

Building Codes & Requirements - At the time the construction drawings were prepared, every effort was made to ensure that these plans and specifications meet nationally recognized codes. Our plans conform to most national building codes. Because building codes vary from area to area, some drawing modifications and/or the assistance of a professional designer or architect may be necessary to comply with your local codes or to accommodate specific building site conditions. We advise you to consult with your local building official for information regarding codes governing your area.

Questions? Call Our Customer Service Number
314-770-2228

Blueprint Price Schedule

BEST VALUE

Price Code	1-Set*	*SAVE $110* 5-Sets	*SAVE $200* 8-Sets	Reproducible Masters
AAA	$225	$295	$340	$440
AA	$325	$395	$440	$540
A	$385	$455	$500	$600
B	$445	$515	$560	$660
C	$500	$570	$615	$715
D	$560	$630	$675	$775
E	$620	$690	$735	$835
F	$675	$745	$790	$890
G	$765	$835	$880	$980
H	$890	$960	$1005	$1105

Plan prices are subject to change without notice.
Please note that plans are not refundable.

Additional Sets* - Additional sets of the plan ordered are available for $45.00 each. Five-set, eight-set, and reproducible packages offer considerable savings.

Mirror Reverse Plans* - Available for an additional $15.00 per set, these plans are simply a mirror image of the original drawings causing the dimensions and lettering to read backwards. Therefore, when ordering mirror reverse plans, you must purchase at least one set of right-reading plans. Some of our plans are offered mirror reverse right-reading. This means the plan, lettering and dimensions are flipped but read correctly. To purchase a mirror reverse right-reading set, the cost is an additional $150.00. See the Home Plans Index on pages 286-287 for availability.

One-Set Study Package* - We offer a one-set plan package so you can study your home in detail. This one set is considered a study set and is marked "not for construction." It is a copyright violation to reproduce blueprints.

****Available only within 90 days after purchase of plan package or reproducible masters of same plan.***

Shipping & Handling Charges

U.S. SHIPPING - (AK and HI - express only)	1-4 Sets	5-7 Sets	8 Sets or Reproducibles
Regular (allow 7-10 business days)	$15.00	$17.50	$25.00
Priority (allow 3-5 business days)	$25.00	$30.00	$35.00
Express* (allow 1-2 business days)	$35.00	$40.00	$45.00

CANADA SHIPPING - (to/from) (plans with suffix 062)	1-4 Sets	5-7 Sets	8 Sets or Reproducibles
Standard (allow 8-12 business days)	$25.00	$30.00	$35.00
Express* (allow 3-5 business days)	$40.00	$40.00	$45.00

Overseas Shipping/International - Call, fax, or e-mail (plans@hdainc.com) for shipping costs.

* For express delivery please call us by 11:00 a.m. Monday-Friday CST